# Praise for *Hack Yoi*

"As the medical director of the Ross Center, with treating thousands of people with anxiety, I am so pleased to have a unique new resource for patients that emphasizes the positive power of our anxiety response and very clearly shows how it can be harnessed and used to our benefit. The explanation of the neurobiology behind anxiety, the case vignettes offered, and the tool kit provided are all clearly laid out such that the anxiety is understood, hope is instilled, and a change in perspective is possible. The reader is provided a clear path to taking back control of anxiety and seeing it as an incredibly useful tool to help them along the path toward self-fulfillment. Thank you, Alicia, for this thoughtful and thought-provoking new take on anxiety!"

—*Beth Salcedo, MD, medical director of the Ross Center and president of Anxiety and Depression Association of America*

"In *Hack Your Anxiety*, Clark faces off against the central challenge of modern life. Anxiety, stress, and trauma have been shown to affect all levels of our mental, physical, and spiritual health from the first days of gestation. If we are to survive in our fast-paced, information-based world, we will have to learn to domesticate our primitive fear circuitry and use our minds to change our brains. *Hack Your Anxiety* will provide you with straightforward, no-nonsense ways of hacking into this circuitry and regaining control of your brain."

—*Louis Cozolino, PhD, author of* The Making of a Therapist *and* The New Science of Psychotherapy

"Alicia Clark offers a refreshingly renegade perspective on anxiety. In a world where many individuals and couples are not operating out of secure functioning and anxiety has been linked to insecure attachment, this is welcome news. In fact, research in neuroscience, especially as pertains to nervous system arousal regulation, supports the notion that it is possible to manage anxiety in a way that leads to happier, more fulfilled lives. Clark's book includes a helpful introduction to some basic neuroscientific principles, along with a recommended process for handling anxiety. With Clark's tool kit, anyone suffering from anxiety can draw new hope."

—*Stan Tatkin, author of* Wired for Love

# hack your anxiety

# hack your
# anxiety

## How to Make Anxiety Work for You in Life, Love, and All That You Do

**ALICIA H. CLARK, PsyD**

**with Jon Sternfeld**

Ⓢ sourcebooks

Published by Sourcebooks, Inc.
P.O. Box 4410, Naperville, Illinois 60567-4410
(630) 961-3900
Fax: (630) 961-2168
sourcebooks.com

Library of Congress Cataloging-in-Publication Data

Names: Clark, Alicia H., author. | Sternfeld, Jon, author.
Title: Hack your anxiety : how to make anxiety work for you in life, love, and all that you do / Dr. Alicia H. Clark, with Jon Sternfeld.
Description: Naperville, Illinois : Sourcebooks, Inc., 2018. | Includes
  bibliographical references and index.
Identifiers: LCCN 2018010617 | (pbk. : alk. paper)
Subjects: LCSH: Anxiety.
Classification: LCC BF575.A6 C634 2018 | DDC 152.4/6--dc23 LC record available at https://lccn.loc.gov/2018010617

Printed and bound in the United States of America.
VP 10 9 8 7 6 5 4 3 2 1

# Contents

**INTRODUCTION**     xiii

**CHAPTER ONE**     1

*The Big Picture*

**CHAPTER TWO**     17

*Waking Up to Anxiety's Purpose and Power*

**CHAPTER THREE**     30

*The Power in Knowing*

**CHAPTER FOUR**     45

*Anxiety through Time and Place*

**CHAPTER FIVE**     63

*Ten Myths and Misconceptions*

**CHAPTER SIX**       89

*The Avoidance Myth*

**CHAPTER SEVEN**       106

*Taking Control*

**CHAPTER EIGHT**       131

*The Power of Perception*

**CHAPTER NINE**       149

*The Brain and the Body*

**CHAPTER TEN**       170

*Anxiety as Signal*

**CHAPTER ELEVEN**       189

*Anxiety as Fuel*

**CHAPTER TWELVE**       208

*Anxiety into Action*

**CHAPTER THIRTEEN**       229

*Social Support*

**CHAPTER FOURTEEN**       250

*Love and Relationships*

**CHAPTER FIFTEEN**                                           **273**

*Parenting and Youth*

**CHAPTER SIXTEEN**                                         **295**

*Work, Money, and Success*

**CHAPTER SEVENTEEN**                                    **317**

*Facing Crisis*

**CHAPTER EIGHTEEN**                                      **330**

*Soothing and Coping*

**CONCLUSION**                                          **349**

**YOUR ANXIETY TOOL KIT**                                 **352**

**NOTES**                                                **384**

**OTHER PLACES TO ACCESS HELP**                         **416**

**INDEX**                                              **419**

**ACKNOWLEDGMENTS**                                   **439**

**ABOUT THE AUTHORS**                                   **442**

**Hack** (*v.*) \\'hak\\

1. To cut or shape clear by cutting away superfluous material
2. To manage successfully
3. To gain access to a network or system

# Introduction

*"Between stimulus and response there is a space. In that space is our power to choose our response. In our response lies our growth and our freedom."*[1]

—**Viktor E. Frankl**

- Obsessing over a low-grade worry that keeps you distracted
- Boundless whirling from task to task to quiet the nagging pressure of stress
- Pushing down anxious thoughts in whatever way possible, wishing they would simply disappear

**If you're reading this book,** chances are good you've tried the above or similar strategies to make your anxiety go away. Or maybe you're looking to help a loved one whose anxiety seems to weigh him or her down. Perhaps you are simply curious about anxiety and how you can better harness it in your life. I get it; I work with anxiety every day, and I have spent the better part of my life immersed in it.

My grandmother worried so much that she shook. Literally. Her body would subtly tremble from this mysterious and overwhelming force of worry inside her. She was a petite southern lady with impeccable manners who favored all things pink and floral. Her short, curly hair framed a round face with fine features and a generous smile. At her warmest, it was a magnet for others. Yet worrying was her natural state of being, like breathing.

What did she worry about? Well, nothing. And everything. She was worried about all the lovely things that grandmothers tend to worry about and likely countless others that remained unspoken:

*Do you have enough to eat?*

*Are you cold?*

*Do you need salt and pepper?*

Her voice was softly feminine, so listeners often had to lean in to hear her. I always imagined she liked the intimacy it afforded. I can see her now, hovering over our Sunday dinner to make sure all the grandchildren and cousins are happy, comfortable, and satisfied. When we were at ease, she was at ease. Or, rather, as at ease as she was capable of being.

The grandkids started a running joke: *Granny, can we pass you the salt and pepper?* Her anxiousness would deflate at the teasing; she'd smile and flush with embarrassment. We were showing our appreciation and poking fun, releasing the valve on her tension. She was never a burden; we accepted and loved her for who she was.

She was the consummate people person, always curious, invested, and connected. I have clear memories of returning home with my family to hear her voice through the tinny speaker of the answering machine: "Hi, it's me again. Just wondering how you're coming along…" She required regular assurance that things were, indeed, all right, and she preferred to hear it firsthand. If she could take care of things for someone, even better.

I later learned about her rheumatoid arthritis, which she seldom mentioned, much less complained about. Instead, her worries were pointed outward, about others, and they were rarely serious. As she aged, her anxiety seemed to escalate as she became less able to put it to use. There was no way for her to release that anxiety, so it stayed inside of her. It seemed to be a force that expanded and overtook her, almost crippling her with worry.

When I search for my early associations with anxiety, the image of my grandmother always pops into my head. When I studied the subject in graduate school, I'd think about her shaking. When I taught students on the topic or met with patients suffering from it, a picture of her face would flash across my mind. As I spent more time exposed to and studying anxiety, I began to understand my grandmother better, and I began to see how pervasive anxiety was throughout my family. It set the stage for me to understand how much anxiety—and people's responses to that anxiety—was affecting their emotions and behavior.

Though no one else in my family shook as my grandmother

did, we have all carried that anxiety in our own ways. Even behavior that appeared to be the opposite of anxious was borne from it, formed in reaction to its presence. Anxiety seems to be the center point of everything.

A whirling dervish of action, my mother's response to anxiety is doing, seemingly always on the move. That feeling is the ultimate motivator; it pushes her to *do*. Whereas my grandmother's anxiety could cripple her, my mother's anxiety seems to spring her forward. She has always known there was something else ahead. Internalized from her own mother, her high standards fuel an anxiety in me that is, at its best, motivating.

My father, on the other hand, was the opposite. Whereas my mother was a constant release valve, my father was a giant balloon; his stress built up over time. He had no way to manage or use it. He could be impulsive, too, aiming too often to soothe his unrest rather than solve his problems.

My family, like many, is a spectrum of extremes. However, in hindsight, I see anxiety as the hub of it all. My grandmother was consumed by it, my father attempted to numb it, and my mother chose to act through it. To my knowledge, no one in my family was ever diagnosed with an anxiety disorder, but if they had been, I imagine they would have been told that anxiety was simply a symptom to tolerate and ignore as much as possible. They would have been advised to take it easy and perhaps been prescribed antianxiety medications to help calm their nerves. Like so many people diagnosed with anxiety disorders, my family members would have likely felt the shame and stigma that go along with mental health issues, including people thinking something was "wrong" with them. Of course, nothing was wrong with any of them—they simply noticed and felt things deeply, weren't always sure what to do with their experiences, and tried many things to cope that didn't always help. Just like so many people I meet every day in my practice.

· ·

Through my experience and my work as a psychologist, I have developed a perspective on anxiety that seeks to embrace its value. I have come to understand anxiety as a powerful resource, encompassing important information. Anxiety can prompt us to pay closer attention to the message at hand and provide the motivation to take control. On a continuum of responses to anxiety, ranging from impulsive to avoidant, I tend to aim for the middle—*taking control*. This is where I do my best, where I try to steer others and, ultimately, is the purpose of this book.

*Hack Your Anxiety* suggests and demonstrates that *taking control* can be the solution to anxiety—as long as it's coupled with an awareness that helps *solve* the issue anxiety is signaling. Time and time again, I've been amazed at just how adaptive this process can be when it comes to harnessing anxiety. This book is about showing readers how to make anxiety work for them.

One of the most important things any of us can offer another person is hope. At my best, I am an eternal optimist, a believer in finding the positive and seizing opportunities. In helping people in my clinical practice as a therapist, I have come to recognize anxiety as the unsung hero in the path to success and happiness. Rather than simply being a primitive response to fear, anxiety can be an efficient tool for growth.

My hope is that this book speaks to the millions out there currently struggling with anxiety and the loved ones who want to help. Especially for those who may not realize anxiety's role in their struggle, I hope they, too, might find a new way to frame, process, and utilize their experiences.

• •

I have yet to meet a person—in life or in work—whose anxiety doesn't significantly drive his or her pain or dysfunction. A cursory look at the psychiatric "bible," the most recent *Diagnostic and Statistical Manual of Mental Disorders*, reveals that some form of anxiousness is present in virtually every diagnosis. Even depression appears to be an outgrowth of anxiety, a type of learned helplessness from feeling there isn't anything you can do to lessen your unease. A recent article in *Scientific American* noted that "nearly 50 percent of people diagnosed with depression can also be diagnosed with an anxiety disorder, and vice versa."[2] Psychiatrists regularly prescribe the same medication for the depressed and the anxious, revealing that the differences between the two are not as wide as our labels may indicate. The management of anxiety, therefore, is critical to maintaining overall mental health and happiness.

But *how* do you manage it? The common perception is that anxiety is a problem that needs to be conquered. Yet seldom is the problem contained in just the anxiety itself. Beyond the experience of anxiety and the problems that drive it is so often the potential fallout: The self-loathing that results from believing you can't seem to manage your experience better. The guilt and shame that you are somehow broken. The public condemning that "you should snap out of it." The fear you will never be okay. Repeatedly, well-meaning friends, health reports, doctors, and self-help experts advise anxiety sufferers to calm down, fight it, release their tension. Avoid it, ignore it, let it go. We have gotten the message loud and clear. *We must make it go away.*

But what if we're working from a faulty premise? What if anxiety is not a monster to be tamed but a resource to be tapped? What if we've been falsely viewing anxiety as the enemy? What if we should be *steering into* the skid?

. .

I have honed effective methods to help people use their anxieties to transform their lives for the better. In turn, they feel happier and more confident, and they enjoy more success in their lives. One of my professional missions is to restore anxiety to its rightful place as a positive resource.

Few professionals talk about this upside of anxiety, the anxiety that is grounded in reality and adaptive. If we open our understanding, we can see anxiety arises because something we care about is at risk and needs protecting. Rather than viewing anxiety as a force to be targeted and eliminated, I propose a more positive perspective, if we know how to use it. Anxiety can be harnessed as a positive force for change.

There are countless books on anxiety and even more articles and studies addressing its negative impacts. Yet, they often come from a similar perspective of wiping out the anxiety, quieting the voice, and attacking and snuffing out the anxious feeling. I offer a counterintuitive but fruitful option—embrace it tighter. *Hack Your Anxiety* takes the bold step in proposing that our anxiety is biologically protective and motivating, and it can ultimately be beneficial. Accept it, listen to it, and use it to achieve your best self.

To hack something is to gain access in order to manage it—often through a side door or through a way you hadn't even considered. Because of the unpleasant emotions associated with anxiety, solutions have often been tied up with shutting it down, avoiding it, or making it go away. I propose something unique: find a way into your anxiety. Embrace it. Hacking means turning it on its head and making it work for you.

I have worked with hundreds of executives, thought leaders, public servants, students, and parents. Through our work, they have learned to rethink their anxiety and convert it into a springboard for success. Continuously, I hear how people feel better, more energized, and less overwhelmed as they implement these strategies. Through a review of relevant research, psychology thinking, and client stories,* I hope to teach you to use your anxiety more constructively and tap into the hidden internal resource that exists within.

---

\* All the stories are composites of clients I've worked with; all identifying information has been changed to protect their privacy.

In chapter 1, we will look at the state of anxiety today, which will give us a better sense of what we're dealing with. Chapter 2 will set the stage for how anxiety can be beneficial. In chapter 3, we'll explore various types off anxiety, before taking a quick trip through the history of anxiety and how it has been historically viewed in chapter 4. In chapter 5, we'll knock down ten towering myths of anxiety, and we'll discuss the biggest myth in chapter 6. We will then look at how our control, perception, and brain and biology factor in to our anxiety in chapters 7 through 9. Then we'll look at how anxiety operates as a signal, fuel, and a catalyst for action in chapters 10 through 12. Chapters 13 through 16 will zero in on anxiety's role and benefit in various life situations, including our social circles, families, relationships, and our professional lives. We will end with a look at anxiety and trauma in chapter 17 and soothing techniques in chapter 18 that can help get your anxiety to a manageable level. At the end of the book, you will find a tool kit that will offer tangible strategies and steps to start making anxiety work for you.

If you are in need of immediate help managing anxiety, you may want to skip ahead to the Your Anxiety Tool Kit section, which begins on page 352. There, I walk you through how to take control of your anxiety step by step, so you can put it to use in your life. There are questions you can ask yourself as well as brief descriptions and references back to sections of the book where concepts are explained more fully. Some steps will be easier than others, but remember to be gentle with yourself as you learn the method. With practice, you will get where you want to go.

My hope is that you read this and feel a desire to approach your anxiety differently, optimistic that it can stop creating problem in your life, and motivated to embrace it as resource you come to value and trust.

## CHAPTER ONE

# The Big Picture

*"Reality is the leading cause of stress amongst those in touch with it."*

—Jane Wagner[1]

**Anxiety is both the feeling** of realizing something we care about may be at risk *and* the arrival of the resources we need to protect it. That is, anxiety is both the signal of the problem and the elements of the solution. But to best take advantage of anxiety in this way, we must first acknowledge how it is currently understood. Far from being seen as a tool for active coping, anxiety today is often bound up with the idea of needless angst and the quicksand of mental illness, exacerbated by the crush of modern problems in this country.

# American Angst

The World Health Organization ranks the United States as being the most anxious country in the world—by a wide margin. Americans are more anxious than citizens of places like Nigeria, Lebanon, and Ukraine, places that face daily challenges far more serious than what most Americans encounter.[2] Yet, the fact remains: we are an anxious people. Almost one third of residents in the richest and most powerful country in the world are likely to suffer from some form of anxiety at some point in their lives.[3]

We are—at the core—a nation of immigrants striving for more. Many of us are blessed by abundance, and we *care* about having a life of plenty. We have eaten the proverbial apple and want more. That often translates into something akin to mass societal anxiety about having enough.

Anxiety has become a haunting and crippling force for the forty million Americans (18 percent) who have a diagnosed anxiety disorder, making it the most common mental illness in the country.[4] However those numbers do not include all of those who are undiagnosed but who regularly experience significant

## A Note on Terminology

Anxiety takes on many faces and many names. Whether we call it anxiety, fear, stress, angst, worry, uneasiness, neurosis, agitation, nervousness, apprehension, tension, panic, or any other of its more than thirty synonyms, it is a universal human expression of caring.

Throughout this book, I will interchangeably use the word *anxiety* with many of its synonyms. This is to reflect the many faces of anxiety that are as unique to each of our experiences as our experiences are themselves.

anxiety, an increasingly common and prevalent feeling among the population.

According to the Anxiety and Depression Association of America (ADAA):

- 40 percent of Americans experience persistent stress or excessive anxiety in their daily lives;
- 30 percent with daily stress have taken prescription medication to manage stress, nervousness, emotional problems, or lack of sleep; and
- 72 percent of people who have daily stress and anxiety say it interferes with their lives at least moderately.[5]

As a society, we've never been more stretched and distracted with demands on our attention and time pushing our limits. A comparative study across America conducted by Carnegie Mellon showed an almost 30 percent increase in stress over the past thirty years.[6] With more information than ever at our fingertips, we are looking for answers. Sometimes secretly, sometimes haphazardly, sometimes desperately. Over the past eight years, Google search rates for anxiety have more than doubled, and those searches in 2015 were the highest since they were first tracked.[7] Compounding our anxiousness is the fear of the negative effects of that anxiety—on productivity, on our families, and on our health. Everywhere we look, the tide of anxiety is on the rise.

## Modern Problems

Demands on our attention come from all directions, creating stressful scenarios in which it feels as if everyone's needs must be addressed and answered all at once. "Attention," writes Mihaly Csikszentmihalyi in *Flow: The Psychology of Optimal Experience*, "is like energy in that without it no work can be done, and in doing work is dissipated. We create ourselves by how we use this energy… It is an energy under control, to do with as we please; hence attention is our most important tool in the task of improving the quality of experience."[8] Philosopher Michael B. Crawford goes so far as to argue, "Distractibility might be regarded as the mental equivalent of obesity."[9]

Our basic one-to-one communication has become a stressful cacophony of buzzing, ringing, and dinging. A friend telling us he is on the way, running five minutes late—something that was not required (nor even possible) twenty years ago—is now just proper etiquette. And of course, we are all guilty. We've all had the experience of having to restrain ourselves from checking our phones at the dinner table or our email during a time of sustained engagement (I myself am fighting it right now as I write this chapter).

Sharing a funny video or inspiring quote through social media can be benign, but it starts a chain of distractibility: many people feel a compulsion to check their Facebook, Twitter, or Instagram feeds repeatedly to see if someone has weighed in. Repeated studies have exhibited how social media responses hit us with a dopamine surge, the neurochemical associated with reward and wanting.[10] Simply connecting with others seems to be what we're built for. The trouble is we are drawing from an empty well—trying to get the digital space to satisfy our human needs, which doesn't always work.

We are getting so out of the habit of face-to-face interactions that we're even becoming afraid of them. Millennials often confess to me their discomfort with a phone call, how it's intimidating to speak to someone when they have grown up almost exclusively texting. As we send information into the ether, we are longing for connection—and perhaps validation.

## The Rise of "Option Stress"

We have all had the experience of sitting down at the end of a long day to watch a television show or movie. Not too long ago, we'd flip channels to see what was on or maybe throw in a DVD we had rented. We might even take a peek at our modest personal collection and rewatch a favorite. Even though those days are a little more than a decade old, they feel like ancient history. Things have sped up to a dizzying degree. Now the unlimited options of where to watch, what to watch, and how to watch have made even leisure time a somewhat stressful experience. It's not abnormal to spend half the time selecting what we want to watch. We don't want to waste our time...so we end up wasting it.*

---

\*    A similar side effect has accompanied the rise of streaming music and the end of the CD. We have access to everything that's ever been recorded, which is... somehow a problem.

If we go on vacation, we now have no reason not to research every hidden gem, restaurant, or experience that awaits us in advance. After all, what excuses do we have? We have access to everything that's ever been written by anyone who's ever been there. But that too is exhausting. Part of us just wants to show up and play it by ear, though we sense we'd feel guilty during our trip, like maybe we hadn't maximized it. Like our vacation's purpose is to "produce" for us.

We search online to find a birthday present for someone, and somehow because we can literally buy just about anything that's ever been made, the decision is difficult. We often end up purchasing a gift card, transferring the responsibility of selecting onto the receiver.

We seem to be starving in a field of excess. Both the tiny house and back-to-nature movements have generated a healthy following among those who have begun to live the philosophy that there is inherent value in having less.[11] Books such as Barry Schwartz's *The Paradox of Choice* and Gregg Easterbrook's *The Progress Paradox*, both based on extensive studies, address the declining nature of our joy and comfort as our options increase.

A National Institutes of Health (NIH) study led by Kathleen Vohs found that the increase in choice has dampened satisfaction across the board, mostly because there is a biological underpinning to that overwhelmed feeling from a flood of choices. Specifically, "the self's executive function relies on a limited resource that resembles a form of strength or energy."[12] When we have to expend energy choosing from among a hundred salad dressings, we lose it elsewhere. As Barry Schwartz explains, "Each new option makes us feel worse off than we did before."[13]

This is not an entirely new concept. The anxiety of choice was a great focus of the early modern philosophers, especially Søren Kierkegaard, who spoke of the "dizziness of freedom" back in 1840. The feeling has just increased exponentially with the choices. Critic Louis Menand recently described anxiety as "the price tag on human freedom."[14]

In a recent *New Yorker* article, "When It's Bad to Have Good Choices," Maria Konnikova highlighted the work of psychiatrist Zbigniew Lipowski, who in 1970 identified this "veritable vicious cycle" that comes from the stress of too many choices. "Faced with enticing options," Konnikova summarizes, "you find yourself unable to commit to any of them quickly. And even when you do choose, you remain anxious about the opportunities that you may have lost: maybe that other stack of hay tasted sweeter."[15]

Not incidentally, Lipowski grew up in war-torn Poland, had to escape under treacherous conditions, and was sprung to his field of study after confusion about why his newfound American brethren didn't seem any happier. If this phenomenon was present almost fifty years ago, one can only imagine how much it has increased since then. After all, we've gone from *Should I have the chicken or steak?* to *Where should I go to college?* to *Which podcast should I listen to while I work out on which machine?* to *Who should I date among the thousands of singles in my network?* and so on. We are anxious and exhausted at having to choose all the time.

## Our Phones, Ourselves

Over the past fifteen years, the internet, smartphones, and social media have taken hold, and they now occupy the integral center of our lives. Their ubiquitous presence has led to an increase in anxiety triggers: from constant news updates to the lurking threat of identity theft to the warning that what we don't know about something we do every day "just might surprise us."

There is also a rise in the general feeling of not being able to keep up, colloquially known as the *fear of missing out* (FOMO), something three out of four teenagers say they experience.[16] A recent University of Pittsburgh study determined that depression and social media use are correlated in young adults, finding that "highly idealized representations of peers on social media elicits feelings of envy and the distorted belief that others lead happier, more successful lives."[17] There have also been studies linking social media to depression in adults as well.[18]

We now live in a world where our friends' parties and vacations are posted online for us to track and envy. There are indeed genuine communities that develop online, but there are residual negative effects to so much sharing and checking and liking. Our social lives have become "public" in a way that our forebearers could never have imagined.

A recent *Guardian* article highlighted the anxiety brought about by a seemingly efficient invention, the read receipt, which tells the sender that his message has been opened.[19] In the silence between communications, there is a lot of room for fantasy, doubt, and irrational fear. It seems that texting has opened a new kind of fear of social rejection, a *Why am I being ignored?* feeling. It can't be a coincidence that the most connected generation in history is also the most anxious. Digital communication styles certainly are playing a role in the skyrocketing rates of social anxiety on college campuses.

Alan W. Watts wrote, "The miracles of technology cause us to live in a hectic, clockwork world that does violence to human biology, enabling us to do nothing but pursue the future faster and faster."[20] Watts's words, from his groundbreaking book *The Wisdom of Insecurity* encapsulate the chaotic and demanding nature of American life in the twenty-first century—yet they were actually written in *1951.* In the sixty-seven years since Watts and others spoke of the way technology has sped up our lives, the frenetic energy of society has increased exponentially. And it has happened—and continues to happen—at a rate that even the most prescient thinkers could not have imagined. There have been great gains and progress in the decades since, but the trade-off for humanity has been substantial. It is as though the bill is finally coming due and more of us are beginning to feel the pain of payment.

## Political Anxiety

"A great man once said that the true symbol of the United States is not the bald eagle," said Ruth Bader Ginsberg, associate justice of the U.S. Supreme Court, after the divisive 2016 U.S. presidential election. "It is the pendulum, and when the pendulum swings too far in one direction, it will go back."[21] Political swings are *always* uncomfortable, and the associated anxiety has a wakening affect: it alerts the electorate to the need for action or change, often motivating us to get involved. Politics becomes more central to our lives than during easier times: we argue, we discuss, and ultimately (in one way or another) we are heard.

The 2016 U.S. presidential election caused a great deal of anxiety but also a great deal of political engagement, especially after the results rolled in. Taking the long view—whichever party you belong to—this is ultimately a good thing. When political anxiety can be turned into action, the country at large ultimately benefits: more voices being heard and more people getting involved. It often takes a hard shake—an element of discomfort—to wake us from complacency.

Edie Weiner, one of the world's leading futurists, holds that as a civilization we are in the midst of seismic change, evolving at an exponential rate. Large-scale resistance; gridlock in forging agreements; and avoidance of divergent ideas, people, and culture are all natural.[22] Fear is in our blood. We don't want anything that threatens our status quo or equilibrium. Yet in our wise moments, we can stop and recognize that these times are just part of a natural progression. The breaking before the changing.

In *Anxious Politics*, Bethany Albertson and Shana Kushner Gadarian examine how, in an environment where terror threats seem to surround us, it is the seeking out of information that calms our anxiety. Seeking information is a powerful way to channel anxiety and gain a sense of control. But how we take in the information, and what we do with it, can be important too. When too much information bombards us, the message gets blurred, and we become overloaded. Fear of another recession, mass shootings, and homegrown or foreign terrorists, for example, occupy a great deal of the modern anxiety palate. Because of our habit to weigh things we've just heard about as being more prevalent than they are (known as recency bias) and our tendency to latch onto easily remembered examples (known as the availability heuristic), many Americans believe they are in more danger from crime or terrorism now than they actually are.[23] Cognitive psychologist Robert Leahy has written extensively about our unfounded fears, which are compounded by "non-events," all the things that go right that we never hear about. We receive an unfair sampling of how dangerous the world is. It is helpful to remember when we watch the news that it is mostly a highlight reel of bad things that happened that day—not a random sampling of events. This alone is a useful way to keep things in perspective.[24]

## City Life

The increase in city dwellers around the world has also led to an uptick in anxiety. A recent study at the University of Heidelberg in Germany demonstrated that "people living in cities risked experiencing anxiety and mood disorders at a much higher rate than noncity dwellers, from 29 percent to 39 percent more." The trend is heading in one direction; statistically we are more likely to live in cities in the future and that "by 2050, about 70 percent of the world's population will be urban."[25] City life is vibrant and exciting, but it's hard for the average person to absorb this environment all the time—during a tough breakup, a busy morning commute, a desire for a moment alone. The same city that can bring us energy and purpose can also be the cause of our tension and stress.

The vigilance that comes with accustoming oneself to city life manifests as low-grade anxiety. You have to be alert to live amidst the hustle and bustle, fight your way onto a metro or subway car, into a traffic lane, or through a grocery line. Even the most extroverted and gregarious among us can find it hard to bear everyone at once.

Our major metropolitan centers also seem to be designed to make sure we never focus on something for more than a few seconds. This can gradually translate into a general and genuine feel of discomfort and anxiety. Even at the end of the day, behind our apartment door, the effect lingers.

## How We Deal

Xanax is the fifth most prescribed drug in America,[26] and nine out of the top ten most widely prescribed psychiatric medications target anxiety symptoms.[27] There are also a staggering number of over-the-counter products and strategies on the market aimed at ridding or suppressing anxiety.

Clearly there is a place for medication in alleviating immediate suffering and for extreme cases where anxiety becomes regularly overwhelming. Medication can be useful in pulling anxiety back into a moderate range, so that sufferers can activate sound thinking and decision-making.

Short-acting drugs like Xanax, Valium, and Klonopin target immediate anxiety relief, and longer-acting serotonin reuptake inhibitors (SSRIs) like Zoloft, Prozac, or Paxil work to increase neurotransmitters in the brain associated with feelings of calm and well-being.

These medications are tools that help turn the volume down on everything—emotions simply are not as severe when the medications are working properly. Some clients say it allows them a bit of breathing room to use the strategies they are learning in their work with me. Others describe it helping them feel more like themselves when such a feeling has gone missing for too long. For everyone, the effect of medication is slightly different, dependent on each person's individual situation and neurochemistry. One of the downsides of medication is that it risks masking emotions that can be useful. We'll discuss how tamping down the anxious response actually hampers the message that anxiety is trying to send us.

Furthermore, more and more relatively healthy people in the United States are taking medications long term. And while medication has been shown to increase our brain's capacity to soothe itself, long-term use can have unintended consequences. Helen Fisher is an anthropologist who has joined many scientists in warning of the overuse and long-term effects of antidepressants, which kill dopamine, the sex drive, and the release of attachment chemicals that come with sexual release.[28]

Fisher's concern about the long-term use of SSRIs for example, is in their dulling of passion and love. These drugs raise levels of serotonin, which subsequently negatively impact the dopamine circuitry that is associated with desire and reward. Fisher's warning: It's all connected. By tampering with one part of the brain system, we are tampering with others, some of which are at the very heart of being human.

Others turn to avoidance and numbing strategies that only make the situation worse. Millions self-medicate with cigarettes or drugs. Alcohol consumption, especially by women, has been steadily increasing in recent years,[29] a period that has included higher rates of binge drinking and drunk-driving arrests.[30] These habits launch destructive feedback loops where the problem masquerades as the solution. "The problem is that the same alcohol that takes the edge off anxiety tends to exacerbate depression," Andrew Solomon explains in *The Noonday Demon: An Atlas of Depression*, "so that you go from feeling tense and frightened to feeling desolate and worthless. This not an improvement."[31]

Clients of mine who are "anxious" drinkers know that alcohol actually increases anxiety and irritability as it exits the system, leaving a person slightly more anxious than before the first drink. This is the foundation of tolerance building: you need more and more to do the trick of relaxing, and in turn the detox is more and more anxiety producing.

Various other forms of escapism are proliferating as well. Many of us are eating more and reaching for more sugary and processed foods to cope, a habit that is both growing our waistlines and disrupting our overall health. Upwards of 40 percent of American adults are considered obese according to the Centers for Disease Control and Prevention (CDC),[32] while as many as two out of every three adults are overweight.[33] Diabetes is also on the rise, as well as the myriad health complications that accompany it.[34] Even a sedentary lifestyle is causing us health trouble, with new data supporting the health risks of sitting for long stretches at a time.[35]

We are also watching more and more television: the average American watches more than five hours per day,[36] and even more of us are zoning out online, on our ubiquitous, portable screens. In 2013, digital usage surpassed television viewing for adults as we've reached 5 hours per day online, with an average of 2.5 hours per day spent on nonvoice mobile activities alone (texting, social media, and games).[37] By 2016, Americans were spending more than *ten hours* a day in front of screens. We do more and more—and *live* more and more—in the digital space.[38] The nature of progress itself means we can expect the speed of society, technology, and our daily lives to only increase—and at a faster rate.

"What looks like relaxation could be exhaustion," author and scientist Robert Sapolsky writes.[39] Therefore, a trend that is not so surprising is the booming relaxation industry. Bloomberg recently reported that relaxation drinks, soft drinks with natural and not-so-natural ingredients with calming properties, are the next billion-dollar industry.[40] It's illuminating if we stop and think about the growing popularity of these products after twenty years of energy drinks flooding the markets. The pervasive feeling that we need to get going and keep up is now counteracted by our desire to slow down and process. We are desperate to feel relief from the pressures of modern life and we will take whatever we can to get it, even if it offers just a brief respite. Perhaps we are in the midst of a giant societal hangover, a malaise about how much is expected of us and how much we expect of ourselves.

Of course, there is nothing wrong with relaxing pursuits, but relaxation as a primary objective is just another form of avoidance. It doesn't succeed at keeping anxiety at bay. In fact, sedentary activities could be exacerbating the problem. A recent study linking inactivity to anxiety—the first of its kind—was led by Dr. Megan Teychenne, out of Deakin University in Australia,[41] which found a positive correlation between the two.[42]

This is also true anecdotally. Ask anyone with anxiety: the more we avoid something the scarier it gets.

Anxiety seems to be a natural reaction to a 24/7 world where it's become increasingly harder to find peace and balance. It is more difficult to shut things out and focus on what matters.

It comes at a time when it has never been more necessary.

So how can we turn on the *power* of anxiety?

## CHAPTER TWO

# Waking Up to Anxiety's Purpose and Power

*"The human mind is the very idea or knowledge of the human body."*

—**Baruch Spinoza**[1]

**When I was twelve years** old, I was asleep in my family's Long Island cottage when I was jarred awake in the middle of the night. It was the Fourth of July; the distant popping of beach fireworks had ceased and even the late-night revelers were asleep. Throughout my childhood, I had battled stifling asthma. That night I woke with an acrid taste in my mouth, a stuffing of my breathing. Something wasn't right. I had that elemental feeling of not getting enough oxygen, but it felt different than my typical asthma attacks.

Half asleep, I wandered to the bathroom to rinse my mouth out with water, but the taste stubbornly remained. A slow panic rose as I realized I couldn't breathe. I got back into my bed, and as my body began to awaken, I realized what was in my nose and mouth: smoke. The house was on fire.

My sister and the babysitter—both soundly asleep—were in the cottage that night. I rushed to wake them up, and when we opened the glass back door, flames rose behind us. We then struggled with the screen door, which was stubbornly jammed in place. We pulled and pulled at the handle, but it wouldn't budge. In that terrifying moment, I felt trapped. It was an old two-bedroom cottage, makeshift, with old and brittle wood. I didn't know much about construction, but I instinctively felt it was the kind of place that burned rapidly.

All three of us finally kicked down the screen door and ran to a neighbor's. Before we even reached the nearest house, our whole cottage went up in flames. I remember watching from that safe distance as the place was engulfed in a raging fire. The image will never leave my mind.

When I reached graduate school and later worked toward my doctorate, my clinical interests often circled around trauma. The fire never veered from my mind. I carried it with me as an experience that shaped how I think about trauma, and I was curious to better understand how people deal with and recover from such situations and the anxiety that lingered. It was not until later that I realized perhaps the most important part of the story: the waking up.

## Anxiety's Message

Anxiety is not a noise (*Cover your ears!*), but rather a signal (*Look over here!*). True, the signal is sometimes misunderstood and no doubt it can be distracting, but that doesn't mean we should shut it out. It means we should *clue in.* Waking up to anxiety's message allows us to use it most effectively. I know there's wisdom and information in anxiety, so I try hard not to shut it out when it comes knocking and have successfully worked with my clients to do the same.

In the fire that night, I couldn't ignore my discomfort and go back to sleep—I woke up and did my best to make sense of what was happening. My anxiety helped activate me to solve the problem by waking up the others and escaping the house. I have often seen this experience as both an indication and a larger metaphor for the way anxiety is a protector, tool, and growth enhancer.

As an adult, I have learned to tune in to my anxiety to harness a deeper understanding of what needs my attention, as well as helped clients, friends, family, and colleagues do the same. Sometimes, it can be less productive. But most of the time, my anxiety keeps me focused on where my attention is needed.

"[T]hrough watching and learning," Michael A. Tompkins writes, "you'll understand that your anxiety doesn't come out of nowhere—even if feels that way sometimes."[2] We don't grow without stretching and we don't change without discomfort. Our anxiety manifests as something unpleasant, but it is trying to protect us, motivate us, and educate us. It takes a commitment to a new mind-set to see this. Understanding that anxiety holds the

seeds of growth can help develop an attitude of curiosity and cultivate a more conscious experience of it.

The more I have on my plate, the more anxiety I will feel,
and, frankly, the more I need. I need the extra reminders when I
am stretched thin, and I rely on them to keep me focused on the
most important to-dos: coordinating homework duty, arranging
transportation for upcoming appointments, organizing the family
calendar, managing kids' schedules and extracurricular activities,
evaluating client progress, grading student work, brainstorming
writing ideas, paying bills, attending to family and friends' needs,
completing errands, scheduling household repairs, answering emails,
organizing travel plans, getting to the gym, and meeting deadlines.

Like the list that swirls in all our heads, some of these tasks
are immediate, some are longer term, some are diffuse, and some
are minute. Especially when life's responsibilities bubble beyond
my capacity, anxiety keeps me abreast of what matters most at any
given time. It reminds me when the juggler is in danger of dropping
a ball and what might be plan B. Allowing anxiety to be a signal and
an engine has taken work and habitual practice, but I have developed a relationship and understanding with it. I know it can help
me, so I have come to rely on it rather than fight it.

We have been relentlessly conditioned to view anxiety as a
monster, an uncontrollable force we must shut down. But my
personal and professional experience offers a more nuanced and
multifaceted impression. I have grown to see that anxiety is really
a sign that something we care about is at risk and we might not be
able to protect it. However it manifests itself, anxiety is grounded

in a cause. "Mood is like a fever," Dr. Michael Khan writes. "It's a signal your system is giving you that something isn't right."[3]

As we will learn later, we can alter our biology and brain chemistry by what we think about and do with our experiences over time. Contemporary thinking about anxiety has given us the idea that we need to rid ourselves of it, that it's a failing we should work to ignore or conquer. I believe, however, we can trust our senses and heed the natural instincts that are trying to tell us something important. There is wisdom in this elaborate and efficient system we already have inside of us.

Mindfulness expert Jon Kabat-Zinn beautifully frames the power we have to change. "Like subterranean water, or vast oil deposits, or minerals buried deep within the rock of a planet," he writes, "we are talking here of interior resources deep within ourselves, innate to us as human beings, resources that can be tapped and utilized, brought to the fore—such as our lifelong capacities for learning, for growing, for healing, and for transforming ourselves."[4] The human mind and body have enormous capacities and hidden strengths. Anxiety can be the catalyst and motivating force for ultimate growth, success, and maybe even peace.

## Anxiety's Stigma

People feel little shame in saying they are "stressed out." Stress is something people brag about, and they often wear it like a badge of honor. It means *I'm busy, I'm important, people depend on me.*

It also communicates worth—whether to our social circles or to our bosses. A recent Columbia Business School study examined this ubiquitous societal shift in the twenty-first century: from bragging about our leisure to bragging about our *work*. "By telling others that we are busy and working all the time," Silvia Bellezza explains, "we are implicitly suggesting that we are sought after, which enhances our perceived status."

Anxiety, on the other hand, comes with a degree of secrecy and shame. To be busy, even stressed, is just a modern, cosmopolitan state. But to be anxious? It is often treated as a private prison we carry with us, one we're afraid others will discover. And that fear only adds to the problem.

But anxiety is still biology reacting to circumstance. If we tease out what is triggering our anxiety, we can see how it makes sense and can thus become beneficial, just like our threat response protects us when we are in danger. Once we recognize anxiety's message and embrace it as a map and a tool, we can use this sensitive and dynamic force to keep us operating at our best. With it, we are tuned into and energized by what is truly important. Our anxiety helps us adapt to life's changing demands and motivates us to strive for what we want. It is not something that should carry any shame—anxiety is the engine that is motivating us and the track that is keeping us focused.

## Moving from Shame to Embrace

In becoming an expert on anxiety, I have become its champion. As a psychologist, I meet every day with people who tell me they have anxiety. It doesn't take a lot of digging to find that they're almost always anxious for a reason, whether they are conscious of what that reason is or not. More importantly, they mostly feel like there's nothing they can do about it. In fact, it was hearing this so often that led me to question the assumption. A classic sufferer of an anxiety disorder is miserable in their experience of anxiety and thus does whatever they can to avoid feeling it. This can often prompt exhausting efforts to avoid potentially stressful, scary, or humiliating situations that are ultimately, counterproductive.

I also noticed something else, especially in patients who were the most anxious. Once they started doing something, anything, the changes were immediate, quantifiable, and inspiring. What really seemed to make the difference was how willing they were to be brave and how willing they were to take action. So, the issue becomes *what did it take to get them there?*

First, they have to realize they are in control.

## The Driver's Seat: On Control

"No control lies at the heart of everything stressful, to a greater or lesser degree," writes health and wellness author Thea Singer.[5] The more we perceive control over the future painful event, and trust in our resources to cope with it, the less distress we will feel. And how do we take control? Through action.

The severity of anxiety then appears to be largely determined by how much control we perceive we have and whether we can handle it—two key ideas we will explore in detail in later chapters.

A 2004 meta-analysis of studies on college students' sense of control compared those who believed they were in control of their destinies to those who believed luck and the actions of those in power determined their fate. The results support the theory of learned helplessness: there is a negative feedback loop where depression and powerlessness reinforce each other. The study found that those who felt less control over their lives showed lower academic achievement, ineffective stress management, and higher levels of depression.[6] When we don't feel control, we don't take control. However, if we are open to approaching our anxiety differently, we see that we don't have to be a passive victim—if we make the choice not to be. Before we get out of any hole, we must first decide that we can.

## Spent Attention

It comes down to listening to ourselves. Our anxiety is asking us for our undivided attention. It's no coincidence we use the verb *paying* when discussing attention. After all, attention is not a bottomless pit but rather a finite and valuable resource. In his latest book *Incognito,* neuroscientist David Eagleman discusses the concept of change blindness in vision. In study after study, researchers have determined that we don't notice something changing in our field of vision—even deliberate and obvious changes—unless we're looking for them.[7] One of the most famous examples of "inattentional blindness" is the Harvard experiment that asked people to watch a video of six people passing a basketball around. Before it began, the viewers were given a prompt: *Can you count how many passes are made?*

Incredibly, a man in a full gorilla suit walked through the frame, stopped and did a little dance in the middle of the screen, and then he continued passing through. Focused on counting the passes, half of the participants *did not see the gorilla at all*.[8] Why? They simply weren't looking for it. Eagleman himself recognizes the larger applicability and the metaphor. "In fact, we are not conscious of much of anything until we ask ourselves about it," he writes.[9] Attention is not something we just have; it's something we give. For anxiety, its very existence is a demand for us to clue into it, and use its energy for focus and problem-solving.

High performing athletes know well the need for intentional focus. In his book *Focus: The Hidden Driver of Excellence* psychologist Daniel Goleman refutes the famous ten thousand hours of practice concept introduced by Malcolm Gladwell.[10] It's not the amount of practice that achieves mastery: it's the type. The practice itself needs to be direct and focused or it doesn't lead to much at all. Goleman looks at a variety of studies and experts (including Anders Ericsson, whose work birthed the ten-thousand-hour concept) and concludes: "Optimal practice maintains optimal concentration." It's about overriding our automatic behaviors or creating new ones.

Habit-change researchers also note the same dynamic—what

you pay attention to is what gets solved, improved, or mastered. When you pay attention to your anxiety, you're on the path to channeling it into usefulness. You are using it to focus on something that needs solving. Sometimes that focus is best directed to our present action, so our thoughts of the future don't distract us. Other times, we should focus on the anxiety itself, so we can understand what it is trying to tell us.

We live in the era of constant multitasking, grasping onto the faulty idea that we can share our attention between focal points and get twice as much done. Science has repeatedly proven this to be an unproductive, imaginary, and in the case of distracted drivers, dangerous idea.[11] In its less dangerous form, our efforts at multitasking are reminiscent of the spork, a utensil that aims to be both spoon and fork but cannot adequately perform the task of either.

Daniel Goleman compares our attention less to a "stretchable balloon" and more to a "narrow, fixed pipeline."[12] We only have so much of it, and how we deploy it matters. Numerous studies show switching back and forth between tasks takes more time and energy than attending to one thing at a time.[13] We end up doing neither task efficiently nor competently because each activity is being processed as a distraction from the other. It is no wonder that multitasking makes us anxious—neither thing is being attended to, and our minds know it.

# The Monkey and the Green Banana: An Invitation to Be Gentle

This book is an invitation to be courageous but also a reminder that we must be gentle with ourselves. "Our culture's epidemic of self-criticism has left us woefully unskilled at self-compassion—that essential anchor of sanity, which both grounds and elevates our spirit," Maria Popova writes in her insightful "Brain Pickings" column.[14] We are in the habit of seeing the negatives, the glasses half empty, and we feel stuck. Stuck and sometimes rigid in how we think about it too.

There is a story shared in various communities—from business to yoga circles—regarding how natives in Africa and India trap monkeys. Hunters place a green banana inside a hollowed-out coconut, which is chained to a tree. An opening is made just big enough for a monkey's paw. The monkey reaches into the coconut, grabs the banana, and by making a fist around the banana, traps itself. Its open hand can always fit through the hole, but its clenched fist is too large to pull out. The monkey doesn't let go; it remains stuck, screaming and struggling to free its fisted paw. The monkey is trapped by a stubborn force of its own creation.

Force doesn't always make things better, and it can often damage things far past their original problematic form. Yet many of us believe that we simply need to force ourselves through our fears and all will be better. This is simply not the case.

Empathy, curiosity, and compassion must be our trusted allies along the way; they will nudge us to stretch our preconceptions and grow our awareness. Harshly judging ourselves or trying to force solutions not only escalate anxiety, but they limit our progress, willingness, and effectiveness. As *Anxiety and Avoidance* author Michael A. Tompkins reminds us, "true motivation is an invitation, not a push."[15]

Being gentle with ourselves is not just emotionally important, it's also a practical facet of the work I do. It's the approach that promotes maximal growth. We must continuously look for ways our experience is understandable, reasonable, and even predictable. Where can we soften our perspective or effort? Where can we be kinder, and how can we be more accepting of ourselves?

Gentleness is not about coddling, permissiveness, or a lack of discipline. It is finding the sweet spot in our effort where we can stick with it, attaining the necessary momentum and confidence to keep going.

Feelings *always* make sense. Always—even if some digging is involved to figure out how. Our job in assessing our anxiety is to understand the source of those feelings and what to do with them. Know that you can listen, that you can bear it, and that it gets easier the more we do it. "As we gain more experience doing something and it becomes easier for us," social psychologist Heidi Grant Halvorson writes in *Succeed*, "we often start to see it in a more abstract *why* way—more in terms of meaning or purpose."[16] Developing this new habit of making use of our anxiety requires a larger understanding of this feeling inside of us. It helps if we take a detailed look at the various names we have for it and the various ways it manifests itself to us.

## When Self-Compassion Is Difficult

For some, self-compassion may be harder than it sounds. This can happen when we get tired of feeling anxious or just feel sick of ourselves and living in our skin. It is in these spaces where being kind to yourself may feel indulgent, or even downright impossible, but might be the most important thing you need to do before doing anything else. Three strategies to try:

**Fake it till you make it:** This is where acting-as-if can be strategy number one. There is strong research supporting positive action yielding feelings of positivity. For example, when we force a smile on our face, our brain receives a signal that we are happy. Try playing the part and you'll be amazed at the work momentum does for you.

**Invert the Golden Rule:** We are often much harder on ourselves than we would ever be on a friend or loved one. Envisioning your problems as those of a confidante can help you access your natural compassion and bypass negative self-talk. What if your mother, brother, or best friend came to you with your problem? What would you say to them? "Learn to be more compassionate company," writes Anne Lamott, "as if you were somebody you are fond of and wish to encourage."[17]

**Give your feelings some *character*:** Create distance between you and the feeling. Try thinking about your anxiety as a character in story, giving it a name and an identity. Is it a devoted but needy friend? A prickly coach? Your wise but always dissatisfied mother? Personifying your anxiety can help you engage it as someone who is trying to communicate a message to you.

## CHAPTER THREE

# The Power in Knowing

*"Fear is wisdom in the face of danger."*

—**Sherlock Holmes**[1]

**In learning how to harness** anxiety, the first step of recognizing it can be harder than you'd think. We're going to look at all the ways to know anxiety in this chapter, from the common physical reactions traced back to our ancestors to how we speak of anxiety and then how we feel it. Finally, we will look at three common ways that anxiety makes itself known using three stories from my practice.

Despite its ubiquitous nature, anxiety can be surprisingly beguiling to define. Language can be double-edged that way: it both crosses bridges and creates them. Identifying anxiety can be a challenge, as it presents as a variety of experiences, can masquerade as other emotions, and can pop up unexpectedly with little warning. Anxiety is a complex full-body experience that is as individual as we are as people. Is it a feeling? A series of thoughts? A physiological reaction? How do you recognize it in your body?

First, we must get a handle on what it means to feel anxiety in order to utilize it.

## The Physical Experience of Anxiety

Stress and anxiety can promote important chemical changes in the body, including the production of a variety of hormones needed by the body under threat. Understanding the biological and physiological responses to anxiety can help demystify it. The autonomic nervous system, which governs internal organs, regulates our physical bodies by activating and suppressing certain bodily functions in response to our needs. It is divided into two parts that are commonly explained through a car metaphor: the sympathetic nervous system (SNS), which acts as the "accelerator" and the parasympathetic nervous system (PNS), which acts as the "brakes."

During times of stress, the SNS activates the release of catecholamines, including adrenaline, that promote physical readiness for the body to respond. It gives you a surge of energy, including "increased cardiac output, skeletal muscle blood flow, sodium retention, reduced intestinal motility...and behavioral activation."[2] Your body is preparing to engage and respond. Blood leaves your gut and fuels your limbs for action—a sensation sometimes described as butterflies in the stomach.

At the center of our threat response is a very small area of the brain called the *amygdala*. Neuroscientist Joseph LeDoux, dubbed by one science writer as the Lewis and Clark of anxiety,[3] first identified the amygdala's role in activating the SNS, and he went on to call the resulting neurological chain reaction the *fear circuit*. The circuit includes a variety of physiological and neurochemical responses along the hypothalamic–pituitary–adrenal (HPA) axis, what we now call the fight-or-flight response.[4] The production of neurochemicals that aid in this response have been widely studied, and include cortisol, which is often referred to as a stress hormone. The fight-or-flight response has been best described as a "carefully orchestrated yet near-instantaneous sequence of hormonal changes and physiological responses that helps someone to fight the threat off or flee to safety."[5]

LeDoux believes that our physiological response to threat is a nonconscious one that precedes our labeling of it. Think of the instantaneous reaction to slam on the brakes when an animal darts in front of your car well before you even processed the threat. Recently, he has proposed that we distinguish between the physiological response to threat and the emotions of fear or anxiety that we identify with them. What we call the "fear circuit," he notes, should more accurately be described a "defensive survival circuit."[6]

When our threat response fires, an increased heart rate assures efficient delivery of needed oxygen and nutrients to muscles and the brain, and shallow breathing allows for an abundance of needed oxygen. Vasopressin triggers conservation of the body's water supply (and suppresses thirst) allowing the body to regulate temperature and metabolism. Norepinephrine heightens needed focus and attention, and oxytocin orients us toward connection with others. Our physiological stress response is an impressively complicated biological feat that readies us for protective action.

These physiological reactions, while reserved for rapid response to immediate danger, can become habit through nonconscious association and repetition. "When something bad happens, the brain leverages the entire body to register that feeling, and that feeling becomes associated with the event," David Eagleman writes. "When the event is next pondered, the brain essentially runs a simulation, reliving the physical feelings of the event."[7]

Everyone's anxiety response is different, and responses will vary with circumstances and severity. While some acute anxiety can be severe and intense, not all anxiety triggers a full autonomic threat response. Some anxiety produces only a portion of a threat response, and some anxiety can produce no physiological symptoms at all. One person's digestive issues might be another person's sweaty palms, which might be another person's butterflies.

While we are still learning how emotions are created, we have a good understanding of the "defensive survival circuit," and we are expanding our understanding of other stress responses as well. We now understand that after our initial biological and chemical reaction, in choosing how we interpret our experience, we thus choose how we will experience it and what we're going to do with it.

# The Naming

As science discovers more about our minds, we are learning that many of our experiences—like stress, desire, and awareness—are not as simple or as one-sided as we once thought. Anxiety is turning out to be another misunderstood experience that, when framed correctly, can be more of a help than a hindrance. So much hinges on our reaction and, inevitably, our choices.

In fact, LeDoux explains that anxiety is actually created through language, and the meaning we ascribe to our experience.[8] He explains that anxiety (along with all emotions) is a cognitive construct of neurological data comprised from various areas of the brain, including the amygdala, and in this way is formulated by the cortex. Other researchers have shown that naming anxiety alone can lessen it, which helps us take better control of the feelings associated with it. [9] The areas of the brain involved in processing emotional words—the insula and the medial prefrontal cortex—are also involved in regulating emotions, suggesting that naming our feelings can moderate our experience of them.

Whether synonyms, or simply different expressions for the same construct, there are several emotions within the anxiety "family" that merit clarification: fear, anxiety, stress, and worry. While these emotions have different dictionary definitions, they appear to share similar physiology and have been used inter-changeably in much of the scientific literature. These emotions are often experienced interchangeably and with considerable variabil-ity among individuals. In this book, I will use the term *anxiety* as I do in my practice—as broadly as possible—to intentionally encompass all iterations of the synonyms of fear, stress, and worry that apply. In order to delve deeper into our understanding of these feelings, I will attempt to clarify those terms here:

**Anxiety** is an emotion characterized by feelings of tension, worried thoughts and physical changes like increased blood pressure. People with anxiety disorders usually have recurring intrusive thoughts or concerns, often about situations outside of their control. They may avoid certain situations out of discomfort and worry. It can present itself as "butterflies" in the stomach, or a lump in the throat, or sweaty palms. Other physical symptoms might include trembling, dizziness, or a rapid heartbeat.[10]

Anxiety is both something each of us might define a little differently, and yet something we know when we feel it. In practice, I think of anxiety as the experience that arises from conflict about future unavoidable pain as well as the perceived threat to something we care about. It is also that sense that something isn't quite right, that we've neglected something important, and even sometimes a sense of dread. We conjure up a scary image in our mind; we think a threatening thought; we recall a painful situation. With this brain activity, our bodies respond. Anxiety "washes over one in formless waves," author Patricia Pearson writes, "pulls one under until the pressure and constriction are tangible and panic rears: *I'm in deep. I'm going to drown.*"[11]

**Fear** has been the emotion most commonly ascribed to the physiological threat response known as the fight-or-flight reflex, or defensive survival circuit; it is nearly automatic in its function to ensure our survival. Science has often separated fear from anxiety, placing fear in the moment. "*Fear* is the emotional response to real or perceived imminent threat," according to the *Diagnostic and Statistical Manual of Mental Disorders (DSM-V)*, "whereas *anxiety* is anticipation of future threat."[12] In fear, the link between stimulus and response has often been considered a straight line: direct threat leads to fear. In the category of anxiety, the lines can get crossed, lost, and tangled as anxiety has been understood as a more conscious, thought-based emotion. The subtleties have made their way into various languages. For instance, in German there is a clear distinction between *angst* (something unknown makes you afraid) and *fear* (you know what makes you afraid).

Fear is more often associated with surges of automatic arousal, thoughts of immediate danger, and escape behaviors, whereas anxiety has been associated with muscle tension and vigilance in preparation for future danger and cautious or avoidant behaviors.[13] And yet the physiology of anxiety shows so much overlap with the physiology of fear that "fear and anxiety are undistinguishable… perhaps because their definition of fear does in fact include all the more biological aspects of anxiety."[14]

**Stress** has been defined as an excessive demand on our resources, a definition coined by scientist Hans Selye in 1936.[15] In studying laboratory animals subjected to bright lights, loud sounds, extremes in temperature, or protracted frustration, Selye noticed patterns of pathological physical changes he defined as stress, or "the nonspecific response of the body to any demand for change."[16]

Stress, like fear and anxiety, has also come to mean something physical—a pulling or a force, which itself offers a useful image. We are being alerted and are resisting this alert, as though someone is grabbing our shoulder trying to get us to pay attention.

Though Selye dealt with the physiological response, he understood the role that approach and perception play when someone is under stress. "Adopting the right attitude," he wrote, "can convert a negative stress into a positive one."

> **Selye's Dedication**
>
> Incidentally, Hans Selye, who first coined the term *stress* in 1936, was not personally disconnected from the subject he spent his life studying.
>
> The dedication to his 1950 book *Relief from Stress* read: "But most personally, this book is dedicated to my wife, who helped so much to write it, for she understood that I cannot, and should not, be cured of my stress but merely taught to enjoy it."

Just because there are physical components to our stress doesn't mean they're unavoidable or unchangeable.[17]

It's interesting to note that we often say that we are "under stress," as though it were a force on top of us or maybe even a spell we're caught in. Stress seems to indicate a known external force bumping up against our own reaction to it. We commonly refer to anxiety as a stress coming from inside of us, in reaction to something that we cannot easily name or locate.

There should also be a distinction between the force of the external world on us and our reaction to it.

**Worry** is often the word we use to describe what the anxious person might spend too much time doing—to the detriment of productive action. Everyone worries; it is common and always treated as a temporary state. "We worry because we are intelligent beings," Norman Doidge writes. "Intelligence predicts, that is its essence; the same intelligence that allows us to plan, hope, imagine, and hypothesize also allows us to worry and anticipate negative outcomes."[18] This conception strikes me as simple and direct: we worry because we are human. No matter how it manifests itself, I believe we are anxious because we love, because we desire, because we hope, and because we care.

## Faces of Anxiety

Whether anxiety is experienced loudly as fear, quietly as worry, or physically as stress, it is an undeniable presence and force in all our lives. Getting a handle on what it is, what it feels like for us, and what we call it is fundamental to harnessing it. Anxiety can show many faces. To help illustrate this point are several people's stories to highlight how anxiety can lurk in many different corners of our discomfort.

## The Yell

Cecilia* came into my office on a gloomy winter day visibly distressed. Soon after sitting down and exchanging in some small talk, she dove in. Struggling to keep her composure, she told me she was privately a wreck. Cecilia worked as a communications

---

\*     All names and identifying details have been changed throughout the book to protect privacy.

director for a government agency and she had been offered a communications directorship at a West Coast company—a higher paying job in the private sector. There was no guarantee the job would work out and she felt guilty about asking her family to pick up and move for her.

Her husband told her told she should do what made her happy, but putting the onus on her just made her more apprehensive. Cecilia had committed so many years to her career that she felt she owed it to herself to keep at it. But she also didn't want to burden her family. The decision was affecting her sleep, her mood, and her health—she couldn't shake her anxiety—it was with her twenty-four hours a day. Cecilia's distress was what I call the **yell** type of anxiety.

As our session continued, the conversation drifted away from her family and she admitted there was something else. She admitted that there was a fear that she would fail or not fit into her new role; if so, it would compound her guilt. The idea of failing at both her career and upsetting her family was too painful for Cecilia to accept or even contemplate.

Cecilia's anxiety was loud, unmistakable, and excruciating; it was keeping her up at night, interrupting her appetite, and confusing her. She had lost her ear to her feelings. Her anxiety was at a point that it was yelling too loudly to be understood or to be of use.

The yell strain of anxiety is likely to show up along with major unexpected adversity or change—navigating crises, intense shifts, personal "earthquakes," loss, and other seismic shifts in life that spike numerous fears and concerns. Yelling anxiety won't be ignored, and insists on taking over just about anything else you might be thinking about or trying to do. It is relentless and exhausting.

Those of us who do public speaking know this experience where the sheer anxiety of facing a large audience can stunt our ability to think about anything. The feeling seems to hijack your experience. It becomes impossible to think of much more than how frightened you feel. Rage and temper tantrums work much the same way too; they are emotional storms that threaten to take over your thinking and ability to accomplish much beyond riding them out. Though we might not call these reactions fear, they do share a physiological similarity in that they all involve some activation of the autonomic threat response described above.

In an autonomic threat response, all our body's resources are readying for survival action, making it hard, if not impossible, to calm down. This sort of excessive anxiety can also be seen in normal responses to traumatic or highly upsetting events. In such situations where the mind is wrestling to make sense of an unexpected and painful loss, anxiety can run higher than is needed, and normal daily functioning can be impaired.

When our system is overwhelmed and activated toward survival, we need to be gentle with ourselves so that we can move and grow through it. There are numerous calming techniques— to be discussed later—which include deep-belly breathing, mind-body scanning, laughing, and other calming techniques, which all stimulate the parasympathetic nervous system (PNS), known as the "brakes" of the threat response.

Often, this kind of excessive anxiety is partially heritable and may require a variety of coping strategies. There are also effective medications that can help. (Remember that taking medication, or doing something to lessen anxiety, is taking important action toward a solution.) There is a direct relationship between how much confidence you have in your ability to handle your anxiety and its ultimate effect on you, as we will discuss later. The more you believe you can handle, the less likely you will be overwhelmed by the rush of anxiety.

## The Chatter

Deanna was one of my most anxious clients, originally coming for help to manage the fallout from a recent promotion and her father's declining health. She was a forty-five-year-old corporate executive who had worked her way up, often by letting her anxiety fuel her. She came in early, worked late, and used weekends to catch up on any tasks left over from the week. Any time she found herself worrying about something that needed doing, she tended to it. Having earned a reputation for hard work and careful attention to detail, some people dreaded working with her, labeling her a perfectionist. Others were grateful to have her on their team, knowing the job would be well done and trusting her leadership.

Everyone noticed her anxiety—it was part of who she was. Always looking around the corner, anticipating the next issue, she was quick to point out concerns and potential issues. She couldn't explain how she did it; she just knew that when she started to sense something was off or around the corner, she needed to pay attention, take note, and take some sort of action. It kept her on her game.

But despite her many successes, Deanna saw her anxiety—what I call **chatter anxiety**—as a problem. She hated the discomfort of it, that she couldn't seem to turn it off, and the angst she was feeling as her roles in life and work were shifting.

Chatter anxiety is distracting. It is easily identifiable, neither too loud that you can't block it out if you have to, nor so quiet that you miss it. You can work alongside it, and sometimes it acts as a running commentary or reminder of what needs to be done. It's the chatter to hurry up and finish that writing because you have to leave to pick up your son (like me right now) or that nagging sense of needing to finish the project that you haven't even started. The anxiety is there, you are aware of it, and whether you realize or not, it is spurring you along. Decoding it will help you focus on what it is telling you to do. It is often anxiety's constant presence that makes us afraid to take it on.

## The Whisper

Jamie's experience was less straightforward. A recent college graduate, her anxiety wasn't so much a feeling as an inference; it let itself be known through her thoughts and actions, or more accurately, her *lack* of action. Anxiety for Jamie was often experienced first through her avoidant behavior and temptations to numb her experience. This was especially significant because she struggled with prescription pills in the past.

Jamie was at the entry level of a promising business career, which had her working ungodly hours. She was often too busy to engage in much else, but at some points—especially weekends—she gave into her temptations to indulge her fatigue and avoidance, staying in bed all day, calling in sick a few Mondays, and putting her future career (and sobriety) at risk. Jamie learned to recognize the early signs: the first sign of danger was procrastination, an important cue of anxiety and a signal that action was needed.

Nowhere was it harder for her to push past her anxiety than when she was faced with menial and boring administrative tasks at the office. She also struggled to ask for help until it was too late to do so, feeling as a woman in the business world she had to prove her worth. She would lose confidence in her abilities, and her internal whispers about being a fraud would amplify: she would surely get fired, waste her degree (and her parents' money), and prove she couldn't hack it.

Jamie believed herself to be no match for the vicious cycle of avoidance she had created. She felt helpless to break free and impotent to take action. Yet, no matter how powerless she felt, Jamie understood that getting out of this vicious cycle always required action. And for her, that action started with changing her perceptions about the situation.

**Whisper anxiety** can be hidden in impulsive acts like reckless spending, eating, and sex or numbing pursuits like alcohol or drug use, computer and video games, online surfing, or social media. The anxiety is quieted temporarily, only to return with a vengeance when the activity ends or the substance wears off.

Whisper anxiety looks for quiet, restful moments to show its face. It's the early morning anxiety about the call you keep putting off, the resume still not updated, the friend you have been meaning to reconnect with. It can show in dreams that remind you of situations that need attention. It can manifest itself as frustrations with others who remind you of yourself. This is not often identified as anxiety per se, but is instead a quiet discomfort that is avoided, placed "on the back-burner," never truly addressed head on. Irrational thoughts of not being able to handle something are almost always part of whisper anxiety, which fuel the avoidance. Just as with the other anxieties, whispering anxiety keeps reminding you of unattended issues you care about, and can keep you on track if you pay attention.

Whether your anxiety is the yell, chatter, or whisper type—and we will return to all of them—your goal should be to listen. To determine. To act.

Now that we've looked at the various ways that anxiety manifests itself, it is helpful if we look at the history of how it has been viewed and treated. Though we like to think of anxiety as a modern phenomenon, it's been taken on by many scholars, thinkers, and scientists. Understanding that winding path is a useful exercise that can help us get our heads around how anxiety has been conceived and interpreted. We now turn to them.

## CHAPTER FOUR

# Anxiety through Time and Place

*"The curious paradox is that when I accept myself just as I am, then I change."*

—**Carl Rogers**[1]

**Over time, the understanding of** anxiety has expanded and evolved, the perceptions have altered, and the specifications have increased. Whereas 1980's *DSM-III* had fifteen pages on anxiety disorders, 2013's *DSM-V* spends nearly one hundred pages on it.[2] It's not just the understanding of anxiety that continues to change; the symptoms themselves do too. Though anxiety has consistent physiological elements, it's fascinating how its features have adapted to the context and to the culture in which it arises.

The symptoms can also be culture specific. As Allan V. Horowitz writes in *Anxiety: A Short History*, "Conditions that are widespread and well recognized in one era, such as hysterical paralyses of limbs and fainting spells, disappear and reappear as another era's panic attacks and social anxiety."[3] Even within the same era, anxiety's features can shift by geographical or cultural space. Thus, anxiety exists—has always existed—at the intersection of how we are and how our world operates. It's a moving target shaped by the time, place, and circumstances.

## Ancient Wisdom

The earliest-known writings about anxiety come from sixth-century BC Chinese philosophers Confucius and Lao Tzu: both believed anxiety to be a natural result of a life lived unwisely. Confucius described anxiety—*yu*—as being a product of longing for material things and wealth that formed what he called a "petty life," which yielded distress and an increase in *ch'i*, or energy, that needs taming and direction.[4] The pursuit of a noble life would yield peace and calm, *tang*.[5]*

Lao Tzu presaged the idea that modern anxiety comes from an abundance of choices. He promises that if we do not want, we do not hurt. Lao Tzu seemed to understand anxiety as a product of thought, rather than faith in the *Tao* ("the way"), which is devoid of anxiety.[6] This foreshadowed the beginning of a commonly

---

\*    "The Noble Person has neither anxiety nor fear." "Being without anxiety or fear!" said Niu. "Does this constitute what we call the Noble Person?" The Master said, "When interior examination discovers nothing wrong, what is there to be anxious about, what is there to fear?" (Taylor, "Confucius and the Age of Anxiety.")

invoked theme in many Judeo-Christian religions: faith is the antidote to fear, a concept that has been adopted by group likes Alcoholics Anonymous and its outgrowths.

In ancient Greek cultures until the third century BC, Stoic philosophy espoused the importance of facing life as it presents itself, rather than allowing ourselves to be controlled by our desires and fears, which were believed to be based in false judgments.[7] Emotions were believed to be derailing, and the happiest and most elevated people relied on their will, or rational thought, to live a life of virtue that would bring happiness.

## The Existentialists

"All existence makes me anxious…" Soren Kierkegaard wrote. "I myself most of all." Kierkegaard was the father of existential thought, and in 1844 he became one of the first modern philosophers to directly tackle the meaning of anxiety with his book *The Concept of Anxiety.*

One of the beliefs of Existentialists is that having choices inevitably provokes anxiety, because we fear making the wrong ones. Kierkegaard understood anxiety as an expected fixture of life, calling it "the dizziness of freedom." He speculated that it is the natural reaction to being able to chart our own course and the endless possibilities therein. Forever vulnerable to imagining the possibilities, Kierkegaard maintained humans could not escape the anxious guilt that flows from all those choices. His work was steeped in Christianity, so he believed this angst was part of the human condition that we all have "inherited" from Adam's original sin.

He describes anxiety in its early form as desirable, even positive, by referring to it as "sweet apprehensiveness." And like any seduction, this often gives way to more dangerous feelings of entrapment, vulnerability, and confusion that limit freedom. This is the kind of devastating anxiety that scrambles one's energy, and it makes functioning seem impossible. Kierkegaard believed that since anxiety is a natural feature of man, there can be a middle ground where its usefulness is embraced. "Whoever has learned to be anxious in the right way has learned the ultimate," he argued.[8]

## Industrial Anxiety

The Industrial Revolution and the accompanying "speeding up" of the world in the mid-nineteenth century brought a new type of anxiety to the population. In 1869, George Beard coined the term *neurasthenia* to define the physical reaction that arose from the mental state created by a modernizing world. He defined neurasthenia as "nervous exhaustion"[9]—*nervous* as in the nervous system—and best understood as the precursor to modern anxiety.[10] It was frequently diagnosed at the time and was heavily weighted to women, who were universally seen as less able to handle the modern world than their male counterparts.[11]

Beard saw a direct connection between the urbanization of America and the rise of stress, even titling one of his books *American Nervousness*. "The chief and primary cause of this development and the very rapid increase of nervous-ness is modern civilization," Beard wrote, "which is distin-guished from the ancient by these five characteristics: steam power, the periodical press, the telegraph, the sciences, and the mental activity of women."[12]* Beard's recommended treatment, which gained global traction, involved separating oneself from the stresses of modern life: "withdrawal from the pressures of urban life, rest, and a simpler, healthy lifestyle."[13] This prescription does not sound far removed from certain back-to-nature and simplicity movements gaining traction in the twenty-first century.

## William James

William James is considered the first American psychologist, because he taught the first psychology class in the United States (at Harvard in 1869) and later penned a classic psychological text (*The Principles of Psychology* in 1890). One of James's major contribu-tions to the field was his expansion of the idea that a thing's value should be measured by its usefulness rather than its truth, and by its impact rather than its source. According to his pioneering theory, the James-Lange theory of emotion, emotions occur as the result of physiological reactions to events, *not* the other way around.

To use a modern-day example: If you are driving along and a

---

* Beard was, of course, a man of his time, and this reference likely meant the novelty of women having goals and pursuits beyond the home.

dog runs out in traffic, you slam on the brakes to stop and avoid the crash. Only after an impressive chain of protective actions to avoid a feared crash do you then identify feeling a surge of anxiety. Physiological reactions prompt thought, which then prompt emotion. James understood that since emotional reactions, anxiety in particular, were physiological reactions that were influenced by our thoughts, they could be *altered* by them as well.

James understood that thoughts were powerful determinants of how we would experience emotion and that to a large extent we had control over them. James also believed in using the power of action to change one's experience. Behavior remains within the realm of control, and James believed that by controlling our actions, we could alter our feelings:

> So to feel brave, act as if we were brave, use all our will to that end, and a courage fit will very likely replace the fit of fear. Again, in order to feel kindly toward a person to whom we have been inimical, the only way is more or less deliberately to smile, to make sympathetic inquiries, and to force ourselves to say genial things. One hearty laugh together will bring enemies into a closer communion of heart than hours spent on both sides in inward wrestling with the mental demon of uncharitable feeling.[14]

James believed in the propulsive power of action to take over and redefine one's anxiety "to wrestle with a bad feeling only pins our attention on it, and keeps it still fastened in the mind: whereas, if we act as if from some better feeling, the old bad feeling soon folds its tent…"[15]

As an example, he referenced speaking anxiety. "Who are the scholars who get 'rattled' in the recitation-room?" he asks. "Those who think of the possibilities of failure and feel the great importance of the act… Who are those who do recite well? Often those who are most indifferent. *Their* ideas reel themselves out of their memory of their own accord."[16] In many areas James was presciently ahead of his time, including his recommendation to "make our nervous system our ally instead of our enemy."[17] Reading James today is illuminating. It is almost as if with the great strides in biological and natural understanding over the years, we have become too apt to give ourselves over to the predetermination of our biology or early experience. We have forgotten about our own role in the process— our capacity to take action—and therefore change ourselves, something that excitingly is being proven by brain scientists today.

## Darwin

In his groundbreaking works on natural selection in the mid-nineteenth century, Charles Darwin maintained that all emotions are part of the evolutionary process. Every organism on the planet is continually adapting to environmental demands and the competition for resources. Every physiological response could then be understood as adaptive, an inherited tool of survival passed down from previous ancestors.

Scholars speculate that the early death of his mother and an abusive father contributed to young Darwin's own anxiety, which he suffered through most of his adult life. Darwin's focus was mostly on fear, what he called flight from threat (fight or flight, as later coined by Walter B. Cannon). In studying emotions, Darwin showed that in all species there existed physiological manifestations, unconscious and habitual, which occurred between an environmental stressor and a pattern of responses. These "associated habits" were not learned, but rather inherited vestiges of previous ancestral adaptation.

"Habits easily become associated with other habits," Darwin wrote in *On the Origin of Species*, "and with certain periods of time and states of the body. When once acquired, they often remain constant throughout life."[18] To the extent that instinctive habits are adaptive, they will be preserved by natural selection. Instincts, Darwin believed, were no different than other physiological structures; they behaved similarly from an evolutionary perspective. Darwin further distinguished between a habit's origin and its action, noting that instinctive habitual actions can be outside of awareness, though they can be "modified by the will or reason."[19] Not surprisingly, the part of the brain associated with will and reason is the prefrontal cortex, unique to humans, and the most anterior brain structure, believed to be the last brain structure to evolve. (It is also the only brain structure we do not share with other mammals.)

It is noteworthy that though he is the name most often associated with the biology of man, Darwin believed in the cognitive capacities of will and reason in determining action. Like James, he felt that it was ultimately in our hands whether anxiety benefited or weakened us.

## Freud's Riddle

At the turn of the twentieth century, Sigmund Freud popularized anxiety as an area of study, calling it "a riddle whose solution would be bound to throw a flood of light on our whole mental existence."[21] The founder of psychoanalysis believed anxiety to be, in LeDoux's words, "the root of most if not all mental maladies and central to any understanding of the human mind."[22]

Freud was one of the first theorists to espouse that humans are driven to reduce tension. He further speculated that avoidance (what he coined "defense mecha-nisms") actually *increases* anxiety. Catharsis—release—was the way to restore one's harmony. The systematic study of underlying psychological forces—both conscious and unconscious—that

**Messy Progress**

Something to keep in mind as we tour through what the great minds have "concluded" on anxiety: *conclude* is the wrong word. "There's a perception that science proceeds in a very directional, linear manner," neuroendocrinologist Bruce McEwen writes, "with an accepted knowledge base and people toiling to inch the edifice away from great falsehoods toward The Great Truth. In reality though, what scientists often have to do is lurch knowledge toward a great truth to counteract their field lurching too far, nearly capsizing, with an enthusiasm for a different great truth."[20]

Each scientific movement doesn't necessarily build on previous knowledge and sometimes tries to pick it up and run with it in another direction, or "lurch" in McEwen's formulation, which best captures the approach. Progress is messy that way.

influence emotions and behavior is known as psychodynamic psychology. The term *psychodynamics* refers to energy that drives our complex brain, an idea originating from nineteenth-century physics presented to Freud in his training at the University of Vienna by Ernst Brücke.[23] Psychodynamic thinkers have since built on Freud's views, theorizing that tuning *into* anxiety's message can pave the way for addressing it in a way that removes the discomfort.

Freud wrote of a "signal anxiety"—neither automatic nor involuntary, but created by thought; it readies an individual to face danger, mobilizes energy, and aids in adjustment to the threat. He describes anxiety as both an emotion and also an energy that needs to be discharged, a framing that echoes Darwin. Freud asserted that anxiety "on the one hand produces the character of unpleasure, and on the other finds relief through the acts of discharge already mentioned."[24] Freud's belief that anxiety was the result of internal conflicts between one's desires and the demands of the world is a concept still widely accepted.

Psychodynamic therapists today agree that insight into one's unconscious processes is believed to help cure anxiety, and that tuning into anxiety's messages is the surest path to ridding one of the associated feeling. Freud believed that we could only tolerate so much in our awareness at any given time, and that many of our feelings and thoughts thus occur outside of our awareness, in a place he called the *unconscious*. Defense mechanisms serve to protect us from the discomfort of our emotional conflicts, but are ultimately unsuccessful in solving those conflicts—a failure that manifests as anxiety.

Freud believed that relief from anxiety came from experiencing its source consciously; only then could it be processed. Therefore, this insight is believed to drive down conflict, delivering relief and a cure of anxiety symptoms. Though much of Freud's theorizing about sex and drive has not stood the test of time, his thoughts on anxiety continue to inform therapeutic practice and are being supported by the latest brain science, especially the idea that naming anxiety has been shown to reduce it. Psychodynamic thinkers would call this *processing anxiety*—making the unconscious conscious.

In psychodynamic psychotherapy, anxiety is taught as conflict. Since we're always feeling unconscious conflict, anxiety serves as the measure of our conflicts, whether we know or it not. When we can start understanding the conflicts, making decisions about them and, finally, doing something about them, we are on the road to progress and improvement.

## Behaviorism

Behaviorism grew out of a frustration with the psychodynamic focus on the mind, which could neither be known nor measured. Instead, behaviorists targeted observable facts. Scientists in the 1950s began to experiment and study how animals learned. Famously, Ivan Pavlov always rang a bell before he fed his dog and soon enough, the dog would salivate to the sound of the bell, whether the food was there or not. This is called classical conditioning: once a stimulus becomes associated with a response, similar stimuli will produce that response. Anxiety is thought to be learned in much the same way. One anxious experience can stimulate the same feelings when a similar scenario presents itself again. My mother, for example, nearly missed colliding with a motorcyclist early in her driving life, a horrifying experience for her. To this day, she still feels intense anxiety whenever she approaches a motorcycle on the road. The two have become permanently linked for her.

Another behaviorist, B. F. Skinner, created a box in which he put rats or pigeons and taught them to press or avoid levers by offering food or electric shocks. His experiments demonstrated that behavior could be manipulated and measured, and most importantly, it can be learned. Skinner's research further demonstrated the impact of rewards and punishments on learning.

To behaviorists, every experience is learned and can therefore be unlearned, including anxiety. They believe that anxiety is strengthened through the avoidance of a feared stimulus, therefore, it can be reduced through systematic desensitization. Behavioral therapy works along these lines, focusing less on the source of these thoughts and more on modifying their effects.

## Cognitive Theory

To many psychologists in the 1960s, it became clear that avoiding the domain of the mind and one's thoughts limited the effectiveness of behavioral treatments. Cognitive theory developed in order to explore those thoughts, yet it strayed from the

descendants of Freud by avoiding the deep recesses of the unconscious. Cognitivists turned their attention to active thinking and
mind processes that could be known and verbalized.

In the 1950s, one of the earliest cognitive psychologists, Albert
Ellis, defined the negative impact that irrational thoughts can have
on our mood and experience. Ellis developed an action-oriented
method of improving emotional well-being by changing irrational
beliefs to rational ones, called *rational emotive behavior therapy*.[25]

Aaron Beck, considered the father of cognitive therapy, also
believed that feelings and behavior flow from thoughts and overriding belief systems he called *schemas*. These schemas organize
how we perceive the world and are constructed during our early
life experiences.[26] For example, a routinely punished child, who
seldom receives encouragement, might adopt an early core belief
that she is a bad person. She could construct a schema of inadequacy that then shapes her every interaction with the world. Her
schema leads her to avoid situations that require effort or social
engagement, fearing failure and perhaps painful rejection. Isolation
and withdrawal, masquerading as self-protection, reinforce her
schemas of inadequacy and keep her stuck. Our schemas are the
stories we tell ourselves, almost unconsciously, about who we are
and how the world responds to us.

## Humanism

Humanistic psychology focused on will, responsibility, hope, and self-acceptance. The movement never gained mainstream scientific traction in that it dealt with ideas that were difficult to empirically prove. Carl Rogers, one of the founding fathers of the movement, described a threatening situation as one in which there is incongruity between an image of yourself and your immediate experience of yourself—between an ideal self and a real self. This conflict naturally produces defenses and perceptual distortions. So much of anxiety, he posited, can be attributed to our distorted ideas and perceptions about ourselves. Indeed, self-acceptance is well-known to deliver anxiety relief and offer a modicum of peace.

Rogerian psychotherapy thus aims to move a person toward self-acceptance and trust of the self, where such distortions are no longer necessary:

> Often, I sense that a client is trying to listen to himself, is trying to hear the messages and meanings which are being communicated by his own physiological reactions. No longer is he so fearful of what he may find. He comes to realize that his own inner reactions and experiences, the messages of his senses and his viscera, are friendly. He comes to want to be close to his inner sources of information rather than closing them off.[27]

In the 1960s, Abraham Maslow, the other father of humanistic psychology, argued that both psychoanalysis and behaviorism were overly concerned with symptom relief rather than satisfaction and growth. Maslow believed in human potential and our need for self-actualization.

In Maslow's essay "Neurosis as a Failure of Personal Growth," he explains neurosis as "a kind of moving forward, a clumsy groping forward toward health and toward fullest humanness."[28] That is, anxiety alerts us there is more out there. He believed that meeting one's needs was a normal growth-enhancing process, and that ignoring our needs, or repressing them, was unhealthy.

Maslow believed our needs were tiered hierarchically, ranging from our most basic (i.e., food and shelter) to our highest aspirations (i.e., purpose and meaning). A person's primary tension or anxiety would therefore reflect his or her lowest unmet need and would cease exerting pressure once those needs are met. A person without food or shelter could not feel tension about higher tiered concerns like self-actualization, whereas only a person whose lower tiered needs for safety, love, and esteem were already met could feel anxiety about lacking purpose or meaning. According to Maslow's theory, a satisfied need creates no tension or drive. Needs consequently only drive anxiety where there is a deficit. "Conflict itself is, of course, a sign of relative health," Maslow wrote, "as you would know if you ever met really apathetic people, really hopeless people, people who have given up hoping, striving, and coping. Neurosis is by contrast a very hopeful kind of thing."[29] It's a construct supported by the latest research on happiness: as we stretch toward meaning and grow, we become happier.

# The Search for Meaning: Positive Psychology

The end of the twentieth century saw a rise in brain-based strategies for dealing with anxiety and stress. A new genre of self-help exploded, focusing on how we change our brains by changing our thinking and our actions. The positive psychology movement is concerned with how "human beings prosper in the face of adversity."[30] Unlike humanism, which came up against skepticism due to its lack of scientific foundation, positive psychology arose simultaneously with the explosion of brain science, which documented the power of the brain's capacity to change, known as plasticity.

As psychologist Martin Seligman tells the story, he was motivated to study happiness and founded a movement dedicated to it after his daughter asked him to become less grumpy.[31] Founded in the late 1990s, the positive psychology movement continues to spread, focusing less on mental illness and more on mental health and happiness. Seligman's book, *Authentic Happiness,* became the cornerstone of the movement. In a paper with *Flow* author Mihaly Csikszentmihalyi, Seligman wrote that positive psychology is "about valued subjective experiences: well-being, contentment, and satisfaction (in the past); hope and optimism (for the future); and flow and happiness (in the present)."[32]

Harvard-trained psychologist and science writer Daniel Goleman became fascinated with the emerging trove of research on emotions and the brain, spurring the birth of his bestselling book *Emotional Intelligence* in 1995. The book outlines the importance of emotions in life and their impact on almost every area of it. He discusses basic brain structure surrounding the emotional and thinking aspects of our brains, describes the current neuroscience of the time, and argues that our emotional thinking might be one of our most powerful resources when it comes to success. Our thinking capacity as measured by our intelligence quotient (IQ) should no longer be the only way to predict success in life. How we understand and handle our emotions, those of others, and those of organizations, he argues, are far more salient predictors of success in life. Sometimes known as emotional quotient (EQ), emotional intelligence has given us a frame to value and further understand the inherent social skills that facilitate our relatedness as humans. Businesses, schools, and organizations rely on Goleman's theory to improve social harmony and grow success.

Unlike IQ that is believed to be hardwired, emotional intelligence is believed to be software that can be learned and cultivated. It is the ultimate reminder that none of us are finished products and of the optimism that comes from embracing our collective capacity for growth.

· ·

Looking through the history of how anxiety has been viewed demonstrates a key point: each new idea required a breaking down of old models. I'd like to propose that we are on the precipice of a new framework.

In order to move forward, to embrace anxiety as a beneficial tool, we must first take on the myths and misconceptions about it that act as walls in our way.

## Quick Reference

**Ancient Wisdom:** Are we made uncomfortable because there are too many choices? Is anxiety this discomfort? Are we indulging irrelevant feelings?

**Existential:** Are we simply wrestling with the bigger questions of life; searching for meaning; and trying to reconcile the implications of freedom, responsibility, and existence?

**Industrial Anxiety:** Is the speed of change causing us to feel anxious?

**William James:** What is anxiety's usefulness?

**Charles Darwin:** Is our anxiety signaling a need for us to adapt?

**Sigmund Freud:** Are we feeling conflict reminiscent of earlier ones?

**Behaviorist:** Is our anxiety learned and amplified by our habits?

**Cognitivist:** What irrational thoughts could be fueling our anxiety?

**Humanist:** Could our anxiety be based in our struggle for self-acceptance and meaning?

**Positive Psychology:** How can our thoughts and behavior help us grow and become happier?

## CHAPTER FIVE

# Ten Myths and Misconceptions

*"The Chinese believe that before you can conquer a beast you must first make it beautiful."*

—**Kay Redfield Jamison, *An Unquiet Mind*[1]**

**To reevaluate what our anxiety** means, we must directly challenge certain myths that remain implanted in the public consciousness and our minds. This is not just an informative step, but it is also a necessary one: how we feel about our anxiety can be as much of a problem as the anxiety itself—maybe even more so.

"Although anxiety is a negative emotion because it feels bad," Dr. Julie K. Norem has said, "it is not a negative emotion in that it's bad to feel it."[2] Anxiety has suffered our collective misunderstanding. Because of its discomfort, it has been treated as a negative force, something to overcome or avoid. Obviously far too much anxiety can be crippling, but its very presence need not be. In fact, in many areas and disciplines, the heightened arousal that comes with anxiety is a positive force, which is a concept we will explore. Yet anxiety's benefits remain muted if we insist on demonizing it or trying to push it away.

As the epigraph of this chapter states, we must remove a beast's ugliness, and once we do, we see it's not a beast at all. The ugliness was not there as a matter of fact but of perception. The myths surrounding anxiety, and the problems and fallout from those myths, make our struggle to tame it that much more difficult. Let's take a look at ten of the most common anxiety myths:

## Myth #1: Anxiety is a sign of imbalance

This misconception is only half true. Anxiety is indeed a sign but not necessarily of something negative.

Here's one way to think about it: One time I was driving to pick up my daughter from school, already running slightly late. I'm sure I had a lot on my mind—both professionally and personally—and someone in the lane next to me kept honking. I was unnerved by what I assumed was the driver's aggravation, and I sped up to get away. Sure enough, my lane slowed, allowing the car to pull alongside me, when the driver again started honking.

As we approached a red light, I knew I had no choice but to face the driver. When I looked over, I saw a middle-aged man pointing, motioning for me to roll my window down. I did, quite uncomfortable by this point. "Sorry about that," he said, before I could say anything, "but your back tire is just about flat. Just letting you know." The light changed and he drove off.

Anxiety is the persistent horn, but its message is not necessarily negative. It carries *information*, often a critical message we should notice. But its value is only accessible and usable when this messenger and its message are acknowledged.

## Myth #2: Anxiety is a relic of our prehistoric brain

Another myth is that anxiety is somehow an accidental remnant of our reptilian brain, out of place in the modern world, but our anxiety is far from out of sync. Steve was an Ivy League-educated young lawyer whose anxiety was getting in his way at work. A litigation associate at a big corporate law firm, he was often responsible for proofreading and filing legal documents in accordance with complicated litigation schedules and requirements. He complained to me that as deadlines approached, he often lost his ability to stay focused. Instead, he became distracted by his fear of missing the deadline and all the subsequent fallout. The more worried he became, the less he could think, and the more he fell behind. Once his anxiety started to brew, he knew there was a good chance he would miss the deadline—or come dangerously close to it. Because this was happening now with regularity, he feared repercussions for his client and for his own job.

Such acute anxiety is sometimes labeled an "amygdala hijack." That is, our primitive brain misperceives a threat and hijacks our response in a way that is neither helpful nor adaptive.[3] The amygdala hijack theory holds that our fight-or-flight response has not yet evolved to meet our modern survival needs. When we worry about missing a deadline and respond with the same reaction we would have to a predator—flushing skin, racing heart, shallow breathing, physiological readiness for *action*—we experience a flaw in our survival circuitry, one that has not yet evolved to meet modern threats. Our primitive stress response takes over our higher-order thinking centers by curtailing cortical activity and priming us to run rather than think clearly. Some psychologists consider this an evolutionary flaw.

While this argument has been commonly accepted for decades, modern neuroscience is beginning to suggest otherwise. Knowing what we know about neural plasticity—the ability of the brain to change throughout the lifespan—it is hard to imagine how key parts of the brain could exist without a useful function. Evolution simply does not work that way. Just because anxiety's roots are deep, doesn't mean anxiety is no longer useful. To the contrary, evolution theory holds that systems are *only* conserved for a purpose. As Steven Pinker writes in *How the Mind Works*, "Though our bodies carry vestiges of the past, they have few parts that were unmodifiable."[4] With our brains continually adapting, a conserved neurological circuit such as anxiety must be fundamentally important to our wellbeing, and not just our survival.

Anxiety is a powerful internal system that has evolved over thousands of years to drive adaptation and change. Its primitive origin—in the amygdala—and its capacity to override other systems, underscores its value as a powerful and primary survival tool. Just because our threats are seldom the physical ones of our ancestors doesn't mean our anxiety system isn't constantly updating. In today's distracted world, anxiety still jolts us out of complacency and keeps us focused when we need it.

Survival relies on our brain's capacity to adapt to the demands of our changing environment. Our brain's natural ability to shape itself to these demands is a process that is both uniquely human and lifelong. "Even when we're adults our brain is still changing," David Eagleman explains in his PBS series, *The Brain*. Using the famous example of the cabdrivers of London, who have to pass a complex test called "The Knowledge" before being given a license, Eagleman explores how the years of practice and study literally change the anatomy of the driver's brain, specifically their hippocampus that stores visual memory. (London's streets aren't organized along any kind of grid like many modern U.S. cities.)

"Who you are, and who you can be is a work in progress," Eagleman adds with his customary optimism. "Everything we experience will alter the physical structure of our brain in some way. Meaning that as long as we're alive our identities aren't fixed. They're constantly changing." Eagleman is not coming from a place of self-motivation or inspiration. He's coming from brain science. "On average, about a third of a person's strengths are innate, built into his or her genetically based temperament, talents, mood, and personality," writes neuropsychologist Rick Hanson in *Hardwiring Happiness*. "The other two-thirds are developed over time. *You get them by growing them*."[5]

Our brains never stop adapting. They are always strengthening what we use, and pruning what we don't. Our primitive anxiety systems should be viewed accordingly. Just because we don't yet fully understand its value doesn't mean it is faulty. Not a single human system has ever been proven obsolete.

Anxiety works as a signal to alert us when something is awry—useful in prehistoric times and useful now. Steve's anxiety always started out serving him—reminding him of deadlines and details he needed to attend to. But as he used this signal to focus on future possibilities rather than the work at hand, he moved away from the solution in front of him, driving up his anxiety to the point where he couldn't use it effectively. Nothing was wrong with, or unevolved about, his stress response. The problem was how he was using it.

## Myth #3: Anxiety is a distraction

A popular way of viewing anxiety is that it distracts us from ourselves and what needs to be done. Anxiety is treated as the thing that is getting in the way, but it's actually the opposite that is true. I always wanted to be a doctor. Like the physicians who helped solve my childhood asthma and allergies, I knew I wanted to work with people to figure out what was wrong and help them. I gravitated towards science and math in school, and I was consistently fascinated by how things fit together and made sense, whether dissecting a shark, dissecting musical chords, or working a physics equation.

In college, I felt sure I was on the path to medicine, but then I hit freshman biology, stumped for the first time trying to understand genetics and the science of probabilities. Dismayed by my struggle I started to rethink medicine and shifted to art history. I was drawn to the puzzle of art, the meaning behind imagery, and the symbolism that captured history and culture. But my earlier desire to help people kept gnawing at me. How was I going to help people in art? Sure, it could be done, art therapy, for instance, but there was something missing. There was a tangible void in my goal, and it was distracting me.

As a junior, I felt back at square one, with no tangible idea what I wanted to do with my life. No longer being sure of what I wanted, or able to figure it out myself, I knew I needed help. In taking an interest inventory test and talking to a professional, I was able to make sense of my distracting anxiety, and I began exploring other helping fields beyond medicine. Through this process, my eyes were opened to psychology and the power of applying it for good. Paths started to converge, and I began seeing different opportunities for helping people—perhaps even becoming a doctor. Later, when deciding between applying to medical school to be a psychiatrist and PhD programs to be a psychologist, I realized my interest in helping had less to do with physical ailments and more to do with helping people *feel* better.

My experience of anxiety in college that I initially found so annoying was something I call a *fire-alarm fallacy*. Yes, a fire alarm is irritating and piercing, but its annoyance doesn't make it a problem or in any way useless. In fact, it's the opposite; there's a *reason* the sound of a fire alarm is so distracting. *It's essential that you hear it.* Anxiety is uncomfortable for a reason: so that it gets our attention and helps jolt us out of complacency. Our amygdala is a complicated cortical alarm that is designed to get our attention and motivate us. Anxiety is not distracting you from what needs to get done; it's *telling you* what needs to get done.

The processing of threat is so basic, that when fully activated, it blocks out our thinking. Our cognitive processing is trumped by preparing ourselves for protective action. Anybody who has suffered disruptive anxiety knows the frustration of not being able to think as clearly when it strikes. Indeed, studies using fMRI imaging show less activity in the prefrontal cortex when the amygdala is activated.[6]

When something we care about is threatened, the situation deserves our immediate attention and energy, and sometimes, this is inconvenient and unpleasant. This time-tested, safety-comes-first response has evolved into a sensitive emotional system, one that helps us stay attuned to our priorities. In our increasingly high-stimulus and distracted world, this attentional aid is sometimes exactly what we need to redirect our resources, just like a fire alarm.

The heightened focus stimulated by threat also allows for powerful memory formation and retrieval. In fact, "mild to moderate short-term stressors enhance memory," Robert Sapolsky writes in *Why Zebras Don't Get Ulcers*. "This makes sense, in that this is the sort of optimal stress that we should call 'stimulation'—alert and focused."[7]

"Stress acutely causes increased delivery of glucose to the brain," Sapolsky explains, "making more energy available to neurons, and therefore better memory formation and retrieval."[8] Accessing and creating memory are critical under times of stress. You are adapting to something important and new, and your cognitive skills need to be sharp. This high-stakes decision-making needs to be stored as efficiently as possible too, so that you can call on it the next time you need it. Our anxiety can work as a quick trigger alarm system that helps us focus and remember, always in the service of protection.

## Myth #4: Anxiety is hardwired and inflexible

A common misconception is that those of us with anxiety are simply stuck and there's little that can be done about it. Jenny came to therapy complaining of anxiety, specifically she had developed a fear of flying. An event planner for major conferences held all over the country, she made multiple plane trips a year that were unavoidable and increasingly miserable. Believing she would never be able to fly without fear, she was thinking of leaving her job. "I'm a pretty anxious person," she admitted to me. As such, she just assumed there was nothing she could really do about her anxiety—that it was inflexible. What she wanted to learn was how to manage it better, and this was her opening request in our first session.

In spite of growing evidence to the contrary, anxiety is still viewed as something outside of our control that we must suffer through. "Perhaps, as the discoveries about the power of directed mental effort systematically to alter brain structure and function attract public awareness," Jeffrey Schwartz and Sharon Begley write in *The Mind and the Brain*, "we will give greater weight, instead, to the role of volition."[9] Volition, that is, control. Control plays a key role in anxiety; it is something we need not relinquish. We'll delve further into this idea in chapter 7.

Anxiety is not a hardware, but rather a "software" that can be altered, sculpted, and redirected. Science consistently has proven that our brain is more malleable than we had ever thought, and it continues to shape itself throughout life. What we practice, how we think, and what we repeatedly do continuously alter neural connections and pathways in our brains; these neuronal circuits mold our brains at the cellular level. As we connect experiences, thoughts, and actions with stimuli, our brains create links between neurons that are strengthened with each repetition. "What fires together, wires together," as neuropsychologists like to say.[10] (One of them, Rick Hanson, calls it *neural Darwinism*: survival of the busiest.[11])

These circuits become well-worn pathways that establish stronger connections the more they are used. As a result, they become faster and more efficient. This is how we learn. We can use that learning to build habits and strategies that help us live our lives as adaptively as possible. The same goes for anxiety: how we think about anxiety determines how we experience it. In a series of recent studies, Alison Wood Brooks showed how increasing anxiety can be transformed into excitement simply by changing our thinking about it. She notes that anxiety and excitement "are very similar emotional states. Both emotions are high-arousal, signaled by a racing heart, sweaty palms, and high levels of the stress hormone cortisol."[12] It seems that by shifting the perception of what is happening to your body, the sufferer becomes the driver. It gives her back the locus of control. Brooks's studies show that "by focusing deliberately on the positive potential outcomes, you actually are more likely to achieve them."

Professional athletes certainly feel anxiety before they compete, but they have often trained their minds and bodies to reframe that anxiety. They don't seem anxious to us; they appear psyched up and geared to go. When you watch a pregame huddle on television, think about how all that anxiety is being repackaged toward enthusiastic roaring and chest bumping.

Certain amounts of anxiety actually changes us for the better, making us stronger. A recent Stanford study showed how stress triggers the movement of immune cells to needs areas of the body, much like "the mustering of troops in a crisis." As the lead author of the study, Firdaus Dhabar, explained, "Mother Nature gave us the fight-or-flight stress response to help us, not to kill us."[13] Like working muscles during exercise, stressing our mental and emotional resources makes us stronger and, ultimately, more emotionally and mentally resilient—provided we rest and recover. Just like your body needs a rest day, your mind does too.

There is more than enough evidence to prove the point: our brains—and our response to anxiety—are changeable. Neuroendocrinologist and stress expert Bruce McEwen implores us to "remember the evidence that by repeated thoughts and actions, we can alter not only the functioning but also the structure of the neural networks in our brains."[14] Brains can show changes after ten weeks of cognitive behavioral therapy (CBT) with no medication at all.[15] CBT is essentially a boot camp for reframing your thoughts and responses. It can include replacing specific irrational thoughts with rational ones, exposing you gradually to something you fear, or seeing what happens when a compulsion is not engaged.

Changing our thinking works for anxiety as well. "As clinical data and PET [positron emission tomography] scans show," Schwartz and Begley write, "patients can willfully change the amount and quality of attention that they focus on those cerebrally generated feelings of anxiety and stress, changing in turn the way the brain works."[16]

Norman Doidge's book *The Brain that Changes Itself* highlights inspiring stories of people recovering from seemingly permanent conditions like blindness, speech loss, and stroke-induced paralysis through behavioral techniques. "The idea that the brain can change its own structure and function through thought and activity is," he writes, "I believe, the most important alteration in our view of the brain since we first sketched out its basic anatomy and the workings of its basic component, the neuron."[17]

There have even been studies on blind patients whose brains have learned to "see" through electrical impulses through their ears. Over time, part of their auditory system had been "rewired for sight rather than sound."[18] Our brains' permanence and immutability is a myth that keeps us stuck in certain patterns, creating barriers to understanding what it is we want and need.

Through our work, my patient Jenny discovered that her anxiety about flying was not something predetermined, or an experience that she would simply have to tolerate. When she felt discomfort bubble up, rather than focusing on how trapped she felt, she reached instead for practiced cognitive solutions that she knew would help. In learning to change how she thought about flying, she started changing her *experience* of flying. She learned to think rationally about the questions that often fueled her anxiety (e.g., *What did common sounds mean? Does turbulence mean the pilot is out of control?*) and remind herself of the answers, rather than her fears. By learning to focus on the facts, she replaced her creative fears with information, which was empowering. For other worries that were possible but unlikely—like unexpectedly crashing or undergoing an emergency—she learned to focus on the *probabilities* rather than the *possibilities*.

With practice, Jenny turned her vivid imagination to focus on all the likely scenarios in which her fears were averted by procedural regulations, aircraft safety features, and professional skills of the pilot and crew. She worked to overhaul her thinking about her experience of flying in general. Instead of dreading a flight, she learned to focus on the upside of flying—an opportunity to get to a destination quickly, while sitting in peace, unburdened by work demands, where she could look out the window or enjoy the luxury of doing *whatever she felt like doing* with no interruptions. In choosing to view her flying differently and employ the strategies she knew would help, she no longer felt out of control when she faced airline travel. She learned how to take control and let her anxiety cue the strategies she needed to direct it productively.

## Myth #5: Anxiety is dangerous and unhealthy

In exploring how anxiety can be used as a benefit, I interviewed Jo, an active duty officer in the Navy SEALs. Jo described anxiety to me as something he and his teammates have had to learn to work with and harness. "To me, anxiety is kind of like being on the starting block for a race," he told me. "The whole race is flashing through your mind, 'I gotta do this and that' but once you start you just go."

Thriving under pressure is something SEALs practice; Jo, like others, calls it being in "the zone." He tells me it's an experience that can come with an unexpected occurrence and when the pressure and intensity of the battlefield "adds stress." Active combat naturally triggers stress and anxiety, but through their training, team members learn to "actively work through it." When this kind of anxiety crops up during a mission, he describes how he uses it:

> It is all about working the fundamentals in your head
> from the individual level (What am I looking at? How
> am I holding my gun?) to the leader level (Where
> are my forces? What should I order if X happens or
> Y happens?). When something does happen, always
> go back to the fundamentals and execute, then

*reevaluate, execute, then reevaluate. Don't get stuck*
*with overcoming the big problem at once, chip away*
*at it until it is manageable.*

For Jo, anxiety is the engine keeping him focused. Rather than trying to deny it, he makes use of it natural energy.

Certainly, too much anxiety is problematic, but that holds true for just about anything. Anxiety, in moderate amounts, is neither dangerous nor unhealthy and can actually be good for you. "It turns out that during the first few minutes (say, up to thirty) after the onset of a stressor, you don't uniformly suppress immunity— you *enhance* many aspects of it," Sapolsky writes. "Physical stressors, psychological stressor[s], all appear to cause an early stage of immune activation."[19] Our anxiety operates as a type of armor— preparing and protecting us.

Under stress, Bruce McEwen explains, "the infection-fighting white blood cells attach themselves to the blood vessel walls, ready to depart for whatever part of the body is injured." Of course, too much stress and they all depart for the heart and lungs, to keep us alive.

Secondly, any damage or issues from the feelings of stress and anxiety are likely from our thinking on it and not from the anxiety itself. In a series of studies at Yale, Alia Crum showed how it is not that stress itself is harmful; it is our *perception* of it that does the damage. That is, we control its effect. "All of our good efforts to warn people about stress might be creating a mind-set that makes it more damaging,"[20] Crum says. The more positively you think about stress, the less damage it does to you.

The famous Whitehall Study, published in the *European Heart Journal*, examined civil servants in London and found "the perception that stress affects health, different from the perceived stress levels, was associated with an increased risk of coronary heart disease."[21] For those who thought their stress was dangerous to their health, it turned out to actually be dangerous. In fact, the risk of heart attack went up by 50 percent simply by carrying a belief that one's stress is unhealthy. There's a self-fulfilling prophecy at work; we think it's true, so we make it so.

## Myth #6: Anxiety limits your performance

Many anxiety sufferers feel that anxiety is getting in the way of them being their best selves, especially in high-stakes situations. Erika is a public-relations representative who has to meet with media and high-level investors on a regular basis. As her responsibilities have mounted, so has her anxiety, often to the point that she blanks out and looks like what she calls "an idiot." She describes herself as a confident person, secure in who she is. But when her anxiety kicks in, she stumbles over even the most basic information—like the name of the company she works for and the product she sells. She went on to question how something like that could happen, having trouble with basic talking points and blanking on fundamental job information.

Erika's experience of anxiety always limiting her performance is a pervasive one: we're anxious and we're worried that our anxiety is harming us—whether it be in front of a crowd, during a job interview, or in any high-stakes situation. However, anxiety can actually be a source of optimal performance.

A now-famous 1908 study, led by two Harvard psychologists, Robert M. Yerkes and John D. Dodson, studied the effect of stress on performance in mice. They discovered that, up to a point, performance *increases* with physiological arousal: "A moderate amount of anxiety can actually be motivating and energizing."

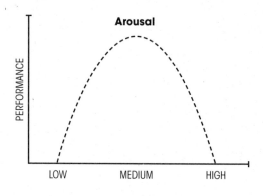

YERKSES DODSON CURVE (SOURCE: WIKI COMMONS)

The high on that curve, where medium arousal meets max performance, is called the "sweet spot." The U.S. military follows this theory, training soldiers to achieve that optimal sweet spot of stress. In addition, a popular color-coded system, created by gun fighting expert Jeff Cooper, that pinpoints optimal stress continues to be widely used across the military, athletics, and other physical performance arenas.[22]

In his groundbreaking 1990 book *Flow*, psychologist Mihaly Csikszentmihalyi picked up on this idea and showed how effort, struggle, and anxiety are necessary components of performance.

To achieve optimal performance, what he called the *flow state,* your body requires the arousal that comes from stress. That arousal allows for a hyper-focus where the task itself becomes reinforcing and self-stimulating. *Flow* suggests that consistently reaching this state is the ultimate secret to happiness—and anxiety seems to be a key part of the recipe. "Most enjoyable activities are not natural," Csikszentmihalyi writes, "they demand an effort that initially one is reluctant to make. But once the interaction starts to provide feedback to the person's skills, it usually begins to be intrinsically rewarding."[23]

As the Yerkes-Dodson curve shows, too little stress can harm performance. If we were to populate the curve with common experiences, on the lowest left-hand side of the curve would be rest, where there is neither arousal nor performance. Further up the left-hand curve—about midway—would be boredom, a state characterized by arousal without performance. In fact, studies have shown that boredom is a hidden but moderate form of stress.[24] Neuroscientist James Danckert found that subjects were more likely to exhibit stress from a boring movie than a sad movie. He described boredom occurring "when someone is motivated to engage with their environment and all attempts to do so fail. It's aggressively dissatisfying."[25]

Likewise, too much arousal or stress can curb performance as well, demonstrated by the lower right side of the curve. When you are experiencing an acute autonomic anxiety response, your higher order thinking is temporarily curbed while all your body's resources are readying for survival action of fighting or fleeing the feared situation. This sort of excessive anxiety can also be seen in normal responses to trauma, where the most important goal is safety. In such situations where the mind is wrestling to make sense of an unexpected and painful loss, anxiety can also run higher than needed, and normal daily functioning can be impaired. This kind of intense anxiety would be represented midway down the right-hand side of the curve, where arousal is high and performance becomes impaired. A pronounced autonomic reaction, if prolonged without breaks, has been well-documented to—over time—increase blood pressure, strain your cardiovascular system, cause obesity, and impair memory.[26] The furthest right side of the curve would indicate an experience of panic, where arousal is at its peak and no performance is possible.

Science has regularly documented that maximal functioning occurs under conditions of moderate stress and arousal. Sports and productivity coaches maintain that the right amount of stress helps optimize performance. Indeed, some of the most accomplished people in the world are anxious; some—like Charles Darwin and Thomas Jefferson—were famously so. They didn't let the fear paralyze them; instead they engaged it, and they used it to grow.

Erika's anxiety was like so many others'—uncomfortable, inconvenient, and even embarrassing. But I reminded her she was more resilient than she gave herself credit for; her errors were relatively minor, and she could laugh them off. Her company believed in her, and if she could avoid the pitfalls of self-criticism and doubt that escalated her anxiety and instead focus on her growth, she could continue to build stronger skills she can rely on.

# Myth #7: My mother/father was anxious so that's just how I am

Many anxiety sufferers feel a victim of biological circumstance, doomed to carry the same anxious genes carried by our parents. Though no one else in my family shook as my grandmother did, we all have carried anxiety in our own ways. Unlike my grandmother, my mother—her daughter—is a doer. When I was growing up, she was a whirling dervish of action. I remember thinking as a kid there was nothing she couldn't do. People would ask in school what my mother did, and I would reply, "Everything."

In those pre-Amazon days, she could get every errand done before dusk, all while driving carpools and keeping her nails perfectly manicured. She'd prepare delicious homemade meals every night with candles and tackle her ironing or dishwashing with the long-wired kitchen phone tucked into her shoulder, catching up with friends and family while she worked. My mother was a multitasking master long before that was even a thing.

At Christmastime, she could decorate not just her own tree but her mother's, too and prepare a twenty-five person lunch with pressed napkins, individual favors at each seat, and identifying labels in front of the serving dishes. Before you really knew you needed something done, she had done it: name-tapes sewed into camp clothes, cabinet hinges repaired, appointments made, and birthday parties planned and executed.

As her daughter, I found it was impossible to keep up with her and to this day can still marvel at her energy. Somehow, she learned to keep moving and doing; she seemed pushed to act.

It's important to remember that biology is not destiny. Anxiety certainly ran in my family—taking on different forms in my mother, grandmother, and father. Yet, it would be a false assertion to claim that any of our anxiety directly "came" from anyone else in the way one inherits eye color. Studies have documented that anxiety can be heritable with similar anxiety responses often running in families, but "what is inherited is the potential for anxiety, not anxiety itself."[27]

Our genetic makeup indeed contributes to how we perceive and respond to threatening stimuli. Researchers have even discovered the 5-hydroxytryptamine (serotonin) transporter (5-HTT) gene, playfully called the "Woody Allen gene," because it had been linked to neuroticism. However, having a genetic propensity doesn't guarantee its expression. The science of epigenetics continues to show that our environment and our choices have profound effects on how our genes are *expressed*.

Genetics are much more in our "control" than we may believe—as we've said in myth number four, how we *think about* something can play an important role in how we *experience* something. (This idea will be the focus of chapter 7.) Happiness researcher Shawn Achor writes: "The belief that we are just our genes is one of the most pernicious myth in modern culture—the insidious notion that people come into the world with a fixed set of abilities and that they, and their brains, cannot change."[28]

Research also shows some propensity for anxiety can be inherited by ancestors' exposure to trauma. Experience can change how our genes express themselves, a process known as encoding the genome; these changes are then passed down, which affect how cells read the genes.[29] This is Darwinian adaptation at a cellular level.* For certain, we can inherit a propensity for anxiety, but it's what we do with it that determines how it impacts our life. At her best, my mother learned to channel her anxiety into action. In this way, I have had a wonderful example of the how powerful our choices and habits can be.

## Myth #8: Anxiety pushes others away

Another myth about anxiety is that it keeps other people away, creating an isolation that makes it worse , but this is not always the case. In graduate school I learned about how babies look to parents to organize their world. Any parent knows the familiar scene of a toddler falling and immediately looking up to see how to feel. A look of concern from the parent, and the child will start crying; a smile or look of calm and the child will get back up without faltering. At the time, I was a bit skeptical. Like so many other theories of child development, I could only really understand it by seeing it action.

The first time my daughter bumped her own head with a toy, I tried it. I put a smile on my face and said, "Uh oh. So silly that toy bumped your head!"

To my amazement, she smiled back.

---

*    Epigenetic changes are heritable changes in gene expression (active versus inactive genes) that do not involve changes to the underlying DNA sequence—a change in phenotype without a change in genotype—which in turn affects how cells read the genes.

Like all toddlers, my kids had seemingly endless experiences—falls, bumps, and surprises—that invited distress, but my children were more malleable than we could have ever imagined. Whenever my husband or I could offer positive reframing, or even successful distracting, the impact was profound.

While anxiety can certainly contribute to withdrawal and isolation, it is also integral to helping us bond with others and organize our world. Children read the expressions of others as a way to reflect back and organize their own experiences. Infant psychiatrists note this is the way a child internalizes resources of their caregivers.[30]

This carries on to adulthood as well. Throughout life, the discomfort and confusion of anxiety propels us to our support systems for help. Leaning on others helps marshal additional resources. It also cultivates intimacy and connection with the people that matter most to us.

Recent science has uncovered that stress has a built-in fail-safe: oxytocin, the "cuddle hormone," which promotes connection. Under stress, the pituitary gland stimulates oxytocin, which primes social behavior, including expressing our emotions. Not only do many of us feel a strong drive to express ourselves under stress, but we also want to feel understood and look to others for support.

Anxiety can also trigger a desire to help and protect others. What has been recently labeled the "tend-and-befriend" response turns out to be an alternative response to stress and anxiety, especially in women but shared by all genders.[31] Stress prompts us to protect loved ones and facilitate the social networks we need to do this.[32] Think about a parent watching a child struggle in the water and instantly rushing to help while also signaling to the lifeguard. The response is immediate and selfless.

In the laboratory, social behavior like trust, trustworthiness, and sharing has been shown to be substantially higher during acute social stress than in people not under threat.[33] As social beings, we thrive in relationships and rely on partners and our social networks for survival, especially protecting our offspring and those we love.

## Myth #9: Anxiety is ultimately about selfishness

Anxiety sufferers are sometimes mistaken as being self-involved, so caught up in their own worries that they don't leave room for others' needs. Jane and Amy were a couple who came to see me together. Jane explained that so many things seemed to irritate Amy, and Amy's controlling behavior had come to feel oppressive. Jane felt shut down in the relationship, missing the connection they used to feel. While Jane understood the pressure Amy was under at work and the toll it took on her energy, Jane still resented how Amy's moods and criticism had dominated their relationship. Jane wasn't sure how much more she could take of having to tiptoe around her.

Amy was surprised, and ashamed, to hear how alone Jane had been feeling. While she wished Jane had felt more comfortable disclosing her loneliness, she understood why she hadn't. Tearfully, Amy admitted she was frightened by Jane's withdrawal and frustrated by her own failures in connecting. Amy felt paralyzed and clueless about what to do. In trying to ignore her feelings, she ended up feeling more overwhelmed and frustrated. They both could see how their respective anxieties were pushing the other away.

In regards to relationships, anxiety can be confusing. Often cloaking itself in withdrawal and self-protection, anxiety can isolate us at the times we are overwhelmed and most need support. *The Highly Sensitive Person,* a popular self-help book by Elaine Aaron, lays out the argument that overly sensitive people—*empaths,* she calls them—notice things others don't and feel things more deeply. Empaths also notice others' experiences and infer their feelings more easily.[34]

I see a lot of these types of people in my practice, those who are born sensitive to their bodily experiences (texture, discomfort, noises, and bright lights), as well as to their emotions. They feel everything more acutely, and because of this, they are prone to feeling more anxiety. Sensitivity appears to be a marker of sorts for anxiety, and the two appear highly connected. There's a vigilance in the empath's personality that comes from *caring* about so much. I always try to remind my readers and clients that one upside of anxiety is to know that you care deeply. I was reminded of this after reading an article written by the ten-year-old daughter of a colleague called "Why My Anxiety is My Superpower." I was moved by the way she embraced this quality in herself; it makes her more sensitive than others, noticing things others don't. She maintains that she is a better friend because of it.

There are more aggressive types of anxiety as well—the kind that triggers tantrums, argumentativeness, or rage—but it is a mistake to assume that anxious people don't care. They care deeply but perhaps aren't allocating their resources effectively. Often, they are so overwhelmed by trying to manage or ward off their anxiety that they don't realize how they come across to the people they love, or worse, are too consumed by it to risk showing vulnerability. This was the case with Amy and Jane and is for so many other relationships. The OCD husband who yells at his wife and kids because his fears for their safety feel unbearable to him. The stressed-out law partner who can't seem to be kind in his frustrated criticism to his colleagues. The high-strung mom who flips at her toddler for chasing a ball into the street. This kind of intense anxiety can't happen if we don't *care*. The behavior might come off as frustrated and angry, but the internal experience is anxiety.

• •

In order to fruitfully and confidently make use of our anxiety, it's essential that we both know and believe why these myths are false, even insidious. However, some are stronger and more pervasive than others.

The final myth is so widespread and all-encompassing that I am going to dedicate the entire next chapter to taking it down.

## CHAPTER SIX

# The Avoidance Myth

*"Use your fear… It can take you to a place where you store your courage."*

—**Amelia Earhart**[1]

## Brian

Brian, a normally poised client in his early forties, sat in my office one morning noticeably distressed because of an incident that had happened a few days earlier. Unlike Cecilia's yelling anxiety and Deanna's chatter anxiety (see chapter 3), Brian often experienced anxiety in a less acute, quieter manner. He was still working to recognize what it was: the signal was not always clear and he was often tempted to avoid or ignore the feeling. Through our work, he has learned that these temptations are reliable signals of anxiety that need to be mobilized into more productive action. Pushing past his fears into brave social action had always been hard for him. All these struggles came to a head one warm autumn day when his wily cat, Barney, scratched a neighbor's child.

As was required by Brian's apartment complex, Barney was an indoor cat. A few days earlier, Brian stepped out to get the mail, and Barney got out. It was unlike him to do so, so Brian didn't notice until he heard a young girl screaming and the high-pitched *rawr* sound that his cat made. When Brian peeked out the door, he saw a girl of about six or seven in the hallway, throwing down the cat and yelling.

Through the girl's screams, Brian tried to determine if the girl was hurt or just terrified. The girl seemed physically fine. However, she happened to be the daughter of a neighbor whom Brian sensed already did not like him. "He scratched me! He scratched me!" the girl was screaming, but Brian could not see any marks anywhere on her.

The mother came running out of her apartment and took the girl inside, mostly ignoring Brian's apologies and concerns. At a loss, Brian just picked up Barney and went into his own apartment, panicked and terrified the neighbor would call animal control and have Barney put down. He kept waiting for the doorbell to ring and for the mother to barge in and yell at him. He thought about going over to check on the daughter, but decided not to, preferring not to face the mother.

Instead of lowering his anxiety, this avoidance caused his anxiety to mount and then snowball. For the rest of the evening and through the night, he could not stop ruminating over the incident: his guilt over getting distracted and not noticing Barney getting out, the daughter's possible trauma, what would happen to Barney, how this would color all future interactions with his neighbor. Brian woke up consumed by dread the next morning. His avoidance did nothing but cultivate and fuel even more anxiety, which only made taking action more terrifying.

Two days later, he was sitting in front of me. (We will return to Brian at the end of the chapter.)

## The Avoidance Fallacy

One myth large enough to merit its own chapter is the myth that anxiety can be avoided, ignored, and ultimately, eliminated.* Resisting anxiety, while an understandable attempt to relieve its discomfort, is a fruitless exercise. It merely drives the negative feelings up, thereby making them more difficult to overcome.

For one, we simply can't *not* think of something. As famed social psychologist Daniel Wegner, who first introduced the concept of trying not to think about the white bear, put it, "Why

---

*    Ignoring is considered mental and avoiding is considered behavioral, but they are often used interchangeably in the literature and can have overlapping meanings.

   Ignoring/avoiding can be either adaptive or maladaptive. Avoidance of a dangerous situation can be undeniably adaptive (i.e., our "fight-or-*flight*" response to actual danger). We don't fight our fear of suffocation when under water for too long, we come up for air. Likewise, ignoring can be adaptive (e.g., ignoring our growling stomach in a business meeting).

   For this chapter, I use these terms interchangeably and largely focus on the risks these strategies pose to our natural anxiety response when deployed too liberally or consistently.

is it that trying so hard sometimes seems to guarantee not just a failure of control but its ironic reversal?"[2] The answer lies in a shift of what we mean by control. When we cannot control our experience, we must focus on controlling our behavior.[3]

When the thought is an unpleasant one, it's even harder. In a controlled study of college students, suppressing anxious thoughts was shown to drive anxiety symptoms up.[4] Countless other studies have shown that thought avoidance or suppression as a coping strategy simply doesn't work. Often, it just reinforces and escalates the negative emotions.[5]

As author Tara Brach, who has written extensively about coping with depression and anxiety, has said, "A false refuge may provide a temporary sense of comfort of security, but creates more suffering in the long run."[6] Anxiety is so unsettling that it can fuel fears that the experience of anxiety itself is dangerous. So many of my clients come in uncomfortable with their anxiety, but they are also deeply concerned that their anxiety is bad for them. Unfortunately, attempts to do whatever we can to make it go away—avoid, distract, ignore, dull—ultimately do little to help in the long run and can make matters worse.

Avoidance keeps at a distance the very thing you need to confront, process, and understand. "Because you avoid your anxious response," *Anxiety and Avoidance* author Michael A. Tompkins writes, "you know less about it than you think you do."[7] If we are going to understand why we react the way we do and how to respond more adaptively, avoidance is the worst possible choice. The problem becomes twofold: the feeling fills us with anticipation—we know we must eventually address it—and it leaves us at the mercy of a force we don't understand.

As happens with many phobias, the more a dreaded situation is avoided, the stronger our fear of it becomes. We think if we keep it pushed down long enough it will suffocate or drown—but all the pushing does is strengthen its force. The more you avoid flying, for example, the scarier it, and even the thought of it, becomes. Anxiety and Depression of America cofounder Martin N. Seif has written on how avoidance is the very thing keeping the phobia present: "The 'active ingredient' for overcoming phobias is exposure to feared triggers. It's important to note that avoidance keeps your phobia alive and intense."[8]

Attempts at avoiding the fear creates a feedback loop: it can escalate into problematic phobias that drive life-disrupting anxiety symptoms. I call it the *avoidance fallacy*: Attempts at avoiding our fears often cause more distress than the feeling itself. What can start out as a coping strategy can end up being a significant cause.

## Ignoring Nature

When we try to push, submerge, or otherwise ignore our anxiety, not only are we doing something futile, we're also operating against what we need: anxiety's natural energy is lost and diverted away from its purpose. It takes energy to mount a defense against anxiety. "When it comes right down to it," Jon Kabat-Zinn writes, "facing our problems is usually the only way to get past them."[9]

If anxiety is a characteristic of all civilizations, then ridding ourselves of it seems counterproductive and, most importantly, impossible. Since Darwin, evolutionary biology has argued that anxiety is our body's way of communicating important, and arguably critical, information. If we aim to eradicate it, we risk losing this important information, its function, and ultimately what it is driving us to *do*.

Worse, efforts to repress its natural function are at odds with its purpose, creating further tension that drains our cognitive and physical resources. So, while anxiety is almost always uncomfortable, it is not in itself negative. Anxiety is simply a message, experienced as discomfort (much like a buzzing alarm clock) that continually points us in the direction of action. "When we deny our stories and disengage from tough emotions," Brené Brown writes in *Rising Strong*, "they don't go away; instead, they own us, they define us. Our job is not to deny the story, but to defy the ending."[10]

## The Problem with "Let It Go"

"If only" my client Jeanette could follow her husband's advice and just let go of her worry, she told me at our first session. A successful lawyer and mother of two toddlers, Jeannette believed perhaps she was just making things up to worry about. Of course, nothing could be farther from the truth: she navigates significant developmental issues with both of her boys, keeps up her responsibilities at home, and manages to bill a great many hours at the office, all while her husband builds his career, often requiring fifteen-hour days and frequent business travel.

Her worry is not some invention she can discard on a whim. She has reason for it and it is serving her, keeping her focused on the most important things in front of her, and fueling her energy to keep it up. She might hope for an ideal time where she can "let it go" but doing so isn't possible or useful. In our work together, Jeannette has begun to accept this. She feels relief in accepting her anxiety as reality-based, therefore she has been more willing to give herself a break and find as much balance as she can along the way.

What she has learned to let go are her expectations, not her feelings. Even the wildly popular Disney song "Let It Go" is about self-acceptance and liberation from expectations, not our feelings. The concept of letting it go has gotten so much traction in recent years, Jeanette isn't alone in wishing she could simply drop it, as if she were supporting it and just needs to detach herself from it. But it's a false construct. Once our neurons are firing, we can't stop the energy, and it is counterproductive to try. It's like asking someone to suddenly stop caring, a difficult—if not impossible—thing to do.

## Tips for Redirection

If we cannot let it go, then the best we can do is redirect it. For example, there are myriad studies and research on successful diet and drug rehabilitation through substitution, which turns out to be a more efficient option than abstinence. We always prefer choice over denial or withholding. Actively thinking about something different, growing it, and visualizing it helps redirect our always-firing associations and build new pathways.

The suppression fallacy is well-documented with things like food cravings. When we outlaw thoughts, we make ourselves more vulnerable to them. The more you suppress thoughts of desired food, for example, the more vulnerable you are to cravings. Research suggests this is why restrictive diets might not work.[11] Emotional regulation is not just an issue of willpower. When people want to stop a worry, escape a bad mood, or stop thinking about a temptation like food, they fail again and again. Studies of self-control demonstrate a paradoxical reaction when we try to control our emotions. In the case of overeating, subjects show a decrease in controlling their behavior after trying to control their emotions. Those subjects who did not try to control their emotions demonstrated more subsequent self-control.[12] The attempt to control the feeling is more detrimental to your goals than just experiencing the feeling itself. Again, this is proof of the benefits of steering into the skid in order to straighten out.

## Secondary Anxiety

Not only does avoiding anxiety not work, it leaves the sufferer on edge—not about the original stimulus so much as the anxiety itself. I call this *secondary anxiety*, when the stressor is the anxiety itself, and it is impossible to ignore. Resisting anxiety requires a level of vigilance, which actually drives up the sensation. This is not uncommon among panic attack sufferers, some of who experience the anxiety about having an attack as potently as the attack itself.

The fight against its signs and symptoms escalates, creating a larger, unpleasant force that is even harder for us to imagine confronting. It's why Brian's sleepless night about his cat scratching the neighbor girl reached a peak by morning. It gained more power the longer he stayed away from confronting it. His initial anxiety was compounded by the avoidance, which created a feeling that he was unable to do anything about the situation. Brian's case reveals an important point about resistance: the flaw is in thinking we can't handle it. It's the false assumption upon which everything else builds.

Understanding secondary anxiety's escalating role can be particularly helpful in taking control, especially for people who suffer panic attacks, who are all too familiar with the overwhelming cycle of anxiety. Cognitive psychologists call this *metacognition*, the ability to think about one's own mental processes or thoughts, and it is foundational to gaining ownership over our experience.

For example, scanning for what feeling you are afraid of is a useful and direct way to get at your fears. Ask yourself, *What experience couldn't I handle?* and you are likely to come up with areas in your life about which you feel conflict and escalated anxiety.

This secondary anxiety can make the difference between anxiety that is useful and anxiety that is overwhelming. Just as with external stressors or a feared social situation, resisting internal stressors like the experience of anxiety itself ultimately multiply the anxiety. Being so afraid of the *experience* of anxiety can fool us into believing we can't handle it—a fear that is always based on an illusion. We may not want to handle it, but that's not the same thing. We *can*.

## A Note about Panic Attacks

Panic is one of the most debilitating and frightening forms of anxiety that exists. It is a full-body experience that can include sweaty palms, ringing ears, racing heart, blurred vision, and often a belief that you are dying. It is terrifying—something that no one wants to ever re-experience once they've had one. While efforts to resist the experience may feel protective and helpful, the avoidance drives up your vulnerability to panic. The mistake here is believing you can't handle it when in fact you can. You may not want to, but you *can*. Knowing panic is a feeling you can handle—even if it is horribly inconvenient and uncomfortable—is what helps protect you from a full-blown attack. It's another example where we should turn into the skid.

When primary and secondary anxiety work in tandem, they feed off each other, and they escalate each other's impact. Secondary anxiety isn't additive, it's exponential: $1 + 1$ does not equal 2, but rather something higher than 3. "I can't handle this" mixed with any uncomfortable feeling can make an experience feel intolerable. Combine this with a fearful resistance to anxiety, and you will quickly spin yourself into something resembling panic. This is how anxiety can be an emotional accelerant.

You might be so convinced that you can't handle what is happening in your body that your fight-or-flight reaction triggers more discomfort and distress. These panic symptoms can trick you into thinking you are dying (a very common complaint among panic sufferers), which only elevates your anxiety further. This is why first-time panic sufferers often go to the emergency room fearing a life-threatening heart attack. According to the *DSM-V*, panic disorder is characterized not just by the presence of panic symptoms alone, but by the *fear* of panic symptoms recurring.[13]

Not only is secondary anxiety a driver of almost certain misery and panic, but in producing so much distress, it often obscures the primary anxiety and the signal it is trying to send. There is seldom an adaptive side to panic, and few people who panic can clearly articulate what fears triggered the anxiety to begin with. Panic turns anxiety back onto itself—an escalating boomerang effect.

Dialing down the secondary anxiety is always necessary to access and use the primary anxiety for its intended problem-solving purpose. Unchecked, secondary anxiety renders primary anxiety useless and destructive.

## Avoidance and Confidence

Amy Cuddy, who has studied and popularized the effect of confident body posture, which she has coined *power posing*, has talked extensively about the negative confidence effects of avoidance:

> *Two systems are believed to drive most human feelings, thoughts, behaviors, and even physiology—approach and avoidance (i.e., inhibition). When our approach system is activated, we are happier, more optimistic, more confident, more creative, more likely to take action, more likely to seek rewards and opportunities, more physically energetic and less inhibited… Activation of the inhibition systems leads to the opposite effects… power activates the approach system, whereas powerlessness activates the inhibition system.*[14]

Approaching our experience gives us power and grows our confidence, whereas shrinking from our experience grows our sense of powerlessness, and thus drives up anxiety.

In addition to her writing about anxiety and depression, Tara Brach has written extensively on the neuroscience of mindfulness, which is ultimately about accepting the thoughts you have in order to make peace with them. Avoidance works against us, and she points to such examples like avoiding a stressful work relationship or an unpleasant work interaction. While the hope is to find a refuge of safety, it comes at a cost: low self-esteem and a sense of being trapped.[15]

Edward A. Selby describes avoidance as "self-sabotage"—a tactic that feels like safety but actually causes damage—to your personal environment, your desires, and your self-esteem. "Each time you attempt to accomplish a goal, but you let the fear take control and back down," Selby explains, "you are avoiding and thus negatively reinforcing yourself."[16]

We are also triggering certain biological habits when we avoid. Joseph LeDoux has found that the neurotransmitter dopamine has a role in reinforcing avoidance. Every time a behavior avoids a negative result—in this case anxiety—we reinforce the behavior. This is called *negative reinforcement*, reinforcing a behavior through avoiding a negative consequence. Dopamine is most likely in the mix here. A neurotransmitter related to reward-seeking behavior, dopamine is known to be a powerful player in addiction, love, hunger, thirst, and now avoiding anxiety.[17] LeDoux has demonstrated that avoidant behavior is partially controlled by parts of our brain having to do with dopamine.[18]

Moreover, dopamine is well known to play a powerful role in the complicated process of learning. Every time we successfully thwart feelings of anxiety—or any other negative consequence—we learn to do it again, thanks to the impact of dopamine. A type of learning accelerator, dopamine strives to ensure the same rewarding behavior will recur, even outside of our awareness. This appears to be why dopamine is involved in such automatic, unconscious action, like eating or drinking when we are thirsty—and avoiding anxiety. Dopamine levels are highest when animals are food deprived and seeing food—it's about reinforcing survival.[19]

When it comes to anxiety, relief comes from action, not avoidance. We avoid because we are naturally resistant to change even if anxiety is a signal that something needs to be changed (or knowledge that change is coming). It is so easy to cling to the familiar for dear life—even if we consciously recognize the need for a new path. And yet clinging to avoidance only diminishes our confidence. If we think back on our lives, chances are pretty strong that every single good thing that has ever happened to us was preceded or triggered by an uncomfortable change.

Yet, as Robert Sapolsky helpfully points out, humans are not built to learn from good experiences—only from bad. The good tends to pass through us, while the bad sticks around.[20] This is known as the negativity bias, and it kept us alive for millions of years. In *Hardwiring Happiness*, neuropsychologist Rick Hanson deftly explains how this bias evolved:

*Our ancestors could make two kinds of mistakes: (1) thinking there was a tiger in the bushes when there wasn't one, and (2) thinking there was no tiger in the bushes when there actually was one. The cost of the first mistake was needless anxiety, while the cost of the second one was death. Consequently, we evolved to make the first mistake a thousand times to avoid making the second mistake even once.[21]*

Even if we are prone to overly focus on negative experiences and avoid them, it is an illusion that avoidance is always safe or risk free. Consider the consequences of your avoidance. What price are you really paying? What if instead of avoiding the feelings of arousal that come with stress, you instead aimed not to feel victimized by it? Avoidance amps up the passive victim framework that is likely making us anxious in the first place. Harnessing anxiety is about finding our sense of agency and control, which requires a different framework.

"You get the right amount of stress and you call it stimulation," Robert Sapolsky says. "The goal in life isn't to get rid of stress. The goal of life is to have the right type of stress because when it's the right type we love it."[22]

## Next Steps

So, if avoidance and ignoring often backfire, what is the answer? As we will discuss in the rest of the book, the relief is in doing. Taking action actually lowers the physiological anxiety response— breathing slows, color returns to face, calm ensues. Think about how much calmer you have felt whenever you have taken brave action. Taking action relieves conflict and halts the anxiety escalation fueled by avoidance.

Action allows a reality of control. When you take control of what you can, you feel the control anxiety so often robs you of, and anxiety immediately lowers. Feeling control leads to greater efficacy and confidence, whereas perceived lack of control drives up the negative effects of stress.[23]

## Brian

Brian understood that as the hours after the cat incident passed, he was feeling increasingly worse and avoiding the situation. His own anxiety was growing and his concern about the neighbor's daughter increased as well. He wanted to knock on his neighbor's door, but he was afraid. He was afraid of so many rational and irrational possibilities, and mostly he was afraid that he would expose himself to his neighbor's hostile judgment. The *possibilities* were taking over the *probabilities,* and it was hard for him to clarify what he really wanted and what he should do.

In our session that first day, we identified the source of his anxiety and teased out the rational piece: he needed to follow up because he was concerned. Then we teased out the irrational piece: his neighbor would be angry, might retaliate, or judge him harshly, and that he couldn't handle it.

The rational anxiety was that he cared about the daughter's well-being and doing the right thing, and his avoidant behavior wasn't allowing him to act on that. Sure, he was afraid of how angry they might be to see him, but he was *more* afraid of how they would view him—and he would view himself—if he didn't follow up.

As is so often the case with translating anxiety into problem solving, he had two uncomfortable options: a false refuge that would avoid confrontation but amplify his distress and an opportunity to face confrontation, risking discomfort by doing the right thing. (Note: This was *his* definition of the right thing. His anxiety about avoiding checking on the girl signaled that he felt it was the ethical act.)

A week later, Brian came in noticeably calmer. He recounted feeling immediate relief when he went over to talk to the neighbor, and he was confident he had done the right thing. He found out that his cat indeed had scratched the young girl through her clothes (the mom showed a picture of the wound to him), that the little girl did not need stitches, but she was seen by a doctor and prescribed antibiotics. While feeling horrible that the girl indeed has been scratched, Brian also learned that both mother and daughter seemed fine, and the mother even shared her own story about being scratched by her family cat as a child. While he was relieved, he was also surprised by how well the family had handled the situation. After his numerous apologies, the neighbor told Brian to "not worry about it."

Only after taking action was Brian truly able "not to worry about it." Not because the neighbor gave him permission, but because his anxiety subsided. It had done its job, and could now stand down. His anxiety had focused him on what really mattered to him—that he cared and was sorry—and fueled him to take action, even if he was afraid. Seeing one more time he could handle being brave, he felt that much stronger and that much clearer about how to use his anxiety next time.

## CHAPTER SEVEN

# Taking Control

*"We can choose courage or we can choose comfort,*
*but we can't have both. Not at the same time."*

—**Brené Brown**[1]

## Craig

"I don't know what this is that I'm feeling, but I can't seem to do anything about it. It's like I'm going crazy. And everything I've been able to do up until now hasn't been working lately."

Craig was in his early fifties, a recent retiree from the military that he had built his life around. A trustworthy and principled man, Craig was raised by stern Catholic parents with high moral standards. He came to see me a few months into his retirement, because he was experiencing severe anxiety, which he regularly described as panic. "It feels like I'm losing my bearings—dizzy, almost as if the ground is moving beneath my feet and I'm float-ing," he explained during a session. "And my heart starts to go, and I feel completely overwhelmed with terror that I'm not going to be okay."

Though the anxiety had recently gotten worse, it had always existed. For years, he had been able manage it on his own, just through reading self-help books. The message he took away from these books was that anxiety was irrational and must be confronted aggressively. He should yell at it and shut it down. In describing this method to me, Craig would make a fist gesture and strike his hand hard into his palm. He was harsh with himself, really rough in his self-talk. But since his retirement, this approach was no longer working. In fact, it was making it worse.

His anxiety was spiking way past usefulness, and the first goal had to be to dial it back. In one of our early sessions, he arrived in the midst of a panic attack, so I was able to introduce active breath-ing as a tool. When I asked him to breathe all the way in to his belly, he could only breathe shallow breaths into his chest. It was too hard for him to lengthen his breathing during the attack. Afraid he might not get enough air, he was trying to force the air in. In fight-ing his anxiety, trying to smother and force it away, he was making it worse. He was frustrated that his efforts weren't working.

Eager to get rid of his anxiety as quickly as possible, Craig engaged actively in our sessions, spent time between them reading and thinking about his anxiety, and committed to working hard at facing his anxiety head on. He started thinking more carefully about his feelings, and he challenged himself to tackle the things

he couldn't accomplish while he had been working: finding a
volunteer community that gave him a sense of purpose, making
more friends, and finding a life partner.

Over the course of those first few weeks of treatment, it
seemed the harder he tried, the worse his anxiety got. As much as
he wanted to move through his anxiety once and for all, pushing
himself was having the opposite effect on his anxiety, and the
overstimulation was holding him back. So, a month or so into our
work together, I introduced the idea of medication, as it became
clear this would be a powerful step in taking control of his anxiety.
I referred Craig to a colleague to handle that aspect of his treatment, and we continued with our sessions.

Though the effect wasn't immediate, the medication eventually took the volume down enough that he could start to hear what
his anxiety was telling him. Resetting his chemistry in this way
helped him reach that sweet spot. We continued to work on being
gentle with himself and listening, rather than pushing himself too
hard. Finally, we were ready to dig into the source of his anxiety.
*What was it trying to say?*

At the core of Craig's anxiety was loneliness. It was
something that had always been with him, but it had come to
dominate his life since retirement. He was unprepared for it, and
he had no other relationships or structure to lean on. Once he
left his job, his anxiety was front and center in a way that it had
never been before.

In order to pinpoint anxiety's message, I asked Craig when
his anxiety flared up the most. He said it was definitely when he

returned to his home in the evening. He'd go out on a run and do errands and when he came home, his home was empty. It had always been empty, but now his life was emptier as well. His anxiety's message was *I am scared to death of being alone forever.* The television had become such a companion that he became anxious if he shut it off before going to sleep.

Craig opened up about the fact that he wanted a partner, a real relationship. He signed up for a popular dating site, and though the thought of dating still scared him, he did it. He took it slow and with every date, his confidence has built and his anxiety has lessened. He has learned how to take control and push himself where he can, but he has also learned how to listen to himself and be kind when he goes too far. Not only is he learning how to use his anxiety effectively, but he is learning how to be the man he wants to be—for himself and for others.

## Stepping Away from Helplessness

A common thread for anxiety sufferers is the feeling of being stuck: trapped by circumstances, emotions, or biology. The passivity of this outlook can give way to a sense of helplessness. And if we are helpless, there is nothing we can do to heal.

There is seldom a situation in which clinical anxiety is wholly outside of one's control. At some level, there is always a degree of control. We may feel a sudden sense of worry or dread, but if we get frightened of these feelings, we will escalate them. How we think about anxiety is so critical, and it is often an internal conflict we are not fully aware of. Fighting anxiety escalates it and makes it worse—furthering the feeling that is beyond our control. And the cycle continues.*

Change is nearly impossible if we don't embrace the choices we actually have. We can go back to bed when we can't breathe easily or we can not, we can hope our mysterious flu symptoms will just go away or we can not, we can wish our abusive relationship will magically change or we can not. As I work with people wrestling with difficulty in their lives, it continues to strike me that the more stuck they are in life, the more asleep they are. It comes down to this: we must *wake up to our choices.*

## Setting Our Minds

In her seminal book, *Mindset*, psychologist Carol Dweck contrasts two mind-sets, each of which predict future success and happiness. The **fixed mind-set** is an approach to the world that essentially says we are who we are, with our strengths and weaknesses, and not much can be done to change that. However, an individual with a **growth mind-set** sees opportunities to stretch and learn and improve. The growth mind-set *seeks out* challenges and doesn't back down from resistance.

Research has repeatedly shown that those with a growth mind-set, who feel they are in the process of becoming challenged,

---

\*   This does not discount those who need medical help or are taking medication. Our body chemistry can get out of whack and getting it back in better balance is often an important step. Seeking treatment is a key way of taking control.

and *moving forward* as a result, are in a better psychological place than those with a fixed mind-set. Dweck follows the implications of this research from education to business to love: the insights are broad.[2] For those with the growth

**The Serenity Prayer**

God grant me the serenity to accept the things I cannot change, the courage to change the things I can, and the wisdom to know the difference.

mind-set, failure leads to success, because it's how we learn. Risk can be the reward, because it leads to the next version of you. It's all in how we choose to view things, whether we can see the new paths instead of the roadblocks.

It takes insight to understand where and when we have choices. We can watch the patterns repeat themselves and hope for a shift, or we can identify our choices and try a different path to get where we want to go, even if it's uncomfortable. We get to choose, but anxiety nudges us along.

Anxiety appears to be a necessary component of seeking this process and in seeking a life that matters. A 2013 Stanford study published in *The Journal of Positive Psychology* attempted to discern the difference between happiness and meaningfulness. Researchers found that the areas where we seek meaning— such as raising children—bring the most fulfillment, but they also bring the most anxiety and stress.[3] It's something I think we implicitly know but don't always act on. Growth really can't happen without stretching out of our comfort zones, and (as anyone who has ever taken a yoga class knows) stretching is uncomfortable. Healthy and purposeful, but uncomfortable. It's *designed to be*—that's how we create a life that's meaningful and satisfying. That's how we grow.

Reinhold Niebuhr's words, which became known as the Serenity Prayer, have been a comfort and guide to the Alcoholics Anonymous organization since the 1940s. But the words carry much further than that. The Serenity Prayer poetically condenses a simple truth: navigating our issues comes down to understanding—and coming to terms with—where our control lies.

As long as self-help has been around, the Serenity Prayer has been part of the landscape. Its simplicity offers an accessible road map for working toward change *where it is possible*. Given the sizable research on the psychological value in taking control, the paradigm of the prayer continues to resonate today. Dr. John W. Reich's recent book *Mastering the World, Mastering Yourself: Living the Serenity Prayer* collects a great deal of professional therapeutic literature on the usefulness of the prayer in clinical practice. He writes, "The bottom line of these studies is that personal control is teachable." This is key—it's not about whether we can or can't; it's about whether we choose to or not.

## Cultivating Courage

> *"Courage is resistance to fear, mastery of fear—not absence of fear."*
>
> —**Mark Twain**[4]

Of course, once we figure out what we can change, we need to muster the courage to do so. Courage is fundamentally the decision to focus on something more important than our fear, along with the realization that we value it more. Especially for the anxious, when we are facing what is hard and scary, courage gives us the boost to face it front and center.

Linda, a client of mine, came to me because she had trouble getting started and staying with things. Her anxiety wasn't direct—it manifested through avoidance. She avoided dating, all manner of conflict whenever possible, and unpleasant tasks at the loan office where she worked. One of her jobs was rejecting businesses that needed money. It was hard because she came to know these people, felt for them, and understood that her call was going to devastate them. She dreaded having to tell them they didn't make the cut, and she would often put off these calls until they piled up.

One of the strategies she used successfully at work was to tell herself to "put on her big girl pants, and just do it," reminiscent of the famous Nike ad. The *just* is the key: it implies that there are reasons to wait, avoid, overthink it. *Just* means resist the temptation to ruminate and take a step forward: make the call, send the email, go to the meeting. She trained herself to decide to be courageous and do the difficult thing, even when she didn't want to. She knew she had to: she owed it to them. And so, she did.

We borrowed her strategy to call up courage and applied it to the other areas of her life that needed help. After distilling the tasks she was putting off or avoiding out of anxiety, we added in the step of deciding to be courageous. It became part of the process. Giving herself a mini pep talk at the moment of truth turned out to be an important strategy to ensuring she would follow through.

Sometimes courage is simply a way to manage fear and cope in spite of it.[5] A reckoning of your fear with what you must do, courage can help sublimate that fear into something more important. How we think about our fear turns out to be important when it comes to cultivating courage. In an interesting Israeli study, volunteers were asked while lying in an fMRI machine to bring what they thought was a live snake as close to them as they could. As subjects made decisions about moving the snake closer or further away, the researchers measured their reported fear, their physiological reaction of fear (via sweat) as well as their brain activity. What they found was that people's assessment of their fear, and the physiological effects of that fear, had to *disagree* in order for a person to be courageous. *The conflict* is what created the courage.

If they were admittedly afraid *and* sweating, subjects were not able to act courageously and bring the snake closer. But those who claimed to be unafraid but were sweating, and those who claimed to be afraid but were not showing it, were the ones able to be the most courageous. "[A]s long as these two disagree, you would act courageously," the researchers noted. "It is as if you have two brakes. Release either one, and you could drive on."[6]

The area of the brain activated when bringing the snake closer was a small area called the *subgenual anterior cingulate cortex*, sgACC, an area also associated with emotional regulation, empathy, and helping others.[7] This finding implies that it is an area of the brain "particularly tuned to controlling and monitoring generosity."[8] Not only is courage a decision to overcome fear, it may also be tied to empathy and generosity. Whether it be bringing a snake toward us, pulling on "big girl" pants, or summoning our own brand of bravery, courage is a decision to act on behalf of something or someone we care about more than our fears. And it is a decision born from conflict and fear. Our fears may not be as important as we think they are; we just imagine them to be. As the stoic philosopher Seneca wrote, "There are more things, Lucilius, likely to frighten us than there are to crush us; we suffer more often in imagination than in reality."[9]

## Our Tigers

While too much anxiety can be problematic, not enough can keep us stagnant and unfulfilled, as the previously discussed Stanford study on satisfaction and happiness suggests.[10] We simply can't grow toward our goals in life without making productive use of our anxiety. Our ancestors had to take control in dangerous situations to survive. Indecision, hesitation, or doubt would have ensured peril. In modern times, inaction can be dangerous too, and it is becoming an increasingly common response to the more nuanced and complicated threats of modern times.

The experience of anxiety may not be new, but its causes are a relatively modern phenomenon...as in the last ten thousand years. Our hunter-gatherer ancestors had similar physiological reactions, though they were likely less complex. They experienced fear in response to direct danger. It was only when basic human survival became the norm that man could make room for higher-level needs. Before that, we never really called it anxiety. It was just the fear of being eaten. Though it was no doubt terrifying, it didn't require much parsing or understanding. It just was.

"Sustained psychological stress is a recent invention," Robert Sapolsky writes. "We can experience wildly strong emotions (provoking our bodies into an accompanying uproar) linked to mere thoughts."[11] The title of Sapolsky's book, *Why Zebras Don't Get Ulcers,* cleverly demonstrates this wide divide. "For 99 percent of the species on this planet," he says, "stress is three minutes of screaming terror in the savannah, after which either it's over or you're over with."[12]

The saber-toothed tigers of the past have evolved into the subtler financial, relationship, and status threats of today. Our tigers no longer bare literal teeth or threaten immediate death, but we should not underestimate them. They still need to be addressed—and the fear and anxiety that we feel in their presence is still very real. Deciding whether to take action or to flee from a modern threat is not always as cut and dry as it was for our ancestors, therefore it's harder to know how to react. Modern life is complicated, and knowing where and how to take control isn't always easy. Indecision can compound the threat we feel and diminish our power. When we resist taking control, we open ourselves to more tigers. We become an easy prey.

Anxiety coming at us invites us to pay attention and stimulates energy. When we can view anxiety as an open door inviting our participation, rather than a thick wall stopping our progress, we begin to change the story we tell ourselves. We partner with the anxiety itself. As we engage anxiety, we move from feeling stymied and stuck into taking necessary action. Harnessing our anxiety, we neither fight nor flee. We take control and grow.

# Mark

When Mark came to my office for the first time, he described himself as ambitious and, ordinarily, deeply motivated. But over the last few months, he had felt bored and frustrated with his life, particularly at his job. As a sales associate, his lackluster attitude and poor performance were impacting both his mood and income. He described spending much of his time with work friends, several of whom were very unhappy and regularly complained. Morale was so low that he had started wondering if he really wanted to stay in his job, even though he was due for a major promotion. He just didn't know what he wanted anymore, and he missed feeling in control of his life.

Underlying all of this were health worries. He had been feeling chest pains for the past two weeks, twice acute enough to warrant ER visits. Diagnostic tests revealed no obvious cause of his pain, and he was referred for a follow-up with a cardiologist and a psychologist. Did he have a latent underlying heart condition, was it panic, or both? Even talking to me about it clearly upset him.

Although an anxious person by nature, he had never before had a panic attack and was understandably skeptical to attribute his physical symptoms to panic. But at the same time, he didn't want to overreact and waste more time seeing doctors who might confirm nothing was physically wrong. His anxiety had reached a fever pitch when he began to worry that he could die in his sleep.

The fear came through his voice and I could see he was desperate for tools he didn't think he had. He needed a way to understand his panic, and he needed to know what he could do about it. I explained secondary anxiety: how his fears about what he was feeling could powerfully exacerbate his anxiety, even flash it into panic. We discussed how fighting anxiety strengthens it, whereas embracing his fears can transform them into something useful. He was relieved to learn anxiety was just a feeling—even if an extremely uncomfortable one—that on its own could not hurt him.

Over time, he came to understand that he could take control of his experience by accepting and breathing into the panic, rather than resisting it. Like a fire requires oxygen to burn, panic required his fear to sustain itself. Robbing its fuel source was as easy as adopting a new attitude. *Bring it on. I can handle it.*

As he stopped avoiding his anxiety, or even trying to, his panic attacks began to diminish. We moved on to what else was scaring him, and what all his anxiety was trying to tell him. In discussing his past and his physical health, he revealed his father's near-death experience with heart disease when he was young.

As he told the story, he began to make the connection about his own heart, and his inability to accept nothing was wrong. In this way, his anxiety was working for him; it was stirring the productive kind of conflict. It was reminding him of *why* he was worried about his chest pain in the first place—what if he shared his father's deadly heart condition? His anxiety was spurring him to *take control* and seek answers.

He needed to hear from the horse's mouth that he was fine. He knew neither he nor the ER doctors were really capable of ruling out a latent heart condition like his dad had—he needed cardiac specialists. His health anxiety had a purpose all along. Getting clear about his anxiety that day helped him take control of it and with that, his anxiety transformed itself into power. We will return to Mark at the conclusion of the chapter.

## Leaning into Discomfort

Author and research professor Brené Brown has spent her life's work researching how we can come to terms with what we often classify as "negative" emotions like fear, vulnerability, and loneliness. In one of her studies, examining a variety of fulfilled and successful people, she found a common denominator among them. "They recognize the power of emotion, and they're not afraid to lean into discomfort."[13]

In *Rising Strong*, Brown writes about the value in "navigating hurt." Simply put, it means to *feel your feelings*. We are trained from a young age to disguise or distract from those "unpleasant" feelings, but navigating through these emotions is precisely where strength lies.

If you didn't experience pain when your bone was broken or hunger when you needed to eat, you wouldn't act. Discomfort is the impetus to notice your experience, and take control of it in response. We hold and breathe into a challenging yoga pose not to promote distress, but to allow the discomfort to do its job: stretching us toward more flexible, healthy bodies. Choosing to approach our discomfort helps to turn passive misery into active control.

Similarly, emotions are not things that happen to you without your control or consent—you make a choice, conscious or unconscious, to define and engage them. In *How Emotions are Made*, Lisa Feldman Barrett explains the theory of constructed emotion. Stimuli in our bodies combine with our experience, thoughts, and cultural beliefs to create something we decide to call an emotion, "a product of human agreement."[14]

We are not passive vessels for anxiety or any of our emotions. We are in control—though it takes habitual recognition, shifting of perception, and practice to make this work for us. "You might think that stress is something that happens to you," Barrett explains, "But stress doesn't come from the outside world. You construct it."[15] Because we are constructing it, we can control, manage, and use it. We are not its victim. We are its conductor. Similarly, when we experience the "trap" of anxiety, we must remember that we are the authors of our experience and can always write our way toward a solution.

## Autonomy

In his book *Drive*, Daniel Pink notes the importance of autonomy, the ability to make your own decisions about life. Besides our two most basic drives—survival and extrinsic rewards—Pink highlights the role of the important "third drive—our deep-seated desire to direct our own lives, to extend and expand our abilities, and to make a contribution."[16] We all carry an intrinsic motivation to live lives of meaning, which propels us forward. New research confirms our mind-set about work predicts our performance. People who view their work as a calling find it more satisfying, work harder and longer, and are generally more successful.[17] "We know that the richest experiences in our lives aren't when we are clamoring for validation from others," he writes, "but when we're listening to our own voice—doing something that matters, doing it well, and doing it in the service of a cause larger than ourselves."[18]

Pink believes that anxiety relates to the ineffective expression of our deepest drives. Control, growth, and altruism are the tools he recommends to focus anxiety. Influenced by Maslow's hierarchy of needs, he notes meaning and autonomy are paramount. Similar to our earlier discussion of courage, meaning can transcend the grip of fear.

Pink's work builds on the ideas of Edward Deci and Richard Ryan, who developed a theory of motivation called *self-determination theory*. Self-determination theory is focused on "people's sense of volition and initiative" and how that contributes to their overall well-being.[19] Their theory holds that when it comes to human potential, nothing is more powerful than intrinsic motivation, defined as "the inherent tendency to seek out novelty and challenges, to extend and exercise one's capacities, to explore, and to learn."[20]

Taking control and seeking challenge is essential to healthy development as well as a joyful and vital life. We are happier and more motivated when we are in control, stretching toward our own goals. Free choice and intrinsic motivation are so powerful that studies have shown that external rewards can backfire if they are at odds with our internal drives.[21]

## Drivers and Pilots

*"Joy is the feel of our power increasing."*

—Frederic Nietzsche

As studies have shown, it's less the reality of control than the perception that matters. A 2012 Harvard study on stress found, "When people believe they possess sufficient resources to cope with stressors, they experience a challenge response, but when situational demands are seen as exceeding resources, individuals experience threat."[22] A sense of power has also been shown to reduce the physiological experience of stress. According to Galinsky and Schweitzer in *Friend and Foe,* who worked on the studies, "power reduces physiological stress as measured by heart rate and systolic blood pressure."[23]

Anxiety decreases with a sense of mastery over its cause and its solution. In a surprising study in England, researcher David Lewis compared the stress response of commuters in traffic to pilots and police officers in training. Incredibly, he found—through heart rate and blood pressure readings—that the *commuters* were more stressed-out. It appears shocking until you realize that it actually makes perfect sense. What's more stressful than the world trapping you in and not being able to do anything about it? Especially in a situation where you are ordinarily in control—think about how we use the term *the driver's seat* as shorthand for the idea of control itself. This is why car traffic is so maddening. We are sitting where we often have control—"behind the wheel"—but we are utterly helpless to control the stressor. The only thing we can control is how we react to it.

"Workers' stress is exacerbated by their inability to control their situation,"[24] Lewis said, a fact that any casual commuter understands. This is also true in animal studies where a lack of control over consistent, but unpredictable, stressors has been found to cause apathy, withdrawal, and a depressed response to rewards.[25] Gaining control lowers the stress response in such a way that we would all benefit from finding ways to do so.

It's not about controlling what is happening. We cannot control traffic, but we can control what we do when it happens. Working with our anxiety and refocusing on what we can do, is *how* we take control. So, it often may not feel like we are in the driver's seat of life, but we are. We have so much more control than we can sometimes see.

## Control and Happiness

Martin Seligman, the father of learned helplessness theory and cofounder of positive psychology, has dedicated much of his career to studying the concept of control and choice. Feeling a sense of control is a key part of coping with anxiety and stress. Seligman believes that how much we feel we're in control can shape how we feel about everything else. Cognitive research has documented the positive effects of having an "internal locus of control," the belief that you can impact outcomes and the world around you.

Those who carry "the perception that they are masters of their own destiny...are more resistant in experimental models of learned helplessness,"[26] Sapolsky writes. The more control we perceive, the less willing we are to succumb to feeling overwhelmed or hopeless. As a consequence, the more able we are to manage our uncomfortable feelings.

Taking action allows both a sense *and* a reality of control. How much calmer have you felt whenever you have taken brave action, be it on the sports field or at the gym, in the classroom or boardroom, or even with someone you care about? Taking action relieves the conflict and the anxiety escalation that comes from avoidance; it allows you to own the feelings you are having and make sense of them.

There is scientific proof that even the illusion of control has tangible, positive effects. One study gave sufferers from panic disorder a mix of $CO_2$-enriched air. One group was led to believe they could decrease the mixture at certain points with a dial, while the other group never had that option. Though both groups received the same amount of $CO_2$—the dial was fake—it was those who thought they were controlling it who had fewer panic symptoms.[27]

Other studies offer broad support as well. A sense of control is protective in new parents with regards to mental health symptoms of depression and anxiety.[28] Similarly, for middle-aged men, those with internal locus of control beliefs responded "more adequately" to stress than those with an external locus of control.[29] And among college students, having an internal locus of control was "significantly negatively correlated with both depression and debilitating anxiety."[30]

## When Taking Control Is Difficult

Taking control still isn't always easy, and for some, it is tough to see or feel any sense of control when life always seems to happen *to* them. This is called having an external locus of control, and cognitive scientists have found that it is correlated with higher experiences of anxiety after negative events.[31] An external locus of control also has been linked to higher rates of anxiety disorders and social challenges. A study focusing on anxiety disorders found that "externally oriented patients also scored higher on neuroticism and trait anxiety and scored lower on social adjustment… Locus of control may be of importance in the formulation of therapy and prognosis in patients with anxiety disorders."[32]

In studying personality factors and brain size of a healthy population, researchers found, "Poor self-esteem and low internal locus of control have been related to 12 to 13 percent smaller volume of the hippocampus,"[33] the area of the brain responsible for memory storage as well as turning off the stress response.[34] Reduced hippocampal volume makes it more difficult to learn how to use anxiety effectively, whereas larger hippocampi have been associated with better problem solving under pressure. London taxi drivers' oversized hippocampi show they have developed resilience through practice and preparation.

Taking control wherever we can is how we use our anxiety effectively and improve our ability to keep doing it. The more control we take, the more we use our anxiety to grow. Successful London taxi drivers don't waste time and energy focusing on the difficulty of the task ahead, or their powerlessness over the daunting situation, they identify the choices they have and focus their efforts on learning and growing capacity.

Learning to deal with stressful situations can make future ones easier to manage, according to a large body of research on the science of resilience. It's the idea behind Navy SEAL training. During BUD/S (Basic Underwater Demolition/SEAL) training, the goal is to inoculate SEAL team members to build capacity. "Repetition in stressful environments allows you to understand what you are capable of," Jo, a Navy SEAL, explained to me.

SEAL training includes plenty of stressful environments and situations that challenge people mentally, physically, and emotionally at incredibly high levels. Repetition in stressful environments is how these elite soldiers learn not to get mired in the bigger problems. They train their minds to stay focused on executing and then reevaluating, executing then reevaluating.

As you repeatedly encounter and work effectively with pressure, you simply get better at it. Jo called this "mental fortitude…the capacity to cope with, and push through, things that you didn't think you could accomplish while maintaining cogni-zant ability to function and utilize fundamentals." Through taking control, and repeated practice, we can keep our anxiety at a manageable level—one where its information and energy can best be utilized.

While few of us will ever get the training and exposure to extreme stress that Navy SEALS do, many of us do the same thing when we practice doing something that starts out nerve-wracking and becomes doable—like public speaking, test taking, or dating. Taking control where we can is how we use our anxiety to help us.

## Controlling Your Reaction

Looking for what we *can* control and not allowing ourselves to get stuck in thinking nothing will ever change, or that we are powerless, are the challenges when it comes to taking control. One solution is to change how we think about our emotions. Chris Hadfield is an astronaut who gives talks on preparing and thinking through unexpected moments of fear. While on his first spacewalk, he temporarily went blind when his eyes teared up—and because of the lack of gravity in his spacesuit, the tears *just stayed there,* creating a giant tear bubble around his eye.

Panic in such a situation can be deadly. To ward off panic, and thus ensure his survival, Hadfield identified the key compo-nent he had to control to carry out his responsibilities: his fear. He had to think his way through his fear—something astronauts specifically train for. Hadfield distinguishes between danger—not in one's control—and fear, which is in one's control. *Fear is a reaction.* We should not always automatically trust our fears, he believes, and instead be able to think in the face of it.[35] The tears themselves weren't dangerous, but if he panicked and threw out his training, it could have been catastrophic. Preparing for the unexpected, and recognizing the difference between his fear and actual danger, helped him resist panic. Instead of giving in to that feeling, he leaned on his other working senses and his teammates for help.

Coping doesn't just happen in the moment, it is often something planned for and practiced in advance. I've written before that worrying can operate as a form of pre-coping. Essentially, you're preparing yourself—and your body—in advance by thinking through the outcomes. A study in *Emotion* found that "participants who suffered through a waiting period marked by anxiety, rumination, and pessimism responded more productively to bad news and more joyfully to good news, as compared with participants who suffered little during the wait."[36] Our worry—if it's accompanied with thoughts about contingencies, options, and preparation—can act as a form of armor.

Preparation becomes the magic bullet. In *Why Zebras Don't Get Ulcers*, Robert Sapolsky references a famous study of Norwegian parachute trainees.[37] Researchers found that it was not jumping out of an airplane that caused their stress and anxiety; it was, at first, the *novelty* and the *not knowing* that created the stress. Once the trainees were prepared and expected the jump, and had habituated

to it, "their anticipatory stress-response went from being gargan-
tuan to nonexistent."[38]

## Mark

A cardiology visit and stress test later, Mark had received the
good news that his heart was healthy. He faced the realities of
his health risks, took control of what he could, and transformed
his anxiety into solutions. Relieved, he also regained emotional
strength. He described to me that he felt lighter and more relaxed,
he was no longer afraid of dying in his sleep, and he was able
to breathe without chest pain. He had used his health anxiety
to address the problem it signaled, and he no longer *needed* that
particular worry.

He continued to be uneasy about his work situation, and
he knew that some of his situational fears were problematic. We
identified what he could control and what he couldn't. He decided
to cut back on time with his negative colleagues, asking them when
they were together to limit their complaints. He also decided to
talk to his boss about his goals, and together they discussed ways
he could jump-start his performance. Taking control and setting
firmer boundaries helped him regain a feeling of control and
autonomy at the office.

Mark used his anxiety to figure out and act his way through
reasonable solutions and grew in confidence. He came to *know* he
could handle his anxiety and stopped being afraid of it. He sees
it now as a source of motivation and something he can harness

toward effective solutions. His productivity at the office came back, and his smile did, too.

So much of it comes down to how we choose to react to our thoughts. As Lisa Feldman Barrett insists in *How Emotions Are Made*, "You are an architect of your experience."[39] This takes us to the first thing we have control over, which is the focus of our next chapter: our perception.

## CHAPTER EIGHT

# The Power of Perception

*"The important thing in science is not so much to obtain new facts as to discover new ways of thinking about them."*

**—Sir William Lawrence Bragg**

## Layla

Layla was a petite and impeccably dressed woman who sat on the edge of her seat in our first session as she uncomfortably described her debilitating anxiety at work. Her answers were quick and polite, but her breathing was shallow, like she seemed uncomfortable in her skin. Her anxiety was a palpable force in the room with us, and it seemed to attach itself to me and our session: *Was I going to judge her? Would she say the right things? Did she make the right decision to seek help?*

This was how she usually felt. As the only female associate at a commercial real estate group, Layla likened the professional culture at work to a sports locker room. Despite her stellar performance, she was starting to lose her confidence. Recently, she found herself questioning minor decisions, rechecking major ones, and staying up late to meet deadlines. Her anxiety was beginning to take its toll on her productivity and mood; she feared it might ruin everything she had built.

Layla's secondary anxiety—her anxiety about her anxiety—was making it hard to tease anything useful out of her anxiety. I discussed with her the range of anxiety and how not all of it is detrimental. As I often do in the first session, I broke out my white board and drew the Yerkses Dodson Curve (see page 79), using it to explain how peak performance exists with moderate anxiety, the "sweet spot" between boredom (on the left side of the curve) and panic (on the right side).

This sunk in quickly for her. She admitted that her anxiety was still moderate, fueled by her drive to do a good job and the weight of her responsibilities. But her secondary anxiety was escalating her experience well past the sweet spot. She had been afraid of how she was feeling, and thus distressed by it. We discussed in chapter 6 (see page 89) how secondary anxiety operates as a vicious circle: we carry the false assumption that we can't handle what we're experiencing, and this resistance to anxiety generates more worry about it, which in turn drives up our suffering. But the fact is that we can *always* handle our experience, even if we don't want to. Knowing we can handle something is a way of taking control, and it can powerfully drive down our anxiety to a manageable level.

I challenged her to think about how her anxiety was serving her, how it gave her a helpful edge. As she refocused her lens on the adaptiveness of her anxiety, she created a rather compelling preliminary list of benefits: it fueled diligence in research and attention to detail, it alerted her to potential pitfalls in her analysis, and it signaled delicate interpersonal politics to navigate.

As she engaged with me in this perception overhaul, I could see small changes in her body language. Her shoulders softened, her body fell back a bit into the sofa, and her breathing slowed. She nodded and smiled, somewhat uncomfortably, but I could tell she was taking it in. Reframing her perception about her anxiety was powerful, and I watched it change her emotional experience in the room that day. Seeing the value in her anxiety seemed to ease it.

## What You See Is What You Get

We all know that how we think about things matters, but it's possible we are underestimating how much this is true, especially for emotions like stress and anxiety. When we believe stress is hurtful, we compound our fear of it, exponentially increasing its power.

Stanford psychology professor Alia Crum and her colleagues conducted a series of studies that showed how much our stress mind-set determines how we react to stress and how it manifests itself.[1] In one study, the researchers first determined how positively or negatively the subjects viewed stress. Then the subjects were shown short movies promoting the idea of stress as either helpful or harmful. Finally, the researchers measured the subject's physiological reaction to a stressful situation afterwards. Those individuals who endorsed a stress-is-enhancing mind-set reported better health, fewer symptoms of anxiety and depression, higher levels of energy, workplace performance, and life satisfaction than those who endorsed a stress-is-debilitating mind-set. The results were significant, driving home how much our belief systems can impact the stress equation.

"Unlike a placebo, which tends to have a short-lived impact on a highly specific outcome," Kelly McGonigal writes in the *Upside of Stress*, which references Crum's studies, "the consequences of a mind-set snowball over time, increasing in influence and long-term impact."[2] McGonigal cites the new body of research that shows stress in its own right isn't destructive or stifling; it's our constant harping on how negative it is, and our inability to shake the association, that cripples us.

In fact, changing our thinking about anxiety can actually boost our energy. It can transform it into a productive outlet as well as conserve the energy otherwise wasted on resisting it. Anxiety can feel like the beast wearing you down, making every decision pregnant with importance. But that exhaustion is not the result of anxiety itself, but rather *the energy we dedicate to fighting it.*

Contrary to its reputation, anxiety itself isn't necessarily affecting our health at all—how we think about it is. In a recent wide-reaching British study, the researchers determined that no robust evidence remains that unhappiness or stress actually increase mortality.[3] Those who perceive their stress is unhealthy partake in a self-fulfilling prophecy: the stress becomes unhealthy *because* of that perception.[4]

In a large-scale study at the University of Wisconsin, researchers found that subjects' perceptions of their stress was directly correlated with how unhealthy it actually turned out to be. Those who claimed to have a high amount of stress *and* thought that it was unhealthy were at a higher risk of mortality than those who simply reported stress.[5] These were not minor discrepancies—the gap was substantial: "Those who reported a lot of stress and that stress greatly impacted their health had a 43 percent increased risk of premature death."[6] In describing this study, McGonigal notes, "It wasn't stress alone that was killing people. It was the combination of stress and the belief that stress is harmful." When stress is not resisted, she further explains, blood vessels are relaxed and the profile looks more like "joy and courage."[7] Anxiety can be helpful when we perceive it can be.

Moderate stress is essentially neutral energy; what makes it a plus or a negative is our response to it. Those who suffer from what I call secondary anxiety, stress about their stress, are the ones who suffer health problems. The *European Heart Journal* found that those who thought their stress was unhealthy were 50 percent more at risk for a heart attack than those who did not, even after adjusting for other factors.[8]

## It's in Your Head

"[P]sychology has shown that mind-set doesn't just change how we feel about an experience," Shawn Achor, one of Crum's research partners, writes in *The Happiness Advantage*, "it actually changes the objective results of that experience."[9]

Achor highlights the "nocebo," or reverse placebo, effect illustrated by an oft-cited Japanese study. Thirteen subjects who were allergic to poison ivy rubbed their hand on a harmless shrub they were told was poison ivy. Incredibly, all thirteen developed the classic rash! When the same group rubbed their other hand on actual poison ivy and told it was harmless, only two got the rash.[10] As neuroscience writer Sandra Blakeslee noted about this and other studies, "As in the outside world, people's internal states have inherent ambiguity."[11] Of course, there are genetics and predisposition, but we're learning more and more about how the cognitive piece—our thinking—can tip the balance. This is emphasized most dramatically by the famous study by Fabrizio Bendetti, who determined that the popular antianxiety drug Valium, "has less effect when patients are unaware they are taking them."[12]

How we think about something impacts *how* we experience it, and by extension, what it is. When we believe that we can get better, we usually do. If we believe a treatment will work, we give it a significant advantage. "If threat, anxiety, and negative suggestion can induce symptoms of pain and sickness," writes Jo Marchant in *Cure: A Journey into the Science of Mind over Body*, "then it follows that feeling safe and secure, or believing that we are about to feel better, will have the reverse effect."[13] As we discussed in the last chapter, we have far more control than we think we do. And as we will learn more about in the next chapter, how we think we will feel has a powerful effect on *how we do feel.*

## Awareness

Daniel J. Siegel's ideas about mental awareness are at the heart of what psychologists have longtime called *insight*, and more recently, *mindfulness*. The idea is that the more we can observe and understand ourselves, the more we can ultimately control our experience. Siegel writes in *Mindsight* about "a kind of focused attention that allows us to see the internal workings of our own minds. It helps us to be aware of our mental processes without being swept away by them, enables us to get ourselves off the autopilot of ingrained behaviors and habitual responses."[14] The changes become "transformational at the very physical levels of the brain."[15]

Although we are built to think that our negative emotions bring vital information—that they are somehow more real—we can benefit from embracing and tuning into our positive emotions as well. Barbara Frederickson, a researcher who has studied the effect of positive emotions, such as joy, love, and laughter, writes: "Positive emotions, however, are adaptive over the long haul. They expand our awareness so that we can survive and grow, give us more tools for our survival tool kit and help us become better versions of ourselves."[16] Finding the positive in something is not just about attitude, it's about productiveness. The old adage "it's all in your mind" is literally true—and it should not be underestimated.

That doesn't mean finding the positive is easy. In fact, we all have a negativity bias, and *this* reflexive negativity has deep ancestral roots that are partly physiological. We are born and trained to notice the negative, so we can make sure to avoid it whenever possible. It's one of the keys to our survival. We give negative experiences more weight, assuming they carry more information and value than positive stimuli when it comes to ensuring our success.[17] But this isn't actually true.

Anyone in a marriage who wonders why their mistakes are always noticed more than their triumphs will find this reassuring. It isn't personal; finding the negative can come quite naturally even if it isn't healthy or helpful. If left unbalanced by positivity, negative evaluations can be destructive especially to relationships. Gottman's Magic Ratio, made famous by John Gottman's research on couples, has determined that the ideal ratio is five positive interactions for every negative to maintain a healthy relationship of any kind.[18] The negatives are just stickier and it's the reason we have evolved as we have.

Putting in the effort to find the positives isn't just a mood-enhancing activity—it's an efficiency one: it frees up more coping mechanisms in the end for the challenges at hand.[19] In *Hardwiring Happiness*, Rick Hanson takes things a step further by not even calling the typically stressful experiences negative; he calls them positive because of the end result. "For example, the pain of a hand on a hot stove, the anxiety at not finding your child at a park, and the remorse that helps us take the high road make us feel bad now to help us feel better later."[20] We could all gain some peace of mind by approaching the stressful situation as a positive one, something that will support and trigger growth.

## The Pull of Perception

> *"It is not events that disturb people, it is their judgments concerning them."*
>
> —Epicetus[21]

The hardest part of gaining control over our experience is simply believing that we can. "Your brain can be subtly manipulated in ways that change your future behavior..." writes neuroscientist David Eagleman. "This effect is called priming: your brain has been primed like a pump."[22] If changing our perception in the moment feels too difficult, we should work on laying the groundwork beforehand. Just like the Norwegian parachute trainees gained control over their fears by preparing for the jump, we can prime our brains to expect, or even welcome, anxiety so that we can feel more control when it arrives.

A recent study led by Alison Wood Brooks on "anxious reappraisal" explains the elegant simplicity of this. Brooks worked with subjects who were nervous to perform on stage in front of a crowd—in this case, karaoke. She asked them to shift their nervousness by repeating to themselves *I am excited* over and over again. Rather than trying to numb or ignore the rush of chemicals they were feeling, Brooks trained them to redirect the feeling simply by *renaming it*. This technique actually lowered subjects' heart rates.[23] How we interpret and name our experience has a more powerful effect on how we feel it than we had previously thought possible.

Similarly, University of Rochester researcher Jeremy Jamieson conducted experiments on test anxiety, examining whether or not treating the arousal as fuel (rather than denying it existed) would work. He has also studied similar effects with the Graduate Records Examination (GRE), employing a reappraising technique: choosing to react to stress as the excitement of a challenge.[24] The researchers discovered that if they told subjects in advance they could handle it, rather than telling them to calm down, their performance improved by 33 percent.[25] "Little" things like reappraisal are not so little; they can tip the balance and change the experience.[26] Jamieson and his colleagues find:

> In stressful situations, signs of increased arousal (e.g., racing heart) are frequently construed as anxiety, nervousness, or fear. These negative appraisals encourage people to perceive demands as exceeding resources, triggering a maladaptive threat response. Thus, modifying resource appraisals may help improve physiological responses.[27]

A study from the University of Illinois published in *Emotion* found that people who regularly engaged in reappraisal reported diminished anxiety compared to those who suppressed emotions.

According to study coauthor Nicole Llewellyn, reappraisal is when you ask, *What are the ways I can look at this and think of it as a stimulating challenge rather than a problem?*[28]

Llewellyn surveyed 179 men and women about how they dealt

> **Language Matters: Anxiety Reappraisal**
>
> Replace "I'm worried about" with "I care about."
>
> Replace "I am nervous" with "I am excited."
>
> Replace "I am afraid I can't" with "I am going to find a way to..."

with anxiety or managed their emotions in various situations.[29] The research team then analyzed the results to determine whether certain strategies were linked to lower levels of anxiety. What they found was that the individuals who engaged in emotional regulation in this way had less social anxiety and suffered from less anxiety in general.

The data suggest that people who suffer from anxiety can gain some degree of control over their symptoms simply through reappraisal. And this type of emotional regulation can be taught, regardless of one's genetic predispositions. Suppressing or "bottling" emotions can be beneficial in the moment (like when your boss shouts at you), but over time, suppressed emotions can have compounding negative consequences.[30] We will learn more about why this is in the next chapter, but for now, know that how you perceive your feelings, and how you name them, matters. A lot.

# Layla

When Layla came back the second week, she was again impeccably dressed and again sat at the edge of the seat. But this time, she
wore a slightly different smile, less self-conscious. She didn't seem
quite as uncomfortable to be sitting in a therapist's office, to be
sitting with me, or perhaps sitting with herself.

She recounted having had a better week, noting the positive
impact changing her thinking about her anxiety had had on her
performance. Simply knowing she could handle her feelings had
helped her tolerate them. She told me that reframing her anxiety
as energy had helped her avoid the procrastination that had bedeviled her the last few weeks and helped her push through a big
project to completion.

Layla opened up about how when her anxiety struck, she
made a conscious choice to view it as a tool: it helped her access
important nuances in her work. She was enjoying thinking about
her concerns in a new way, not as a symptom of something wrong
with her, but as evidence she was doing the best job she could.
Cautiously, Layla admitted loving the idea that her anxiety was
a powerful tool that could *help* her compete and execute on the
things that mattered most to her. She admitted it would take time
to train herself for this seemingly counterintuitive approach, but
she seemed open. A simple change in perception already was
helping her feel freer from what had been developing as a burden.

# Paula

Changing our view of anxiety can help us feel more control, creating the courage to tolerate the discomfort long enough to embrace it. By virtue of showing up to their appointments, my clients are courageously facing their anxiety. Allowing the discomfort to wash over them, really digging into its source and message, takes guts and practice, and it isn't always easy.

Paula is among my bravest clients—having sought help during her journey of substantial weight loss. In our sessions, she realized just how afraid she was of her feelings—all of them—because she had used food for so many years to numb them. To lose the weight, she had to learn new ways of understanding and expressing her feelings that had for so long eluded her. She had to embrace the power of naming her emotions, and find control in her perception, rather than her avoidance of them. Shifting her control to her awareness and perception has broadened her coping; she has learned what it means to tune in and use her feelings, and her anxiety in particular. It has taken time and practice, but she continues to thrive.

"Anxiety is not paranoia," Andrew Solomon writes in *The Noonday Demon*. "People with anxiety disorders assess their own position in the world much as do people without. What changes in anxiety is how one feels about the assessment."[31] Again, it all runs back to what we can control and how we see it. Avoid the traps and dig anew with courage and self-compassion.

# Looking Ahead with Hope

Anxiety is a feeling whose source almost always lies in the future. Of course, we can't avoid thinking about the future. Defining long-term goals and dreams are an important part of motivational direction, and without them people can lose a sense of purpose and drive. But letting the future override your present and dominate your thoughts is a destructive way to live. The future, after all, is infinite and there are just too many scenarios and options to consider to ever feel like you have a handle on them. I do find that anxious clients do better to look at things closer to the present when conceptualizing time, or at least acknowledge that their concept of time or what the future may hold could be inaccurate.

Overgeneralizing, taking today's experience and applying it indiscriminately to the future, is a habit that significantly worsens anxiety symptoms. If today's circumstances are difficult, and we extrapolate and assume that the future will be the same, our anxiety worsens. Putting ourselves in the future too frequently can exacerbate the feeling that we can't handle things, including our anxiety.

A common strategy used in Alcoholics Anonymous, "one day at a time," describes the idea that you can stay sober for today. Paula ran a half marathon this way—when she felt like quitting, she took it one minute at a time. When she felt her anxiety about not being able to keep going, she made a deal with herself to keep going for the next sixty seconds and then reconsider. The next sixty seconds and then reconsider. Literally minute by minute, she kept at her goal until she finished.

Breaking down the future into manageable chunks became a powerful metaphor in our work as to how she could build her tolerance for a variety of frustrations: one minute at a time, even one breath at a time. When we allow ourselves to start cataloging the future, and how much pain we will feel, we work ourselves into useless anxiety and fear that ultimately gives us an excuse to sabotage our efforts now.

I attend physical therapy for a chronic shoulder injury/arthritis. At the end of a fatiguing shoulder workout (that I jokingly liken to torture), my therapist told me to hold a plank position and then transition to a side plank. As I watched him demonstrate the move, my anxiety immediately fired, suspicious I was not ready for such a strength pose and might reinjure my shoulder I had worked so hard to rebuild. But I also knew I trusted him. So, I used my anxiety to check with him, negotiating to put my knee down for support if needed, and I decided to give it a try, just to see. Much to my surprise, I found that I *could* do a side plank once again, and not only that, I could do more than one on each side. When I had completed two on each side, I asked him how many he wanted me to do—confident (hoping) he would say I was done, or just one more. When he said five, which was more than twice what I had already done, my anxiety soared, and I immediately put my knee down, giving into my fear.

I was tired and had forgotten to take each move at a time, letting my head get in the way. Recognizing I had sabotaged my efforts, I mentally regrouped, rested for a few seconds and negotiated with my therapist that I would try one more on each side. I then hauled myself into the plank once again and was able to complete a final round, noting my physical fatigue but also my strength. I didn't need to be afraid of not being able to do it. My body was telling me what I needed to hear, and one more was the right amount of strain to continue to build strength.

## Fatima

Fatima is a longtime patient in her forties from an immigrant family who often feels a bit lost in identifying who she is. Her story is about finding her self-confidence, emotionally regulating herself, and making healthier relationship choices. In learning how to better interpret and manage her feelings, we have noticed that Fatima's perception of time can be a significant source of anxiety. Time is one of those variables that can play a key role in how we perceive our experiences, especially when we look into the future. When things are going badly, it can feel like they will be that way forever, a perception that triggers more distress and anxiety. This happens regularly for Fatima. When she is feeling disappointed, ashamed, or particularly alone in her relationships and friend-ships, she is prone to believing she will never feel any differently in the future. That she will remain alone, disappointed, and pathetic. That if she hasn't made quality relationships yet, she won't ever make them.

Fatima has had to learn to resist the urge to overgeneralize her current feelings far into the future, and to instead shorten a time horizon to this afternoon, tonight, and tomorrow in order to regain control. Predicting the future is a risky proposition anyway. There are simply too many variables involved in the future to feel any real sense of control, and the further out we allow our thoughts about time to go, the more powerless we feel. The opposite is true as well. When we keep our thoughts on where we are now and what we can control and influence presently, we allow our anxiety a needed outlet and we can measure our success. Small manageable steps keep our expectations in check and keep us motivated.

I have a friend who uses a similar time trick for his own anxiety by seesawing his perspective as needed. When the little details are a struggle, he shifts to the big picture, which is usually a worthy goal. When the final result—the big picture—is scary, he focuses on the little things in front of him. He calls it *Thinking big when small bothers you, and thinking small when the big bothers you.*

Pulling your time horizon closer to present will help you see what is in front of you that is in your control. Few of us feel control over the distant future, but most of us can see what we have control over right now. We can literally envision what we need to do in the next five minutes, hour, or day, but too far into the future gets harder to visualize. It can easily become too conceptual, and we can lose clarity on our sense of self. Tuning into our future self can be important when it comes to executing goal-oriented behavior. Self-control has even been called empathy for your future self: "The Present You taking a hit to help out Future You."[32] The further away the future you, the harder it is to identify and control.

"The power of prospection is what makes us wise," Martin Seligman and John Tierney wrote. "Looking into the future,

> ## Hacking Your Time Horizon
>
> When you think about your fears, when are they? Where is your time horizon?
>
> Move it closer to boost control and reduce anxiety.

consciously and unconsciously, is a central function of our large brain, as psychologists and neuroscientists have discovered—rather belatedly, because for the past century most researchers have assumed that we're prisoners of the past and the present… Therapists are exploring new ways to treat depression now that they see it as primarily not because of past traumas and present stresses but because of skewed visions of what lies ahead."[33]

Viktor Frankl, whose quote opens this book, was a psychiatrist and neuroscientist, in addition to being a Holocaust survivor. In his seminal book *Man's Search for Meaning*, he wrote, "Everything can be taken from a man but one thing: the last of the human freedoms—to choose one's attitude in any given set of circumstances, to choose one's own way."[34]

Now, let's look at the what is going on inside of our brains during moments of stress and anxiety and how understanding this process can help us gain more control of our anxious reactions.

## CHAPTER NINE

# The Brain and the Body

*"In each of us there is another whom we do not know."*

—**Carl Jung**[1]

**At its foundation, anxiety is** a complex brain-body system that has evolved over millions of years to help ensure our survival. Anxiety expert David Barlow goes so far to say that anxiety is "largely responsible for the survival of the species."[2] We depend on anxiety for self-preservation, and we rely on it to fuel adaptation.

Dr. Jeremy Copland, professor of psychiatry at SUNY Downstate, conducted a study that found that anxiety likely evolved alongside intelligence. "Worry may cause our species to avoid dangerous situations," he says, "regardless of how remote a possibility they may be. In essence, worry may make people 'take no chances,' and such people may have higher survival rates. Thus, like intelligence, worry may confer a benefit upon the species."[3]

Your body knows what you need even if "you" do not. Think of the pounding heart preparing to meet a challenge. It is delivering more oxygen to your brain to focus attention and energy to the concern at hand. Anxiety is not so different.

From what we know about the brain's ability to change and adapt, and the emerging science about how we construct emotion, our feelings are purposeful. They reflect the things we care about most and our understanding of how we are interacting in the world. But science hasn't always understood anxiety this way.

## The Brain as an Apple

Much of anxiety treatment has been based on the idea that anxiety is an ancestral ghost, a specter haunting modern man. Because the threat response involves the most primitive parts of our brain that we share with other animals, a belief has held that anxiety is generated by a primitive brain system out of step with modern needs. Much of this thinking comes from a model of the brain called the *triune brain theory.*

The triune brain theory holds that our brain's architecture reflects our evolution, noting three main areas of the brain have evolved from the base outward, from old to new:

- **Inner Layer:** Hindbrain (reptilian brain, reflexive, instinctive, automatic)

- **Middle Layer:** Limbic brain (emotional and mammalian —social relationships have adaptive value)
- **Outer Layer:** Neocortex (uniquely human: awareness, analysis, logic, reason, self-management)

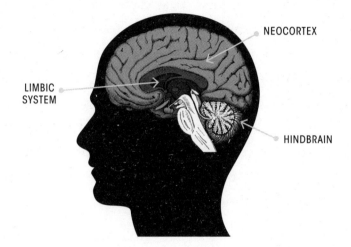

Think of it as an apple: the flesh is our neocortex, which has allowed us to build cities and cure diseases; the core is the adaptive part of our brain that formed communities and friendships; and the stem is the instinctive part of our brain that we share with other mammals, regulating basic functions like hunger, thirst, procreation, and self-protection. Our assumption of a hierarchical brain is so ingrained that even the vocabulary we use reflects this: "reptilian brain," vs. "*neo*cortex," (neo as in new), "primitive" impulses vs. "higher order" thinking.

This framework has informed neuroscientists' research and the treatment for anxiety. The theory posits that although we are no longer on the savannah of Africa, our "primitive brain" is still reacting like we are, like it's a leftover bug from a previous operating system. Likewise, the current thinking around how to treat anxiety has been aimed at eradicating its symptoms, since it must be habitually misfiring.

But with what we know about the brain's capacity to grow and change, why—for all of modern humanity—would we conserve an inadequate system? Every other part of our brain is constantly adapting and changing to the shifting demands of our environments. Why wouldn't our anxiety system likewise adapt? Our brains are designed to continually shape themselves so that functions are reinforced and conserved for a purpose. Anxiety too must be adaptive to the here and now—our brains are too malleable and efficient to allow otherwise.

## Constructing Ourselves

New research has shown that emotions, including fear and anxiety, are not "gut" reactions, but they are actually full brain constructions. "Thinking and feeling are not distinct in the brain,"[4] Lisa Feldman Barrett writes in *How Emotions Are Made*. Barrett, a neuroscientist and professor at Northeastern University, takes on the myth that our emotional reactions are somehow alien from our thinking selves, a "break" from who we are. "Emotions are not temporary deviations from rationality," she writes. "They are not alien forces that invade you without your consent. They are not tsunamis that leave destruction in their wake. They are not even your reactions to the world. They are your constructions of the world."[5]

We are constantly creating ourselves, including our emotions. They don't come out of us fully formed—we engage with the process. It might *feel* like we're taken over by grief or rage or panic, but that's simply not true. Emotions of course begin with stimuli and sensations, but the brain then makes sense of those sensations by weighing them against our knowledge and experience. This is how we make judgments about their meaning.

I notice I am feeling cold sensations on my bare legs in summer air conditioning and determine that I am cold. I feel the air, compare it against my experience and knowledge, and respond. I get to determine if the cold air feels uncomfortably cold or comfortably cool. There may even be a middle ground where I am uncomfortable, but decide I am not *that* uncomfortable. The stimulus is happening, there is wiggle room in defining how we feel, and we get to decide. It's not unlike how the baby looks to his mother's facial reaction to decide whether a new bump is worth crying about.

We notice the sensation of an internal experience and name it. And in this way, we are in control. There is a feedback loop at work. Emotions only become what we think of as "emotions" when we consciously think about and name them. While our minds are constantly tuning into and sorting stimuli, we aren't always aware of it. We can feel uncomfortable before we know what's happening. We can even respond to these stimuli before we know quite what we are feeling, but we are still deciding. We have all had the experience of getting a bad feeling about a person or place. It feels "in the air"—but of course, it's not. It's in *us*.

Naming our anxiety can be a critical first step in perceiving and understanding it. When we name our feelings, we activate parts of our brain that help us process emotion, a process that psychiatry professor Daniel J. Siegel calls "Name and Tame."[6]

The more we can name and understand our emotions, the more we can tolerate and ultimately control them.[7]

## The Gas Pedal

The threat system is activated largely by the amygdala, two pea-sized areas located deep in our forebrain, the brain region that controls our thought and emotions. When we are afraid or acutely anxious, our amygdala activates the autonomic nervous system along the HPA axis to create a threat response commonly known as our fight or flight, as we discussed in chapter 3. The threat response signals various other parts of the brain and body via the sympathetic branch of the autonomic nervous system, which gives us the energy and resources we need to defend ourselves from threat.[8] A good way to think of the sympathetic branch is as the "gas pedal," propelling us into action.

The amygdala "receives not just simple signals (such as loud noises) from the lower stations of the brain," writes Steven Pinker in *How the Mind Works*, "but abstract, complex information from the brain's highest centers. The amygdala in turn sends signals to virtually every other part of the brain, including the decision-making circuitry of the frontal lobes."[9] The message is an alert: *prepare for a response*. At its most severe, in the case of jumping out of the way of a car or reaching after a falling child, this response is full body and automatic.

The amygdala is acutely sensitive, quick, and in times of imminent danger, it operates outside of our awareness. Rapid response is so critical that the process tends to skip our thinking brain to provide us the most rapid response possible. This is known as the "bottom up" response. The amygdala drives the response "up" the neurological chain, activating the HPA axis, which inhibits our thoughts and steers our biological response, including sending blood to our extremities and increasing respiration to increase oxygen levels.

## Bottom Up vs. Top Down

Anybody who has suffered disruptive anxiety knows the frustration of not being able to think clearly when it strikes. It's not an illusion; there is a biological reason for this. Studies using fMRI technology show less activity in the prefrontal cortex, the part of our brain that is associated with planning, reasoning, and prosocial behavior, when the threat response is activated.[10]

We all have had the "I just did it without thinking" explanation of how we've reacted in seemingly urgent situations. Under conditions of uncertainty or threat, messages from our primitive cortical areas are released.[11] It's as though there is usually a gate that keeps them at bay. When danger strikes, we automatically unlock it, unleashing the primitive side of us that just knows how to react. This is the "bottom up" theory at work.

For example, you see a snake in front of you on a path and you jump back well before you register the danger. Likewise, a dog running into the street ahead of our car elicits an automatic response in you to brake. We jump back and stop the car long before we can think about it. These are our protective reflexes at work. We feel and respond before we are even consciously aware enough to label our experience, much less govern it.

"Top down" theory suggests the opposite, that most emotions and responses can be controlled by our thinking and perception. The theory posits that our higher-order brain centers can control our more primitive emotions by governing how we process them and what we do with them, through various circuits that exert control over the amygdala.[12] There are things we would do as humans that virtually no animal would do, like get on a roller coaster or cross a footbridge. Likewise, a dog will swim in a riptide or an ocean unafraid of sharks, whereas humans would not— because of what we know about what lurks in there.

Current thinking is that neither bottom up nor top down wholly explain the interplay between our reflexive responses, our thoughts, and the emotions that result.[13] There is continued debate around how the amygdala can be influenced.

## Chemistry of Anxiety

The chemistry of our bodies is equally important in the way we feel, exhibit, and respond to anxiety. As Bruce McEwen explains, "Hormones associated with stress protect the body in the short run and promote adaptation."[14] Under stress, cortisol, a powerful chemical that supplies glucose and supports our immune system, is released in the brain and detectable throughout the body.

Not only can humans adapt to chronic stress and build resilience,[15] but acute, non-repetitive stress has also been associated with increases in memory, adaptivity,[16] and neural growth.[17] All the chemicals released under stress facilitate coping, bolster our immune system, provide energy for action, and compel interpersonal connection. (It is when it never shuts off that cortisol can become damaging.[18])

Oxytocin, called the *cuddle hormone*, is also triggered by the stress response and is believed to help regulate it. Not only does oxytocin play an important role in cell repair, but it promotes social engagement, attachment, bonding, and helping.[19] Be it rallying a team to tackle a problem or securing a hug from a trusted friend, oxytocin is working to help us make use of our support networks and solve our problems at a chemical level.

Chemicals in our brains called *neurotransmitters* also play important roles in the experience of anxiety. Neurotransmitters transmit messages between nerve cells and have been associated with a variety of mood experiences. Serotonin, for example, has been associated with feelings of calm and well-being, whereas dopamine is linked to feelings of desire and reward. While the role of these neurotransmitters in anxiety disorders is not yet fully understood, they have been the target of many commonly prescribed antianxiety medications. The suggestion—pushed by drug company advertising—is that such disorders could be the result of an underlying chemical imbalance. However, it's more complicated than that. As an article in *Scientific American* puts it, "Just because a drug reduces symptoms of a disease does not mean that those symptoms were caused by a chemical problem the drug corrects."[20]

Most antianxiety medications aim to deliver better balance in our neural synapses of the neurotransmitters thought to be involved in anxiety. When effective, these drugs quiet anxiety by adjusting the levels of these naturally produced neurotransmitters. However, not all anxiety issues are helped by adjusting these neurotransmitters, and the search for better chemical solutions continues.

## Shifting Gears

Just like the sympathetic nervous system (the "gas pedal") kick-starts your threat response, your parasympathetic nervous system shuts it off, telling your body it can relax. In this way, it operates like the "brake pedal." Most antianxiety strategies have targeted this neurological off switch, since it is so hard to gain a sense of control when the gas pedal is pressed all the way down.

The threat response (fight-or-flight) only shuts off when stimuli are considered safe, and this is where our perception and thinking come in. When we change how we view our anxiety, even our most acute anxiety, and interpret it as harmless or even helpful, we make it less threatening and can therefore gain more control of it. Much like using downshifting, rather than the brakes, to slow down a car, this is how thinking activates resources to calm and refocus our anxiety. When we recognize our anxiety as familiar—as "friend" instead of "foe"—we are less alarmed by its arrival, and we can better think through what we can do about it. Believing anxiety is safe (and won't harm us) allows our threat response to stand down (brake), while thinking through anxiety helps access more of our cognitive resources that slow down our anxiety (down shifting), and deliver more control. This is how we can use our thinking to *respond* to anxiety rather than simply *react* to it.

## Rethinking Anxiety's Physiology

However, the human experience of anxiety is much more nuanced than an intense and automatic threat response—and can produce a variety of responses. New research suggests that the amygdala may serve the purpose of directing our attention, and prioritizing resources, rather than generating fear.[21] The amygdala's threat system might be better called an *attentional prioritizing system*: novel and emotionally significant stimuli draw our focus. I use this metaphor with my clients: Anxiety is like an alarm clock that will snooze but not turn off. You can ignore it temporarily, but it will always come back on. It won't stop until you wake up, get up, and turn it off.

New York University researcher Joseph LeDoux has been at the forefront of this new fight-or-flight research. He differentiates between our threat response and what we call anxiety. There is our animallike detection of a threat—pumping our adrenaline or speeding our breathing—and then there is the conscious feeling to which we assign words. This naming step opens broader access to our thinking brain and all its resources. There's even research that if we talk about ourselves in the third person, it makes it easier to shape our experience and calm our anxiety.[22]

Feelings only become feelings when we are conscious of them and can name them. LeDoux explains how we each construct emotion through a collection of elements that we choose to put together, like making a soup:

> Fear can be thought of as emerging in consciousness, much the way the character of a soup emerges from its raw materials, its ingredients. Start with salt, pepper, garlic, onions, carrots, and chicken. Add roux and chicken soup becomes gumbo, or add curry paste, and it shifts it in a different direction... Similarly, emotions emerge from nonemotional ingredients, events that exist in the brain and body as part of being a living organism of a particular type.[23]

LeDoux's work has gained widespread support, especially since there is consensus that our survival reactions are quick and automatic, whereas the conscious feelings are slower and more deliberate. It further supports the efficient nature of our brain's organization:[24] survival first, awareness second.

# Tend and Befriend

When life's demands seem to outweigh our ability to cope, we have another stress response that seeks help and draws on our network of friends and family. Dubbed the *tend-and-befriend* response, this response is based largely on oxytocin's role in weakening the HPA stress response, *fight or flight*.[25] Given the importance of our social networks, it only fits that we would lean on and protect these connections when we're threatened.

Jumping into a dangerous situation to assist, or otherwise risking our safety for that of another, is behavior promoted by stress thanks to the release of oxytocin.[26] Look no further than the courage and bravery we see on battlefields or in crises. During these times, there are always people compelled to help. Beloved children's TV host Fred Rogers so understood the power of crisis to fuel compassion and altruism that he believed it could help heal a community. He would often advise distressed onlookers to notice the helpers, noting "if you look for the helpers, you'll know there is hope."[27]

Anxiety can also fuel help-*seeking* behavior. When anxiety gets to be too much, it compels us to look for help from the people around us. Whether to a doctor to help manage our symptoms, a therapist to help work through a crisis, or trusted loved ones for comfort and support, reaching out for help is a powerful way our anxiety motivates solutions and fosters connections.

## Meeting a Challenge

Many benefits of moderate stress have been documented, including neural growth[28], memory improvements, and strengthened immunity functioning.[29] This has led some researchers to hypothesize other adaptive responses beyond the HPA response conserved to protect our physical safety. When resources are sufficient to meet demands,[30] stress and anxiety can produce what some researchers call the Challenge Response (see page 123), where the stressor is perceived to be a *challenge* rather than a threat.[31]

A challenge response is another way to describe the sweet spot in the Yerkses Dodson curve (see page 80) where moderate stress and anxiety fuel peak performance. The more we practice harnessing anxiety for optimal activity, the better we get at meeting challenges.

Exposure to stress can also be a form of strength building, which is what chemists call *hormesis*.[32] The purpose is to build resistance to that stressor, as when a doctor gives us vaccines with low amounts of antigens to build up our immunity, or we strain muscles to fatigue in order to build them back stronger.

## Using Our Whole Brain

When it comes to anxiety and our well-being, our drives aren't the whole story, nor are our threat response, our genes, or our experiences. We have much more control than we think we do, and our brain is far more complex than an animal brain with a prefrontal cortex layered on top as suggested by the triune brain theory. The control is built-in. By the time we are aware we feel anxious, our thinking center is already engaged. Once that happens, we have access to more than just our habitual responses. We have access to choice. This is the start of control and change. Not just the perceptual kind, but the hardwired kind. Researchers have even put a number on how much control we actually have: 40 percent. According to data compiled by positive psychologist, Sonja Lyubomirsky and detailed in *The How of Happiness*, approximately 50 percent of variance in happiness is determined by genes, 10 percent of variance in happiness is determined by circumstance, and the rest of our happiness is determined by our actions.[33] This is powerful information. "To understand that 40 percent of our happiness is determined by intentional activity," Lyubomirsky writes, "is to appreciate the promise of the great impact that you can make on your own life through intentional strategies that you can implement to remake yourself as a happier person."[34]

Developments in neuroscience are uncovering that our emotional responses, and anxiety in particular, are the result of a fully integrated system with complex interactions between all its parts. Anxiety is not simply a hijacking of a primitive system that has not yet evolved to the demands of modern time. It is a sophisticated, full-brain experience that we actively participate in.

When we notice and think about anxiety—rather than simply react—we engage more of our whole brain. We construct our experience of anxiety, therefore we can create our responses to it. It might be beyond our control when our amygdala grabs our attention, but *what we do* with that signal and how we think about it certainly is not.

We might be alerted, even alarmed, but we don't have to be scared. We can instead be motivated, excited, eager, challenged, or compelled to help. We get to decide how we interpret our experience. Our threat system confirms that it is far more than just a fear response. We can make it work for us.

## The Plastic, Automatic Brain

"What fires together, wires together," is a much-invoked phrase made famous by Donald Hebb in 1949 that is still used by neuropsychologists to describe the fundamentals of habit formation in the brain.[35] As we associate experiences, thoughts, and actions to stimuli, our brains create links between neurons that are strengthened with each repetition. This capacity to "hardwire" experiences is how we absorb new learning and is called *plasticity*: it is how our brains change and grow. Think about learning a new skill or starting a new habit. We learn, and then we practice. The repetition that accompanies these activities actually strengthens the new connections we are forming. Simply doing something different, thinking new thoughts, or practicing new behaviors creates and strengthens new connections that rewire our brains.

Signals are transferred from nerve cell to nerve cell via the space between them called a *synapse*: axons are the part of the nerve that send information into the synapse, and dendrites are the part of the nerve that receive them from the synapse. Neurons "connect" to each other by sending signals to one another, creating a chain of connections referred to as a *neural pathway*.

Every nerve cell has only one transmitting axon, but it has as many receiving dendrites as it needs. Dendrites allow neurons to connect to as many as ten thousand other neurons. Under microscopes, dendrites look and act like tree branches—growing or pruning with use. Our dendrites are the most malleable part of our brain's wiring, allowing for new connections and pathways to be formed. The more we use a pathway, the stronger and faster it becomes; repeated use makes the connections stronger, more efficient, and less effortful. You can be a gifted athlete, but if you don't practice, your dendrites will prune themselves and will not allow for new connections and fast growth. But if you continually practice, and make more connections, the neural pathways become more diverse and stronger—more automatic.

*Automaticity* refers to what we do without consciously thinking about it. The most basic example of this is walking; we wouldn't be able to function if we had to think about every step. Much like airplanes and cars carry out simple and routine functions automatically, reserving only the most important for the pilot or driver, our brains work the same way. Humans are not built to do everything—even most things—consciously. Some things get set to autopilot. Our limited attentional resources demand that we rely on automated responses;[36] these are the things we can "do without thinking." The easier and more familiar the stimulus, the more likely we will respond automatically, conserving resources for more challenging demands.

Your brain is always striving to clear space for new thinking and more complex mental processing. It wants to relegate as many tasks as possible to the "automatic" parts of your brain, so it can conserve mental resources for other things.[37] The more items that can be left simmering on the back burner, the more space we have for more complicated or novel tasks.

Think of driving a car. It is quite a complicated task, as any new driver can tell you. It requires focus, coordination, planning, motor skills, and synchronized movements. It is a full brain activity when it is being learned. But over a relatively short period of time, the task of driving requires less and less mental activity. (So much so that drivers look to other stimulation to pass the time while driving!)

What was once a new and daunting full-brain activity becomes something so routine that we can do it without active thought. Your brain is executing the task of driving, but it's happening in the background, beyond your conscious control, freeing up attention and space for other things.

## The Toggle Switch of Anxiety

"There is also no doubt that we can use our brain to change our brains,"[38] anxiety experts Margaret Wehrenberg and Steven Prinz explain in *The Anxious Brain*. The habits of our brains are well-worn neural networks that are created and strengthened by use, and they are designed to make following them increasingly effortless. As Charles Duhigg writes in *The Power of Habit*, "Habits, scientist say, emerge because the brain is constantly looking for ways to save effort... When a habit emerges, the brain fully stops participating in decision-making. It stops working so hard, and it diverts focus to other tasks."

The opposite is true as well: it takes energy and focus to interrupt a habit, forge new neural pathways, and practice a new behavior to the point where we do it without thinking. In his book, *Moral Tribes,* neuroscientist Joshua Greene uses the analogy of a camera to explain different brain functioning: the automatic setting allows for quick and effortless action whereas the manual settling allows for consideration and flexibility.[39] According to Duhigg, "Unless you deliberately *fight* a habit—forge new routines—the pattern will unfold automatically."[40]

We now come up to a powerful idea: What if anxiety is there to jog us out of our complacency, offering us just enough help to fight a habit and forge something new? So much of our brain is geared toward autopilot; what if anxiety is precisely the catalyst it takes to snap out of it when necessary?

A key part of the cycle of adaptation and plasticity, I would suggest anxiety acts as a toggle switch, shifting us from automatic to manual mode. It alerts us to focus, assess, and take new action so that we can adapt to the challenges ahead. Anxiety wakes us up from the reverie of autopilot, signals us to pay attention and act, and then abates as we build automaticity back in. It is a vital part of how we grow new habits, and evolve.

## Digging New Riverbeds

Habits can be adaptive…or not so adaptive. With things like parking a car, or saying "good morning," our automatic behaviors are useful; we can do them without thinking, and they help smooth out our day. However, other times they aren't quite as helpful to our overall goals, like eating sugar-heavy food or snapping at a loved one. In these cases, we can feel stymied by our maladaptive habits and bugged by the whisper anxiety these unhelpful habits tend to generate.

A good metaphor for the neurobiology of habits is a concept of a riverbed. Over time, water flows along similar paths, creating crevices that are deepened and widened with use, reinforcing the path. Similarly, old and reused paths direct our experiences, responses, and emotions. Neural pathways forged in our brains early in life—and reinforced by repetition—continue to operate automatically unless they are consciously altered through new thoughts and actions. That is, of course, unless a force diverts the path. This is where anxiety comes in.

I worked with an elderly client named Richard who routinely talked to me about changing his mental riverbeds. He was working to build new cognitive habits and resist old destructive thinking that felt so familiar and tempting. A childhood of being shamed for sickness had left him feeling responsible for his various physical illnesses. It took a long time, but he worked hard to resist these familiar, inaccurate thoughts and choose more rational ones. A science buff, he liked to visualize how he was rerouting his neural pathways every time he redirected his thinking. By focusing on his mental choices, he used his anxiety to change negative thoughts into more positive ones, deepening the neural tributaries he was forging. It was a regenerating process: the more he did it, the easier it became.

Like water, our minds seek the path of least resistance. We tend to react how we've always reacted and our experiences continue to shape how we will react to the future. "Your past experiences," Lisa Feldman Barrett writes in *How Emotions are Made*, "give meaning to your present sensations."[41] Just as old, dry riverbeds remain long after the water stops flowing through them, these experiences and patterns never really go away. They are, after all, the products of our memories and our experiences; we can't just erase them. These patterns of behavior exist in our minds, but they do not need to keep driving our choices. Our personalities are *not* so entrenched and our ways of behaving are *not* so ingrained. We can react differently and learn new behavior—*if we want to*. And at its best, anxiety is there to nudge us along in finding better solutions to how we approach life.

We can avoid the riverbeds of negative thinking by not allowing our minds to continue too far along the tributaries there. We can change how we understand and view our experiences, and in so doing we create better options. Brain science continues to prove that our brains are designed for efficient adaptation, and they are more malleable than we ever thought. What we practice, how we think, and what we repeatedly do create and strengthen neural connections and pathways, changing them at the cellular level.

The more we create and reinforce habits, the more we can change our minds—from the outside in. This is physiologically the way we grow our brains throughout life, and anxiety has an important to role to play in this process. Let's now take a look at the first thing anxiety can become for us when we're tuned in: a signal.

## CHAPTER TEN

# Anxiety as Signal

*"Sometimes when people are under stress, they hate to think and it's the time when they most need to think."*

—**Bill Clinton**[1]

## Cecilia: Yell Revisited

Let's return to Cecilia from chapter 3, who experienced what I call yell anxiety, the kind that is constant, deafening, and distracting. She was offered a great job opportunity to move from Washington, DC, to the West Coast but was feeling anxious about the decision. It was a rare opportunity and a significant boost to her career. However, she felt guilty about burdening her family and annoyed that her husband wasn't communicating with her about it.

My work with Cecilia focused on the actual reason for the anxiety, which was getting lost in the noise. We had to sort through the yelling and name her various feelings, which for her became an empowering experience. What eventually came out had less to do with the move and her family's response to it, and more to do with the job itself. She liked the prestige and opportunity but was ambivalent about the man who would be her future boss and the other members of her future team.

She felt she was *supposed* to love this new job, but she couldn't lie to herself: she didn't love it, and this was causing anxiety. She ended up turning down the job, and more importantly, took ownership for the reason for that decision. The yell anxiety that was keeping her awake, killing her appetite, and not letting her concentrate required the opposite of shutting it out: it required tuning in.

## The Big Shift

As we discussed, shifting from automaticity to plasticity is the key to making changes in ourselves, but we are so wired to operate autopilot that we probably need the occasional jolt, or whisper, of motivation now and then. There simply has to be some sort of catalyst, *some* sort of push. And anxiety most certainly fits this bill.

When we *choose* to view anxiety as our body coping, alerting, or signaling opportunities to us, we can see anxiety not as a burden, but as a finely tuned system trying to signal our attention when and where it is needed most. With every firing, anxiety is an invitation—perhaps even a mandate—to notice and do something different, new, and bold.

This is its purpose, and *using* it is the only way to make its discomfort stop. We have to be honest with ourselves: Aren't we most often *forced* to change our habits? *Could it be that we actually need some level of anxiety to change anything at all?*

## All Emotions Have a Purpose

According to Berkeley's Greater Good Science Center (GGSC), a research center that studies the science of a meaningful life, each emotion—even the ones we think of as "negative"—has its purpose. The GGSC's Dacher Keltner was an advisor on the Pixar movie *Inside Out*,[2] which takes place primarily inside of the head of a twelve-year-old girl, Riley. The five main emotions/characters—Joy, Sadness, Anger, Disgust, and Fear—interact, coordinate, and argue about how young Riley should react and behave. Throughout the film, Sadness is treated as a burden, especially by Joy. However, one of the key takeaways at the end of the film is that sadness is purposeful; in fact, sadness is the key player that helps Riley even recognize joy, bond with her friends and family, and create memories. It's an astute and dramatic distillation of how each emotion has a clear purpose that helps complete the whole.[3]

Psychologist Gregg Henriques, author of *A New Unified Theory of Psychology*, suggests that emotions are the result of disconnect between what is and what we want, therefore they compel us to set things into proper balance.[4] "Emotions send signals about our goals, and they prepare us for action," he writes. "Desire, joy, and excitement are positive emotions that orient us and send signals that there are good things out there to be approached… Fear and anxiety tell us that there are threats out there, and they prep us for defensive action."[5] Think of our emotions as signals about how we are doing in relation to our hopes, desires, and goals—they're the impetus for us to set things in balance and *do* what needs to be done to achieve it.

## Investigating Ourselves

As we learned in last chapter, rethinking an emotion by identifying it differently is not just a mind trick. It's physiological. "Giving a name to an emotion as we experience it reduces activation in the parts of the brain like amygdala that light up under duress," writes Matthew Lieberman at University of California, Los Angeles (UCLA). "Identifying and naming what we feel helps us process and let go of our negative emotions. In fact, correctly naming our emotions is one of the powerful steps in dealing with those emotions."[6]

Understanding how anxiety works allows us to reframe our thinking about it, tap into it, and put it to work. But we have to be willing to make sense of it and accept that it is not some accidental misfiring or reptilian relic; instead, it is something we can understand and use. The commitment to understand it opens the door. As Alan Watts wrote: "Doing something about a problem [that] you do not understand is like trying to clear away darkness by thrusting it aside with your hands."[7]

Rather than trying to push it away—a nearly impossible task that actually increases it—investigating our anxiety allows us to transform it into something useful. Instead of experiencing anxiety as a scary symptom, thinking about anxiety changes it by engaging more of our whole brain, which in turn can better direct our response.[8]

In studying the differences between our right and left brain, scientists have discovered that the left hemisphere is more closely associated with positive emotions and the right brain with negative ones.[9] In particular, activation in the left prefrontal cortex (our naming of experience) has been associated with a more positive effect and may be important in dampening and controlling amygdala response (the part of the brain associated with negative emotions and the threat response).[10] When we activate the language part of our brain, we take control and can powerfully shape our experience.

## Catherine

Catherine was a sixty-year-old senior partner of a successful consulting firm. One of the main issues that bedeviled her was how incapable she felt at getting her needs met. She struggled to speak up for herself or allow herself to seek what she actually wanted, and the result was a fairly constant state of anxiety and conflict that was making her miserable.

A great deal of this inhibition came out of her anxiety about doing the wrong thing or being judged. It manifested as something unique: jealousy of others, especially those who were having fun. She was both drawn to their lifestyles and disgusted by them at the same time. Consequently, she found herself consumed by the enjoyment others were having: her colleagues, her husband, and especially her friends. The jealousy had become quite painful and all-consuming, leaving her feeling ashamed and inadequate despite her many successes and accomplishments.

Jealousy is actually a sign of anxiety. Our jealousy is never about the object of envy; it's about our own conflicts regarding that person and what she or he represents for us. The feeling is directed at someone else, but it is always about us.

Catherine and I spent many sessions discussing the origins of this anxious jealousy, how it signaled a deeper dissatisfaction with her own life. Part of it came from her aging body, which prevented her from living the active life she once embraced. Part of it came from looking ahead at what she really wanted and what could actually improve her happiness. Her sense of helplessness was compounded by her unwillingness to speak up for what she wanted to the people who mattered. Sometimes, she even struggled to identify what that was.

We focused on how she could enjoy her life inside of new constraints, not what she wished he could do, or what she might have been, but what she could do now. We also started defining more of what she wanted and what kinds of pursuits could bring her the satisfaction and joy she was seeking. A key step we took was coming up with a list of things that she wanted to try—hobbies, charities, leadership opportunities, yoga, and travel. Slowly she started creating a plan: a way to stay active and focus on what she can add to her life instead of brooding and resenting others. In listening closely to her anxiety, she saw that she wanted what others had: satisfaction and variety. As she identified what her anxiety meant to her, what she needed to do became clearer, and she transformed her anxiety into motivation and solutions.

Today, Catherine is involved in numerous charities, holds leadership positions, and enjoys a few recreational hobbies. She is grounded and happier, and jealousy no longer overtakes her joy. When jealousy flares, she has learned it signals she is falling down on her commitments to herself and sensing a new challenge ahead. She now recognizes how invigorating new challenges can be, especially when they are born of a personal curiosity or passion, and she takes the calculated risks she needs to channel her anxiety into sustaining growth.

## The Needed Jolt

Anxiety is a message—almost an alarm—to which we must pay attention. This alarm bell framework is a constant in my work. I help clients view their anxiety as a needed jolt out of automaticity, into doing something different. Our brains learn by doing something new; anxiety, discomfort, and unrest are all catalysts to new learning and new living.

Dr. Dale Archer's *Better than Normal: What Makes You Different Can Make You Exceptional* takes on and reframes what we stereotypically view as negatives or deficits. He posits that anxiety can be akin to that rush of skills that come instantaneously when you think you're about to have a car accident. "The sudden surge of energy allows you to heighten your reaction time and propels you to take rapid, lifesaving actions," Archer writes. "In similar ways, anxiety often represents an early warning sign that something is amiss in your life and needs to be addressed. In healthy proportions, anxiety keeps us alert and on our toes when we sense threats to ourselves, and it can motivate us to behave in positive, often highly constructive ways."[11]

Archer notes vigilance, intuition, preparedness, and observation as skills of the anxious person. "Lack of anxiety may give you a false sense of security…you might miss important opportunities" and it makes you a target "for unscrupulous wheelers and dealers. They don't bother looking at the hidden underbelly of things." Anxious people have an extra layer of protection, a built-in alarm signal, that helps them navigate potentially harmful situations. Today's increasingly complicated challenges demand ever-nuanced awareness and perception—something anxiety facilitates. I can't help but agree that in today's world, this is indeed a strength.

## Anxiety as a Sixth Sense

As we touched on earlier, our anxiety is reading signals that we may not consciously be taking in. In this way, our anxiety can operate as a type of sixth sense. In a famous study out of the University of Iowa, neuroscientists demonstrated how our bodies can react to things we don't consciously realize, and our anxiety can point us to something we haven't even noticed. In the study, subjects were asked to choose cards from various decks, with a payout system for certain types of "good" cards. The players weren't aware of it, but two of the decks were stacked in favor of the players, and two of the decks were stacked against them. The scientists tracked the subjects' anxiety responses through their skin via sweat. FMRIs were later used to determine which part of the brain was activated in the choosing.

As the game went on, players' anxiety spiked when they reached for the decks rigged against them—even though they never gave a conscious explanation of why. Their anxiety was out in front of them, knowing things that they consciously did not. (Interestingly, those with amygdala damage didn't seem to distinguish between the two decks.)*

This is more powerful evidence illustrating how much we take in below our conscious awareness. "Before they had conceptualized the reason but after their skin response showed anxiety about those decks, something in the brain was acting as a sort of intuition generator."[12] Players were never able to explain why they avoided the bad decks, even though they kept doing it. Like the earlier example about us slamming on the brakes before we are even consciously aware the pedestrian in the street, their bodies just knew.

Other scientists have documented similar perceptual speed and accuracy that defies consciousness of process, most famously Malcolm Gladwell in *Blink*, who looked at, among other things, the way art experts could spot forgeries before they even had a chance to think about it.[13] Something about them just felt off—a type

---

* Of course, the amygdala does more than spot card patterns; it lays the foundation for what we do and do not fear. In 2010, a fascinating patient, known as S.M., made science headlines when it was reported that her missing amygdala—from a genetic disease—took away her capacity for fear, to the point that it endangered her life.

of anxiety about the work was speaking to them—and this told them they were fakes. If science is showing us that conflicts, and our emotional reactions to them, can be outside of our immediate awareness, then how are we to understand what is happening? How can we put our anxiety into action if we can't be outright conscious of it *in the moment*?

Nobel Prize winner Daniel Kahneman conceived of two systems of thought that compete for control of our behavior: System 1, which is fast, emotional, and instinctive, and System 2, which is slower, rational, and deliberative. As he asserts in his bestselling book, *Thinking Fast and Slow,* complex judgments most often rely on fast emotional reactions, detailing just how easy it is for us to swerve away from rationality.[14]

Some argue that the conflicts that cause us anxiety could be occurring so fast that they are outside of our perceptual capabilities, and that we make complicated decisions and judgments without being fully aware. Anxiety often occurs so quickly that we seem to react without even being aware of the cause. Becoming aware of our anxiety, and consciously naming it, is how we activate our thinking and take control over what we do with it. And getting good at noticing the signal takes practice.

## The Masquerade

Anxiety is not always loud and clear in identifying itself. Often it is hidden in other emotions like anger, frustration, sadness, or even boredom and excitement. In my work with patients, I have found that when we break down a person's emotional struggles into its various component emotions, we often find anxiety. It seems to be the common denominator among most of the emotions that carry unease and discomfort signaling a needed change. For one thing, helping people detangle their fears of anxiety from the anxiety itself is always helpful. Sometimes, simply recognizing that anxiety isn't itself harmful is enough to dial it down to where it can be useful.

When anxiety is buried in different feelings, it can act as an escalator of those other emotions. I sometimes refer to anxiety as a "volume control" of other painful emotions; the higher the volume, the higher the anxiety. "Like a volume knob on some emotional radio," biologist John Medina writes in *Brain Rules*, "the more the loss of control, the more severe the stress is perceived to be."[15] Intense emotions like anger, frustration, boredom, and loneliness almost always have an element of anxiety to them. Consider the agitation of waiting aboard a delayed flight, an evening at home with seemingly nothing to do, or a lecture that simply doesn't grab your attention. Your discomfort in these situations is often the extent to which you would rather be somewhere else, doing something else, avoiding the frustration of the moment, and how much you are working to ignore it. In other words, you are fighting your experience.

Anxiety kicks in and escalates your discomfort when you allow yourself to think that you can't tolerate what's happening, and the more you focus on how intolerable the situation is, the more agitated and upset you become. As with virtually every uncomfortable feeling, anxiety ratchets up your discomfort.

Look for places where you experience intense feelings and you will often uncover anxiety. Emotions are accelerated by anxiety's signal that you can't, or don't want to, handle them. So, sadness becomes anger when the source of your sadness feels intolerable. Anxiety's message of "danger ahead, beware" gets misunderstood as "I just can't handle that!"

Here are a few more questions to consider as you look for anxiety in your escalated feelings:

- What makes me mad or brings tightness to my chest?
- What brings me to tears? Is it part of any situation I have just described?
- What feelings are so intense that it feels like I can't handle them?

Anger is often the result of pain fueled by the fear that if it continues you won't be able to handle it. In anger, the sadness piece is about disappointment, and the anxiety piece is about doubting our ability to handle what is to come. This comes up a lot when people feel overwhelmed by their feelings and just don't think they can manage a given situation. Exasperation with a spouse, for example, can happen when worry and concern meet *I can't handle this much longer*. It's as if we send the message that we're upset, along with the warning to *please, make it stop*. In those moments, we can't always access—or really want to—what we can do to change things.

This also comes up with those struggling with irritability, temper issues, and intense emotional pain. They are often masking a broader anxiety problem. Solutions for irrational and scary thoughts involve transforming them into rational but tolerable ones. For example, *I can't handle it* becomes *I do not want to handle it, but I can and I will.* Translating any irrational fears into rational ones allows you to understand more clearly what concerns still face you and determine where to focus the energy of your anxiety.

These strategies are a key part of finding the productive middle ground of anxiety, especially when it feels too unwieldy to be either useful information or energy. Once anxieties are distilled and sorted, and irrational fears are translated, what's left starts to make sense. Rational anxiety rallies focus and inspires motivation to cope and forge solutions, even if we don't always want to.

## — Highlighting Our Feelings

Paul Zak, who studies trust and prosocial behavior, has dubbed oxytocin, a key hormone in regulating compassion, the "moral molecule." His research has also shown people who cry during movies are more socially aware and empathic than those who hold their emotions inside.[16] The social fluency of tears can come in handy when it comes to understanding intense emotions, both in ourselves and in others.

In my practice, I liken tears to highlighter pens. Whenever a person is moved to tears telling a story or talking about an issue, it is a signal of its importance and meaning. Tears are a window into our deepest personal values; they can help us better understand our emotions. A powerful signal of deeply felt emotions, they can help us uncover the thoughts and feelings that most impact us. Whenever your feelings are jumbled and confused, crying can help illuminate important signals as well as produce oxytocin that orients us to seek and give help.

Another strategy for detangling emotions and getting at core fears is scanning for what emotion you are *afraid* of feeling. Ask yourself, *What experience couldn't I handle?* and chances are you will come up with a few areas in your life about which you feel conflict and anxiety. This is staring directly into the beast's eyes and seeing that it's not a beast at all.

Tuning into feelings of stress or discomfort is another way to access anxiety's signal. Dr. Simon Ravicz uses the term *prostress* to distinguish between the stress that wears us down and the kind we view as a challenge, excitement, or engagement.[17] (Previously, Hans Selye coined the term *eustress* for the same idea.[18]) This is the chatter anxiety that keeps us on track: the motivation of a deadline, the needling reminder of something important, the surge of awareness that rescues something in our memory. Stress can clue us into our priorities and keep us on track

Discomfort can also signal subtle whispering anxiety. In his book *Hit Makers*, which attempts to decode the science of popularity, Derek Thompson discusses the concept of *disfluency*, which is a marketing term for when someone feels difficulty or discomfort in processing information. Thompson describes disfluency as "a subtle alarm, piercing the calm of automatic processing, summoning a higher level of attention."[19] Whispering anxiety creates a sense of disfluency where we benefit from paying closer attention.

When we dig into our anxiety's source, we take control, and can transform its energy into something useful, finally freeing us from the negative feeling of its grip.

## Anxiety as Compassion

My grandmother used to say, "I worry because I care," without even realizing how literal she was being. Caring is part of a complicated system of being involved, noticing, and protecting what matters most. Anxiety can operate as a barometer of how engaged we are in the various areas of our lives, letting us know what we care about and what needs our attention and focus. This anxiety stays with us, keeping us aware of how close or far we are to what we need. And just as high-performing athletes focus on what needs attention in their games, so must we zero in on the issues that need addressing.

Our anxiety holds tremendous tangible information if we can tune into it. Without it, we'd grow complacent and disengaged. With it, we are tuned in and energized. Like a baby's cry, anxiety drives us to find or create a solution that will quiet it.

Babies' cries signal a hardwired response to stop what we are doing, determine the need, and attend to the baby until the cry stops. This could mean changing a diaper, feeding, or simply soothing with a simple touch. Determining the signal requires a quick read of what's going on, including how wet she might be, how long it's been since she last ate, and a best guess at what is most needed to soothe her cries. The goal is not silencing the child permanently (!) or to move her out of earshot: you simply want to understand what the child needs in that moment, and do it. We don't condemn the noise and try to ignore it—we figure it out, and *address* it. And amazingly, all it takes is the cry to tell us we must act.

## The Power of Dreams

Freud called dreams "the royal road to the unconscious," and it's where our anxiety can manifest itself in symbolic realities. I was recently interviewed by a reporter about one of our most common dreams, which follows us deep into adulthood: not having studied for a test. I speculate that since test taking and test preparation are some of our earliest experiences with using anxiety, the imagery tends to hold, even as the context of our anxiety moves. Though the science of dream interpretation is speculative at best, the emotions triggered inside our dreams can offer important clues to our deepest desires, needs, and conflicts.

This common dream of showing up to a test you're not prepared for—which may manifest years or even decades after you were last in school may not be as odd as we may think. During the time where our school experiences become stressful—adolescence—our brain is developing rapidly and laying down classic pathways. The test dream gets lodged at a ripe time and can stay there as a primal anxious experience we recall when other similar experiences present themselves.

In *The Storytelling Animal,* Jonathan Gottschall discusses the universality of dream language. He highlights studies of office workers that found "the workaday activities that dominated their waking hours almost never featured in their dreams. Instead, they dreamed trouble. Trouble is the fat red thread that ties together the fantasies of pretend play, fiction, and dreams, and trouble provides a possible clue to a function that they all share: giving us practice in dealing with the big dilemmas of human life…"[20]

We will spend about six total years of our lives dreaming.[21] Though everyone dreams as part of normal REM sleep cycles that occur multiple times per night, many people seldom or never remember their dreams. If you are a vivid dreamer, or simply someone who remembers your dreams, consider yourself lucky. You have another tool at your disposal to use in harnessing anxiety's messages. Think of your dreams as emotional processing snapshots. We often dream a heightened version of our concerns and fears, hopes and desires. If we can access the feeling that prompted the dream, we are halfway there in understanding what it is signaling.

## Sarah

Dreams often demonstrate in Technicolor the worries that lurk outside our awareness. I will never forget Sarah's recurrent dream that involved her harried arrival to the airport terminal, the long security line, the run to her gate, only to be followed by long stretches of waiting in the terminal to board a plane. Time would go by, planes would come and go, and still, Sarah would be waiting. For some reason, she simply couldn't bring herself to board the planes that were available to her, despite her rushing to get there. She would instead sit and watch as plane after plane took off without her. Rushing to wait.

In both her personal and professional life, Sarah ultimately struggled to take decisive action. She felt and used a lot of anxiety in her life around keeping balls moving and getting things done, but when it came to the most important things in her life, like being in a satisfying relationship or a better job, she felt as if she was being kept waiting, hoping for things to change and being disappointed that they never did.

Sarah could not bring herself to leave her relationship or her job, even though she could identify both as necessary steps toward happiness. She felt stuck and miserable with anxiety as she watched opportunity after opportunity go by in her life, much like the planes in her dream. Sarah came to understand these patterns of behavior that were exacerbating her anxiety, and she identified different more reasonable solutions.

When at last she mustered the courage to leave her relationship, Sarah felt relieved and free, accepting that her anxiety was trying to guide her. Over time, as she addressed her conflicts, her experience of anxiety diminished (as did her recurrent dreams). About six months later, as we came to the end of her therapy, she remarked that she supposed she no longer needed her waiting dreams since she had learned how to stop waiting in her life.

Once we recognize that anxiety is in fact a signal and not noise,

we are on the path to making use of it. The next step is to understand that the anxiety itself is not just an indication of a problem,
but its fuel is part of the solution.

## Tracking Your Dreams

When you can remember a dream, as soon as you can
after waking, be ready to take notes. As we move from
a sleep state into a waking state, the memories of our
dreams often fade quickly. It can be useful before you
do anything else—get out of bed, go to the bathroom,
drink water, even roll over—to take notes on the answers
to these questions:

How did I feel immediately after I woke up?

What happened in the dream that provoked these
feelings?

Who were the main characters in the dream—and how
did they reflect people in my life or parts of myself? How
do I feel about them?

What conflicts played out? And how did they parallel
other conflicts in my life both with others and within
myself?

## CHAPTER ELEVEN

# Anxiety as Fuel

*"Be patient toward all that is unsolved in your heart and try to love the questions themselves, like locked rooms and like books that are now written in a very foreign tongue. Do not now seek the answers, which cannot be given you because you would not be able to live them. And the point is, to live everything. Live the questions now. Perhaps you will then gradually, without noticing it, live along some distant day into the answer."*

—**Rainer Maria Rilke**[1]

## Deanna: Chatter Revisited

Let's look again at Deanna, a client of mine who was experiencing chatter anxiety. Deanna had gotten pretty good at using her anxiety, which kept her on the ball and detail-oriented at work.

But as her workload increased and she was put in charge of taking care of her elderly father, the chatter of the anxiety was starting to worry her. Quite simply, it wasn't working for her as well as it once had, and she suspected she was missing something.

The way Deanna had previously coped with work stress was by allowing herself more time in her personal hours to complete work things that she wanted to get done: researching trends, preparing reports, and completing nonurgent items that kept her ahead of the game. She often let her chatter anxiety propel her forward, and when she felt she had gotten far enough "ahead," the feeling would subside.

However, between her father's declining health and a recent promotion at work, she was losing the ability to engage in this coping strategy. She no longer had the free time she once used as a resource.

Not surprisingly, her anxiety didn't really let up either. It was unnerving to feel so many new demands; she was constantly stretched for time without being able to catch up, which produced her consistent anxiety. She couldn't make more time, so she had to be more efficient with the time she had. And this is where we worked to steer her anxiety.

Deanna needed to carve out different spaces in her schedule for catching up at work and look for other caregivers who could visit her dad on the days she really needed to stay at the office or rest. Her weekend schedule became a particular focus, and she knew she had to be more deliberate with how she scheduled her time.

Instead of spending most of both days with her father and

never having a chance to relax or catch up at work, she arranged to see her father on Friday evenings and Sunday afternoons and for an aide to come take her father to physical therapy on Saturdays. She learned to structure time for herself on the weekend to catch up on chores, spend time with her husband, and relax. She also found a few hour-long windows during the week to address other administrative tasks that were weighing on her. Deanna realized the tasks she regularly put off—and worried most about—were the ones she should address first thing in her day, when her energy was at its peak. Aligning her tasks to her energy levels made her more efficient and ultimately calmed her chatter anxiety back to a usable level.

Deanna hadn't appreciated just how adaptive her anxiety had been. She needed it to help juggle her many priorities, and it had been there for her all along. In learning to identify and claim her anxiety as a tool, she felt better about the important role continued to serve in her life even as her responsibilities evolved. Once she understood and could steer it, the chatter anxiety became what it had wanted to be all along—fuel and motivation. Last chapter, we explored how anxiety is a signal. Now let's look at how it is energy.

## The Nudge

Despite its reputation as something holding us back, anxiety—especially the chatter type Deanna experienced—operates as a type of fuel, something best understood as motivation. David Barlow, founder and director of the Center for Anxiety and

Related Disorders, calls anxiety "an ambassador of responsibility, nudging you to taking care of the things that you need to take care of."[2] Think about it for a second: What would life be like, and how would we get by, without that motivation?

During his presidential address to the American Psychological Association in 1906, William James was asked why some people can utilize their resources to their fullest capacity while others cannot. He responded by saying that two questions needed to be answered in this regard:

1. What were the limits of human energy?
2. How could this energy be stimulated and released so it could be put to optimal use?[3]

As with many other things, James was far ahead of his time. He was already thinking in terms of *optimal* use. How we think about anxiety, and what we choose to do with it, drives the difference between its helpful and harmful effects.

Anxiety's motivating characteristics are starting to be better understood. "While fear of failure can be a paralyzing force, sometimes it can provide the push we need," says scientist Amanda Phinbodhipakkiya, who argues against the idea of a backup plan or plan B when facing a scary situation. When we take away that safety net, the stakes are raised. This provides us with that jolt of motivation we sometimes need to push ahead. Think about a child who is terrified when the training wheels come off only to learn that she can balance just fine—the pedaling will keep her from falling.

Phinbodhipakkiya references a study[4] that determines "the more negative emotions you anticipate feeling if you fail to reach your goal, the more driven you might be to achieve it."[5] Essentially, she recommends we get comfortable working without a net. Having no plan B activates your anxious self—and utilizes that motivated energy for good. It's lifting the free weight without a spotter nearby or walking a high rope with nothing to fall onto but the hard ground. It hyper-focuses your mind and body, motivating us to find and execute solutions and perform optimally.

## Motor for Change

When it comes to change, anxiety can also help us along. Would any of us actually do something new, challenging, and possibly life-changing if we didn't have to? Anxiety is our body readying for action and nudging us along. With every firing, anxiety is an invitation—perhaps even a mandate—to do something different, something new, something bold. "Recognize that the panic and stress you feel as you try to create isn't a sign that everything is falling apart," writes Charles Duhigg in *Smarter, Faster, Better*. "Rather it's the condition that helps make us flexible enough to seize something new...anxiety is what often pushes us to see old ideas in new ways."[6]

When we embark on a new beginning—a project, a writing assignment, or even just returning to the gym—we have no momentum at the beginning. There is no automaticity for our minds to lock into, no predug riverbed through which the water can flow. This is part of what makes it so hard to upend old habits and create new ones. The starting is perhaps the hardest part and energy is never more needed than at the beginning. This is what anxiety provides. *Energy to engage;* it's offering that needed first push to create some needed momentum. After all, what could be more energizing than your threat response firing?

We learned in the last chapter that anxiety is the signal. Now let's look at the biological and chemical ways that anxiety is *energy* we can use to plow through the walls of our old habits and into a new self.

## The Push/Pull of Dopamine

Dopamine is a powerful neurotransmitter involved in desire and motivating behavior. It continually drives us toward rewards. If we didn't want anything, we wouldn't do anything to get it.

We often think of anxiety as getting in the way of our progress, so this requires a shift in our thinking. Anxiety is seldom associated with motivation or reward, but there are many physiological connections that science is uncovering between them. It turns out the neurochemical cascade of anxiety involves the activation of brain circuit involved in motivation and effort. While this circuit that regulates the production of the neurochemical dopamine has been associated with addictive behavior (short-term reward but long-term problems), it is now understood to regulate more wide-ranging motivation.[7]

According to Mercè Correa, coauthor of a scientific review of the dopamine center in the brain:

> *It was believed that dopamine regulated pleasure and reward and that we release it when we obtain something that satisfies us, but in fact the latest scientific evidence shows that this neurotransmitter acts before that, it actually encourages us to act.*[8]

Anxiety not only harnesses our attention and focus, but it activates our motivation. We *want to act*, we *want to do something*. This is our brain circuitry priming us for action. As anxiety summons our attention, it is also activating dopamine to *keep* us motivated to act. The reward is solving the problem to remove the stressor, and dopamine helps us keep our efforts focused. This is how our stress becomes fuel.

Animal studies further suggest that we might need dopamine to keep us motivated for high-effort tasks and strenuous decision-making.[9] A recent review of dopamine's association with the stress response proposes that dopamine could play an important role in coping with stress by activating responses motivated to reduce or avoid the stressor.* Controlled by the medial prefrontal cortex (the area of our brains in charge of determining stress), dopamine "supports the expression of active coping strategies."[10]

Dopamine is associated with both pleasure and pain, specifically in motivating behavior to optimize internal balance and has been shown to increase under stress and perceived threat.[11] "Many

---

* This refers to the Mesoaccumbens circuit between the midbrain structure (meso) ventral tegmental area (VTA) and NAc, which is dopaminergic, meaning it uses dopamine as a neurotransmitter.

of the same mechanisms that cause you to shrink in horror from a predator are also used when you are having sex," writes John Medina in *Brain Rules*, "or even while you are consuming your Thanksgiving dinner. To your body, saber-toothed tigers and orgasms and turkey gravy look remarkably similar. An aroused physiological state is characteristic of both stress and pleasure."[12]

Humans are goal driven, and our anxiety and dopamine systems work together to keep us motivated to protect what we care about. When faced with obstacles, dopamine kicks in to keep us focused and ready for action, leaving our thinking and planning centers to direct the show. Embracing what we want and are passionate about, and tolerating discomfort as we stretch, is how we grow and cultivate capacity.[13]

Author of *The End of Stress* Bruce McEwen also discusses the connection between anxiety and change in noting how plasticity is primed following moderate stress.[14] Anxiety invites a readiness to engage something new. We are jolted out of habits and there is a breaking of that cement—it again becomes the wet clay we can use to mold something new.

## Marlene

Marlene grew up as something of an intellectual prodigy, excelling at an early age and skipping multiple grades. As a driven woman in her late twenties, she was a go-getter and a doer. However, when she came to see me, she had places in her life where her anxiousness could take over—especially at work.

Marlene worked crazy hours as a political fund-raiser, where she had to organize quarterly fund-raising campaigns with enough moving parts and details to keep anyone up at night. During these events, her self-care just fell off the table. She'd get up early in the morning and not leave the office until eleven o'clock at night. She lost control over what she ate, with no time to exercise and barely time to think.

Her challenge was to recognize that she was in this place where things weren't going to get better for weeks, but she had to keep pushing through. It's tough when we're too tired to let anxiety fuel us without getting negative in our thinking: *Why am I doing this? What's wrong with me? This job is my life, but is it really what I want to do? I can't focus, and I can't think straight. I screwed that thing up and now this person is angry with me.* And on and on and on. All those little and not-so-little concerns that flash up in the fatigued brain. Fatigue is fertile soil for negativity.

Teetering on the precipice of burnout, Marlene worked to make sure she stayed strong and focused. She recognized that this was a difficult and uncomfortable time, but it was going to be over soon, and she just needed to propel herself to the finish line.

The fact was, her anxiety was getting the job done. She was fortunate to work in a setting where the superiors recognized the pressure everyone was under and offered positive feedback as a constant source of support.

Internally, Marlene had the struggle of fighting the fatigue and the niggling worries that came up, and the fact that she couldn't do anything about them. She couldn't start dating, an exercise routine, a diet—she had to stay focused on what she had to do until it was over. It was the mental discipline, always fueled by an anxiety, that helped her stay on track.

## Unleashing Strength

As discussed in chapter 9, in an effort to conserve energy and attention, we are pulled toward the familiar or routine. Automaticity, which the brain favors, frees up resources to do more of what it most likes to do: tune out.[15] The brain has designed itself to favor efficiency, so that maximal time can be spent in this default mode.

Known as the default mode network, tuning out is actually one of our favorite neural pastimes.[16] Scientists believe it may be one of our most valuable survival tools, and is adaptive to engage whenever possible. Associated with social cognition, self-awareness, and goal setting, tuning out actually helps us better attune to an ever-changing social and technological landscape.[17]

Accommodating to something new requires attention and energy, finite and valuable resources. Our cognitive attitude when it comes to taking resources away from what we want to do seems to be: *It better be important.* Much of the research on changing behavior in the last few decades has focused on the importance of thinking—how you are thinking and what you are thinking. Indeed, our thoughts are a huge part of how we interpret information, and they also drive much of our behavior. How we think about things has even been shown to change how we feel about things, as we discussed in the chapter on perception. But thoughts aren't the whole picture when it comes to controlling what we do. Automaticity and motivation are very much part of this complex equation.

"Motivation is underappreciated in psychology generally," writes Roy Baumeister and Kathleen D. Vohs, two prominent researchers in the field of self-regulation, "no doubt partly because the cognitive revolution of recent decades has induced the majority of researchers to think in cognitive rather than motivational terms."[18] The fact is, sometimes we do things because we *want* to, or simply *feel* like it, and not necessarily because we've put a lot of thought into it. Consider the almost nonconscious action of opening the refrigerator when we're hungry, or rolling out of bed into our gym clothes by force of habit. We don't have to think about everything. Sometimes, our automatic habits just kick in.

Essentially, our brain wants to do as little work as possible so it can switch into automatic whenever it can.[19] However, we can't rely on an automatic reaction to process new stimuli; we have to pay attention and respond, spending costly resources. This is another way anxiety becomes helpful: the stress of a new situation can rally the energy we need to focus.

Consider a driver zoning out on a rural highway with flat scenery, attuned to the relaxing voice of an audiobook on her car stereo. With little warning, a rainstorm deluge starts hammering down from the sky. Visibility is minimal, and the sheer distance between exits lets her know that a skid out would be a logistical nightmare and a legitimate safety issue. The windshield wipers are at full speed but of little use. The anxiety of the situation is a palpable force, and her heart beats like a steady drum. But rather than distracting her, the anxiety unleashes laser focus and attention to the road. The driver's sharpened mind helps her identify the obscured lane markers and the tail lights of other nearby vehicles to stay in her lane at a safe distance. She hasn't even noticed the audiobook still playing, as the needling sound of the rain and the whoosh of her wipers have her locked on the task at hand.

We naturally pay attention to what's new. Novel stimuli disrupt our automatic routines, create uncertainty and stress, and deliver the focus and attention we need to address the task at hand.

As Tara Bennett Goleman writes in *Emotional Alchemy*, "Our attention, which determines what we notice, is limited. The mind continuously selects some aspects of the world around us to bring within the narrow beam of our attention."[20] Focus requires energy, and the anxiety implicit in a new situation can deliver results. The stress of something new can create the energy we need to exert focus on it. Perhaps it can also provide the boost we need to try something new.

As we focus and respond to the novel stressor, we use our anxiety to fuel adaptation, creating new neural connections that are strengthened with repetition—this is the foundation of the brain's plasticity. Every time we practice new skills and thought processes, we exercise our brain and grow new dendrites, new tributaries leading to new, healthier riverbeds.

# Shaun

Shaun, a driven man in his early thirties, had a demanding workload and a developing relationship. Then, like with a lot of my clients, the precarious balance that was holding in place began to teeter. Suddenly, he found himself besieged by a compounding crisis.

Shaun got word that his brother, who lived in rural Indiana with his mother, was gravely ill. He had suffered a heart attack, and he needed exploratory bypass surgery. Shaun was agitated that he couldn't be there to help his brother and his aging mother whose health was also in decline. While the surgery was successful, Shaun grew uncomfortable with the ongoing cardiac treatment options available to him in their area, and he started to make arrangements to bring both of them to the Washington area where he lived.

Shaun assembled a medical team for his brother and, in the process of learning about his brother's undiagnosed heart defect, decided to have his own heart tested as well. He learned he had a mild heart condition that required further work. On top of all the work and worry related to his brother and mother, Shaun also had to change his diet and manage his own health anxiety.

In supporting his brother's tenuous recovery and his mother's health, he felt unbalanced. Like in the movie *Speed,* he told me he felt like he was thrust behind the wheel of a speeding bus without any training on how to drive it or any idea of where he was going. All he knew was that he had to keep moving to avert disaster.

"But the bus is going where it needs to go," I told him, "even if it feels too fast." The anxiety was already translating itself into fuel;

the only challenge was where to keep steering it. This metaphor became a powerful way for him to reframe his anxiety. He took control of what he could and used his anxiety to guide him toward solutions. The visualization allowed him to trust in his decisions regarding his family—making sure to check in on his brother, meet with doctors when he could, and make room for his own self-care. The bus was moving fast and he was doing his part to keep it progressing on the road. He stopped feeling scared of his anxiety and continued to use it as a tool to help achieve his goal: getting his family the best care possible.

He dug deep, letting anxiety fire and fuel him, but making sure to rest and be gentle with himself. His brother's health continued to improve, and his recovery allowed him to rebuild his professional life and work toward making a home locally. Shaun learned relatively quickly how to use his anxiety, and the bulk of our work focused on cultivating balance and being gentle with himself. His anxiety allowed him to unleash more inner strength than he even knew he had.

## The Strength of Butterflies

As we learned in chapter 9, activation of the threat response triggers a complicated cascade of neurochemical responses in the brain and body. The brain releases chemicals—including adrenaline and cortisol—which facilitate immediate delivery of physiological reinforcements to key areas, like our muscles and respiration. These chemicals facilitate coping, bolster our immune system, provide energy for action, and even compel interpersonal connection.

Digestion becomes secondary to physical readiness, and as blood leaves the stomach for the extremities, "the muscles surrounding the stomach and intestine slow down their mixing of their partially digested contents," as one scientist explains. "The blood vessels specifically in this region constrict, reducing blood flow through the gut."[21] This is what we commonly call "butter-flies" in our stomach. Adrenaline promotes physical readiness for the body by giving us a surge of energy. Those butterflies are there for a reason. Research suggests that this kind of "challenge" stress actually fuels our best performance and peak learning.[22]

We are designed to protect ourselves. More accurately, we are designed so that the resources to protect ourselves are available to us. In effect, anxiety fuels the energy we need to act and gives us the push we need to execute solutions. Once the anxiety response is activated and its energy is engaged into action, anxiety's power starts to diminish. No longer needed for survival, it subsides.[23] This is how anxiety works—priming us to perform and receding when no longer needed.

## Misdirection

When anxiety is misdirected or directed back on itself, the opposite can happen; anxiety is preserved and even escalated. Dopamine motivates our behavior toward reward, so we are sometimes tempted to choose the wrong path. When the stress response kicks in, we are vulnerable to short-term choices that deliver quick rewards at long-term costs.[24] For example, a stressful meeting with your boss can tempt you to indulge in the office candy supply, a snarky rant to a coworker, or a stiff cocktail. Likewise, a looming stressful computer project can tempt procrastination in even the most disciplined, thanks to the pull of our many digital distractions that lurk in our digital devices.

Choosing the "hard right," over the "easy wrong," takes courage and determination. Many soothing behaviors don't start out being unhealthy or even addictive; they simply calm us down in the short term. They are temporary strategies of avoiding what is troubling us—and they do the job for a short while. But as the root of anxiety remains unsolved, anxiety festers, and we find ourselves clinging to addictive behaviors with increasing urgency. As our tolerance grows, we need to up the "dose" of our addictive habits, and we drift further and further away from the solutions. Sometimes, we get so far out that when we look up, we can no longer even see the shore.

A common example of this kind of numbing behavior is compulsive overeating. Obesity is at an all-time high, and more and more of us eat for comfort rather than sustenance. For many of us, food can be a temporary salve for the anxiety that we feel every day. Not just the delicious tastes, but the sugar itself can produce feelings of pleasure and calm, along with a numbness that ensues as our bellies fill to the point of stretching. Many of us know this experience from overindulging at a delicious meal or restaurant. But for a compulsive overeater, the sensation of being full is one that is sought also for its numbing properties, which ease emotional discomfort that is often felt in one's belly. I have many clients I've worked with over the years who have struggled with this behavior. Overeating can be an effective way to temporarily numb feeling, but its boomerang costs to one's health, confidence, and self-esteem continue to climb.

These behaviors might deliver temporary relief, but they aren't solutions for the problem fueling the anxiety. Angst and frustration add to the underlying problems, driving up anxiety to higher and higher levels. Addictive behaviors almost always exist alongside anxiety, and they ultimately force us to pay attention, and reconsider our choices.

No matter how misdirected our choices might be under stress, we always have the opportunity to redirect our behavior. Anxiety will make sure of this. Like a trusted (but perhaps annoying) friend, anxiety will let us know when we don't direct it effectively, hassling us until we do.

## Nia

Misdirected anxiety is not just limited to our mental and physical choices. Our fears can prompt us to make easier, but less healthy, choices in many areas of life, including our relationships. Nia struggled with this, and she came to see me because she was consumed by the fear of being alone. Ashamed of being single, she wanted to lose those feelings of inadequacy, but she also wanted someone who made her feel loved and comfortable with herself. She was also anxious about being with the wrong person and often noticed her various relationships could make her feel worse about herself. These conflicting anxieties confused her. When she agreed to date men who were interested in her, she almost always felt temporary relief of her anxiety.

But over time, as they inevitably disappointed her, she became more anxious about lowering her standards and worried about a future spent with the wrong person. Her anxiety about her single life persisted and nudged her to continue dating in spite of her frustrations. When she opted to stay in the relationship, she reasoned she was better off with someone inadequate than no one at all.

However, her anxiety always said otherwise. As she stayed in relationships that disappointed her, her fear of being unhappy generated anxiety that made her more and more miserable. No amount of rationalizations or subsequent dates quieted her anxiety; it only worsened the longer she hung on. Her fear of being unhappy continued to generate discomfort, which nudged her toward ending things and braving her fear of being alone.

While Nia disliked being alone, the anxiety of being with the wrong person always kept her attention until she took action. This anxiety kept steering her toward healthier and healthier relationships as her confidence and decision-making continued to spiral up. This is how anxiety can keep at us, nudging us toward growth.

• •

As sensitive and elaborate of a response anxiety can be, getting clear on what anxiety actually means requires practice and decoding. Luckily, when we take action that isn't on target, anxiety lets us know. Just like the baby that continues crying until its needs are solved. With practice, and trial-and-error solutions, we learn what each cry means and what is needed to quiet it for good. One thing always remains certain: until we get its solution right, the cry won't stop, and neither will our motivation to stop it. In the next chapter, we'll address what action we can take to adaptively channel our anxiety.

## CHAPTER TWELVE

# Anxiety into Action

*"Action may not bring happiness...but there is no happiness without action."*

—**Benjamin Disraeli**[1]

## Jamie: Whisper Revisited

Let's take another look at Jamie, my client who was experiencing what I call whisper anxiety, which is low-level and often buried in other feelings. Jamie's anxiety was essentially one of avoidance. She wouldn't come into my office and say, "I can't stop worrying"; she'd come in and say, "I can't stop procrastinating." Her avoidance behavior was starting to add up, creating a life that was making her miserable.

Jamie was getting increasingly riskier with her work behavior, turning things in late or not at all. On the weekends, she was doing nothing at home, often under the influence of various pills, which kept her sedated. She'd spend Friday evening to Sunday night lying around or sleeping. Then, feeling terrible about herself, she'd roll into Mondays teetering on the edge of depression.

She knew it was unhealthy—her procrastination and blown -off weekends meant something was wrong— but even recognizing the signals didn't help her. She knew she needed to do something, or there would be consequences she didn't want to face.

With some prying, she admitted she was ready to take action—not on her substance abuse, but on her procrastination. The solution we came up with was for her to break things into small manageable pieces, which would help generate momentum. She would force herself to do one thing, decidedly, even when it didn't feel great or effective. This would begin a process where it would become easier to do the next thing, then the next.

She had to address her first step, the gateway behaviors that could set her down her habitual paths. In Jamie's work life, she decided to complete each work assignment on time, not letting one deadline pass that would get her behind the ball. If she was falling behind, she would communicate a solution with her boss, but agreed to herself she would no longer passively avoid turning in assignments without explanation or acknowledgment. She wouldn't let herself leave the office until she had gotten traction she could pick up again the next day.

On the weekends, her promise to herself was to get out of bed, shower, and make plans that would *compel* her to get out of the house. While her solutions may have been simple, they were in no way easy for her. She knew there was no other way, and the risky gateway behaviors of staying in bed in her pajamas or leaving the office before finishing her work had to be avoided at all costs. Like an addict must always swear off that first drink, she knew these were the new behaviors she had to cement. Getting them started was tough, but once they got going, she knew she could continue. I call it the *magic of momentum*. We commit to the struggle to get that boulder rolling down the hill, and gravity helps us do the rest. In the case of Jamie's anxiety, she committed to taking active steps early in the process so that it didn't require as much energy later when her unaddressed anxiety became unmanageable.

## Insight plus Energy

Chapter 10 looked at anxiety's role as a signal—of information and of conflict. Insight itself is powerful, and it delivers a needed sense of control. But insight alone cannot fundamentally change a situation or help us direct our anxiety. Chapter 11 focused on anxiety's energy as a motivating force; but of course, that alone won't get us to a comfortable place either.

When I work with patients on examining their anxiety sources, they will sometimes say to me, "OK, I get it. I really do. But what can I *do*?" They understand

> **Mindful Action**
>
> Getting the solution right requires mindful action, which is the subject of this chapter. Anxiety is a signal that delivers us information and the energy to get us to change. Put those two together and we get an equation for utilizing anxiety:
>
> Insight + Energy = Mindful Action

anxiety's message and feel anxiety's motivation, but they know they need *action* to carry them further.

Neuroscience is now confirming what clinicians have long seen in practice: feelings of anxiety are as individual as each of us, and only subside through individualized solutions. There is no one-size-fits-all approach.

## My Mother

When I was a kid I was convinced there was nothing my mother couldn't handle. Sometimes I thought it was keeping herself busy that propelled her forward. But I now understand that she simply loved the satisfaction of getting things done, and she hated the sensation of—or criticism about—leaving something undone.

My mother's high standards fueled an anxiety in me that was motivating at its best. Her proactive approach to life's challenges was an early model for me on the advantage of doing what needs to be done. Don't put it off, *just do it*, like the Nike ads told us for all those years. When faced with the choice between doing it now or doing it later, my mother has almost always chosen now.

But blindly *doing* wasn't always the answer either and sometimes valuing *now* over *how* got complicated. When I was in grad school, and she was trying to help me get settled into a new apartment, she took on some quick touch-up painting of some battered dining room chairs. However, when she got out the paint thinner to clean up the brushes without putting on gloves, she noticed her red nail polish had loosened just enough that while drying her hands on her clothes, she smeared the red nail polish all over herself and her cotton pants. It was summer, and she was wearing white, and anyone who has worked with paint understands it is nearly impossible to remove it from cotton. What started out as a get-it-done moment to avoid delays and help, ended up costing her a trip home to change, a rather expensive pair of pants, and not a small amount of frustration. We laughed about it—and still do—but it was a revealing moment of how *doing* needs to have some *thinking* steering it.

When thinking takes too much of a back seat, doing can become impulsive and risky. As my mother has aged, and life's demands have softened, she too has slowed down and can now afford more time to think. Her energy is more limited, and so she has to more carefully weigh the value of her efforts, as we all do. In watching her I am motivation for action whenever possible (unless it involves paint thinner and nail polish).

## The Reward of Action

Whether it's completing a work assignment hanging over our heads, making that nerve-wracking phone call we've been putting off, or finishing the home project that we keep meaning to get back to, there is an intrinsic pleasure in taking productive action. As my mother knows: in things big and small, few things are more satisfying than *getting it done.*

"It is when we act freely, for the sake of the action itself rather than for ulterior motives, that we learn to become more than what we were," writes *Flow* author Mihaly Csikszentmihalyi. "When we choose a goal and invest ourselves in it to the limits of concentration, whatever we do will be enjoyable. And once we have tasted this joy, we will redouble our efforts to taste it again. This is the way the self grows."[2] Action begets action, until momentum takes hold.

On a basic level, inaction doesn't *feel* good. Research shows we don't regret the things we do in the short term, but we regret the things we *didn't* do in the long term.[3] This is yet more evidence that we are wired for action.[4]

Harnessing our feelings for action stretches us, provides our anxiety the productive outlet it needs, and gives way to satisfaction and confidence. "A person who has achieved control over psychic energy and has invested it in consciously chosen goals cannot help but grow into a more complex being. By stretching skills, by reaching toward higher challenges," Csikszentmihalyi writes, "such a person becomes an increasingly extraordinary individual."

## Get Uncomfortable

When faced with challenges, difficulties, and fear, we must rely on our internal resources—something that is impossible to do without some pain and uncertainty. Most of us think of this discomfort as being inconvenient, distracting, or even a hindrance to moving ahead. But there's plenty of evidence proving that this discomfort and uncertainty are *keys* to our effectiveness, so long as we harness our anxiety for solutions. "Emotionally painful instincts are a call to action, a challenge to overcome, a pathway to self-improvement,"[5] writes Jeffrey P. Kahn in *Angst*.

As we discussed in the last chapter, anxiety is a powerful and unrelenting *energy* source, one that delivers needed resources to drive productive action. Anxiety about social threats, for example, has been shown to trigger areas of the brain associated with action.[6] Reading dissatisfaction on your boss's face can make even the most confident—or lazy—employee itch to fix the situation. Energy is so fundamental to anxiety that the Merriam Webster's dictionary definition of anxiety includes the element of action: "Fear or nervousness about what might happen; a feeling of wanting *to do* [my italics] something very much."

But this press toward action has somehow gotten lost in our collective understanding. My grandmother, for example, often used expressions like "I'm anxious to get going." Like a lot of people of her generation, she intuitively understood that her anxiety would alleviate if she did something. I fear we have lost this crucial connection between anxiety and motivation. Perhaps the stigma of *anxiety* has stopped us from embracing, harnessing, and using it this way. Still, anxiety lessens as we take action.

To use a basic example from my own work life: I have an "anxiety" Google alert set up that keeps me abreast of developments in the field through emailed news stories. It's a fantastic resource, which can itself become anxiety producing if the information simply collects. I notice that if I utilize what I've learned— with a client, in a blog post, or in this very book—I feel a sense of progress and productivity. However, if the alerts accumulate in my email folder, if they have nowhere to sit but in my head, the anxiety alerts become…well, anxiety producing.

## Switching Tracks

We can either figure out ways to manage our stress—a passive activity with limited results—or we can actively cope. Proactive coping helps moderate the amygdala response[7] and is controlled by our prefrontal cortex, the part of our brain that thinks, plans, and directs. Joseph LeDoux calls the prefrontal cortex "the switch that controls the track on which the train travels… Active coping and agency…helps the person control the accelerator, brakes, and the track switches."[8]

This is the call of adaptation: to improve our efficiency at interacting with our environment. How we think about our future, the possibilities we can visualize, and the solutions we can conceive are at the heart of who we are and a key strategy we can use to harness anxiety's power for change.[9]

## Thinking through Solutions

Following one's curiosity and investigating opens the door to control. Sometimes action steps present themselves clearly. Jamie, for example, understood that blowing off deadlines was dangerous, as was staying in bed through the weekend under the influence of prescription drugs. Her action steps involved meeting deadlines and getting out of bed—it was certainly not easy for her do, but it was easy enough for her to figure out she had to do it to see improvements.

However, sometimes action steps aren't as obvious as this, and they take more exploration and problem solving to identify. Luckily, chances are good that if you struggle with anxiety, you are also intelligent,[10] a good problem-solver,[11] and will likely make more conscientious decisions.[12] When solutions aren't immediately obvious, embrace the challenge and look to see your anxiety a bit differently. Ask yourself two questions:

1. What information is your anxiety trying to tell you?
2. How can you use your anxiety to solve that problem?

## Miranda

In my work, I actively engage my clients' rational thinking and deductive reasoning to determine the causes of their anxiety. We act as codetectives, looking for clues, themes, and situations that come together to create their unique anxiety.

Miranda was a professional in her late twenties, in a serious relationship, and working at the entry level of a law firm. She came to me with rising complaints of irritability and frustration that had recently flared up. Bored by work and in her relationship, she was frustrated that she didn't feel like her normal enthusiastic self. Getting up in the morning had gotten hard, and staying engaged at work was even harder. Even hanging out with her boyfriend had become a chore.

Concerned she might be depressed, she admitted wanting to get away from it all and check out. Yet none of her go-to salves were working anymore. Alcohol wasn't taking the edge off, and marijuana wasn't calming her the way it used to. Often quite libidinous, even sex could no longer quiet her mind. She simply couldn't snap out of it, and she was frustrated that things weren't coming easy to her as they often did. She confessed to me that she never had even thought about seeking help before and even carried self-judgment about doing it.

Miranda's racing thoughts and irritable mood were clearly giving her information, and she was eager to understand what was happening and how she could feel better. I asked her if there was anything in her situation that was frightening her, trying to assess if her anxiety was hiding amidst her other emotions.

Miranda hesitated, seeming to genuinely wonder about it. As we began to explore, she spoke—almost as if just discovering it—about how terrified she was. She feared she would not be able to cope with the hardships of a career and life, and that she wouldn't measure up to her own aspirations as well as the expectations she put on herself because of the success of her father, a high-powered attorney.

So disturbed by her fear of failure, she found herself struggling to engage. Yet she was surprised to watch what seemed like a self-fulfilling prophecy unfold before her eyes. Anxiety for Miranda took the shape of irritability, agitation, and apathy, all mixed together, and its relief did not come until she faced her core anxieties and harnessed her fear with productive action.

She was almost haunted by an undefined motivation: She had to tap into what she wanted. But what was that? What did she value most—success, happiness, or esteem? Did she want to be like her father, or did she just want her father to like her?

She also complained of being disinterested and annoyed with her boyfriend. However, what revealed itself as we dug into her feelings was that she was actually *jealous* of his drive. She wanted to be more like him, and that made her envious. Attracted by what he had, she didn't know how to get it. Her boredom at work and her irritation with her boyfriend were emanating from the same source: her desire to do something fulfilling and the feeling that she wasn't.

As we got clearer on the source of her anxiety, potential action steps became clearer. We talked about her entering more intellectually stimulating fields and potentially going back to school. While she was uncertain at first, she realized she wanted to be good at something, an expert like her dad, so she began thinking more about school and the options it could open for her. By recognizing that her work and relationship issues were part of the same issue, we were able to come up with a solution that addressed both.

## Make a Plan

Research has shown that the dissipation of anxiety to a manageable level comes not just with the completion of the act, but even just the *starting* of it. The very decision to take the action can be helpful. An example of this would be just calling and making an appointment with a professional and then putting that task on your calendar. If the anxiety is brewing and you direct it toward an outlet—making that call, setting up that meeting, or writing a draft of that email—you will feel better. A study of anxious college students found that when they actively addressed their negative thoughts and actively picked apart their meaning, their anxiety distress went down.[13] Naming and sorting our emotions is taking control and it itself doing something.

Considering possible solutions and planning action is also taking action. It begins the channeling of anxiety's energy. As Christine Carter explains in *The Sweet Spot: How to Accomplish More by Doing Less*:

> Research shows that simply making a plan to deal with an unfinished task makes a huge difference in our ability to focus on other things without being constantly reminded by our unconscious mind about what else we need to do. It's not so much about deciding what to do—by making a list or something—as it is about deciding when to do it... As it turns out, our unconscious isn't nagging us to do the task at hand, but rather to make a plan for when we will get it done.[14]

That nagging reminder buzzing in your ear, a type of daily whisper anxiety, is most likely anxiety that you will forget to do something important. Planning for *when and how* we will do it can quiet the whisper. The anxiety might not be about doing the task so much as it's about *forgetting to do it*. Scheduling a time or conceiving a plan to organize and send our tax information to our accountant is a more reasonable solution to our anxiety than to stop what we're doing there and then and launch into such an intensive project only because it popped into our heads.

Robert Epstein, who studied under founder of behaviorism B. F. Skinner, conducted a wide-ranging survey to determine which stress-prevention techniques were the most effective. The winner? Planning. Epstein points to the effectiveness of "fighting stress before it even starts, planning things rather than letting them happen."[15] I see this over and over in my sessions with clients: anxiety diminishes just through the planning itself. Just the thought of action allows the reality of our own control to sink in. This brings a much-needed dose of confidence.

## Fatigue and the Power of the Checklist

Of course, it can be hard to maintain motivation when we are tired, and it can be even harder to be positive about it. Acute anxiety— like a sudden threat—can override fatigue, as anyone knows who has been driving on a long, lulling stretch of road only to get a surge of adrenaline when a car swerves into your lane.

Anxiety can provide just the boost we need at times when fatigue is looming. Between the surge of stress-related blood sugar and the neural dosing of dopamine's motivation, anxiety can deliver a potent cocktail of energy when we need it most. A backup battery of sorts.

Rest and rejuvenation are the best suppliers of energy, but anxiety works as a temporary stand in, especially if we recognize its usefulness and don't deplete its energy by fighting it. Using anxiety effectively when we are tired can be tricky, especially since it can be hard to regulate our thoughts and assumptions when we're physically depleted. Likewise, mental fatigue has been shown to impair our capacities to regulate and control our emotions.[16]

When we are tired—and potentially fueled by anxiety's motor—is when we need to be the most careful and gentle with ourselves. The temptation to be negative is often strongest under anxiety's influence.[17] This is when a cheat sheet of sorts can be useful. When we are too tired to avoid our own mental traps, it can help to have something to stand in for our fatigued decision-making and lapsed self-control. Digital reminders of cognitive reframing, keeping schedules that are inflexible, committing to "nonnegotiables" of self-care, even encouraging regular "moments to notice progress" can all help us use anxiety productively, even if we are too tired to fully appreciate its usefulness.

Ideally, healthy routines are so ingrained as habits that we don't think about them. We know and stick to our exercise routines, we routinize our grocery shopping to include healthy foods, and we establish and stick to a bedtime routine that allows for adequate rest. But when habits aren't quite established, and we need to rely on consistent effort, checklists can also be helpful, especially when tasks are straightforward and simple. James Murphy, a business consultant and former fighter pilot, preaches the power of the checklist. He calls it a "memory jogger... It's designed to get pilots pointed in the right direction very quickly by taking an action that pulls them through task saturation."[18] Now, it's not foolproof; putting a difficult or emotionally loaded task on a checklist for example will not necessarily ensure you will do it. But building a habit of manageable tasks will set you up to maximize automaticity.[19]

It comes down to knowing yourself—and your future self— and planning accordingly. Knowing where you will stumble is the key to building strategies that help keep you on task when you need it. For example, I know that on particularly busy weeks, I need reminders in my calendar for tasks I would otherwise remember to do, like getting to the grocery store, sorting mail, or reviewing social media. Inserting normal tasks in my calendar when I know I am likely to forget them helps me stay on track with ongoing goals of keeping my household and business running without hiccups.

Laying down a structure in advance that will keep you on point in your behavior is something called the *Ulysses Effect*, named after the character in *The Odyssey* who asks his shipmates to tie him to the mast before they pass the sirens so he would not be lured in by their seductive song.[20] There are now a variety of online programs based around this premise. One particular program requires you to send money to the website for them to hold while you try to meet your goal—whether it's losing pounds or quitting smoking. At the end of the selected time period, if your goal isn't met, that money is automatically donated to an organization you've selected in advance that you *despise*. The premise is that the extra motivation of already sending away the money and having the "punishment" put into place helps motivate you to achieve your goal.

# How Control Leads to Action

Without adaptive outlets for discharge and solutions, anxiety and negative emotions escalate and fester, further diminishing our sense of control. How much power we perceive predicts the confidence we feel, our social engagement, and how much risk we are willing to take.[21] It can make the difference between whether we attend a networking event and reconnect with colleagues or avoid it, opting for our couch and remote. But as we have learned, nothing in our experience is finite or fixed—we can always look for ways to take control. Even if taking control doesn't feel easy or natural, it's always an option.

As we learned in chapter 7, control—the lack of it and the need to regain it—is central to keeping anxiety usable. Groundbreaking psychologist Albert Bandura, whose social learning theory explains how we learn by watching others, determined that "people who believe they can exercise control over potential threats do not engage in apprehensive thinking and are not perturbed by them."[22] This is reminiscent of the innate wisdom of the serenity prayer: accepting the things we can't change and changing the things we can't accept.

The country of Israel provides a potent backdrop to study anxiety coping, where decades-long fighting rages unpredictably and uncontrollably, and stress levels are chronically high throughout the population. And yet taking action, even if small, can have a meaningful biological effect. A recent Tel Aviv study that considered compulsive behaviors determined that "ritualistic behavior in both humans and animals developed as a way to induce calm and manage stress caused by unpredictability and uncontrollability."[23]

Doing something purposeful, no matter how small, can help us take control.

We must see where we can take control—and do so. Bandura's work demonstrated the more control we feel, the better we initiate coping behavior, expend effort, and sustain it in the face of obstacles.[24] So important is our sense of control that when anticipating negative experiences, we will withstand more suffering if we can be in control.

## Thinking vs. Ruminating

When we set out to think about solutions, it's important to remember that there is a distinction between thinking something through, which is useful and healthy, and ruminating, which is not. Rumination is letting anxiety fuel negative thoughts, creating a spiral which makes us feel worse. It is a symptom of anxiety run amok. Rumination is a case where anxiety drives the thinking rather than the thinking driving the anxiety.[25]

"The dividing line between fruitless rumination and productive reflection," writes Daniel Goleman in *Focus*, "lies in whether or not we come up with some tentative solution or insight and then can let those distressing thoughts go, or if, on the other hand, we just keep obsessing over the same loop of worry."[26] Translating worry into active contingency planning, especially in situations where we have less control, has been proven to reduce distress and increase our ability to cope.

Few situations produce more challenging worry than waiting for high-stakes news. With no control or outlet for our nervous energy, the anxiety of waiting can be particularly distressing. To investigate the impact of various coping strategies on the distress of waiting, researchers at the University of California, Riverside, studied 230 law school graduates during their four-month wait for the results of their bar exam to see how their experiences of anxiety and coping styles predicted distress in waiting and upon learning results.[27]

Researchers found that participants who actively worried about failure during the waiting period and planned for contingencies felt less overall distress while waiting. They also better coped with negative outcomes than those who attempted to ignore their anxiety or simply brace themselves. In perhaps the most surprising finding, participants who felt more anxiety and proactively prepared for failure enjoyed the thrill of passing even more than participants who engaged in more optimistic thoughts and less proactive coping all along.[28]

## Fake It Till You Make It

"We intuitively know that how we feel influences our physical behavior," Adam Galinsky and Maurice Schweitzer write, "but what this research shows is that this relationship also works in reverse; our physical behavior also influences how we feel. In other words, just as we can start a manual transmission car by rolling down the street, putting the car in gear, and releasing the clutch, we can 'roll start' feeling powerful by directing our body in a high-power gear."[29]

Experiencing emotions is a two-way process where our brains send and receive messages to and from our bodies. For example, a frown is both a manifestation of concern or disappointment as well as a signal of it. In one interesting study, Richard Davidson and his colleagues compared response times in women who had used Botox (to calm frown lines) to women who did not use Botox. Each group was asked to identify the emotions represented in a picture. The researchers found that paralyzed facial muscles delayed how quickly the women were able to identify emotions.[30]

## The Low-Hanging Fruit Strategy

One strategy for jump-starting momentum: the low-hanging fruit strategy. The key is to use momentum from the success of an easier but related task, and apply it to the harder task. Your confidence will be boosted, and energy will be released into the tougher task ahead. The idea of borrowing competency from a smaller task and applying it to a bigger task is a helpful trick I sometimes recommend to patients. Not surprisingly, confidence comes from the harder task, not the easier one. It is what we are most afraid of that, of course, fuels confidence and satisfaction when we take action.

It seems that because their faces could not mirror the emotion, they were slower in spotting them. People who think they're only changing their outside appearance are forgetting something: our biology influences our emotional experience and vice versa.

The Duchenne smile,[31] which is smiling with your eyes squinting, has been shown to facilitate faster stress recovery than not smiling or only slightly smiling.[32] Stuck in traffic and late for work? Try holding a toothy, eye-squinting grin for a minute or so. It might help lower your blood pressure and heart rate. Harvard University researcher Amy Cuddy takes this idea a step further, exposing how our posture can impact our feelings. She calls these expansive postural stances *power poses* and has demonstrated their capacity to increase feelings of confidence and power prior to high-stakes social situations.[33] These bursts of courage and confidence can help bring our anxiety to a manageable level, giving us the boost we need step into our anxiety as something we can use.

## Get Curious

In her book *Grit*, Angela Duckworth defines *grit* "as persistence and passion over time for long-term goals." Looking at a wide array of data on the subject, researchers have recognized that "the more grit you have the happier you say you are, the less anxiety you have, the less depression, the less sadness."[34] Resilience clearly improves anxiety coping, but cultivating resilience—or grit—isn't always straightforward.

Christine Carter, author of *The Sweet Spot,* suggests that persistence at anything has to begin with curiosity and joy and be maintained by routine, or what she calls a *groove*. While anxiety might be initially motivating, we can only get so far fearing a negative consequence or failure. This kind of motivation is more likely to lead to perfectionism, something Carter argues is maladaptive and unsustainable.[35]

When we get bogged down and start to feel the anxiety of falling off task, it can help to return to our interest and curiosity. Focus on what's interesting and enjoyable in a task, even if it's getting it done. Research shows effort that is purposeful, and aligned with what we care about most, can be integral to finding the success and happiness we crave. It is in the doing where we assert ourselves and take control over anxiety: we hear its signal, engage its energy, and focus on solving the problems of our lives.

## CHAPTER THIRTEEN

# Social Support

*"The deepest principle in human nature is the craving
to be appreciated."*

—**William James**

## Janet

Janet's social anxiety was not only uncomfortable, it could also
be crippling at times. If she thought about being around people
at parties, family gatherings, or even casual meet-ups with friends,
she started to worry about what people thought of her. These
worries brought her almost constant discomfort: the thought of
these situations was so unpleasant that she avoided them, opting
to be alone. And yet, she wasn't happy.

She thought spending time alone should bring her relief
from feared social interactions, but it seemed to do the opposite.

It increased her worry and self-disappointment. Her loneliness was confusing to her, since she knew she was *choosing* to be alone. Janet's anxiety had a few layers—and fear of other people was just one of them.

In our work, Janet discovered her fear of people's judgment masked another fear: fear of rejection and being alone. Janet's conflicted feelings signaled not a desire for solitude, but rather a deep desire for connection. This new awareness opened her thinking. It gave her the space to come up with a more effective attitude and a new perspective on her behaviors. She had to tolerate her fear of judgment to get in touch with a deeper fear. Only then could her deeper anxiety—about being alone—fuel constructive social behavior.

## Evolve to Belong

Our social connections are integral to who we are, how we survive, and whether we thrive. In *Social: Why Our Brains are Wired to Connect*, neuroscientist Matthew Lieberman explains that our brains are wired for "reaching out and interacting with others. These are design features, not flaws."[1] Social networks have evolved, he explains, as a means of survival and reproduction.

In addition, our sense of self is wholly wrapped up in others' perceptions of us, and as such our connections mean considerably more to us than we may suspect. When those bonds are broken, we feel it in a profound way. In fact, Lieberman's fMRI studies show a similarity between physical and social pain;

rejection and loss can feel just as painful as physical injuries. Meanwhile, positive feedback from others feels as good to us as a monetary reward.[2]

Our social networks are more embedded into who we are than even the most outgoing person might suspect. Lieberman explains that our default mode network, what our brain is running when we're not paying attention, "directs us to think about other people's minds—their thoughts, feelings, and goals,"[3] and our place in our social world. Out of all the things we could have organized around, "evolution made this 'choice'—for the brain to reset to thinking socially."[4] We are powerfully driven to understand and tweak our own behavior through the expectations of others. This practice of "harmonizing" speaks powerfully to our social needs and their primacy in driving us.

In his ambitious book *Sapiens: A Brief History of Humankind*, Yuval Noah Harari discusses the origins of this need for social connection and how adaptive it was. He notes that we are all born helplessly dependent as babies.

> *This fact has contributed greatly both to humankind's extraordinary social abilities and to its unique social problems. Lone mothers could hardly forage enough food for their offspring and themselves with needy children in tow. Raising children required constant help from other family members and neighbours. It takes a tribe to raise a human. Evolution thus favoured those capable of forming strong social ties.[5]*

Being part of a group has long increased our chances for survival, and it still does. It was our ancestors' ability to connect on mass levels that enabled humans to become the dominant species. Over time, we have evolved sensitive methods of protecting these connections. In *Angst,* author and psychiatrist Jeffrey Khan calls it an "advantage for society...that these primeval emotional instincts still nudge people into social harmony."[6]

Social support is a two-way road in its relationship with anxiety: it is an effective buffer against our own anxiety,[7] and anxiety drives us to connect with others, as we discussed in chapter 9.[8] Psychologist and meditation teacher Tara Brach advocates an "attend and befriend" response to stress, one that is more adaptive than our fight/flight/freeze response, which "contracts our body and mind, and separates us from others."[9] We worry because we feel, and we feel because we care. Anxiety is simply the manifestation of the things that matter and our drive to protect them.

## Emotions Are Contagious

There is a great deal of evidence linking social support to overall physical and mental health. The right kind of social support has also been shown to enhance resilience to stress.[10] Though some of us may feel like being alone when we're anxious, biology tells us that we should be reaching out.

Having friends around us can help mitigate our fears of rejection. Few experiences are more stressful than public speaking, where humiliation and public rejection loom large. In one study, researchers at Cornell University found that having a friend in the crowd while speaking in public lowered one's cardiovascular response.[11] Just the presence of someone we're connected to is enough to put us at ease.

Research has documented a variety of key roles social support can play in our lives. Poor support systems are linked to weaker immune systems, cardiovascular diseases, and earlier mortality.[12] Social support is well known to mitigate the negative effects of trauma.[13] As well, it appears to protect people from engaging in more destructive ways of coping—alcohol abuse, drug abuse, avoidance of change.[14] According to happiness researcher Shawn Achor, a positive mind-set + social support = higher satisfaction and lower stress.[15] Together with a good attitude, feeling supported can help us feel and be our best.

Our social connections do a great deal in terms of physical recovery as well. Research has determined that visiting a sick person in the hospital really does improve their health.[16] Feeling a sense of connection is deeply powerful, and a key facilitator of this is our human capacity to feel empathy for others. A special type of neuron we have in our brains that reflects and imitates those around us helps us do this.[17] Mirror neurons are brain cells "that respond equally when we perform an action and when we witness someone else perform the same action."[18] If you've ever been playing a game of catch and recoiled after you made an errant throw (because someone else was about to be hit by the ball), you've witnessed mirror neurons at work.[19]

Mirror neurons and empathy are highly adaptive; they build

understanding and thus our connections to people. If you break into a smile when your spouse smiles at you, your mirror neurons are helping to forge an important connection. Customer-service gurus have long known about the power of mirror neurons and preach their usefulness when trying to calm angry customers.[20] When we feel connected and understood, we feel better.

Emotions are contagious for a reason; it's how we learn about and protect each other. After all, societies large and small are based around the principle of sharing and dividing. We have deep-seated preferences for helping and for fairness that keep these structures intact. Think about the uproar that would result at the office if a boss just walked in one day and gave certain employees flexible hours for no apparent reason—there would be a revolt.

None of us are experiencing emotions in isolation. We co-construct emotions and realities with all those around us. Families intuitively know how much the emotion of one can seep into the emotions of others. All it takes is to be at my kitchen table to watch my family rise and fall on one of our emotions. One of us starts laughing, and all of us are immediately buoyed. Once a second person starts laughing, we are off to a family laughing fit. Likewise, all it takes is one of us to be particularly cranky or irritable to suppress the collective mood of the rest of us.

"We're a social species," writes Lisa Feldman Barrett, "which means we regulate each other's nervous systems. I can make your heart rate speed up or slow down, just by my choice of words."[21] We are drawn to and vulnerable to mirroring what others do around us: this is the essence of our need for connection. And it is also the basis of shared anxiety and second-hand stress. Like yawning[22] and divorce,[23] anxiety can be contagious, too.[24]

## Staying Home

For some, like Janet (whose story opens this chapter), connecting with others can be the basis of such excessive anxiety that they avoid social situations altogether. Their fear of rejection outweighs their desire to connect, and they suffer both loneliness and intense anxiety. *Scientific American* highlighted research by Andrew R. Todd at the University of Iowa that showed "from a broader perspective, it seems that anxiety-inducing social situations are also (ironically) the ones that most demand our empathy."[25] When we think about others and their experiences, it becomes very hard to think only of our own. It allows us to both be a friend for others and gets us out of our own heads—two key tools to use in channeling social anxiety.

How we think about our friendship skills can also fuel additional anxiety. A new study finds that while social anxiety sufferers think their friendships are not of the highest quality, their friends are much more positive about the same relationships.[26] Negative thinking can be a familiar trap when it comes to social anxiety.

## Cynthia

Cynthia was a client who felt a great deal of shame about her anxiety and various worries in both her professional and personal life. It was hard for her to identify her feelings and even harder for her to connect with others when she was feeling vulnerable. When these times struck, she just wanted to stay in her apartment and not see anyone or do anything. She wouldn't return friends' texts or calls—she thought she just wanted to be alone. Part of her withdrawing stemmed from her relationship with her highly judgmental mother, and she tended to react as though everyone was judging her in the same way.

She was so guarded and accustomed to her mother's judgments that she sometimes even referred to herself in the second person as a way to distance herself from her experiences. She made statements like, "Sometimes you just have to do it" or "Sometimes you can't face it." Learning to express herself, and to choose people who could understand rather than judge her, was a key part of helping her harness her anxiety toward strengthening her social bonds.

Through our work together, Cynthia was honest with herself, recognizing that being alone prolonged and worsened the feelings she was trying to avoid. Once she bravely began acknowledging her feelings, she saw how they merely reflected that she cared. In fact, they lent a point of connection to her many friendships. More critically, she realized her friends could understand her. They felt closer to her when she was honest about her experience and didn't avoid them. Letting them into her life, not just when she was feeling good but when she was feeling vulnerable too, was a key part of helping her access and deepen her support system, especially when she was vulnerable. She had to *let* herself lean on it.

When we seek empathy, we should remember that we're never going to find someone who understands us completely. No one knows exactly what we're feeling and this is how it should be. It's part of what it means to be human. Self-psychology founder Heinz Kohut believed that while empathic understanding was critical to the development of the healthy self, perfect empathy was neither possible nor even desirable. He argued that learning to deal with not being completely understood is a key part of developing a strong sense of self.

## Accessing Support

Anxiety primes us, on a neurochemical level, to express our feelings. Because we are biologically wired for emotional expression, we *want* to express ourselves. It's how we get our feelings out and protect ourselves from the damaging effects of built-up stress. As we've discussed, expressing our feelings activates more areas of our brain, as well as more resources, and increases our immune responses.[27] It allows us to understand, and therefore *use*, our emotions adaptively.

One of the most adaptive ways we can use our emotions is to facilitate connections with others. In *Social*, Matthew Lieberman shows how "affect labeling"—literally naming an emotion—both reduces emotional distress *and* enacts empathy from others.[28] The more clearly we express our emotions, the more likely a trusted listener will be able to understand them—and us—and respond with empathy. When we express our emotions, we open ourselves up to be understood with empathy and compassion. Our emotions are doing their job of spurring focus and attention as well as facilitating a collective solution. This helps regulate our emotions and at the same time deepen our most trusted social bonds. Telling someone how we are really feeling allows them access to our world. Without emotions, others have a difficult time understanding—and meeting—our needs. Remember the baby's cry: it grabs the attention of caregivers. Without it, the baby would not get any help. When it comes to getting what we need, sharing our emotions is one of the most efficient tools we can use.

## Being Heard

When it comes to personal connection, and especially intimate relationships, we feel the most connected when we lead with our feelings, which activates others' empathy and compassion. Generally, the more vulnerable we are, the more compassionate people are in response. One of the biggest pitfalls I notice in my clients is when they try to seek support without making their feelings known. It happened with my client Cecilia. She wanted her husband to understand her ambivalence about moving the whole family to the West Coast, but she was not clearly articulating this need. I make this same mistake myself. When trying to solve family scheduling conflicts, I jump past my feelings and find myself debating logistics with my husband rather than addressing our feelings—sometimes he doesn't mind going to the grocery store, whereas I always do.

When we leave out our feelings, we make it harder for our listener to give us what we want—understanding. Describing events instead our *feelings* about them keeps us removed from our experience; in turn, we deprive ourselves of the connection we are seeking. One trick I have used effectively with people is to lead with "I feel…" followed by a feeling—not a thought. For example, "I feel frustrated when you look at your phone while I'm talking," works a whole lot better than "Why do you always look at your phone when I'm talking to you?"

I see many relationships in my work where the lack of communication creates a chasm—with both sides acting out of an assumption of the other's feelings rather than the reality. When we talk about our feelings, we prime others to respond with empathy thanks to our capacity to relate to others and the release of oxytocin ("the cuddle hormone") in the brain.[29] With this chemical's release, we feel a sense of trust and connection, and we are more likely to show compassion and generosity. "Your biological stress response is nudging you to tell someone how you are feeling instead of bottling it up,"[30] says health psychologist Kelly McGonigal. Indeed, the healing power of empathy is one of therapy's most powerful tools. Even in discussing the darkest of subjects and emotions, people feel lighter and better just by having felt the support of a professional and having an opportunity to clarify their feelings and conflicts. The better you express yourself, the more support you will feel.

# Giving Support

We need support and help from others, but there's a reciprocity at work as well. Various studies have shown positive mood effects from giving—money, time, or attention—and how giving supports the health of the *giver*.[31] Offering an understanding ear can relieve our own anxiety as well. Sometimes in listening and supporting others, we find solace and answers for ourselves. It can help us clarify what is going on inside of us.

The tendency to feel empathic joy is associated with a stronger desire to help others thrive and a greater willingness to take action to do so. As Kelly McGonigal explains, "Positive empathy also enhances the warm glow you feel from helping others—making compassion much more sustainable."[32] Thinking about others is a great way to harness our anxiety for good. Not only does it pull us away from our problems, but it nurtures our connections.

Though empathy appears hardwired, we can also pick it up through conscious learning and practice. Empathy can ultimately become an automatic habit thanks to the development of our medial prefrontal cortex.[33] When we think about others, we prepare ourselves for empathy and more control. The same area of the brain involved in helping others is also closely tied to mediating anxiety. The dorsal medial prefrontal cortex helps quiet our fears and increases motivation to help.[34] "Often," writes Robert Sapolsky, "one of the strongest stress-reducing qualities of social support is the act of giving social support, to be needed."[35]

# The Power of Storytelling

> *"Tell me the facts and I'll learn. Tell me the truth and I'll believe. But tell me a story and it will live in the heart forever."*
>
> **—Native American proverb**

Stories are a powerful communication tool that help us feel connected and less alone. We tell stories to ourselves to make sense and give order to our world. We read, watch, and engage with fictional stories that allow us to play out our feelings in a safe environment. The Greeks, who just about invented the idea of story structure, had a word for it we still use: *catharsis*. It's the feeling of emotional release that comes from participating in a resolved story. Research shows compelling stories have the power to impact our brain chemistry, attitudes, and behaviors more than any other mode of information sharing. More than sharing information or conveying simple fact patterns, stories help us understand the *why*.

As a psychologist, every day I listen to people tell the stories of their lives. This is how I come to understand what they're experiencing and how I relate to them. There are characters, plot lines, and hopefully, resolutions. Not only do I listen intently, but I try to retell their stories back to them in a way they can hear. The idea is for us together, in the process of creating their stories, to create satisfying resolutions.

This is how we relate to each other and secure our bonds.

Consider the husband coming home from a stressful workday and simply telling a wife that he needs to be alone. He goes off by himself, but he gives no context to help his wife understand his behavior. There's no story there. Predictably, she struggles to understand or feel compassion. She is more likely to resist his request, or make it about her, compounding any insecurity she may already carry. She tells herself her own story about why he wants to be away from her.

However, think about how different things could be if he were to take the time to explain the why behind his request—to frame it for her in a story. He could tell her a story about a childhood filled with performance expectations he had to learn to handle on his own. He might include how hard his parents both worked to provide for his family, how they weren't around to help him, how he *had* to learn to cope with pressure. He could explain that he did this alone, by putting his head down, withdrawing from whoever he needed to get the job done. To this day, this is how he copes. It is a habit he developed through necessity in his formative years, and he never learned another strategy.

Hearing his story would allow her to understand the *why* of his need. What it means for him, not just for her. The story acts as a bridge, a pathway to empathy. As we connect to the shared humanity of a story, we experience for ourselves what they are experiencing. Stories enact empathy and a sense of closeness, thanks in part to the production of oxytocin in our brains. Paul J. Zak's work has demonstrated stories' capacity to create a sense of trust and connection via the production of oxytocin in the observer.[36]

Scientists believe that this capacity for empathy is an innate and uniquely human trait that may have evolved to secure our survival through human connection.[37]

It is only when we *feel* a sense of trust that we are willing to take a risk. Whether it's sharing a story of our own, extending a vulnerability of some sort, or putting our trust in a person or organization, we make these risk-taking decisions with our hearts—*not* just with our heads. Stories help us bring our hearts into the matter.

## Spinning Your Wheels

Mark, in chapter 7, felt his work colleagues' poor attitude was affecting his own attitude—and he was correct. In listening to their complaints, he was taking on their emotions, and like them, he was feeling stuck. We are always breathing in this emotional mix: our own emotions and the communicated emotions of those around us.

Complaining is really just worry that we express aloud, but it can be toxic. Studies have shown the negative health effects of not only complaining, but listening to others complain.[38] It becomes one of those cycles we fall into, especially when it's the default language of our social circle. We get habituated to the grooves of complaining—the more we do it, the more our brain is drawn to doing it. So many of us are besieged by this seductive, but ultimately unsatisfying, form of release—whether it's about our boss, traffic, or a narrative we tell ourselves about how the world is treating us.

There is nothing wrong with expressing complaints; we

know that bottling up our emotions is linked to higher distress and less emotional control.[39] Indeed, experiments have shown that thought suppression actually drives up unwanted thoughts.[40] But this kind of expression and release needs to have a driving purpose. Is there an art to complaining in a way that initiates change? Is there a way to give constructive criticism to a friend to improve your relationship? Is there a suggestion to make improvements in the workplace?

People don't like to hear complaints; they want to hear your feelings. Feelings encourage empathy, which in turn foster compassion and generosity, both key elements in producing change and promoting action. If you have something difficult or painful to talk about with a friend or colleague, make sure to tell them how the situation is impacting you and how you are feeling—including your desire to find a solution. Avoid statements of judgment about the other person, especially ones disguised as your own feelings. "I feel *that* you aren't really trying" isn't about your feeling at all. It's your conclusion.

At its worst, complaining is an exercise in spinning our wheels in mud—exerting energy that gets us nowhere and leaves us filthy. Venting just to vent may feel good in the moment—but it often leaves us feeling unsatisfied and stuck, whereas using your feelings as a motivator to solve the problems you *can* solve can be helpful. Your emotions are tools that are there to help you fix things when they are out of balance.

What kind of complainer do you think you are? Do you blame? Do you overshare? Do you describe the situation or your experience? Perhaps most important, how do people respond? If you find that people aren't giving you what you are looking for, ask yourself why. If you are bottling things up to the point that you could explode, try expressing them sooner and in smaller chunks. If you are detailing events rather than your feelings, the problem rather than moving to the solution, the past instead of the future, try to shift your focus inward and forward: to what can be done.

## Social Support: Common Pitfalls

Shame might be one of the most insidious obstacles we face in securing the support we need. There is nothing wrong with feeling embarrassed. Embarrassment can be uncomfortable, but it is not something to fear or even avoid, because it is "a moral emotion," says Dacher Keltner.[41] University of California–Berkeley researcher Robb Willer agrees. "Moderate levels of embarrassment are signs of virtue," he explains. "Our data suggests embarrassment is a good thing, not something you should fight… It's part of the social glue that fosters trust and cooperation in everyday life."[42] But sometimes our embarrassment gets dialed up to such a high degree that it becomes a virtual prison. This is what we call shame.

Shame can inhibit your reaching out to people you love. *They have their own lives and problems*, you think, *they don't need to be burdened with mine*. Or worse, *They'll think less of me or will see me as a failure*. Thinking this is likely a reflection of your own discomfort—perhaps thinking that was internalized from others in your life, but it is not likely something you would pay forward. Would you feel judgmental about a friend in need? Shame occurs when we hold ourselves to a different standard than we do others. It derives from unrealistic beliefs about ourselves that can quickly fuel further anxiety and avoidance.

Even with the most supportive friends and family, you might not be able to bring yourself to share. Something holds you back. It warns you of judgment and rejection, dismisses your feelings as exaggerated or even deserved, and blames you for not being good enough in the first place. Shame is a powerful and silencing force.

*I'm not enough* is the language of shame, and at its root it is our basic fear of rejection. In her book *Daring Greatly*, Brené Brown defines shame as "the intensely painful feeling or experience of believing that you are flawed and therefore unworthy of love and belonging."[43] She reminds her readers that unless we're sociopaths, we all have a capacity for shame, and we are mostly all afraid to talk about it. But the less we talk about it, the more control it has over our lives.

I once led a seminar on rebuilding from personal and professional setbacks, inviting the audience of professionals to share their journeys of recovery. Each volunteer described a battle with shame and its attempt to silence him or her. Pushing through shame was critical to them accessing the understanding they desperately needed and the support they required for healing. Their courage and vulnerability were almost universally met with compassion, understanding, and respect from the audience that day. The more vulnerability the group seemed to share, the more connected the audience felt. There was a snowball effect: Their humanity inspired others to share their own stories.

I see this effect among trusted friends, as well as with couples I work with in my office. We follow one another's lead. As others share their vulnerability, we are moved to respond with compassion, and join in taking risks too. As social creatures, we are propelled to connect, and inspired by each other's courage.

## The Right Support

Another pitfall of securing support is seeking it from those we shouldn't. Whom we bring into our lives is an issue we should never take lightly. For example, being open to a judgmental or critical person will not bring you the compassion and support you are craving. In fact, it can be dangerous, setting you up for harm at times when you are vulnerable. An extreme example of this is an abusive relationship, where a partner could use such disclosures as weapons in future arguments. This can happen at work as well, where an effort to be honest with a critical boss about areas for growth could backfire and become criticisms later.

We also should be careful of seeking support from those who *cannot* give it. Not every person in your life is capable of listening and delivering the empathy you need—even your closest loved ones. Some of them might be too hungry for their own support to be able to give it, and some may simply feel too vulnerable giving any other feedback than criticism.

If you aren't feeling supported at the level you need, don't force it. Looking to these people for empathy, and making yourself vulnerable to them, will leave you feeling more alone, unheard, and maybe even judged. It can be hard to accept the limitations of the people we love, especially when we want them to understand us, but accept them we must. The key is to recognize and work with what we have—not what we wish we had.

You may *want* your mother or husband or best friend to be your go-to support, but that doesn't mean they are able to be in every situation, if at all. Sometimes loved ones just don't see where we are coming from, or understand us the way we need them to. Their responses in times of need can be variable at best and inadequate at worst. It doesn't mean they don't love us, it means it's complicated by a whole lot of factors, including how we express our needs as well as their own feelings and conflicts.

Often, we don't want a loved one or friend to solve anything for us; we simply want them to be there. I remember a story of a friend who had sustained a devastating blow to her fledgling company, and of all the advice and help she received from her impressive professional network, the most comforting thing a friend finally said to her was to tell her how much the whole thing stank and to offer her some wine. While the alcohol wasn't necessary to help her cope, it showed he understood just how bad things really were without judging or pitying her.

The friend further shared that he too would be shrinking under the weight of the situation, and this honesty helped her feel not so alone, not so crazy, and in a solidarity sort of way, stronger. It also communicated to her that she was worthy of support and encouragement, which pushed back against her shame. He didn't solve anything, nor did he try to, he simply conveyed understanding and compassion. And this helped her take a bit more of this compassion and understanding for herself and use it to move forward.

The growth of social media in recent years has allowed us to maintain many more social contacts with very little effort. We can stay and feel connected to people far and wide and reap a sense of community that is at our fingertips. But this social connectivity has come at a cost too. Recently, a large Pew study explored the "cost of caring," and it warned about the contagiousness of stress via social media.[44] Think about all the people you don't even really know who are capable of causing you stress—intentionally or not—through nothing but a tweet or Facebook post.

Our social tribe, virtual or in-person, inform our reality, and we adopt our coping from them. Surrounding yourself with people who use their anxiety adaptively can have a strengthening effect. People in my life who are careful listeners help me feel understood, the doers inspire me to keep taking action, and the avoiders tempt me to put things off. Who is in your tribe? And whose strategy for anxiety coping inspires you? A trainer, a friend, a coworker, a therapist? Envisioning what they would do, or what they would say, can help you choose the path you want to emulate.

## CHAPTER FOURTEEN

# Love and Relationships

*"He who has a why to love can bear almost any how."*

**—Frederic Nietzsche**

**We all know what it** feels like to be in love, or at least what we think it should feel like. Perhaps we were once young or naïve enough to believe love should always be effortless. And, in the beginning, maybe it can be. But anyone who has forged a successful relationship knows that effortless love cannot last. Securing and protecting our relationships are so essential to our survival that our anxiety about them can sometimes trump everything else.

In all our relationships, anxiety alerts us to sensitivities—land mines that we need to be aware of and issues that need our attention. Whether it's in our dating experiences, steering our relationships, or coping with loss, anxiety can help us navigate murky, and sometimes treacherous, waters. Anxiety won't allow us to ignore those we care about, and it keeps us attuned to their needs as well as our own. Think of relationship anxiety as the smell they put in natural gas to let us know how aware we need to be of it, how carefully we need to handle it.

## The Propeller

In relationships, one of the most common conflicts arises from the gap of how connected we want to feel and how connected we actually feel. In love, anxiety's job is to ultimately *propel us toward others*. So drawn are we to love, that romantic love is not just a feeling, it's a motivation system; it can even function like an addiction.[1] We are driven powerfully to the rewards that love brings.

Anxiety can emerge when love feels threatened or when we feel disconnected. As we discussed in the last chapter, we must take the risk to communicate it to someone capable of hearing it and in a way they can hear. We have to also be willing to listen to our loved ones and think about their needs. I often teach my clients that opening ourselves up like this is not a weakness, but a strength.

"Vulnerability is the most accurate measurement of our courage," writes author and scholar Brené Brown.[2] We must be willing to make ourselves vulnerable; it's an integral part of our humanity. If not, we will never truly be able to connect.

# The One: Anxiety and Dating

In dating, nerves come with the territory. We generally assume anxiety is just part of the process, that mix of excitement and fear that accompany risk-taking. After all, dating can be stressful: we are putting ourselves and our hopes for connection out there, risking being judged, rejected, and even humiliated.

Social media has changed so much of the arena and ground rules of dating. There's a new layer of anxiety that the previous crop of singles didn't even have to consider. There's no barrier to entry anymore; people we would never encounter or be set up with now have immediate access to us.

It isn't easy to expose yourself to the scrutiny of dating, and anxiety can accompany even the most confident person. We may feel the pressure that comes along with being our best self, or the worry that a relationship will never happen for us. All of it can be enough to prevent us for getting out there at all.

Dating is one of the many common places anxiety avoidance can lurk. It can hide behind typical excuses like "I'm too busy" or "It's not worth the effort." What we're really doing in disguising our anxiety behind excuses is attempting to avoid situations that might trigger it. But if we recognize it's there to help and guide us, we can more easily steer into it.

Dating can be scary, because it opens us up to potential rejection and our anxiety is tuning us into its discomfort. That anxiety is also a signal of an internal conflict inside of us: we don't want to be hurt or rejected, but we also don't want to be alone. Ultimately, dating anxiety can fuel us into action—putting up a dating profile, socializing with people we don't yet know, and taking calculated risks to try new experiences. Dating anxiety is the kind of anxiety that lingers unless we use it for motivation: if we want something new in our lives, we will have to do something different to get it. Doing new things generally requires discomfort, and our resistance can keep us stuck in anxiety if we aren't careful.

Once we begin dating, and find someone we feel connected to, this kind of dating anxiety should diminish. Strong anxiety felt after a date or two deserves our attention. It might be a deep-seated discomfort about the potential relationship or a signal of a poor fit. Malcolm Gladwell's popular book *Blink: The Power of Thinking Without Thinking* is premised on the very idea that our instincts often know things before our conscious minds have even had a chance to take it all in. Remember: *Your anxiety surfaces for a reason*. When we connect with a new person, and our anxiety spikes, it behooves us to listen.

Honor your anxiety if you start to feel uncomfortable at any point in dating, and use its energy to pay attention to its message and protect yourself. Ending a date early is always better than wishing you had. Other kinds of anxiety, especially if you are feeling self-conscious or particularly uncomfortable, can clue you into revealing subtleties about a person, and your interactions with them. For example, overly complimentary people can be off-putting because compliments, while positive, are still judgments. Other judgments, even if unspoken, are likely just around the corner.

Similarly, anxiety can also flag elements of a date's personality or behavior that could be dangerous, such as trust issues, a penchant for secrecy, or hints of dishonesty. Selfish people, for example, can show their colors early on in constant interruptions or never asking questions. How well does this person listen to you, show interest, and relate to what you are saying? How comfortable, and adequate, do you feel? These are some key questions to ask yourself when you are dating. The right partner makes us feel *more* like our best self, not less so. We are accepted and elevated through their eyes, not diminished. If we don't feel that, then our anxiety is presenting us with essential information we need to carefully consider.

## Denise

Denise was a single woman with an intense career whose relationship with her father had always been volatile. Her father had long been a quintessential "button" pusher, knowing which pressure points rile his daughter and using them to exert control. Newly widowed, the father depended on Denise as his sole caretaker. Her relationship with her father, along with her commitment to her career, had long kept Denise from avoiding real connection. She had a deep fear of being infringed upon or swallowed up.

Denise and I began our work by looking at the relationship with her father, how it has intensified since her mother's death, and his ability to push her buttons. When something is stirred up inside us that feels like the past, our old conflicts get activated and our old patterns reassert themselves. Denise and I searched for the connection between present and the past. She wanted to date but was wary; so many men just seemed interested in finding someone who would take care of them. We worked on listening to how her anxiousness was communicating her needs to herself and how she could use it to keep looking, rather than give up. We agreed there are no traps in seeking a relationship; each and every step is her choice.

Some time later, Denise found a man whom she described as having a "soul" that entranced her. He was independent but caring, and he had a way of leaning on humor and joy that she hadn't known before in a partner. He seemed more interested in her than he was in what she could do for him, and as they got to know each other, her worries increasingly calmed. She went from restless frustration to tearful gratitude that somebody could understand and love her for her; this, in time, lifted her anxiety about feeling trapped or alone. With the growing love and trust, Denise's views changed about what a relationship could be and how capable she was of making room in her life to love and be loved.

Over time, her interactions with her father improved in parallel. She became less sensitive to his frailties, and she became gentler in her expectations of him, other people in her life, and with herself. I see Denise less often, which itself is a sign of progress. When we do work together, we talk about her progress, and how she can stretch to stay present with this man she loves, whom—in moments of stress—she can still push away. Working through those reasons prevents her from falling back into her old riverbeds of mistrust and withdrawal.

## The Anxious Relationship

Stressors in a relationship should never be ignored or labeled too minor to address nor should they be dismissed as a product of mental illness. Constant unresolved fighting, poor communication, betrayals of trust, or a lack of safety are all legitimate issues that can be understandable stressors in any relationship. Anxieties about such issues are profound signals of needed focus and attention. Some marriages are rife with conflict and unmet expectations. These are rocky relationships where anxiety can play a key role in drilling into where the problems are lurking, sometimes not so obviously.

Anxiety can fuel and escalate anger, so much so that it can predict future problems, and even divorce. In one study of long-time married couples, hostility predicted 80 percent of those marriages that would end in divorce within the year.[3] Likewise, levels of stress hormones in newlywed arguments predicted future relationship trouble.[4] Even whispering anxiety can portend trouble. Brides having cold feet before getting married were shown to be 2.5 times more likely to be divorced or be unhappy in their marriage 4 years later.[5]

Insecurity, the kind of whispering anxiety that leaves you wondering if you—or your relationship—are good enough, has been shown to be a powerful predictor of chronic marital dissatisfaction[6] and infidelity.[7] When it comes to relationship trouble, anxiety is a powerful warning sign that should not be ignored. If there is poor communication and regular misunderstandings, or anxiety is left to fester, even a solid relationship can lose its footing.

Marriage anxiety can also reveal itself as boredom. Boredom is not just stagnation in a marriage, but the whisper that something is internally wrong—a needling chronic dissatisfaction that is chronic deserves our attention.

A marriage is a fertile ground for avoidance, too: it can manifest in work, substance abuse, chronically separate interests, excessive travel, or infidelity. When we avoid in this manner, we're merely driving up our resistance to our partner when what's needed most is nurturing and compassion. Being honest about our anxieties with our partner and accepting its messages as important are powerful ways to work toward reconnection. If a relationship is to be saved, we must drop the avoidance patterns and examine the anxieties and their messages.

## Rebecca

A working mom of toddlers, Rebecca found herself dreaming at night about having affairs. In the dreams, she felt guilty, though she found evidence of her husband straying, too. However, it was this element—her husband's straying—which caused anxiety when she awoke. Both Rebecca and her husband were deeply in love and fully committed, but in reality they were disconnected due to the demands of their many responsibilities.

Using the anxiety and guilt she felt in her dreams as a starting place, we worked to assess where those feelings were coming from. Quickly we found she felt guilty about not spending more time with her husband, and she was anxious about the diminishing quality of the time they did spend. While cloaked in a fictional drama, her emotions were very real; they were signaling the hunger she felt for connection. She and her husband had recently been disagreeing about finances, childcare, and other weekly logistics; in fact, it had been their primary communication. He traveled frequently for work and dealing with their toddlers from morning to night fell to her. Because she was so exhausted, and they were often apart, their sex life was suffering too. She was "missing" him in almost every sense of the word.

Rebecca and I worked on answering some forward-thinking questions: What could she *do* to help the situation? How could she make more time for fun and for her husband in her schedule? How could she communicate her feelings in a constructive way? Even talking through some strategies appeared to reduce her anxiety—giving her an outlet that was once being choked.

## When Trusting/Sharing Responsibilities Is Hard

Trusting others is difficult, especially when we've learned that leaning on others can lead to disappointment and rejection. Those who internalize this lesson become lone wolves—believing that in order to get something done, they have to do it themselves. In moderation, there is nothing wrong with this sentiment: it fuels responsibility, control-taking, and resilience. But it also can lead to stubbornness, isolation, and resentment.

Asking for help is extremely hard for such lone wolves. Activist Tiffany Dufu describes how anxiety-provoking this attitude can be for women in *Drop the Ball: Achieving More by Doing Less.* Women are especially socialized to take care of others, which comes at a price: our balance falls out of whack, and our needs clash against our belief that we are not allowed to have any of our own.[8] But expressing our needs and sharing the load of running a house are so vital to a healthy home. Indeed, research confirms that division of labor in marriage is a key aspect of marital happiness,[9] with a recent Pew Study confirming more than 50 percent of married adults in the United States believe shared housework is key to a successful marriage.[10]

When we sacrifice too much of ourselves for others, resentment builds; it becomes the kind of anxiety that comes from feeling trapped. But as Dufu describes, taking control of your experience and forging compromises with your partner can rebalance the scales.

## Tim and Richard

Tim and Richard were a couple who came for help navigating how to balance the needs of their relationship with the demands of two executive careers, a busy household, and two small children. They are both doers, accustomed to over-delivering in their responsibilities and receiving positive feedback. The issue was that they were falling short in giving and receiving the support and validation they each needed at home. Both men felt overworked, under-appreciated, and frustrated.

Tim and Richard were both talented and resilient men who

loved each other deeply, but they were not as skilled at emotional communication. Neither had much practice with these skills growing up, and voicing their feelings was still hard. They had settled into household roles that might have been unfair, but more critically, they weren't talking about it. Their frustrations would smolder, until inevitably there was a painful eruption that took days, sometimes weeks, to smooth over.

In our work, both men learned how powerful sharing their feelings could be in facilitating mutual compassion. This was helpful both in working through their conflicts and in avoiding disruptive escalations. Framing their experiences through the lens of their feelings allowed the other to understand and show the empathy each craved. They may not have responded to the touchy-feely aspect of sharing their feelings, but once they saw how efficiently it solved things, they were willing to practice and quickly improved their skills. When they fall into old habits, they now know that their starting place is finding time to talk to each other about how they are *feeling,* rather than what is happening.

## Change and Compromise: Cecilia

Sometimes anxiety in a marriage manifests because of power imbalance or a shift in roles that goes against expectations. Cecilia, my client who was experiencing yell anxiety about her job offer on the West Coast (see chapter 3), wasn't sure what her husband would do out there career-wise. He had an idea, some semblance of a plan, but nothing was a guarantee. Like for so many couples navigating dual careers, finding some sort of solution came down to a common issue: How much does my career happiness matter in this relationship versus my spouse's? How do we weigh whose job, and whose wishes, are more important? Can we even compromise without risking resentment?

She was wholly confused. Uncomfortable being a primary breadwinner while her husband looked for work and hesitant about moving the family three thousand miles away "just for her career," the situation left her feeling empowered but also more than a little anxious. She would be putting her husband in the position of having to start all over, and his communication about how he felt was mixed and unclear to her. She wanted her husband to make the decision for them, but ultimately, she didn't. She just wanted the decision to be easier, and it simply wasn't. Like so many important life decisions, it was complicated and messy, and one they had to make as a team. Over weeks, his ambivalence started to reflect her own. The negatives more reliably outweighed the positives, and she ended up turning down the job. But importantly, she came to recognize that it was their choice and their collective desires that drove the decision. They decided together.

## Ghosts of Relationships Past

*"It is doubtful that we came to feel undeserving on our own. We were helped to feel unworthy. We were*

*taught in a thousand ways when we were little, and*
*we learned our lessons well."*

—Jon Kabat-Zinn[11]

All of us bring our previous relationships—including the one with our parents—to our romantic relationships. These ghosts emerge when feelings become intense, escalating anxiety and driving conflict. We are all engaged in a process of recreating and revising: seeking the best of our past role models in our relationships and looking to improve the worst. We desire the familiar in love, but we are also motivated to heal any unresolved wounds. It is a powerful—if unconscious—motivation in our choice of mate.

Take for example a woman who, raised by anxious parents, was shown plenty of affection, but was never made to feel like she had done well. Her parents' focus was on the dangerous what-ifs rather than the positives, an outlook that she developed as well. Hungry for affirmation, she gravitated toward encouraging teachers and peers. Eventually, she found a partner's protectiveness a powerful indicator of love, but only felt comfortable when she also had his approval. If she didn't receive affirmations, she felt uneasy—sometimes to the bafflement of that partner.

Dr. Gary Chapman, author of *The Five Love Languages*, distills the various ways couples express love to each other and has determined that these "language" preferences develop in our childhoods.[12] The brain wires itself based on our early experiences, and how we receive love is so integral to our growth that this makes intuitive sense. These emotional remnants from our childhood, and the anxiety we feel when these needs are unmet, need not necessarily be a burden. They can help us by steering us toward healthier relationships. As long as we accept and heed them, rather than ignoring them and letting them escalate, we will be able to use them effectively.

Take for example, a woman who grew up with a somewhat absent, loving father who learns to mistake absence for love. As an adult, she could find herself seeking partners who are frequently unavailable; when a boyfriend is never around, it doesn't occur to her that something is amiss. This is what love has always looked like to her. When she finds out his absence is because he has been having an affair, she is shocked and devastated.

In her later marriage, she could find herself drawn to a driven, hardworking man. She is anxious when her husband doesn't come home when he says he will, or if he seems to be more distracted on his computer and smartphone than usual. She understands the heavy demands of his work, but she still feels uncomfortable with his divided attention, since she had been burned by similar behavior in the past. Not knowing how to approach the situation without sounding overbearing or paranoid, she could opt to say nothing. This type of avoidance in turn only escalates her anxiety, allowing it to fester. Her challenge is to focus on what is real in her relationship and find a way to communicate her needs without letting the ghosts of her past take over.

In another case, a man might pull away from a partner's bids for affection, which he finds suffocating, reminiscent of previous relationships when he felt trapped. The man has trouble determining if his anxiety is current or the remnants of a previous relationship. He should neither treat these feelings as entirely real nor shut them out completely. The goal is to find a middle ground where he listens to what his anxieties are telling him about his current situation, without being unnecessarily distracted by previous experiences.

Awareness of your buttons or ghosts from the past can help detangle them from the stressor itself. Once you can determine what is a ghost and what is real, it is easier to focus on what is real and needs your attention: your communication, your shared time together, and your feelings.

It isn't always easy to resist our hopes and expectations, many of which are born in the past: *Why can't he be like he used to be? Why won't she be the person I know she can be? Why don't I have the marriage I always thought I would have?* They are "highlight reels" of what has come before, and the "what-could-have-been" fantasies of the future. As humans, we think, create, and imagine. It is what we do. But when we embrace these imaginings too tightly, we set ourselves up for disappointment and anxiety. "The enemy of contentment," writes columnist Carolyn Hax, "is the refusal to accept your facts as facts, and to keep hoping someone will hand you different ones." [13] It once again echoes the innate wisdom of the serenity prayer in harnessing anxiety—controlling what is controllable.

# Focusing on Faults

We all know people who are quite forthright—even adept—at advising others but who can't seem to get their own act together. We may bite our tongues when they offer advice they would never take themselves. It is *always* easier to focus on others' behaviors and actions than on ourselves, and it is particularly tempting when we feel overwhelmed by our own conflicts. It is true that what we hate in others is often what we hate inside ourselves. It's called *projection*, and it remains largely unconscious, and therefore often immune to insight until we recognize its signs.

Projection is a way of protecting ourselves from uncomfortable internal conflicts. Look closely at any spouse, roommate, or work colleague, and you will find that fundamental irritations in these relationships have as much to do with the complainer as they do the complainant. In general, things only annoy us when they're also a struggle for us—a struggle we would prefer to ignore. For example, your partner's poor cleaning habits will likely only irk you when you are similarly bothered by having to clean up after yourself. Likewise, your partner's propensity to put off decisions may be a particular annoyance when you also struggle with making decisions. Do you view your partner as a control freak? Chances are good you might have control issues, too.

If we are anxious about those traits, we are more likely to notice and be bothered by them in people around us. We may try to suppress such thoughts about ourselves, but they're easily accessible when present in someone else, according to research by Roy Baumeister and his colleagues.[14] We reserve projection for our closest relationships. These people are the lens through which we understand—and come to terms—with our own issues.

Our own inadequacies can be powerful, and our inner conflicts tend to get reflected back to us in loved ones. Focusing too much on others can obscure our self-awareness and thwart anxiety's nudge to take control of what we can: ourselves. When you find your thoughts drifting towards others' behavior, gently bring yourself back to you: *What can I do about my reactions and behavior?*

## Fueling Connection

Renowned marital psychologists John and Julie Gottman advocate that the key to creating strong relationships is maintaining the quality of the couple's friendship, which is the single largest determining factor of marital satisfaction.[15] They also teach that the best protection against adversarial feelings are positive ones.[16] Their research has shown that deliberately focusing on a partner's positive qualities, noticing the small things, saying more thank yous, offering more compliments, and celebrating successes are all powerful ways of keeping marriages strong.[17]

In long-term studies of marital satisfaction, partners who see the best in their partners tend to be more tolerant of their annoyances, and they report stronger ongoing feelings of love.[18] Because no partner is perfect, positive illusions have their place in protecting love. Anthropologist and love researcher Helen Fisher has found evidence that areas of brain associated with empathy and self-control are activated when partners who are in love simply talk about their loved one.[19] Positive illusions help us stay connected, tolerate day-to-day relationship frustrations,[20] and keep us oriented toward the positives in our partner.[21]

But positive illusions can stretch too far when they are accompanied by anxiety. In an interesting study of newlyweds, wives with the most optimistic forecasts also experienced higher levels of stress and aggression toward their partners initially, and they had the steepest decline in satisfaction four years later. The authors caution that "believing that one's marriage will improve does not make it so and instead may paradoxically mask risky relationships among women."[22] Wishful thinking alone will not help much of anything, and often is a hidden driver of anxiety.

Listening carefully, sharing empathy, and being responsive are central to maintaining healthy relationships; they keep us connected to our partners. Anxiety can propel us to pay attention, to listen, to clarify, to help. What is *really* going on with our partners, rather than what we may think is going on? With poor responsiveness being a better predictor of divorce than the level of conflict, anxiety can signal hope and a desire for things to be better.[23] Relationship anxiety can thus be harnessed to facilitate connection: it signals we care and provides the energy we need to pay attention to our partner.

Touch, sexual contact, and intimacy are all well known to fuel connection and stimulate feelings of biological attachment. No matter how alone and shut down you might feel, channeling anxiety into desire and reconnection can be good for your relationship. Thanks to the cascade of attachment hormones that flood your brain during arousal and sexual stimulation, there are few things healthier for a relationship than sex.[24]

Learn your partner's buttons so you can avoid pushing them. Though it might feel satisfying in a moment of anxiety or anger to press them, it will flood your partner with activated emotion that will make finding a solution more challenging. John Gottman reminds couples that if their heart rate reaches one hundred beats per minute*, no matter how hard they try, they won't be able to listen to what is being said. Gottman advises instituting a twenty-minute break to calm someone's physiological response.[25] After emotions have returned to a more normalized place, communication should resume.

Anxiety is a normal and useful part of healthy relationships, marshalling needed attention, releasing and drawing out compassion, and motivating us to solve our issues. Whether a whisper, chatter, or yell, anxiety can keep us tending to the needs of those we care about, especially when other demands compete for our precious attention and resources.

## The Anxiety of Loss and Grief

Few experiences are scarier or more painful than facing life without someone we love. In *Social*, Matthew Lieberman explains how loss can feel like physical pain, and the links between depression and heart disease are well known. A close friend's grandmother

---

\*    For athletes, the threshold is eighty beats per minute.

unexpectedly lost her husband and experienced temporary heart failure, a condition referred to as a broken heart syndrome, also called *stress-induced cardiomyopathy*.[†26] In severe cases, this syndrome can lead to short-term heart muscle failure, yet most patients make a full recovery within weeks.[27]

She was in intensive care for ten days, had heart beats that dropped precipitously, and even flatlined once. Fortunately, a pacemaker, along with an outpouring of love and support, has helped her recover. Her story is a quite literal example of how intimately connected our emotions are to our physical health. It's no coincidence that we describe the feeling of losing love as having a "broken heart." The pain and anxiety is almost unbearable. We are drawn to love so completely that its absence is as painful as just about anything, and it scares us into thinking we can't survive without it.

Helen Fisher and neuroscientist Lucy Brown have studied the neurophysiology of love and found that love operates much like an addiction.[28] So critical is love to our survival and procreation that our capacity for addiction may be *born* from our need to fall in love and successfully rear offspring; it could be that addictions simply hijack the neural circuitry designed for love. In studying the brains of people suffering from rejection in love, they found withdrawal symptoms similar to those found in cocaine users, involving the same brain profile as being in physical pain.[29] Losing love hurts; it creates a cascade of anxiety and pain that can

---

†     This occurs almost exclusively in women.

complicate grief. At its best, that anxiety nudges us toward the support of others, fostering needed connection that helps us heal.

## Barbara

Making a life after a loss is extraordinarily challenging, especially for those in relationships that have lasted for decades. Barbara, a sixty-five-year-old widow, worked with me to resist her urges to withdraw from people when she felt alone. She had lost her husband to a stroke ten years earlier, and she still periodically wrestled with wrenching grief and missing him. She was alone, sometimes lonely, and often scared of connections that could ask too much of her.

Since her husband's death, some of her close relationships involved people who took advantage of her. She enjoyed their companionship, but she ultimately felt beleaguered by their neediness and selfish behavior. In my sessions with Barbara, we often cycled through these questions: *How can I put myself out there emotionally when I've been so disappointed? Is it worth it? What do I really need, and who can I trust?* Posing these questions helped guide her in her relationships, helping her protect herself when called for and reaching out to others when necessary.

Facing and healing from loss is something Facebook Chief Operating Officer Sheryl Sandberg, working with Adam Grant, has detailed in *Option B: Facing Adversity, Building Resilience, and Finding Joy.* It explores her experience of suddenly losing her husband to a fatal heart attack, and her path of coping with grief. Sandberg and Grant describe the importance of accepting negative feelings and "leaning into the suck… That dealing with grief is like building physical stamina: the more you exercise, the faster your heart rate recovers after it is elevated. And sometimes during especially vigorous physical activity, you discover strength you didn't know you had."[30] The anxiety of grief is like any other anxiety: a signal to focus on protecting what matters most to us, and the motivation to forge solutions. Grief requires us to do just that. Face our feelings, experience them, and use them to orient ourselves to others.

Perhaps one of the most moving stories of loss comes from a 2017 *New York Times* article written by a terminally ill woman in search of a wife for her soon-to-be widowed husband. In her article, "You May Want to Marry My Husband," which became a viral sensation, Amy Krouse Rosenthal eloquently detailed the qualities of her husband she had so valued and loved. It is a moving goodbye letter, but it is also a brilliant example of empathy—both in understanding his upcoming pain and trying to solve it down the road.[31] Her wisdom runs deep. Propelled by her obvious love and anxiety for her husband's well-being and the urgency of her illness, she doesn't just wallow in her pain: she takes action. In noticing all the wonderful things about her husband, she chose to do something for him and his future grieving self.

She died a few months later, and I took the time to listen to her TED talk, which was embedded in her obituary. In the talk, she references the power of attention and focus, and where we elect to put it.[32] Not only is her story a beautiful example of focusing on the positives of a relationship, but it is a bold expression of compassion and taking action. Rosenthal's experience is resonant because it echoes something we all seek: meaningful outlets to channel our relationship anxiety for good.

## CHAPTER FIFTEEN

# Parenting and Youth

*"The human brain is born remarkably unfinished. Instead of arriving with everything wired up—let's call it 'hardwired'—a human brain allows itself to be shaped by the details of life experience."*

—**David Eagleman,** *The Brain*[1]

**Preceding the moment of their** births, even before their conceptions, we worry about our children. Whether it is the kind of worry that is protective, or the kind that just circles back on itself, few of us escape the feeling. The expectations on modern parents are vast. Parental communities are full of resources on everything from prenatal care to breastfeeding, through playgroups, playgrounds, and preschool, into pediatrician offices and peer groups and schooling. Every phase can leave parents anxious about the next thing they should focus on and worrying whether they are doing enough.

As parents, we feel pressure to keep our kids safe, healthy, successful, and free of emotional turmoil. We care deeply about them, and we want to give them everything we can. It's not enough to give them what we had growing up, we want to give them more, and this creates an unmistakable sense of pressure. This pressure drives competition, that proverbial chase to "keep up with the Joneses." While it is seldom something we admit, parenting can become a tool to demonstrate competency and worth. It can be an insidious and often subtle trap, one that simply recognizing can help us avoid.

Paul Kershaw has labeled those parents experiencing this uptick of parental stress "Generation Squeeze."[2] We're trying to fit everything into a space that maybe can't handle it. Today's mothers and fathers are constantly juggling competing demands. It leads to a level of anxiety that is hard to use productively.

Stress management has to do with making choices, separating out what we wish were true from what actually is. If our daughter is not interested in soccer, and spends much of her time on the bench or daydreaming on the field, we should accept this reality. If we keep pushing soccer because of our own memories or because we hope she'll land an athletic scholarship, we are operating from our wishes. In this conflict between what is and what we think should be, we're hindering her potential to grow.

We are our children's first teachers and first models. Our responsibility as parents is not just in our interaction with them, but in the environment we create for them. Our own behavior—including our own anxiety—is part of that environment. As a parent, I am as neurotic as the next one, even though I know how unhelpful it is. I do a good job, while also making mistakes right and left. I do things for my kids I know I shouldn't; I forget to keep the limits I set and my supervision suffers when I get tired or distracted.

I am also a long-term worrier regarding my kids' development, so I am quick to spot a habit that could become problematic. However, I always try to keep one key thing in mind: our collective feelings. Tuning into others' feelings is powerfully grounding. I find that the more connected I am to how my family is feeling, the less my anxiety can spin into unhelpful places. No subject is taboo at the dinner table or in the car—the two places we most often discuss what's going on these days. I know communication about our thoughts and feelings is hugely important to my children's developing emotional skills and their sense of feeling understood.

## The Power of Good Enough

For those of us raising children, we must acknowledge how hard we can be on ourselves. We all want what is best for our kids, and we can be ruthless in what we expect of ourselves. I hear it so often in my work with parents, and I can easily feel it myself. Parenting becomes a heavy burden when we're not gentle with our expectations. When it comes to parental anxiety, it can be hard to remember and even harder to accept that we are doing the best we can.

Parenting is at its most challenging when we are worn out and our kids are the least cooperative: first thing in the morning, at the end of a long day, and in the middle of the night. Negative self-talk can take over at these times. As our frustration mounts, we need to remember to be gentle. We must try to be selective about the messages we absorb that we somehow have to do more, and do it better, for our kids to be happy. Believing that we aren't doing enough, or that we aren't enough as parents, can be particularly toxic.

I will never forget an evening years ago when my toddler son was crawling in the kitchen around my feet while I prepared dinner. All the electric outlets were child-proofed, the cabinets with chemicals fitted with latches, and the kitchen doors closed. I had put some of his favorite toys on the floor for him, though I suspected he'd play with other things in the kitchen, including the Tupperware cabinet and recycling bin. I noticed him reaching into the recycling, but didn't think much of it. It was usually filled with plastics and paper.

In a blink, he started howling in pain, having gotten his finger stuck in an empty, half-opened tuna can. He couldn't remove his finger without injuring it further, and it was now bleeding profusely. He was screaming, and I couldn't make it go away. Worse, it was my fault. *What in the world was I thinking? How could I have been so careless? Of course there were more things in the recycling bin than harmless plastic!*

I pulled myself together as I drove to the emergency room, cycling on the guilt, the permanent scar, the stitches, the plastic surgeon, the dread of explaining myself to the doctor. But my anxiety fueled what any parent would do—I got him there. After an initial check of his finger and a lengthy two-hour wait, we were finally seen by a doctor, and sent home with Neosporin and a Band-Aid. No stitches, no Child Protective Services case file, no permanent damage. I felt lucky that night, and I walked away with a recognition that accidents happen. And I was lucky that I would, and could, make mistakes without inflicting permanent damage. Though I needed to do my best to prevent them, I wouldn't always be able to. What mattered was how we would handle the inevitable mistakes moving forward.

Carl Winnicott was a pediatrician and writer who spent his career working with families advocating for "the good enough mother." He understood the negative impact unrealistic standards have on parenting and the shame that results. "Good enough" allows for mistakes, imperfections, and humanity. He warned that aiming for perfection in parenting was detrimental in many ways to the kids as well; it sets an impossibly high standard that they internalize.[3] We can't teach our kids how to accept their struggles if we don't model the same. We may feel anxious that we're not doing every little thing, catching every little problem, or solving every little issue. But this type of anxiety is a negative spiral. Cultivating a standard of *good enough* can provide a powerful ballast against the pressures that threaten our sense of balance. It's also one of the most lasting things we can impart to our children.

## Empathy and Attachment

Parenting is at its most effective is grounded in empathy. Empathy is a quality of reviewing and experiencing situations through others' lenses. As parents, we must think about *their* experiences, not just ours. A UK study on social anxiety disorder found that "children are more likely to be anxious when their parents direct criticism at them, display high levels of doubt, and are emotionally cold."[4]

If we love our children, and we want that love to translate, we need to ensure that our love includes considering their desires and emotional needs. Never underestimate the power of simply letting your child know you understand how they feel and showing them affection. There is power in bearing witness to our children's pains, even if there is sometimes nothing we can do to solve them.

Any connected parent has had that feeling of being hurt for our children in a way that is almost unbearable. If we could, we'd absorb all of it for them. When my daughter was in sixth grade, I was late picking her up from school one day. As I was pulling in, I saw a mother of one of her friends and eight friends leaving the school together. This woman's daughter's birthday was that day, and I knew immediately what was happening. My daughter had not been invited to the party. Not only was she excluded, but she had to watch all her friends leave together. As I pulled in, I saw her standing alone, trying to put on a brave face.

When my daughter finally reached my car, she exploded into tears. She felt so betrayed and my heart broke for her. I wanted to fix it, racing over in my mind how to make it better, but all I could really do was bear witness and support her. I hugged her tightly and let her know how horrible I knew she felt: the rejection, the surprise, and the humiliation of sitting there alone. As I held her there in the car, her sobbing slowed and her tears eventually subsided. The pain was real—and she was getting through it. The most important thing I could do was to let her know she could handle it, and we'd get through it together.

In the face of anxiety, empathy is fundamental in making sure we respond appropriately and help use it to its highest advantage. Empathy is the glue that bonds us to our kids and them to us. It's also the gateway to effective helping and compromises. This is where poor attunement—not being in touch with our children's fears and anxieties—can wreak havoc in a family. Understanding our children's experience helps ground us in what they need; this is how we support their evolving coping skills.

Empathy is hugely important in mitigating anxiety both in parents and kids. Parents need to be careful to not respond to their kids' anxiety with their own—skipping over their kids' experiences in the name of helping execute a solution. The best solutions involve solutions and empathy. Empathy might be one of the most powerful things we can offer an anxious child—the validation of their feelings, the message that we understand, and the signal they can handle it.

*Load sharing* refers to the sharing of stress across a close relationship. In one revealing study, mothers were told to either touch or not touch their daughters' hands before the daughters had to give public speeches. The physical contact alone was enough to lower the stress responses of the daughters; in relationships deemed to be of higher quality, the contact wasn't even necessary—the mere presence of the mothers activated the load sharing.[5]

It is normal for anxiety to arise in our parenting. However, what we do with it can make the difference between helping and hindering our children. It's important to let our anxiety propel empathy and healthy attachment. Too much anxiety can cloud our ability to empathize, but the right amount bonds us to our children, and allows us to shoulder some of our kids' emotional burdens.

The first two years of life, considered a critical "growth spurt" for the developing brain, are heavily influenced by attachment. The more securely children attach to their parents, the stronger their brain development and ability to regulate their emotions.[6] Researcher Beatrice Beebe has intensively documented video (frame by frame—to the millisecond) of parent/infant interactions. Her films capture small interactions between mother and child, "remarkably beautiful moments, such as both partners rising up and up into glorious sunbursts of smiles. It also reveals very disturbing moments, such as maternal anger or disgust faces, or infants becoming frantically distressed or frozen in alarm."[7]

Though these interactions cannot be seen by the naked eye, they are very much affecting an infant's sense of attunement and connection, influencing the child's later development. We can't control every minor interaction with our child; the best we can do is operate from a place of empathy. Showing our children that we understand and can tolerate their experiences teaches them they can do the same for themselves: our empathy gets internalized to help them face adversity later. If we build off an intention to understand our children's experiences, rather than judge or change them, the support we give will be enough for our children to hold themselves up as they grow and face the world on their own.

## Eleanor

Pregnancy and birth can be stressful for a mother, but so can the aftermath. Postpartum anxiety (PPA) is real, and multiple studies have shown that PPA is more common than its more recognized counterpart, postpartum depression. However, because it's not as well known, it often goes untreated. Scientists have debated PPA's causes, but they "suspect that the lack of sleep and fluctuating hormone levels that come with being a new mom may be at play."[8] It would be strange *not* to have anxiety about bringing a living being into the world whom we are duty- and chemically-bound to protect.

When Eleanor first had her daughter, she battled high blood pressure and panic attacks around imagined calamities. By the time her child was around six months old, she had developed a dark imagination: "I can't help but imagine catastrophe," she told me, horrors like a car driving off the side of a cliff. Her mind was trying to work through her anxiety. Instead of aiming to "let it go," replacing a negative with nothing, we worked on imagining a substitute story.

Think of anxiety as a burst of energy we cannot stop but can direct. It's a car with a brick on the gas pedal or a train with the controls stuck. We can steer the wheel or switch the track. When your mind is going to something that will exacerbate your anxiety, you have to change the story, and insert something more likely, different, or positive.

Eleanor and I got to the heart of where these imaginary fixations were coming from. She had a fear of calamity striking at any moment, just as it had in her pregnancy and premature delivery. Recognizing the impulse and emotion as real—even if the imaginings were not—helped her embrace them. Once those were better understood, it became easier for her to exert control over her thoughts and influence them.

## The Carousel of Parenthood

With each developmental stage a child reaches, new challenges reveal themselves. Right about the time we establish a routine that works, a new phase emerges. When kids reach school age, our worries shift from supporting their physical development to their cognitive and social development. *Is my daughter picking up math fast enough? Is my son playing with other kids on the playground? Can he throw and catch a ball? Can she hold a pencil and write?*

Then, we wake up one day and our kids are adolescents. We transition to a supporting role, being there to encourage and pick up the pieces when needed. Hormones are changing their physical bodies every day, and their neural connections are multiplying fast, at a rate comparable to those of an infant.

Adolescence is a time of creativity and power as well as a time of "great boundary pushing that can be challenging and create catastrophes," writes psychologist Daniel Siegel in *Brainstorm*, his book about the teenage brain. "But this pushing back propensity can also be a remarkably positive, essential part of our lives."[9] Adolescents push away from their parents and toward their peers as they begin to define themselves.

As life gets increasingly complicated with increasing demands and responsibilities, adolescents step up, make their own decisions, and face their own consequences. Anxiety is always part of this mix. How can we *not* worry when our child gets behind the wheel of a car? Or goes out on his or her first date?

But anxiety can also alert us to the need to loosen our grip, respect their boundaries, and allow our emerging adults to earn our trust. We want our teens to grow into responsible adults, and anxiety is there to remind us to back off when we overstep and fail at trying to control too much. Teens need our support, not our control, as they pull away, stumble, and succeed on their own terms.

As parents, anxiety accompanies the transition to every new developmental stage as we are stretched to grow as parents just as our children grow. Trusting our instincts, and our worry, becomes a well-tuned resource for navigating the ever-shifting demands of parenting.

# Marie

There is no operation manual for parenting's constantly shifting landscape. With clients who have parental anxiety, I ultimately bring them back to using their anxiety and trusting their instincts. Marie struggled to juggle the demands of two teens with learning disabilities, which she did impressively. She carried an irrational anxiety that she couldn't handle the pressure. Because it wasn't easy, she confused the effort it took, and the fatigue she regularly felt, with not being a good enough parent.

Within that feeling was the rational anxiety that kept her focused on balancing everything properly. There was also the quiet whisper of anxiety when she neglected her own needs too much, and she became vulnerable to feeling taken advantage of. Sometimes this whisper turned into a yell—letting her know it's time to focus on herself, even briefly. An ongoing focus of our work was sorting through her anxieties and directing her energy toward greater balance between her responsibilities and her own needs.

# Anxiety in Our Children

> *"The little world of childhood with its familiar surroundings is a model of the greater world. The more intensively the family has stamped its character upon the child, the more it will tend to feel and see its earlier miniature world again in the bigger world of adult life."*
>
> —Carl Jung[10]

Anxiety is not something reserved just for adults. Children demonstrate a variety of anxious behaviors ranging from normal to problematic. Worries, fears, shyness, phobias, nightmares, and sensitivity are among the many examples of heightened anxiety in kids. Sometimes anxiety isn't always obvious, and it's not always clear to parents, even involved parents, what may be going on. One European study determined that "parents consistently underestimate the intensity of their children's fears."[11] Even a loving parent might stigmatize anxiety and deny what his/her child is experiencing.

In the absence of being able to understand or govern these new uncomfortable feelings, kids look to their parents. With so little of their environment within their control, children are exposed to the stressors without the solutions. This is where we need to step in. As parents, our role is not to protect children from anxiety or convince them to shut it out. Rather, our job is to notice their anxiety as quickly as possible, work with them to name it, and help them cope. It's so easy to tell a child, "Oh, don't worry about that" or "You have nothing to be afraid of," which does little to help our kids. Belittling their fears teaches them to mistrust and avoid their emotions.

Children gain strength from learning to name their fears. Helping kids to label their feelings could be one of the most important things we can do as parents. Young children who can label their feelings have better social behavior, emotional control, and academic competence than children who can't describe their experiences.[12]

According to Patricia Pearson, author of *Anxiety: A Brief*

*History… of Yours and Mine*, "One thing anxious children lack in this culture that has traditionally been granted to them is what psychologists call a 'recipe' for dealing with their dread… An *action* that can be undertaken to offset the almost unendurable feeling of helplessness that characterizes anxiety."[13] Naming their experiences allows kids the control they crave, and it delivers the tools they need to cope.

## The Sensitive Child

Particularly sensitive kids—known as "high reactive"—can experience a significant amount of distress, along with an exaggerated arousal to it. It was once commonly held that temperament was something you were born with—it was part of a child's *nature* and nothing *nurture* could really change. However, modern science has debunked the false dichotomy, demonstrating that they feed into each other: nurture *shapes* nature.[14]

Parents and teachers are critical "brain changers,"* powerful influencers in a child's development, especially regarding stress and anxiety. Research has shown that stress sensitivity and anxiety activation is influenced through experiences—kids who learn to cope with moderate stress fare best.[15] If kids can learn to tolerate imperfection and discomfort, it will build their resilience. If they feel supported and loved, they will navigate these moments more deftly.

In these sensitive children, it's important for parents to

---

*      I first heard this phrase used in a lecture given by Sheila Walker and Bill Stixrud.

cultivate a feeling of acceptance for their natural states—rather than forcing them into some false sense of bravery. Their sensitivity is indeed a strength; it motivates and drives them toward others.[16] Encouraging sensitive children to embrace what makes them special can help them identify the usefulness of their anxiety.

## Being Different

For many children, feeling different is a consistent source of anxiety—as it was for me. Whether it was my health issues, food allergies, or my awkwardly tall build that ensured I was picked last in every game, I always felt different. Slow and uncoordinated, I faked my way through what I could, and I tried hard to get by without standing out.

Looking back, I'm glad I had these challenges that taught me I had to keep trying. Quitting just wasn't an option, as much as I wished it were. Avoiding these sources of anxiety would have compounded them and kept me from developing the skills to face future challenges with courage and perspective.

Dawn Huebner, author of *What to Do When You Worry Too Much*, teaches kids and parents how to cope with childhood anxieties by recognizing the fears that aren't likely and gradually working *toward* them. Afraid of bee stings or going upstairs in the dark? Know that your fear is not the same as being in danger and that gradually you can bravely face the outdoors or a dark basement. Like astronauts learn in their training, fear is not the same as danger.

Facing down our childhood fears is deciding not to grow them by avoiding them. We should face them, name them, and consciously experience them so we get used to them. As Huebner explains, it's like adjusting to a cold pool. The temperature doesn't change, we get used to it.[17] And if we're lucky, we even enjoy it— and can't wait to get back in.

## Preadolescence and Middle School

As children age into adolescence, their worlds start to orient away from their parents and toward their peers. Not every child knows how to make and keep friends, and social exclusion can be especially painful. Bullying at this stage, when sensitivities are so profoundly felt, can be especially devastating. Kids are shedding their childhood skins and are often so self-absorbed they lack sensitivity to those around them.

Bruce McEwen has studied the stress response across developmental stages in animals, explaining that puberty is associated with increased physical and neurological development as well as increases in the stress response compared with adults.[18] Animal studies confirm what most parents of preadolescents know: stress responses are more acute and prolonged in early adolescence.

Life simply feels more dramatic and stress is felt more intensely and for longer periods. With maturity, these painful periods fade; part of growing up is learning how to respond in proportion and learning to take anxiety in stride. But the wounds of youth can linger, and the immature habits of coping can persist.

So important are social skills to our healthy development and mental health that *Social* author Matthew Lieberman envisions a time when school curricula will include social skills training for classrooms.[19] Keeping kids in the arena of trying is crucial at this developmental stage as well. As parents or caregivers, we do not want to appease the instinct for avoidance under the false idea that we are protecting our children.

In *The Confidence Code,* authors Katty Kay and Claire Shipman note that in early adolescence, girls show a greater drop in confidence and are six times more likely to drop off sports teams than boys, a phenomenon that appears correlated with an imbalance in confidence that follows women into adulthood.[20] The authors discuss the critical role social anxiety can play in inhibiting confidence in girls. Without encouragement to take calculated risks, and strategies to assure social connection, anxiety can lead to avoidance.

Girl Scout survey data confirm these results and provide interesting clues to why this might be. In surveying leadership attitudes and barriers for leadership development in almost four thousand girls, almost half (45 percent) of youth not interested in leadership cited simply not wanting to speak in front of others, whereas a third attributed their lack of leadership motivation to a "fear of being laughed at, making people mad at them, coming across as bossy, or not being liked by people."[21]

The challenge of adolescence is to use anxiety to make relationships stronger, solve problems, and stretch. Forging a new path will involve anxiety—this is how we know we care. Anxiety isn't a stop sign or something to be avoided. It's a caution sign we can teach kids to use to protect the things they care about most.

## School Performance

One area that can prompt anxiety in school-age children and preteens is school performance, test-taking in particular. But some research suggests test anxiety can actually be a strength harnessed for performance. One study has found that people who have good memories and who get anxious actually perform better in exams. Dr. Matthew Owens, who led the study, says the results "suggest that there are times when a little bit of anxiety can actually motivate you to succeed."[22]

In another study, researchers explored how labeling and communicating our anxiety can be beneficial. They found "that a brief intervention—writing about their anxiety about the upcoming exams—helped students to do better in the exam. Perhaps by acknowledging their fears, students were able to tame distracting emotions."[23] It's yet another example of when the anxiety can be channeled into performance, rather than being perceived as a hindrance.

## Being Watched and Judged

As a mother of two millennials, I have a front-row seat to the unique pressures facing today's youth. They must manage the same stresses as my generation did, but on a vastly broader, and often public, platform. Their every move is noted, described, and commented on via social media, and the pressure to keep up is enormous. Not only are they living their lives, but they are documenting them and managing their own public relations at the same time. Their social time is no longer reserved to when they see friends or have time to talk on their phones. Because of the ubiquity of smartphones, those lives are always going on, in their pockets, waiting to be updated and responded to.

The ubiquity of anxiety, especially social anxiety, is more understandable than surprising. Teens are defined by their relationships with peers and the anxiety of being left out or rejected looms large. Think about the difficulty that comes from any kind of failure or challenge. Then think about how much harder it is to go through it with everybody watching and sharing their thoughts on it in real time.

Our youth are saddled with expectations we can't even imagine, with social media exacerbating so many of their fears and worries. They are hungry for our empathy and guidance, rather than our judgment. Eighty-two percent of teenagers told a significant lie to their parents in the past year.[24] Yes, sometimes they tell a lie to avoid punishment, but a study out of Pennsylvania State University conducted by Drs. Nancy Darling and Linda Caldwell found the most common reason children and teenagers lie to their parents is to not disappoint them.[25]

Bodies transform, friends change, school and extracurricular demands rise; teenagers experience anxiety as a natural state of being. All this happens while the adolescent brain is still learning *how* to notice what's happening and how to make good decisions under these conditions. Peer opinion and perception become central as kids rely on their peers to define who they will become.

Teenagers have greater social anxiety than adults, which can be reflected on a physiological level. In a study run by David Eagleman, volunteers sat in a shop window to be stared at by passersby. He measured the galvanic skin response (GSR), essentially what a lie-detector does, which he calls "a useful proxy for anxiety." Adults showed a stress response, but for the teenagers "that same experience caused social emotions to go into overdrive: the teens were much more anxious—some to the point of trembling—while they were being watched."[26]

Not surprisingly, social acceptance triggers motivational and reward centers in the adolescent brain.[27] These motivational circuits nudge them toward their goals, as they do for all of us. Anxiety is a key part of this journey: learning to use it constructively can be critical to navigating this developmental time.

## The Young Adult Mind-Set

Data from Cambridge show that people under thirty-five are suffering more anxiety than other age groups, and their anxiety has steadily risen.[28] I've often been asked by journalists to speculate on why younger people are more anxious, and I always cite the litany of huge pressures they feel. Those in their twenties and early thirties may not yet have all the responsibility of an adult life, but they have the pressure to identify, shape, and create that life.

They are at the starting line of adulthood, making choices that will impact them—and their future families—for decades to come. Think about all the undecided factors that burgeoning adults must address: school, career, geography, friends, dating, marriage, family goals, and financial independence. Established adults may look back on this time in their lives nostalgically and fondly, but we'd be rewriting our own history to claim we were at ease back then.

"Anxiety has now surpassed depression as the most common mental health diagnosis among college students,"[29] according to a recent study on college campuses. "More than half of students visiting campus clinics cite anxiety as a health concern."[30] There's evidence to think this generation is having an even harder time coping with pressures. According to the American Psychological Association (APA), millennials, those who have come of age in the twenty-first century, have not "developed proper learning strategies for managing stress," with self-report levels of stress substantially higher than what they consider "average" or "healthy."[31]

## Sam

Sam was a college senior when he first came to see me for help with ongoing anxiety that had recently "flared up." A dedicated journalism student, he was having trouble staying calm as he anticipated the second half of the year when he would have to face finding a job and wrapping up a college experience that had been "ideal." He was having difficulty concentrating on his schoolwork, and he noticed a new kind of social anxiety creeping into his relationships with his peers. He was afraid he was losing his confidence, and he wanted help before it got worse, which had happened during his senior year in high school.

Many standard treatments would aim to contain this most recent "relapse" through a variety of coping strategies aimed at reducing his anxiety symptoms. But we took a different tack: What if we didn't view his anxiety as a mental health relapse? What if his anxiety could be understood as a signal for him to focus on the new and important tasks at hand? What if the anxiety could also be the energy and motivation he needed to solve them? What if his daydreaming about a future job that was distracting him from his schoolwork were an invitation to devote attention to his future?

Could it be that his anxiety flared while playing video games with his best friend was not discomfort, but rather dread about his friend moving thousands of miles away after school, forever changing what had been his social anchor for four years? In viewing his anxiety "flare ups" as signals rather than a symptom, we not only sidestepped him viewing himself a victim of a relapse, but we opened up new ways for him to think about and embrace his anxiety. He could now harness its motivation for growth. He had work to do, and his anxiety was doing its best to keep him on track.

Of course, as we grow into adulthood, our anxiety doesn't vanish but rather refocuses on the big issues we all must face. In the next chapter, we'll take a look at some of the big issues outside of the home that trigger our anxiety and places where we can make our anxiety work for us.

## CHAPTER SIXTEEN

# Work, Money, and Success

*"Money, fame, and influence may be valued more as tokens of—and means to—love rather than ends in themselves."*

—**Alain De Botton, *Status Anxiety***[1]

## Sarah

Sarah woke up nauseated every morning, wondering how she would get through the workday. She was leading a huge project at work—an opportunity she had wanted for some time—but she was wrestling with feelings of inadequacy. Though honored to have the opportunity to climb the company's ladder, she secretly dreaded the work itself. The anxiety had spiked so much that she was considering changing careers.

Her morning anxiety had become a constant struggle, and

her fight to ignore it was making it worse. At the office, Sarah was pushing herself further than she could handle, and her productivity was suffering. Each morning as she readied for another workday, she could only think of how to push herself *harder*. She viewed anxiety as a barrier to be overcome rather than as a directional signal.

In our sessions, Sarah became aware that her efforts were not as efficient as they could be. For one, she had "lone wolf" tendencies, believing that she had to do everything herself. Her reputation and advancement were on the line, but the limits of this approach were revealing themselves.

She set about using her anxiety to solve the problem it was signaling. She needed to learn how to work smarter, not harder— to tweak her process, not her job. She was doing too much, and she was not utilizing her team to the best of its capacity. We worked to find a few strategies: requiring twice daily contact with her subordinates to review the day's to-do list and assign tasks, communicating her progress and asking the same of her teammates, and taking on only the highest and best use of her skills as manager.

As she made these changes, Sarah's morning nausea diminished. The day became manageable and less of an impending avalanche. Interestingly she felt *more in control* of the project as she relinquished control. She gave herself permission to not do everything herself; with that decision, she felt freer to keep going.

# Holding Off the Irrational

Many of us spend half of our waking life—if not more—at work, a place that can magnify our anxieties. At work, anxiety attaches itself to the day-to-day—getting an important task done, managing responsibilities against time pressures, and solving issues with a boss or coworkers. It also latches on to big-picture considerations like career advancement, retirement, and the future. Anxiety's alarm is just awareness of the things you care about as well as the motivation to protect them. It's breaking the glass, pulling the fire alarm, and handing you the extinguisher.

An important strategy for using your anxiety—especially around work issues—is to tease apart rational and irrational anxiety. Irrational anxiety is *I'm not good enough, I'm a failure, I can't handle this.* Aim to continually redirect those into rational thoughts—*I am good enough. Though I have failed here, I am not a failure,* and *I may not want to but I can handle it.*

Label the irrational, and put it aside, so it doesn't flash into crippling anxiety. Once you've determined what the rational anxieties are—*I am unemployed and have bills to pay. I don't know what work is out there but let me look. What have I learned to help me in this situation?*—you can use them. Our anxiety becomes a form of intuition, a manifestation of our "gut."

Once it's managed and heard, anxiety can then become the fuel to help us achieve. Researchers have recently shown that we perform best when we feel a moderate amount of stress and anxiety. Many performers and athletes recognize that their stress, when channeled properly, can act as a motivator and a performance booster. This is a physiological fact. Acute stress helps to "prime" the brain for better performance.[2]

Claudia Batten, a noted entrepreneur and friend, describes anxiety as a constant companion when it comes to innovating and risk-taking. There comes a time in innovating where one must so believe in one's path that we choose courage over anxiety, and take a bold leap from which there is no turning back. This is both invigorating and scary at the same time. Anxiety, and its power, is a part of our continual self-creation.[3]

Growth comes from being stretched. Mihaly Csikszentmihalyi, author of the groundbreaking book *Flow*, notes that we perform best when our stress combines with effort to drive an intrinsically rewarding state. Csikszentmihalyi even speculates that inside this state is where we are most happy. "The best moments in our lives are not the passive, receptive, relaxing times…" he writes. "The best moments usually occur if a person's body or mind is stretched to its limits in a voluntary effort to accomplish something difficult and worthwhile."[4]

What Hans Selye called *eustress*, the positive kind of stress, can help you achieve a state of flow, a heightened sense of awareness and complete absorption into an activity. "Some anxiety in the face of stress can be a good thing," a *Science* magazine article on anxiety in the workplace explains. "It helps us work harder, prepare more thoroughly, and perform with more intensity."[5]

However, the idea that if we could just clear our to-do lists then we'd be happy is a myth that we sell ourselves. Despite the anticipation that we can only relax when we clear our plate, people are actually happier when they are busier—if it's the right kind of busy. This is borne by that the fact that retirement increases the risk of depression by 40 percent, and there's a demonstrable connection between work and personal well-being.[6] Work is not a break from who we are. It's an arena where we work to be the best version of ourselves while engaging challenges and growing. And this can be an optimal experience.

## Patrick

Anxiety can also act as that whisper in the office when we know something isn't right, we are disappointing someone, or we have a bad feeling about where things are headed. This type of anxiety invites us to take note of what's happening and devote more thought and resources to our strategy. It alerts us to the realities of our situation and prompts us to take strategic action.

Patrick was a generous person who carried low self-esteem about his appearance. He was socially awkward and admitted that he was not a great communicator or advocate for himself. Holding a key position in accounting for a national political group, he struggled to please everyone: he was up at dawn, in the office until 10:00 p.m., emailing with his bosses and team until past midnight.

As things heated up at work, and more and more was piled on his desk, he started to miss details. His direct supervisors got on him for these occasional mistakes, more than he felt was merited considering how much he did. Patrick lacked the confidence to defend himself and started to feel anxious about being

sidelined at his organization—or even replaced. His inability
to demand respect set up a feedback loop where he was getting
stepped on regularly.

Weeks passed and projects were taken away from him. Then,
right around the time an outside consultant was brought in to
the workplace, Patrick was given a demotion. The consultant was
particularly hard on Patrick, criticizing him for not managing his
time well. The frustration built, as Patrick had been taking on
other people's workloads and was now being punished for it. Low
self-esteem kept Patrick feeling ashamed and inadequate. He had
gotten to the point where he wanted to leave the job—tired of
being overwhelmed and under respected.

While looking for another job was certainly an option, I
worked with Patrick on managing his current situation. What
could he learn from digging himself out of this space that he had
cocreated? How could he tolerate this discomfort and find what
he had control of? We worked on keeping him grounded so his
anxiety wouldn't wash him away. The goal was for him to take
control, find solutions for work challenges, and learn when self-ad-
vocacy is necessary.

Patrick and I worked to locate opportunities for him to stand
up for himself, to set more limits, and to plan and prepare for the
challenges that overwhelmed him. He was taking control of what
he could, implementing better time-management systems for
particularly tedious tasks, and avoiding the trap of focusing on
other people's behavior. Over time he learned to let his anxiety
breathe—not to fight it—so he could stretch his limitations and

steer toward more effective solutions. Mostly, even as it was hard, he learned to work through challenges without immediately running away. With better boundaries and improved confidence, he was soon ready to seize a new opportunity when it came along and translate his new skills into a fresh professional start.

## Common Workplace Anxieties

**Procrastination** at work is something many of my clients struggle with. One of the hidden reasons we procrastinate is that we're afraid of failing. We don't want to head down a road that will reveal ourselves as failures—to ourselves and others—so we don't even get started. Sometimes we don't even know where to begin. "Courage is not the absence of fear," James Neil Hollingworth said, "but rather the judgment that something else is more important than fear."[7] Knowing where to start, designing manageable steps, and attaching to the greater purpose of the task all can help you muster the courage to begin.

Another common reason for work avoidance is **fear of completion**—we don't want to engage with the next step. By not starting, we are delaying its unpleasant result. Of course, there's also the procrastination that comes from just not feeling like doing it; we don't think it's worth our time or it makes us miserable. The cure here is finding the joy—even if it's small. Even if the only joy is in taking ownership and putting ourselves back in the driver's seat. Recognizing the source of the procrastination is helpful in fueling a way out of our feelings of being stuck.

**Distractions** cause anxiety by interrupting and confusing our attention. As we are pulled away from a task, anxiety escalates. It fires because our hijacked attention puts our original task—what we care about—at risk. Multitasking, as tempting as it may be, has decidedly been proven to be a myth and our attention can only be in one place at a time. [8] So when our singular focus is drawn away, it is anxiety's job to pull us back.

(Writing this book, or working on any large project, are good examples of the challenge to juggle time blocks and the predictable distractions to our attention. Whether away from email, my family, or my own fatigued attention, anxiety has repeatedly hauled me back to the project.)

The trick to managing distractions is to plan for them, limit them as much as possible, and make room for them in places where you can. Setting time limits, availability limits, saying no, turning off email notifications, and shutting your door are all are helpful in wrestling back what might be our most precious commodity: our attention.

**Performance Anxiety** can also be a significant occupational stressor, as mandatory presentations, group meetings, and performance reviews can invite the familiar anxious spiral of *I can't handle it*. Accommodating external demands and expectations can be stressful, and how we think about them matters a great deal. Viewing demands as challenges rather than traps helps us take control where we can and channel our stress productively. A bit of performance pressure can help keep us in a state of optimal challenge, or *flow*, as we discussed earlier.

In survey after survey, public speaking always lands at the top of people's lists of fears—ahead of death.[9] I believe the best salve for speaking anxiety is to clue into what the audience wants, what you are *giving* them, or even better, how you are helping them. The fear of rejection is obliterated by connection. When we think of others, we get out of our own head and approach the situation from a place of empathy and perspective.

Finally, an all-too-common workplace stressor many clients face is **interpersonal conflict** with coworkers. Our interactions at work can be as impactful to our well-being as those with loved ones. As we discussed in chapter 13, those we associate with can powerfully impact our anxiety and overall functioning. Few relationships can be as stressful as those at work, where most of us log regular and long hours together, share the workplace burdens, and often feel little real control over the dynamics of the group. One difficult colleague or client can add stress to a workday, leaving a team feeling frustrated and overly anxious.

## Difficult People

Whether we are dealing with a narcissistic coworker, a passive-aggressive assistant, or a controlling boss, the workplace always presents social challenges. The human dynamics of a workplace can add a heavy burden of anxiety to simply doing our jobs. Just like we don't pick our families, we can't always pick our coworkers; we just have to adapt and cope.

Worries about coworkers' perceptions or reactions is one the most common things my clients mention when discussing their workplace anxiety. We can't control how they view us, which is often at odds with how we view ourselves or how we'd *like* to be viewed. A coworker looking to advance his or her agenda insinuates we aren't competent, and it sinks in a little. A boss neglects to give a deadline but then blames you for not turning in something sooner. A colleague steals an idea and fails to give proper credit.

We put ourselves at the mercy of a workplace and don't have the ability to detach and walk away. We have to find ways to get the job done where we are. Wishing for a different situation may help clarify what we want, but it never solves anything. The trick is to exploit the control we have, and find better ways to work with outside forces—and other people—toward a shared goal.

This means focusing on what we can control and keeping in mind what *is* rather than what *we would like it to be*. A coworker looking to advance her agenda by belittling our efforts will have a harder time doing so when we clearly communicate our contributions to the entire team. If we have a flighty boss who blames us for missing deadlines she forgets to communicate, we can ask her questions about timing when she assigns us a task, preferably in writing. A colleague who promotes our work as his own should become someone with whom you avoid sharing ideas and thoughts with in the future. Such compromises are solutions within our control. They break the cycle of behaviors and patterns at work that are keeping us from being our best.

# Growing through Failure

Somewhere along the way, we have been sold the idea that success comes without pain or uncertainty. We seldom think about how accomplishments are often achieved alongside feelings of doubt, error, and inadequacy. In the process, we forget how integral failure is to success.

"What did you fail at today?" entrepreneur Sara Blakely's father used to ask her at the dinner table when she was growing up. If there was no failure, there was no learning, and he was disappointed. Blakely is now the billionaire founder of Spanx, and she credits this approach with her success. "Failure for me became not trying versus the outcome,"[10] Blakely now says, aware of the poignancy of her father's question. J. K. Rowling, whose Harry Potter series was rejected by twelve publishers before becoming a worldwide phenomenon, echoed this sentiment in her Harvard University commencement speech: "Failure taught me things about myself that I could have learned no other way."[11]

Sometimes the anxiety we feel about failing can be turned outward, stimulating the extra motivation we need to perform at our best. Concern about falling short of our goals can help us dig in a bit more when we might wish we were finished, just as our fear of disappointing a boss or client can spur the impulse to stay focused just a little longer or take a bit more time. Worry about failure can be a useful form of anxiety so long as it is channeled into productive action.

## Reaching Across the Cubicle

As social beings, there is no place we can escape our need for connection. For those of us who work in an office, we must remember that we are part of a community—and we should take advantage of it. The impulse to draw inward is understandable, especially for the socially anxious, but it is ultimately counterproductive.

"Studies show that each positive interaction employees have during the course of the work day actually helps return the cardiovascular system back to resting levels," writes Shawn Achor in *The Happiness Advantage.* "[O]ver the long haul, employees with more of these interactions become protected from the negative effects of job strain."[12] If you are a freelancer or work from home, find ways to connect with others in your industry or company. That reaching out will provide you with a dose of resilience and support that you might not even recognize you need.

In addition, working with others can also improve our performances. Collaboration can bring out parts of ourselves that haven't been needed or compensate for areas where we need improvement. According to Stanford University's School of Business, innovation is at its best when it is the product of small groups working together to identify key problems and develop new solutions. Design thinking is based on the premise that intuition and deep thinking start with a willingness to face the emotions of a problem. Indeed, the first step of design thinking is empathy. Before a problem is even defined, it must first be understood emotionally, an approach that echoes how we understand ourselves.[13]

As for bosses who are looking to make their office a little less stressful—remember your employees need to know where they stand. "Social rank can cause stress, especially where rankings are unstable and people are jockeying for position."[14] Office politics are known to stimulate extraneous anxiety and erode professional confidence, a well-known predictor of success that can make up for skill deficits.[15] Offices that run on intimidation and fear sacrifice productivity and the boss may not even know it.

## Control at Work

Though executives will always claim to be more stressed than low-level employees, stress has often been correlated with how *little* control we have.[16] Think back to the commuters who were more stressed than the fighter pilots—the same applies for the workplace. Having an internal sense of control has been shown to predict not just job satisfaction and performance,[17] but our overall health. In *Why Zebras Don't Get Ulcers,* Robert Sapolsky cites the studies that show negative health effects from "the killer combination of high demand and low control—you have to work hard, a lot is expected of you, and you have minimal control over the process."[18]

At work, just like in our lives, we are all looking a sense of purpose. Psychology professor Paul Spector calls having not enough to do *underload*, which can "cause many of the physical discomforts we associate with being overloaded, like muscle tension, stomachaches, and headaches."[19]

Boredom at the office is a frustration with not serving a

useful purpose or having agency over what we are doing. Daniel Goleman, in his book *Focus*, finds that management, and the workers themselves, would do well to focus on "evoking a sense of purpose and adding a dollop of pressure."[20]

## The Role of Play

Mihaly Csikszentmihalyi also examined what he terms the artificial separation between work and play. "There is no reason to believe any longer that only irrelevant 'play' can be enjoyed," he writes in *Beyond Boredom and Anxiety,* "while the serious business of life must be born as a burdensome cross. Once we realize that the boundaries between work and play are artificial, we can take matters in hand and begin the difficult task of making life more livable."[21] Making time for play means choosing activities that we do for their own sake, not just for their outcomes.

According to play expert Stuart Brown, play is an essential part of creativity and stimulating one's brain: "Nothing lights up the brain like play. Three-dimensional play fires up the cerebellum, puts a lot of impulses into the frontal lobe—the executive portion—[and] helps contextual memory be developed." When we play, we practice cooperation, self-control, and altruism, and we feel connected and happy. "The opposite of play is not work," Brown emphasizes, "it's depression."[22]

# Risks of Pushing Too Far

Especially for overachievers, recognizing one's limits and internal signals to rest are critical. Big gains require big risks, and anxiety is *always* part of the picture. Getting comfortable with discomfort in many ways is a requisite of being successful in innovation and growth. But there is a downside: According to a study from University of California, San Francisco, 30 percent of all entrepreneurs experience depression.[23] Without rest and balance, too much anxiety scrambles and hinders our performance, and it tips moderate anxiety into the debilitating kind. Feeling overwhelmed is our signal we have pushed ourselves too far, and we need to rest to restore our capacity and performance.

Like an inflated balloon, capacity can't be stretched indefinitely without consequence. Lines become limits, and we are all subject to them when it comes to how much anxiety we can absorb and use productively. Where and how clear these lines are have more to do with self-care and balance than innate capacity.

I'm reminded of my friend Ann, a businesswomen and entrepreneur who had reached a point of maximum stretching, especially after a partner dropped out of a major project and left her holding the bag. Though she often felt her anxiety was a useful booster, it had now become crippling. She was on overdrive and had no idea how to stop or even slow down. It had reached a point where channeling it was simply not possible.

Ann was overwhelmed by the constancy of her anxiety, and without some self-care, she was going to crash. The answer was

simple—even simplistic—but it worked. She took control of
something small.

Recently, Ann had been wrestling with how broken down
and unattractive she felt. She decided to reschedule her workday,
"embrace the feminine," and among other self-care items, she
did her makeup—and it worked. She embraced being gentle
and created space in her day or the personal needs she had been
neglecting. In pulling back, she found the energy for herself for the
rest of that day she needed to get back on track. I checked in with
her a week later, and then a week after that, and the small decision
and action had successfully reset her. It was both an efficient use of
her time—doing less led to more—and an empowering recognition that she *could* handle things. Her life wouldn't collapse if she
took a break and some time for herself. In the end, it was less the
action itself than the decision to allow herself a break that reset her
back on course.

## Financial Anxiety

Money is one area of life that can attract a substantial amount of
anxiety for almost all of us—and the upcoming generation seems
to be struggling with it even more so. Surveys find that millennials
are experiencing higher rates of financial anxiety than other age
groups. More than half report feeling high to moderate anxiety
about losing their jobs, which is almost double that of the general
population.[24] For millennials, the conflict between the instinct to
save and the urge to spend is spiking their anxiety to a point that

it is hurting their job performance, mood, and close relationships twice as much as it does for the general population. [25]

Financial anxiety continues to be a stress for people of all ages. The fear of not having enough, or not being able to have the life we want, is powerful. This anxiety leads in one of two directions: it triggers avoidance and detrimental behaviors that set us back even further or it motivates us to get things in line. The fear of not having enough money (for bills, goals, or retirement) can promote protective financial decisions, and it can drive effective budgeting. Conversely, it can spur impulsive spending and denial that makes things worse. This is essentially what buyer's remorse is: a coming-to after a poor decision.

## Jane

A client of mine in her fifties, Jane, actively shook when we first met—just like my grandmother. She couldn't stay still and often sat in the waiting room on the edge of the chair, her anxiety visible in her movement and posture. Jane was entirely focused on her "retirement number," the amount of money in the bank that would let her know she could stop working. The number was her holy grail; it consumed her, building up pressure for her to monitor her expenses, hold regular meetings with her financial planner, and perform at work. Ostensibly, the number's purpose was "so I don't have to worry"—but it had the exact opposite effect. Worrying about the number, and the time it would take to reach it, had become the ruling fact of her life.

As we worked together, her existential anxiety revealed itself: her job was her identity and she didn't know what she would do when she stopped. Since she was older and single, she had no choice but to rely on herself and prepare for retirement. Her work was a productive outlet for her anxiety, and she became concerned about redirecting it as a retiree. Would it just sit and pool and make her feel restless and crazy?

Jane was blind to the fact that she already had the financial security she so craved. Earning and saving money was Jane's *safety behavior*, a term used for phobics and compulsives when they cling to an object or action as a form of self-protection.

Money can catch in the crosshairs of our emotional issues. The way we handle it can mimic the way we handle many other resources in our life like energy, time, and attention. Working with Jane involved helping her see what she was sacrificing in the rest of her life in putting so much energy into her work, something she ironically did to buy security so she could quit her job someday and hypothetically not be so anxious. But it wasn't about her "number"—the anxiety had simply attached to it. Jane was working extra weekends and holidays to get an edge, which robbed her of the opportunity to forge a satisfying social life— something that she craved. Through our work, she began to recognize the security she already had, find more ways to embrace rest, and started investigating other interests. Over time, we worked on teasing out where the anxiety had led her astray and how it could be focused more beneficially.

# The Myth of Having It All

It seems that the secret to a healthy work life includes a healthy personal life. Using examples from Warren Buffett to Oprah Winfrey, a recent article in *Inc.* magazine recommended, "You know what will add even more stress to your already stressful work life? Not having an active life running on all cylinders outside of work."[27] Balancing work and home-life can be a challenge for even the most resilient and principled worker. Money, career goals, or even our boss's demands can throw us off balance and away from our other commitments. Anxiety can show us where we tip out of balance and help us recalibrate our efforts.

In an interview with *The Atlantic* magazine, Indra Nooyi tells a story about coming home the evening she was named CEO of PepsiCo to be met by her mother's ire when she walked in: the household had run out of milk, and it was Nooyi's duty to go back out and get it. Her mother was far less impressed with her daughter's career accomplishments; strongly rooted in her Indian culture, her mother reinforced the cost of her success on her familial responsibilities. Nooyi warned that too many women have mistaken ideas about how easy it is to balance a career and family and should be aware that having it all simply isn't possible. [28]

Research shows that more women are dropping out of the workforce, disheartened by the reality of these conflicts, and potentially afraid of even trying. According to research cited in Sheryl Sandberg's *Lean In*, many women are settling for less satisfying careers in anticipation of future familial conflicts that are perceived as unsolvable.[29] In spite of growing flexibility in the workplace, women still fear making tough choices between career and family, and they seem to be hedging against them in advance. Gloria Steinem even recently asserted that the fight for women's equality is actually being waged in our homes.[30]

American women today are better educated, more empowered, and more independent than ever before. Many young women dive into their twenties thinking time is on their side, and it's too early for choices to be forced or values to be chiseled. Following the flow of opportunity, both women and men leave fantasies about a future life unchallenged. They remain whispering in the background, ready to haunt them later.

Maintaining positivity is important, but only a realistic outlook can lead to concrete plans.[31] Don't be afraid to dream—it's how we clue into what we want. However, a dream is not a road map. Attach your dreams to your values, your opportunities, and your realistic expectations, and go after them.

If you believe that you can make all your meals from scratch and sourced from your garden that you serve at your spotless and stylish table, while thriving in your career and attending every one of your child's events, then you are likely headed for disappointment. Many simply ignore these conflicting signals between what they want and what is likely; they push forward, hoping—or assuming—they can somehow have it all. That if we want it badly enough, it will come. And it is that wishful thinking that is the crux of the problem.

# Anxiety on the Field

Paul Assaiante, the varsity squash coach at Trinity College, is the winningest coach in collegiate history. In his book, *Run to the Roar,* Assaiante describes the importance of facing anxiety head on. The book's title is a reference to a hunting strategy of lions in the wild. When the pack of lions surround the prey, the weakest lion roars, scaring the prey directly into the claws and jaws of younger, more dangerous lions. It's about the *safety* of approaching fears, rather than fleeing them; known fears are far less dangerous than the unknown dangers of retreat.

In teaching his athletes to embrace and move toward their fears, Assaiante demonstrates that anxieties can feel much more dangerous than they actually are. "In moments of tension and crisis—when the lion roars—I teach them to understand that safety is actually found in moving forward," he writes. "They would want the ball. They would not be scared. They would face the old lion."[32]

Phil Jackson, who has won eleven championships as an NBA head coach—the most in professional basketball history—is an adopter of Eastern thought. He taught his players to embrace their anger—which he said manifested as anxiety—in order to be productive on the court. "The more you try to suppress it, the more likely it is to erupt later in a more virulent form," he wrote in his book *Eleven Rings: The Soul of Success.* "A better approach is to become as intimate as possible with how anger works on your mind and body so that you can transform its underlying energy into something productive."[33]

Excellence and optimal performance will always involve

challenge, uncertainty, and anxiety. Recognizing the advantage of the pressure to motivate us can help us reframe our anxiety and use it, whether it be on the field, in the classroom, or at your desk. Anxiety invites us to show up and rise to the challenge.

## CHAPTER SEVENTEEN

# Facing Crisis

> *"Great emergencies and crises show us how much greater our vital resources are than we had supposed."*
>
> —William James[1]

## Hear Yourself

One day when I was nineteen, I started to have strange tingling sensations down the left side of my body. Disoriented, I first thought there was an earthquake, but I soon realized I was the only one trembling. Then it happened again. And again.

The episodes hit with more frequency and they were always scary—almost out-of-body experiences. Numerous specialists, tests, and hospitals could not determine the cause of my episodes; more than once, a doctor suggested that perhaps nothing was really wrong with me at all. It was frustrating—and terrifying. But

I listened to my body, and fortunately, my mother listened too. So, we spent months digging for answers.

It took a three-week stay at the Mayo Clinic, but we finally had the answer: advanced neurological lyme disease, a treatable—if little-known—infectious disease at the time. The anxiety that something was wrong was not a false alarm at all; it was an intense signal. My body knew, and I was able to listen—and be listened to.

I have a close friend with a similar story: a strange pain in his lower stomach that would simply not go away. X-ray after X-ray revealed nothing. Doctors told him more than once it was likely nothing—maybe gas, maybe a strained muscle. But none of those sounded right. The pain was intense and strange. So, he continued going back to doctor after doctor, from one referred specialist to another. "Look, I know I'm not a doctor," he said to the latest one, "but something is not right." The doctor later said that it was those words that made him certain that something indeed was wrong.

By the end of the second week of this, the specialist finally had the answer, and it was the simplest one imaginable. His appendix. It was enlarged and located slightly off the typical spot, so no one caught it. The doctor sped him into surgery and removed it just before it burst.

I'm sure you or a friend has experienced something similar. The point is not that doctors miss things. It's that we can never remove ourselves from the equation—even if we're working off instinct or feeling or without the necessary vocabulary. It doesn't require too much sensitivity to recognize when things are off. Our bodies cannot really be duped, no matter how loud other distractions become.

Health is an area of anxiety commonly experienced by those who aren't normally overly anxious. We experience whisper anxiety about our diets, about our need to exercise more, see that doctor, maybe quit drinking or smoking or eating fatty foods. The anxiety is about the gap between how we feel and how we *want* to feel. We are experts at delaying, procrastinating, and ignoring health concerns. This is where our anxiety raises its head.

If we listen to our bodies, we will know—maybe not specifically what it needs, but that it needs help. There is an embedded honesty and wisdom in there. And we must listen: because we know our bodies better than anyone else possibly could. It's a built-in system of checks and balances to make sure these habits don't get out of hand.

## Without Judgment

As a psychology graduate student, I worked primarily with female victims of domestic violence. I would listen to their traumatic stories, witness their struggles, and try to navigate their current state so I could offer help. But I was baffled by their resistance. If they were being beaten, their children were at risk, and their life was being threatened, it seemed obvious that they should remove themselves from their situations and enter one of our free, hidden shelters. But they resisted. The walls they had put up were solidly built.

Those interactions first exposed me to how powerful shame and avoidance habits can be. I was concerned for these women, frustrated for their situations, and felt like there was nothing I could do to help. They were blinded by a certain wish for how their lives could be instead of seeing what was real, and they were ashamed, often believing the abuse was their fault. They were caught in a cycle of abuse that included a reconciliation and "honeymoon" period, one where their husbands or boyfriends pulled out all the stops to win them back. The women almost universally stuck to the idea that *this* was the real man. *This* version. Convinced by this manipulation, and psychologically beaten down, they would reenter the relationship—only to go through the cycle again.[2] As they returned session after session for help, I realized I couldn't always convince them to leave these men. But I noticed the subtlety of what I was slowly offering: acceptance, connection and hope, the kind that might lead to courage.

As I worked my way through graduate school, the powerful pull of past experiences was never far from my mind. "For each of us, there is a point at which fear crosses the line into trauma," writes Lou Cozolino, "causing severe disturbances in the integration of cognitive, sensory, and emotional processing."[3] Post-traumatic stress disorder (PTSD) is a sustained reaction to a previous event. Long after the person has escaped the danger, the symptoms—the sensory reality of the experience—remain. My dissertation advisor, David Foy, a renowned trauma expert, used to always say about PTSD symptoms, "These are ordinary reactions to extraordinary experiences," words that have stuck with me a long time.

Many of the women I worked with early in my career particularly struggled with distinguishing between the choices they had and the choices they wished they had. This distinction is a hugely important element of deciding a useful course of action. I met so many women who were unsure about their relationships, unwilling to face the painful realities of their situations, wishing their lives could be the way they once were, or the way they *could be* if only someone else would change. The *if onlys* and *what ifs* keep people stuck, circling and swirling, never leading to active solutions. It places the impetus for change outside ourselves when the focus needs to be within us.

When facing a tough situation, hope and support can help us bravely face our truth and muster the courage to cope. Compassion helps us translate anxiety into something we can use. Researchers found that self-compassion correlated with lower PTSD symptoms, as did helping people cope with the symptoms themselves.[4] Getting out of a dark place and into a place of control requires us to accept and embrace ourselves in a way that can be especially difficult for those who experience trauma. Loving ourselves, and taking control of our perceptions, is the key to exiting the tunnel and pulling out into the lighted road ahead.

## Coping with Trauma

Trauma can happen anywhere and to anyone. Estimates are that 70 percent of people have experienced a trauma in their lives—and 20 percent of them will develop PTSD.[5] Be it a traumatic loss, an injury or illness, a dreadful accident, or a natural disaster, trauma can strike at any time with no warning. PTSD-like symptoms are almost universal in the immediate aftermath of trauma, where the "majority of individuals will have symptoms of reexperiencing, avoidance, and hyperarousal initially following the trauma that will extinguish over time," though for some victims, symptoms will persist and full-on PTSD will develop.[6]

The ability to distinguish between current danger and previous danger gets confused in those who develop PTSD. The part of the brain responsible for scanning our physical environments for threat and activating the appropriate response are less active in PTSD patients. One of the most common PTSD symptoms involves misperceiving neutral stimuli as threatening (e.g., loud noises being misperceived as gunfire), suggesting that there could be damage to this part of the brain.[7]

According to neuroscientist Bruce McEwen, "In PTSD the traumatic event engraves itself in the brain, often obliterating more recent, and less significant, memories."[8] Despite the variety of loud bangs that a PTSD sufferer has heard in his life, the gunfire trumps all the others. All loud bangs are gunfire, no matter the reality.

## Reaching Out

Crisis situations are anxiety provoking. The best way to cope is to talk through them in a structured way.[9] Telling someone how you feel, what happened, and what is going on can help you use your support system to process your new reality. Think of it as building up a network of resilience, one that can protect us from developing symptoms of trauma.

Another key to preventing prolonged trauma symptoms is allowing the stress response—which includes cortisol—to work adaptively. So powerful is our cortisol response to protect us during intense stress that some studies have shown high doses of glucocorticoids (a class of steroid hormones, one of which is cortisol) administered in the immediate aftermath after an accident, surgery, or trauma have had protective effects in preventing trauma symptoms.[10]

Whether it's talking to friends, leaning on a medical team, or simply being honest about what you need, actively coping is critical. Otherwise, anxiety symptoms lodge, pull us into sticky cycles of avoidance, and give the symptoms room to linger. Tell your story to those you trust will listen. Translating feelings into words is a powerful coping tool and can reduce needless shame, allowing people around you to provide the support you need.*

Also, don't be afraid to cry as you talk about what is happening. Tears are not just emotionally cathartic, but they boost our immune system, remove toxins, and even elevate our mood once we stop.[11] It can help to think of tears as "highlighter pens" for our strong feelings. Moving into and through our new reality is the challenge of coping with trauma and protecting ourselves too much from its symptoms can plague us further. Despite dated

---

* If you're looking to assist a friend or loved one in facing a crisis, remember though that *forcing* anyone to talk about something painful is ill advised. Talking about a trauma should *always* be on the person's own terms, allowing their instincts about their needs to be valued and strengthened.

thinking about crying being the mark of the weak, studies show a capacity to weep is correlated with emotional strength.[12] It demonstrates our capacity to understand and relate to the world. "He who does not weep," novelist Victor Hugo wrote, "does not see."[13]

## Writing It Down

*"Owning our story and loving ourselves through that process is the bravest thing we'll ever do."*

—**Brené Brown**[14]

Putting our feelings into words can be cathartic, allowing us to release pent up emotion. Often, we don't know how we think until we are made to articulate it. It's one of the reasons that talking about trauma helps us process it. In a similar vein, writing helps us understand our emotions, giving language and structure to what can be scary feelings.

It's a question of healing, not ruminating. How we view our experience shapes what they become. We cannot change what happened, but we are in control of the story we tell ourselves about what has happened, and what happens next.

The psychologist James Pennebaker, in his books *Writing to Heal* and *Opening Up: Healing Power of Expressing Emotions*, was among the first to document the detrimental effects of keeping secrets, noting that among some abuse survivors the act of keeping secrets about an event was more painful and lasting than the event itself. Pennebaker studies how language creates emotional meaning and how writing can work to diminish the remaining stress from a traumatic event. [15] One study even links stress reduction directly to writing a positive narrative. [16] We are creators of meaning and this is true on the chemical level. Both in writing and in speech, embracing a narrative of healing can be powerful in constructing a present and a future not at the mercy of the past.

## The Science of Buttons

While the term *trauma* is clinically reserved for life threatening experiences, the trauma process can be enacted through a host of overwhelming experiences. Often, these experiences are those that happen early in childhood when so much is outside of our control.

When painful associations lodged in our minds are brought up in present situations, our reactions can feel overblown. The present experience feels familiar and our amygdala signals danger. We are triggered, and our reaction is exaggerated. There are times when buttons get pushed and the noise (the yelling anxiety) that results spikes the anxiety to an unusable degree. It's as though our amygdala gets us going before we have a chance to control how we react.

"The amygdala catalogs past threats to apply them to future situations," writes Lou Cozolino in *The Healthy, Aging Brain.* "Unlike our fragile memory for names and dates, the amygdala has a tenacious memory for what has frightened us… Activation results in chemical processes that enhance memory for fearful experiences."[17] Our bodies carry the memory of the traumatic experience in a deep, sensory way, whether we choose to hold onto it or not. It's essential that we get familiar with what our buttons are; once they are activated, we are most likely to benefit from understanding the terrain and recognizing its pitfalls.

## Panic and Phobia

Panic is one of the most debilitating and frightening forms of anxiety. It is a full-body experience that can include sweaty palms, ringing ears, racing heart, blurred vision, and often a belief that you are dying. It's the quintessential expression of what I call *secondary anxiety*—anxiety about your anxiety.

Though panic itself is too loud for you to use constructively, its very presence pushes you to seek to make sure it never happens again. While efforts to resist panic may feel protective, the avoidance actually drives up your vulnerability to experiencing more panic. The mistake is believing you can't handle it. You may not want to, but you *can*. The very act of opening yourself up to panic diminishes it right away, preventing it from taking hold. Additionally, understanding what is driving the panicky feeling to begin with can help you regain control. Panic is never random, though its source is not always clear.

Phobias are a type of anxiety where a fear of something, and its avoidance, creates secondary anxiety. Avoiding the feared object or situation often comes back to bite us. Max is a young man I saw who had anxiety about flying, among other things. One of the things we had to focus on was how to redirect his thinking about what happens in a plane or what could happen. He used an online resource set up by pilots that explained what the engine noises were and how landing works.[18] Information is powerful, and it can help offset the onslaught of irrational possibilities, which the imagination can create. We worked on using the information he learned to challenge the validity of his fears and redirect his imagination of the *possibilities* to the *probabilities*. Knowing what was happening when he heard engine sounds and recounting to himself the safety records of air travel helped him stay focused on facts rather than his fears, helping him to keep his anxiety in check.

## Raphael

A crisis doesn't have to be one single event or situation. Sometimes just the accumulation of responsibilities can overtake us. Getting clear on signals of overload are an important part of keeping anxiety at its proper level. A chronic overachiever, Raphael came in one day for what he termed a "tune up." The rising demands of several family crises were competing with his new executive responsibilities in such a way that he felt he was sinking.

He described a recurring dream he had been having the previous few nights; he would happen upon a horrible accident with needy victims, and he was the only one there to help. After helping a few people, he leaves in the middle to go to the movies with the intent to come back and help. He wakes up annoyed at his frivolous choice, feeling confused and guilty about what it says about his selfishness.

Raphael's new job had him assisting underserved communities. Meanwhile, he was also struggling to support his immediate and extended family manage a variety of relationship, health, and legal troubles. He felt the impact of each problem and obliged to be present for everyone. Under the weight of the pressure to also be a father and husband, he found himself fantasizing about leaving his job. He feared he was burning out, attributing his feelings to work pressures. He seemed not to recognize how the family responsibilities were weighing him down.

His recurring dream had been telling a different story and signaling a different need. Rather than being selfish, and ill equipped for the empathic demands of his job, perhaps he simply needed a bit more time for himself. The work in his session was about reframing the signal that his anxiety was sending: he had to do a better job of balancing his various demands—not simply drop one.

Valuing his own needs as much as others' continues to be a growth area for Raphael, but for the time being he sees self-time as a necessity, not a luxury. He had been forgetting to put on his oxygen mask before helping others.

If your anxiety is overwhelming and becoming chronic, your anxiety may be sending you the message to slow down, to pause, to heal. Remember that the action you may need to take can be seeking help and stopping. Sometimes the best solution is the most obvious: what is needed is rest, recovery, and self-care.

# Failing Up

Coping with trauma, adversity, or any sort of crisis anxiety takes guts and a willingness to take control. We are in more control than we realize, and it can be a self-perpetuating loop. Once we accept we are in control, the control itself becomes easier. There is a resilience that comes from absorbing and growing through crisis.

In *The Happiness Advantage*, Shawn Achor uses the phrase "falling up,"[19] which nicely distills the idea. Post-traumatic growth has been a revealing field of research, with evidence suggesting not just that sufferers return to normal—but that they build themselves back stronger, just like the old adage. "Posttraumatic growth is not simply a return to baseline," write Richard Tedeschi and Lawrence Calhoun, pioneers of this field of inquiry, "it is an experience of improvement that for some persons is deeply profound."[20]

One action we can always turn to is easy in the abstract but difficult in reality: forgiveness. It's helpful to remember that forgiveness is about you—not necessarily about the person being forgiven. And yet the act of forgiveness can release the anger and regret that has been pooling up and has been scientifically proven to reduce distress.[21] Forgiveness can be the ultimate way of stepping out of the past and into the present, and ultimately, the future.

## CHAPTER EIGHTEEN

# Soothing and Coping

*"Our deepest fear is not that we are inadequate. Our deepest fear is that we are powerful beyond measure."*

—Marianne Williamson[1]

## Quieting the Yell

Throughout this book, I've made the case that our anxiety is a supportive friend, not an adversary. However, there is obviously a level of anxiety that is too high to be useful. This chapter focuses on strategies that reduce this type of yelling anxiety to a manageable level, so it can be channeled productively. Just like the sympathetic nervous system (the gas pedal) kicks in your stress response, your parasympathetic nervous (the brakes) system is designed to shut it off. Sometimes engaging those brakes are necessary in order to ensure you are traveling at a safe and manageable speed, and the following are my go-to recommendations for keeping anxiety at its optimal effective level:

- Go easier on yourself
- Find ways to feel and show gratitude
- Draw your attention to the here and now
- Embrace the positive
- Just breathe
- Calm your body to calm your mind; calm your mind to calm your body
- Engage in healthier habits

## Self-Compassion

Think back to the monkey and the green banana: forcing doesn't always make things better. Often it compounds our issues or traps us into rigid thinking. This is true for anxiety as well. Unfortunately, there is a culture out there telling us we simply need to force ourselves through our fears, and then all will be better. *Suck it up. Grind it out.* This simply is not the case. Yes, anxiety must be faced and tolerated to be understood, but it cannot be done forcefully. It's not a question of will. It's a question of compassion and courage.

We hear a lot from the media, from society, and even from loved ones that we need to be tougher on ourselves when we're working on self-control, but perhaps the opposite is true. In one classic experiment on overeating, self-forgiveness actually drove *up* self-control.[2] In making healthier choices, we are usually better off being gentle and compassionate in our efforts than being rigid and self-critical.

So, if you notice yourself feeling stuck, trapped, or rigid, ask yourself *How I can be more gentle? Where can I ease my perspective?* Yoga teachers often ask their classes, "How can you soften your effort to get more from the stretch?" I love that framework: soften to get *more*. Pulling harder doesn't get you where you need to be. You want your mind and body to cooperate with you—think about how we get other people to join us. By being gentle.

A brief warning: gentle behaviors can become indulgences if they don't ultimately solve our anxiety. Keeping your workout easy can help you keep your gym routine, but if we never step up resistance, we'll never build strength. Shopping for a new dress may ease our waistline frustrations, but it can delay actually taking action on our waistline goals. Self-compassion is about making it easier so that we solve the issue, not just making it easier for its own sake. According to Dr. Kristen Neff, self-compassion means "we clearly acknowledge our problems and shortcomings without judgment, so we can do what's necessary to help ourselves."[3]

Two researchers at Duke University, Ashley Batts Allen and Mark Leary, have directly studied the connection between self-compassion and healing from stressful events. "People who are high in self-compassion," they write, "take greater responsibility for their failures and make needed changes while maintaining a loving, caring, and patient approach toward themselves."[4] Self-compassion is not about denying anything—it's about acceptance. Accepting the realities in front of you, so you can productively move forward. It's about "taking responsibility for oneself and for attaining one's goals," note Allen and Leary. It's helpful to remember that these are not positivity gurus, but *research scientists*. Self-compassion is not abdicating or avoiding. It is about facing our experience, upping our responsibility, and taking control.

# Gratitude

> "*Some strengths are innate—built into your DNA— but most are acquired, woven over time into the fabric of your brain... You become more grateful through internalizing repeated experiences of gratitude; you become more compassionate through internalizing repeated experiences of compassion.*"
>
> —**Rick Hanson, *Hardwiring Happiness*[5]**

Robert Emmons, perhaps the world's leading expert on gratitude, posits that gratitude has two key components: (1) it's the affirmation of goodness in the world, and (2) its source originates outside ourselves.[6] Gratitude helps us see that we are supported and affirmed by others, and it underscores a sense of connection that strengthens us. Social scientists believe gratitude evolved as a way to pay it forward. Sociologist Georg Simmel called it "the moral memory of mankind,"[7] while eighteenth-century pioneering deaf educator Jean Massieu memorably called it "the memory of the heart."

Besides helping reframe negatives as positives, gratitude expands our views beyond ourselves; it opens us to our relationships with others and the larger world. This can help pull us out of our immediate feelings and add width and depth to our perception. Gratitude is not just about counting our blessings, it's about digging further into our *experience* of our blessings, the source of them, the interconnectedness of all of us.

Neurobiologist Richard Davidson has noted that the connection between our emotional and thinking selves is an interconnectedness that we can tap into. "The brain's emotional circuits are actually connected to its thinking circuits, which are much more accessible to our conscious volition," explains Sharon Begley, who cowrote Davidson's *The Emotional Life of the Brain*. "So, while you can't just order yourself to have a particular feeling, you can sort of sneak up on your emotions via your thoughts."[8] Our feelings and our thoughts work together. As we discussed in chapter 3, how we think about a feeling actually defines what it is. A feeling is not something that happens to us—we cocreate it.

## Undoing and Grounding

Scientists also recognize "the undoing effect," where positive emotions can reduce negative ones. In one study, when subjects with stress-related health issues were triggered into anxiety, cardiovascular symptoms decreased faster in those who watched positive films than in those who watched neutral films.[9] This suggests watching a few minutes of a favorite comedy show, or scrolling cute animal videos, could promote faster recovery from yelling anxiety. "A quick burst of positive emotions doesn't just broaden our cognitive capacity," happiness researcher Shawn Achor explains, "it also provides a quick and powerful antidote to stress and anxiety, which in turn improves our focus and our ability to function at our best level."[10]

There is also the technique known as *grounding*, which involves attaching yourself to the here and now of your immediate environment. Grounding is about focusing on what's in front of you immediately, like a table's surface, the texture of a carpet, or the light coming in a window. This technique, which is especially helpful for panic, brings awareness to the most concrete things in front of us as a strategy to escape the cycles inside our minds.

## Just Breathe

If you aren't always sure what you are feeling, that's okay. There are things you can do to activate the parts of our brain linked to insight. The simple exercise of becoming aware of your breath has been shown in various studies to activate the insula and the anterior cingulate cortex, two areas of our brains involved in awareness as well as self-regulation of attention and emotion.[11]

When we are anxious and feel threatened, controlled breathing has also been shown to activate the parasympathetic branch of the autonomic nervous system (the brake pedal) that helps turn off the stress response.[12] As the threat response calms, the thinking part of the cortex becomes more accessible. Simple exercises to lengthen and slow your breath can have a powerful effect on increasing your cognitive capabilities.[13] One of the most effective things you can do to physically calm your nervous system is to calm your breath, balancing the short, choppy breathing that accompanies a threat response.

Belly breathing is another specific strategy. While techniques vary, the goal of belly breathing is to slow your breathing and take air into the deepest part of your lungs (which feels like your belly) such that a hand placed just above your belly button would rise with an inhale. Breathe in through your nose to slow your intake (on a count of three to four seconds) hold for one to two counts, and exhale slowly through your mouth at least as long as your inhale, if not longer (three to eight counts). Aim for no more than eight breaths per minute, which means every complete breath (inhale and exhale) should be eight seconds. Timing yourself can help, but counting aloud at roughly one-second intervals works just as well, forcing your whole experience to focus on slowing down your breath. Continue for as many cycles as it takes to calm yourself.

Taking a simple deep breath can stimulate the vagus nerve, our largest nerve that runs from our brains to our abdomens and controls the parasympathetic nervous system (PNS). This can have a powerful calming effect. Neuroscience research has shown in rats that stimulation of the vagus nerve enhances the extinction of fear and alters the plasticity in the pathway from the prefrontal cortex to the amygdala. In other words, rats that received vagus nerve stimulation (VNS) "forgot" a stressful event faster than rats that did not receive VNS. It is feasible to propose that VNS helps patients to reduce their anxiety, because the increased vagus nerve firing will help strengthen the control that the prefrontal cortex has over the amygdala.[14]

It's important to lay the groundwork in advance before anxiety strikes. Developing a simple practice of deep belly breathing during times of calm can help you access this tool when anxiety spikes.[15] While we can't always control our threat responses, we *can* activate our relaxation response.[16]

## Other Calming Routines

Calming your body with your mind is the basis of almost all physiological relaxation techniques. Progressive muscle relaxation, developed by Herbert Benson, is a technique of relaxing your body, muscle group by muscle group, which promotes full body relaxation.[17]

Soothing rituals like a hot bath, sauna,[18] or massage[19] promote circulation and relax muscles, which can in turn soothe our minds. Most parents know the soothing magic of submerging a cranky child in warm water. Fortunately, this relaxation response stays with us for life, and a warm bath or hot shower can work wonders. A cup of hot tea, soaking up some sunshine, or simply hugging someone are some of our grandparents' favorite calming rituals, and they still work today. Science is starting to understand just how helpful some of these remedies can be in balancing our bodies.

Perhaps counterintuitively, cold water can also be helpful in reducing anxiety. Cold water exposure to your face has been found to stimulate a dive reflex, lowering blood pressure and respiration, that can calm the body.[20] Cold water immersion is another example of a type of hormesis, like a vaccination, where you become inoculated to the original stressor such that a little bit of it builds your tolerance for even more.

Yoga and other mindful stretching practices also help promote physiological calm.[21] In a 2011 study by Sara Lazar at Massachusetts General Hospital, participants who took only eight weeks of yoga and meditation classes (less than thirty minutes a day) reported less stress and scans showed a smaller sized amygdala.[22] It was the first study to document changes over time in decreasing the thickness of a brain structure mediated by meditation.

According to an overview of yoga and stress conducted by University of Maryland nurses, an increasing body of evidence documents yoga's positive impact on mental health, specifically because it moderates the body's stress response.[23] Anyone who has practiced yoga understands the mental challenges that rival the physical ones. Breathing into the discomfort grows tolerance, and it also creates greater capacity to think about our discomfort when we are in it, both on and off the mat. A calm body is the path to a calm mind.

A number of newer technologies claim to teach stimulation of the PNS (the brakes) through biofeedback and monitoring heart rate variability (HRV). Biofeedback teaches us the capacity to control our physiological responses simply through real-time feedback of our physiological reactions (e.g., heart rate, skin temperature). By watching what your body is doing in real time, and experimenting with various techniques to calm it, you can find the one that works best for you. Like weighing yourself to check the success of a diet, biofeedback offers data we can use to target our strategies more individually.

Noninvasive vagus nerve stimulation has been shown to lower depression and may soon become available to patients.[24] Audio programs of binaural beats that claim to entrain your brain to stimulate relaxing (alpha) brain waves that are normally only achieved through structured meditation are available. These technological "shortcuts" are a big business but have yet to be scientifically proven.[25]

## Mindfulness and Meditation

The strength of the mind-body connection is the basis of all forms of meditation. Dozens of meditation practices exist that have been shown to improve relaxation and calm. The structured practice of transcendental meditation (TM) has shown improvements in neural connections and coherence in the brain; practitioners of TM report a greater ability to control their thoughts and emotions.[26] TM is about harnessing attention toward the intrinsic pleasure of stillness through a mantra—a repeated phrase. Participants tap into a deeply restful state of consciousness that offers intense rest and restoration.[27]

Mindfulness is a type of meditation that involves focusing without reacting. Being curious about what's actually happening (along with focusing on one's breath) stimulates the processing part of the brain. This, in turn, can reduce stress. The inward focus makes it easier to name our experiences and better control them.

The thinking cannot stop the emotion, but how we think about it can alter the experience: *I know what this is. It's anxiety, it's trying to help me, and I can handle it.*

Importantly, mindfulness is not to be confused with optimism. Optimism can shut out important details and keep us focused on wishes rather than reality. Mindfulness helps us be more aware of the evidence that's available to us. Rather than a reverie in what we want something to be, it is an awareness of what is.

Noted mindfulness and mediation expert Tara Brach offers a helpful acronym for mindfulness she calls RAIN: recognize, allow, investigate, and resume natural presence.

- *Recognize* emotional reactivity.
- Pause by taking three full breaths; *allow* your inner experience to be as it is.
- *Investigate* with kindness whatever feelings are most predominant.
- Resume activity, and notice if there is more *natural presence,* which is understood as the reality *separate from our thoughts and feelings.*[28]

## The Science in Mindfulness

Author and mindfulness expert Jon Kabat-Zinn views emotions as our senses trying to get our attention. "If you're not paying attention, your senses will try to wake you up while you still have a chance," he writes. "The senses are the only way we can know the world."[29] Mindfulness-based stress reduction, as explained in Kabat-Zinn's book *Full Catastrophe Living*, is a practice of being aware of what's happening with curiosity rather than judgment. It is simply the act of tuning into what's happening in your individual world at any given time. "Dropping in" to your experience, as Kabat-Zinn would say. In one study, subjects were taught to not fight the anxiety, but to recognize their negative thoughts, let them happen knowing they would eventually pass, and focus on their breathing.[30] Their goal was accepting it fully with no resistance.

After training participants in an eight-week course, researchers presented participants with self-critical statements (e.g., *I am ashamed of my shyness* or *people always judge me*) while they were in the fMRI machine. They found that the more subjects mentally processed their anxious thoughts, the less stress they felt. In a similar experiment, focusing on the thoughts was more effective at stress reduction than distraction.[31]

Acceptance commitment therapy (ACT)[32] focuses on the importance of *not* changing your thoughts but rather accepting them and detaching from their impact. An example would be taking the thought of *I am a bad person* and reframing it into *I am having the thought that I am a bad person*. By identifying what's happening, you can separate yourself from its effects. You can accept the presence of the thought without believing it.

Distancing oneself into the second or third person can also be an effective tool at managing your anxiety.[33] When subjects encouraged themselves in the third person (using their own names) prior to a meeting or public speech, they regulated stress better and engaged in less ruminating than those who engaged in first person self-talk.[34] I refer to myself by name when I need an extra boost of courage: *Come on, Alicia. You can do this.* It gives you a comfortable distance from the thought and the feeling—a bird's-eye view that spreads the whole out before you.

## The Happiest Man in the World

Psychology professor Richard J. Davidson worked with Matthieu Ricard, a Tibetan monk known as "the happiest man in the world," on a twelve-year study of meditation and happiness.[35] One specific practice, called *compassion meditation,* is in Ricard's words, about "unrestricted readiness and availability to help living beings."[36] The meditation often begins with thinking about alleviating the suffering of a specific loved one and then expands out to everyone.

In his book *The Emotional Life of Your Brain,* Davidson discussed the experiment, where compassion meditation lit up areas of the monks' brain linked to doing. Davidson and Ricard agreed that a loved one in distress conjures a "total readiness to act, to help." A readiness to act makes sense given the strong impulse to tend and befriend under distress as well as act.[37] Another study of monks' brains revealed neural growth of the frontal cortex and other regions associated with happiness.[38]

## Talking It Out

Whether we are talking to ourselves, to someone else, or simply writing, language is critical in helping us process our anxiety. Of all the calming techniques, none will help us understand and "process" our feelings more than talking about it. Journaling, talking with a friend, and attending talk therapy all share the common thread of identifying and understanding one's experiences. Paul J. Zak— who has been at the forefront of discovering oxytocin's role in the brain—has shown that when we engage our language centers and name our experiences, we reduce our physiological arousal.[39]

Naming our experiences also allows us to better understand our choices and needed solutions. It allows us to construct a narrative of hope and healing and gives us the tools and language to reach out for social support, which lowers our threat response and helps guide us toward solutions.

## The Big Three

Let's finally turn to what I call the big three: exercise,[40] sleep,[41] and nutrition.[42] Each of these physical needs have been repeatedly linked to cognitive control as well as emotional regulation, and they are especially important in turning on your awareness to your emotional signals.[43]

# Exercise

"Exercise is stress reducing so long as it is something you actually want to do," explains Robert Sapolsky. "Let rats voluntarily run in a running wheel, and their health improves in all sorts of ways. Force them to, even while playing great dance music, and their health worsens."[44] Exercise has also been shown to mitigate the stress of cravings[45] and increase cognitive control and self-regulation.[46]

Beyond the mental and emotional boost, exercise can help you practice being uncomfortable or even tolerate pain. This practice of tolerating discomfort in the physical world can spill over into the emotional world. *The Power of Habit* author Charles Duhigg calls exercise a "keystone habit," which "changes our sense of self and our sense of what is possible."[47] There's a debate as to how long it takes to create a habit (one recent scientific study found it to be sixty-six days),[48] but all agree that a key to maintaining healthy coping is converting positive coping strategies into habits.

# Sleep

Americans are chronically sleep deprived, with a full 40 percent getting less than the recommended amount of shut eye.[49] Scientists have recently discovered a tiny network of fluid-filled channels that clear toxins from brain cells that only activates during sleep,[50] leading one *Science* magazine writer to dub sleep the brain's housekeeper.[51] Unless the brain sleeps, its cells cannot get cleaned, yet many of us don't get the "housecleaning" we need to function at our best.

Sleep loss saps energy, efficiency, concentration, and emotional control.[52] For people who already wrestle with anxiety, inadequate sleep can make things worse, particularly escalating anticipatory anxiety.[53] A brain without sleep struggles to think clearly and manage emotional reactions. The part of the brain associated with this function, the medial prefrontal cortex (mPFC), is impaired with inadequate sleep.[54]

On the other end of the continuum, extra sleep has been shown to help athletic performance[55] and "super-high-achievers sleep significantly more than the average American," according to Christine Carter at the Center for the Greater Good, a science facility at UC Berkeley dedicated to studying happiness and compassion.[56] While getting enough sleep isn't always easy for an anxious person besieged by insomnia or early-morning waking, getting enough sleep, or at a minimum sleeping when you are tired, is critical to building healthy cognitive and emotional habits. Pushing through fatigue is a recipe for unwieldy anxiety, and often sleep difficulties, that can be avoided by doing simply what our bodies want us to do.

## Nutrition

There are also links between nutrition and anxiety that are still being explored. A recent study on mice "found that the bacteria in your gut can affect the molecules in the areas of the brain that are associated with anxiety and depression."[57] It is well documented that a diet rich in sugar, caffeine, alcohol, and preservatives can wreak havoc on our blood sugar, arousal circuits, and metabolism; these in turn impact our brains and our ability to regulate our bodies and emotions. Eating a diet high in nutrient-dense foods can help provide our brain the fuel it needs to keep our bodies running efficiently and smoothly.

But eating healthily is a whole lot easier said than done. It's not always a nutritional or educational issue—many of us *know* what we're supposed to do. It's a behavioral one. Cornell professor Brian Wansink—dubbed the "Sherlock Holmes of food"—has studied eating behavior for his entire career, and he has shown repeatedly that much of our eating process is preconscious, if not wholly unconscious. In order to survive, we eat without awareness. If we were to have to focus on every bite or every stomach grumble, we wouldn't have room for much else in life. We rely on our instincts to eat, and we choose what is convenient and in front of us that's desirable.

It's not an accident that people on diets or new food regimes can talk about little else than eating. They have had to become more aware and more focused on something they're not used to paying attention to. I know many moms—including myself—complain they have to wait until their kids outgrow hot dogs and macaroni and cheese before they can stop eating those things themselves. A son who needs to gain weight? No problem, I can gain right along with him. A pregnant wife eating for two? The husband is all too willing to match her pound for pound. This is just how we are wired. We do so much without noticing. And noticing is a precious commodity and resource. The key to a healthy diet? Your immediate environment.

Wansink has researched our habits related to the proximity of healthy versus unhealthy foods—where we store them—or what is in our line of vision.[58] When unloading the groceries, think about what an exhausted version of you is going to see and grab. Then unpack accordingly. Wansink argues that controlling your environment and the foods you expose yourself to, rather than controlling what you eat, is a more sustainable way to change your eating than a diet or controlled food plan.[59]

## Building Habits

The effect of our environment on behavioral changes goes way beyond food. There is an emerging science of nudges, or choice architecture, that focuses on strategic changes in one's environment that can alter a person's behavior in predictable ways without precluding other choices or incentives.[60] Think of the end of the day when you're too tired to do anything but stare mindlessly at cable news, surf the internet without reading anything, or scour websites to do some unnecessary shopping.

Happiness researcher Shawn Achor coined the "twenty-second rule," which accounted for how far away his guitar was from him, yet he still couldn't practice. When exhausted, those twenty seconds are a trudge. So Achor moved his guitar from his closet to a stand next to his couch to increase likelihood of practice,[61] and it worked.

We are vulnerable to dopamine and decision-fatigue when we are tired. The best we can do is plan ahead and make good choices easier. Design an environment for success to make it easier on your future self. Schedule plans with friends, buy a new book you heard about, pursue a creative hobby, move your body, and have healthy food available. Limit choices by stacking your choices for success. And when you're tempted to go for that cigarette, chocolate bar, or extra drink, just wait ten minutes. Dopamine works best with immediacy. It is tougher to sabotage long-term rewards when we add time to the mix. It's a form of gentle discipline that works.[62]

As we discussed in chapter 8, how we perceive ourselves across time is important, with the latest research suggesting self-control is linked to empathy for your future self.[63] "Empathy depends on your ability to overcome your own perspective, appreciate someone else's, and step into their shoes," an article in *The Atlantic* states. "Self-control is essentially the same skill, except that those other shoes belong to your future self—a removed and hypothetical entity who might as well be a different person."[64]

Have empathy for the you that has to give a presentation in the morning, and pass on that third drink. Have empathy for the you at the gym tomorrow, and skip the chocolate cake. Have empathy for the you that has to get up at the crack of dawn, and shut off the iPad and get to bed. Your anxiety will thank you for it. It has been desperately trying to get your attention, offering a helping hand, and providing you with the information and energy to make you your best self. If we would all pay attention and embrace it for the tool that it is—it may take some time and practice—we'll find that better self.

# Conclusion

*"We either make ourselves miserable, or we make*
*ourselves strong. The amount of work is the same."*

—Carlos Castaneda[1]

**At the heart of using** our anxiety is a simple but powerful
concept: allowing ourselves to think differently. It's about recognizing just how much control we really have—even if it doesn't
feel like it and we have convinced ourselves we don't.

The new science around anxiety, and its empowering message,
is that anxiety can help. It doesn't have to own us, and it doesn't
have to stay hidden in the shadows, stigmatized, and treated as a
burden. Anxiety deserves a rebranding—so much more of it is
healthy than is unhealthy, and seeing it this way only increases our
ability to use it constructively.

Of course, this idea is not really new. It is embedded in the work of Charles Darwin, Sigmund Freud, and William James. We have simply gotten away from embracing the natural wisdom of our bodies, or perhaps we never learned. Thinking about anxiety differently begins the process of building new neural pathways and habits, which in turn grows our capacity to handle more. We can only choose what we think about and how. As Winifred Gallagher writes in *Rapt: Attention and the Focused Life,* "Who you are, what you think, feel, and do, what you love—is the sum of what you focus on."[2]

Anxiety makes sure we stay focused on the things that matter, helping our struggle to prioritize and reminding us when we are off track. Anxiety is like the compliance officer of our attention, reminding us when we are drifting into dangerous territory. Its job is to alert us out of complacency and automaticity, focus our precious attention, and motivate us to take needed action for growth.

Anxiety's impact on us boils down to how we think about it, and what we do with it. Anxiety is not in control—we are—and this is the hope. You are in control. You can hack your anxiety and make it work for you. Anxiety has been there all along, trying to nudge you into doing things that are more efficient and more in line with what you want and need. At this moment, valuing your anxiety as a resource is one of the most effective things you can commit to doing.

We are often far too hard on ourselves, convinced when we look around (and online) that everyone seems to have a better handle on things than we do. This is a collective illusion, and it simply leads us to picture some ideal that we'll one day get to, somehow. But this thinking does not motivate and it does not inspire. It submerges us, drowning us in unreasonable expectations. As the brilliant writer Anne Lamott put it, "Perfectionism is the voice of the oppressor, the enemy of the people."[3]

At the heart of this book is a message I share with all my clients: *You can handle it.* You have inside you the resources to hear anxiety's message, allow it to focus your attention on the things that matter most, and use its energy to solve the conflicts it signals. Once you accept anxiety's value, you are ready for the payoff. You will know strength, confidence, and increased capacity when you embrace it.

Self-esteem is built and strengthened by accepting our emotions' truth; anxiety is part of this process. Anxiety is really an invitation—a gateway for growth and continual recalibration. You have choices about what you do with its information and energy. In our quest for more comfort, joy, and peace, it is satisfying to know that the thing that we thought was holding us back was really—the whole time—pushing us forward.

# Your Anxiety Tool Kit

## MAKING YOUR ANXIETY WORK FOR YOU

**As we've learned in this** book, anxiety is an invitation for growth—a call to step up and face the road ahead. Anxiety gives us what we need to grow and adapt; we *require* it to reach our full potential. Yet, anxiety still signals something we fear and aren't sure we can handle. As we've learned, *this is its job*—to motivate us to take action and fuel solutions.

You can learn how to both handle your anxiety and use it your advantage. This tool kit offers you an overview of how to hack your anxiety, access it, and use it more productively to ultimately improve your life. This section is designed to walk you through the process of transforming your anxiety into action.

The process consists of the following five key pillars:

1. Recognizing anxiety
2. Identifying anxiety

3.  Sorting anxiety

4.  Determining action

5.  Taking action

Each pillar is subdivided into smaller building blocks with examples, clues, helpful hints, and questions to ask yourself.

You may not feel like every step applies to you or that you need as much explanation for every component. Skip over the areas that feel straightforward and dig into the sections that feel the most challenging. Circle back when you feel stuck. This should help you make sense of the material, so you can apply it more easily to yourself.

## Pillar One: Recognizing Anxiety

Recognizing when and how your anxiety is happening is the first step to being able to harness it for productive action. We have debunked many common myths about anxiety and have learned how it can act as a powerful advantage. Now is the time to allow your new thinking to work for you.

### Building Block 1: Reframe your thinking about anxiety

The first step in using anxiety is to broaden how we understand it. Opening up our thinking about anxiety allows us to make sense of it. Simply activating your curiosity and noticing your experience when you are feeling anxious can help enormously. Understanding what is happening also delivers a needed sense of control.

<u>Key questions:</u>

- What have I learned in this book that has changed how I think about anxiety?
- How can I use this learning to adopt a more positive mind-set about my anxiety and the growth it can fuel?
- Where can I bring more curiosity and awareness to my experience?
- In what ways has my anxiety been a help to me in my life?
- In what ways has my anxiety not been helpful?
- How do I handle my anxiety well?
- Where do I want to improve?
- What assumptions about my anxiety could be holding me back?
- What can I learn in the future from my anxiety?

**Building Block 2: Notice how your anxiety speaks to you**
Anxiety can take many forms and operate at varying levels of intensity. When you think about your anxiety, ask yourself at what volume you experience it. Does it yell at you? Does it whisper? Is it more of a constant chatter, like background noise? Be curious. It will help you better identify the types of anxiety you feel, and give you a vocabulary to understand your experience.

YOUR ANXIETY TOOL KIT

## YELLING ANXIETY

If your anxiety is yelling at you, chances are you experiencing it viscerally and with some amount of intensity.* Is it a racing heart, sweaty palms, or a pit in your stomach? This anxiety can be miserable and nearly impossible to ignore. It is our physiological threat response, and it's doing what it's supposed to do—making us uncomfortable enough to take notice, interrupt our inertia, and prod us to take protective action. If it's yelling too loudly for you to understand or use, then work to separate the rational anxiety from the irrational type. You also may need to use calming strategies we reviewed in chapter 18 to reduce its volume to a manageable level.

## CHATTER ANXIETY

For many people, anxiety can feel like the white noise of life— the stress of life's demands overflowing what you think of as your capacity.† Whether you're annoyed by the pressure or doubt you can cope, you don't feel in control. External stressors are common triggers for chatter anxiety: opening up a flooded inbox, juggling the demands of your family and friends, navigating your kids' lives. The pace and volume of life's demands feel outside your control. This anxiety is normal; its job is to help you focus and execute on the challenges most important to you.

---

\*    See Cecilia, whose yelling anxiety is introduced in chapter 3 and followed up with at the start of chapter 10.

†    See Deanna, whose chatter anxiety is introduced in chapter 3 and followed up with at the start of chapter 11.

## WHISPERING ANXIETY

Whisper anxiety lives outside of our awareness, lurking in the shadows of our consciousness.* To harness its usefulness, we must be ready to look in the not-so-obvious places, sometimes the places that house our deepest conflicts. Anxiety can be found hiding in confusing behavior, where the source or reason is clear. It can also be hiding in avoidant behavior, like always arriving late to work, letting your bills pile up, or finishing that bag of cookies when you know you want to feel better in your clothes. Anxiety can bury itself in other emotions, often escalating them. (I sometimes refer to anxiety as a "volume control" of other painful emotions like anger, frustration, or loneliness.)

Key questions:

- How does my anxiety most often speak to me?
- In what sorts of situations is it a yell, a chatter, or a whisper?
- What types of anxiety do I manage well already, and what types of anxiety do I want to get better at?

## Building Block 3: Contextualize your anxiety

Now that you have identified some ways anxiety speaks to you, you are ready to understand more about its context: where, when, and

---

* See Jamie, whose whisper anxiety is introduced in chapter 3 (p. 42) and followed up with at the start of chapter 12.

how you feel it. Look to identify patterns, causes, themes, and a bigger picture for your anxiety. This will set you up for the steps ahead.

Whether your anxiety is a yell, a chatter, or a whisper, it is always about conflict and your fear of it. There is a discomfort to anxiety that energizes you, helps you pay attention, and gets you to find solutions. Like an alarm clock you can't shut off, anxiety's evolutionary job is to keep you focused on threats to the things you care about most in life.

Key questions:

- What patterns do I see in my anxiety? Are there people, places, or situations that trigger it?
- Are there certain places and situations that seem to cause me the most conflict? What threads connect them?
- How do these patterns relate to other important conflicts in my life?

# Pillar Two: Identifying Anxiety

Once you've recognized your anxiety, noticed how it is speaking to you, and understood more about when and where you experience it, you are ready to identify its message.

### Building Block 1: Hear anxiety's message

Just like birds have to turn into the wind in order to fly, we have to turn into our anxiety in order to transform its energy into action.

Anxiety's force can be daunting and intimidating. We may believe the way to weather anxiety's storm is to take shelter and avoid it, but ultimately anxiety can't be avoided.

At times, you will do almost anything to escape anxiety's unrelenting discomfort—these feelings you believe you just can't handle. Or can you? You may not *want* to, you may not *have* to right this minute, but you absolutely *can* handle your anxiety. The key is to not confuse your aversion to it with not being *able* to tolerate it. Anxiety itself isn't dangerous. In fact, it is quite the opposite. Faced head on, it makes you stronger. It's supposed to motivate you to make it stop. This process is there to protect you and it is best done with curiosity.

Key questions:

- In what ways do I resist facing my anxiety?
- Can I identify situations where this strategy makes it worse?
- In thinking about a recent time I was anxious, was I uncomfortable or genuinely afraid that I couldn't handle it? Am I feeling that way now?
- In what ways can I be more self-compassionate and curious, rather than avoid my discomfort?
- Where can I take a control of my thinking and lean into my discomfort?

## Building Block 2: Name your anxiety

Once you have recognized and faced your anxiety, you are ready to identify how you are feeling. One of the best ways of accomplishing this is to put your feelings into words, either aloud or on paper. If you don't have anyone readily available to talk about your feelings with, document them on paper or even talk things out with yourself. Dictation software can bridge the gap between talking and writing, bringing to the page your naturally flowing words. Naming our experience helps us articulate what we are feeling and offers relief in and of itself.

When you talk or write about your feelings, you will notice your experience starts to change. You don't know what's going to happen because you are "processing" your experience. Any list-maker understands the value of getting those swirling thoughts down on paper. The simple act of holding it in creates anxiety as pressure builds; articulating your feelings offers an outlet and the distance to understand them.

As you express your feelings, they will become clarified, distilled, and diminish in intensity. In addition to the relief of expressing your feelings in writing, capturing your experience on paper allows some distance to see what's going on. Noticing both what you see on the page and feel in your body and mind allows distance, which activates more of our thinking resources to bear on the problem.

As you articulate your feelings, aim to be physically comfortable and in a safe, private place. Imagine you are talking to a close friend or supportive teacher. Let your feelings flow: aim to describe how you *feel*, not events that have happened.

If this is hard, remember the goal is simply to ignite curiosity about your experiences and feelings. Think of this process like mining for something really valuable protected by layers of rock and debris. Our feelings, especially the scary, uncomfortable ones, are sometimes buried beneath layers of defenses and avoidant behaviors. If your feelings feel hard to extract, there is likely a reason for this. With persistent excavation, feelings will emerge and become clearer.

Key questions to tease apart your feelings:

- What are the ways I feel uncomfortable, anxious, or unsettled?
- Are there areas of my life that are more stressful than others? My work, family, or relationships?
- Are there areas of my social life that are worrisome or leave me feeling disconnected and unsupported?
- Where do I feel out of control in my life?
- What events or situations past or present have contributed to my feelings?
- What might this mean for the future, and what could happen?
- What am I sure of? What aren't I sure of?
- How do I feel about how I'm feeling?
- As I think about a particular situation that makes me anxious, what feelings are clear to me?
- What am I afraid of?

If you know you are anxious, complete the following:

- I feel afraid of…
- I am scared about…

- I worry that…
- I'm anxious when…
- …makes me really nervous.
- …scares me.
- I wish _____ weren't happening. Thinking about it makes me _____ that _____ will happen, and I will feel _____.

## Building Block 3: Decode anxiety's message

Once you have identified how you are feeling anxious, you can now start the process of decoding its message, looking for the "why" behind it all. You likely have a list of situations, thoughts, and feelings, likely clustering around anxiety and some things you really care about. Break out a highlighter to note the feelings that are part of each sentence. This will help you clarify what is emerging.

Look at the details of your fears, but also look at the overall themes. Is there one area that is worrying you, like your relationship? Or is it something about your performance at work? Are you worried about money and the future? Perhaps there are overlaps, or perhaps there are distinct fears that seem unrelated.

Where is anxiety emerging? Where is the conflict? What might your anxiety be trying to tell you? Sometimes anxiety's messages aren't so obvious, and they need more sleuthing to expose. The following clues can offer further strategies to help you decode what can sometimes be anxiety's confusing presentation.

## Ask open-ended questions:

- If my feelings could talk, what would they say?
- How do I feel at this moment? Try to identify three distinct feelings.
- What might my anxiety be trying to warn me about?
- What future event am I afraid of, and how might I be on a path to it?
- If that scary thing happened, what would happen next?
- If that scary thing happened, what would that mean for me, my goals, or my future?
- Could I handle it?
- What am I afraid of doing but might be wise to consider?

## Ask targeted questions:

- How is anxiety yelling at me?
- In what ways do I feel the chatter of anxiety?
- Where could anxiety be whispering to me? What might it be saying?
- What do I care about that is at risk?
- What can't I handle that could be looming ahead?
- In what ways do I feel trapped and unable to control an outcome?
- What are some things that matter a lot to me and are worrying me?

- What important situations are out of my control and causing me worry?

Where do you feel conflict? Common areas of conflict exist around time management, meeting conflicting demands, feeling pulled by contradictory desires. Anxiety can be both a signal and by-product of conflict, so looking for these clashes makes good sense as a starting place.

<u>Key questions:</u>

- What elements of my life feel at odds with one another?
- In what ways do I feel torn between two imperfect options, stressed about choices, or irritated by the competing demands in my life?
- What inconsistencies in my life are bothering me?
- Where in my life do I feel confused, conflicted, or ambivalent?
- Where do I feel tugged, pulled, even trapped?
- Where in my life do I not see solutions I *like*?

## OBSERVE ESCALATED FEELINGS

Anxiety can be an *escalator of other feelings* too, so looking for places where you experience intense feelings will often uncover anxiety. Emotions are accelerated by anxiety's signal that you can't, or don't want to, handle them. Anger is often the result of pain fueled by the fear that you can't handle it. Look for anxiety in your escalated feelings.

Key questions:

- What makes me mad or brings tightness to my chest?
- What brings me to tears? Is it part of any situation I have already described?
- What feelings are so intense that they feel overwhelming or even confusing?
- Are there feelings or experiences that I'm trying to ignore and avoid?
- What feelings am I having that I'm not sure I can handle?

## NOTICE PUSHED "BUTTONS"

Another escalator of anxiety is when our "buttons" get pushed. We react to a situation almost instinctively, because it triggers something else we remember or are sensitive about. These emotionally loaded experiences bring up feelings about the present as well as feelings about the past. These happen often: your spouse's criticism reminds you of something your mother would say to your father, your friend annoys you in a way your sibling used to, or your coworker grates on you the way a classmate once did.

Key questions:

- Have I ever felt this way before?
- How does this experience remind me of situations in my past?

- How might my feelings from the past be escalating, and possibly conflating, my feelings now?
- Even as the situations feel similar, can I see how they are different?

## IDENTIFY INCONSISTENT BEHAVIOR

Anxiety can also lurk in your inexplicable actions and behavior, those patterns or habits that are at odds with your goals. Did you not prepare for that important presentation even though you're soon up for a promotion? Do you want a strong relationship with your children but turn them down when they ask to play? Confusing behavior can be a powerful signal of conflict, and it can illustrate where you feel anxiety, even if you aren't completely aware of it.

Conflict can also signal ambivalence about doing something you don't believe you can do. Avoiding it only makes it scarier. Thinking you can't handle something is usually your body telling you that you simply don't *want to*. Turning your "can'ts" into "don't-want-tos" can be incredibly powerful, because it reintroduces choice and control. Choice allows for action, and therefore it presents a solution.

Key questions:

- What behavior do I regularly engage in that confuses me, is counterproductive, or is self-destructive?
- What situations or behaviors do I avoid?

- If my behavior could talk, what would it say?
- How might my behavior say, "I want to ____ , but I have to
  _____ ?"
- How might my behavior say, "I believe I want to _____ ,
  (e.g. get to work on time, go to the gym) but I really want
  to _____ (e.g., sleep late, stay on the couch).
- Where does my behavior betray me? Where does it embarrass me or make me feel ashamed?

## IDENTIFY NUMBING BEHAVIOR

Another type of avoidance is emotional avoidance. Look for ways you might numb or detach from your emotions all together. Think about how and when you check out. Perhaps you use substances like alcohol, recreational or prescription drugs, tobacco, or food to relax? Or do you participate in dopamine-enhancing activities like internet surfing, video games, gambling, or pornography to help fight boredom or dull uncomfortable feelings? Do you binge-watch TV when you really don't have time? Or maybe you use healthy activities to excess like sex, exercise, or work?

First, establish how dependent are you on these activities or actions. Are these behaviors something you can take or leave, or are they something you *need*? How hard would they be to give up? This can help you determine how much you use them to deal with other emotions rather than simply enjoying them.

Second, ask yourself if there are any negative impacts of your behavior. Do you actually have the time to catch up on *Game of Thrones* if your mail is piling up, your house is a mess, and your friends are wondering where you have been? Does having that cocktail stop you from being patient enough to help your daughter with her homework?

Last, take a look at how dopamine might be hijacking your attention, fueling you to keep trying for a new life on *Candy Crush* or waiting for more likes on Facebook. Fatigue makes us particularly susceptible to our brain's desire for reward. This is dopamine at play.

Numbing behaviors are often those things we reach for to feel control and distance. Ultimately, they are the temporary escapes from our anxiety. We often settle for this rather than face the confusion and pain of our unsolved conflicts. In the end, not only do these behaviors do a poor job of shielding us from our anxiety, they produce additional frustration.

## PINPOINT HOT-BUTTON ISSUES AND ANXIOUS LANGUAGE

Anxiety can also show up in our language, self-talk, and ways we understand and interpret our worlds. It can lurk in the background of our attention and concerns, clueing us in to the things we care about. Subtle vocabulary choices and common irritants can often uncover the things we care about most and our concerns about them.

Key questions:

- What complaints do I most commonly have? What are the situations that get under my skin?
- Are there national or community issues I care about so

much it upsets me or the people around me? (*When issues start to feel personal, this is a clue that anxiety is at work.*)

- When and where do I rely on anxious language?
- Where do I most use phrases that have to do with fear, stress, and worry?

## PAY ATTENTION TO YOUR DREAMS

Considered an indispensable therapeutic tool, dreams often demonstrate in bright color the worries and concerns that can lurk just outside our awareness. Though everyone dreams, many people seldom remember them. If you are a vivid dreamer, or you can consistently remember them, you have another tool at your disposal.

After waking, be ready to take notes because the memories of our dreams fade quickly. Dreams often amplify feelings and thoughts you have while you are awake. Does the dream of you in public in your underwear remind you of the fear of humiliation anywhere in your real life?

In your dreams, people can represent themselves, others like them in real life, or even manifest different aspects of yourself. This goes for objects and places as well. Don't get stuck in literal thinking—focus on the feeling. Dreams often symbolize feelings and dynamics we are either unaware of or are unable to process in waking life. Getting at dreams' messages can a be a powerful tool in building self-awareness.

Key questions:

- How do I feel now?
- How did I feel immediately after I woke up?
- What happened in the dream that made me feel this way?
- Who was I in the dream? How did I feel as that person?
- Do any of the other people in the dream remind me of elements of myself?
- Where in my life do I feel the same feelings I felt in the dream?
- What conflicts from the dream are true with others and within myself?

Before moving on, take a moment to review what you have identified so far about your anxiety. You now understand how it speaks to you, how often and in what contexts it manifests, it's obvious—and less obvious—messages. You are assembling your conflicts, your fears, and your discomforts, and they are identified on paper in whatever way makes sense to you. This sets you up for the next step: sorting them.

## Pillar Three: Sorting Anxiety

You now have a better impression of the things you really care about. Identifying what you want and what to do to get there comes next. You are ready to sort anxiety's message, and identify the actions that can solve it.

## Building Block 1: Determine rational fears

It's easy to waste time attending to irrational fears at the expense of the rational ones. Some anxiety is almost always rooted in the irrational. Take the common fear of "I can't handle it." Have you ever thought about looking at the evidence? What does it say?* Are you afraid, averse to the discomfort, or is it literally true that you can't handle it?

By contrast, anxiety that signals a realistic threat is considered rational and worth heeding. A good example of this would be, *If I don't finish this project on time my boss will be angry*. These fears are signaling an important problem that needs your attention—and these are worth parsing out. If it isn't immediately obvious what is irrational and what is not, here's a useful hint: any anxiety about not being able to handle things is irrational. Feelings are uncomfortable, painful, even excruciating, but they *are always tolerable*.

Key questions to determine rational from irrational fears:

- Which of my worries are irrational, and which of them are rational?
- Which of my fears realistic? What fears could *actually* happen?
- Where is the evidence that what I'm worried about is true?

---

* This was the work of Albert Ellis, a psychologist who was a pioneer in the practice of cognitive behavioral therapy. Along with other cognitivists, Ellis believed that anxiety was the result of irrational catastrophic thinking.

- If I were to survey the most reasonable person I know, would he or she say my fears are rational or irrational?
- Am I getting stuck in *possibilities* rather than *probabilities*? What could be rather than what is likely to be?
- Has my time horizon skewed too far in advance, confusing what is in front of me right now?

## Building Block 2: Prioritize goals

Identifying your goals requires two steps: (1) deciding what you care about and (2) figuring out how to realistically get there. You might be petrified of flying, but you know that the only way to stop it from negatively impacting your life is to get on a plane, a solution so clear and scary that it both brings relief and anxiety.

Other times it's not so straightforward, and a more delineated process is needed. When you think about the future, what comes to mind? What are your hopes and dreams? Your most important values? Embedded in our aspirations and dreams are our values and the things we care about. Perhaps you want to find a loving relationship and raise children or feel comfortable with your professional legacy. Each of these can drive any number of worries about how to get there, and what to do when you fall off track. Another way of accessing our goals is to look at our fears. Maybe you are afraid of not finding love, being stuck in a lackluster job, or retiring with little savings. Core fears provide insight into our deepest goals and desires.

<u>Key questions to ask in delineating your goals:</u>

- What do I want?
- What are the experiences and achievements that are the most important to me?
- What don't I care so much about?
- What do I wish would happen without my effort?
- What am I afraid of not having?

## Building Block 3: Resist the wish trap

Getting what we want involves parsing the choices we *have* from the choices we *wish we had*. We can't control the past, we can't control others, and there are aspects of our current situation that are simply unchangeable. Taking action toward things you cannot change is wasteful, unproductive, and ultimately anxiety provoking.

So compelling are these fantasies that they can be hard to shake sometimes, and they can even lure you into thinking you are powerless or have no choice other than to be passive. This is a trap of powerlessness that keeps up from harnessing the advantages of our anxiety.

Most of the time, resisting action that needs to be taken is not helpful. Examples of this are staying in an unhealthy relationship while wishing it will go back to the way it was or continuing to engage unhealthy eating patterns hoping someday you will somehow change. Indulging in fantasies stunt your growth. Remind yourself that change, growth, and solutions can only happen within the constructs of reality. With compassion, you will get there.

<u>Key questions to consider in parsing choices from wishes:</u>

- What are the choices I *have*? (Not the choices I *wish I had*.)
- What can I control?
- What can't I control?
- In what ways are the solutions I can't control holding me back from the ones I can?

## Building Block 4: Adjust anxiety's volume

A moderate amount of anxiety is helpful, but too much is unproductive. This is the place where you may need to adjust the volume of your anxiety. Look for ways you may be fighting your anxiety and inadvertently driving it up, rather than facing it head on. Other helpful action steps include traditional techniques of deep breathing, relaxation training, exercise, and yoga as well as good old-fashioned rest. Refer back to chapter 18 for additional resources on soothing.

If your high levels of anxiety continue to impair your sleep, appetite, or ability to do the things you normally do, you may need extra assistance. This is where a qualified professional can help. It can be useful to think of professional or pharmacological treatment as something you can *do* to help yourself. It's no different from using crutches to support you during a healing process for a broken leg.

<u>Key questions to determine excessive anxiety:</u>

- Can I think clearly or am I easily distracted, frustrated, and confused about what to prioritize?

- Do I feel overwhelmed by my anxiety?
- Is my anxiety getting in the way of my other priorities?
- Can I fall asleep and stay asleep?
- Do I feel stuck or powerless?
- Am I so frustrated or worn down, I feel tempted to give up?

## Pillar Four: Determining Action

This part of the process varies tremendously by individual. While determining anxiety's message is different for everyone, so too is identifying smart action. This is where listening to and thinking about your anxiety really matters. Inaccurate perceptions will spin ineffective action: it's fruit from the poisoned tree. Address your evidence-based fears, orient your thoughts toward realistic goals, and identify action within your control.

### Building Block 1: Establish your decision-making style

According to the popular Myers-Briggs Type Indicator, we all make decisions differently. Some persons are introverted types who make decisions easily and alone (I-J)*, while others labor over decisions, preferring to weigh options and the opinions of others to help them (E-P).† The presence of anxiety in itself

---

\*    I-J refers to the first and last letters of a four-part type, "Introverted" and "Judger," meaning that a person gets their energy from being alone rather than with people and prefers to make decisions rather than take in information.

†    E-P refers to the first and last letters of a four-part type, "Extroverted" and "Perceiver," meaning that a person gets their energy from being with people rather than being alone, and prefers to make take in information rather than make decisions.

may compromise your natural decision-making capabilities and require enlisting other nonpreferred decision-making styles.

How you make decisions will impact how you identify action. While making decisions might be easiest with pad and paper, a pensive commute, or long shower, you can also rely on supportive friends, mentors, or a good therapist. Extroverts and introverts alike can benefit from social support; people who encourage and believe in you will restore your belief in yourself.

Key questions to understand your decision-making style:

- Are decisions hard or easy for me?
- How do I make the best decisions, and is this any different under pressure?
- What can I do to ensure optimal decision-making when I am anxious?

## Building Block 2: Identify potential solutions

Now that you (1) know where and how you feel anxiety, (2) have identified the choices you have rather than the choices you wish you had, and (3) know a bit more about how you make decisions, you are now ready to identify solutions. Remember, anxiety's job is to keep bothering you until you take action. Let's consider what actions make the most sense for you.

For many, the process of understanding anxiety points to somewhat obvious solutions. Anxiety about being alone necessarily invites solutions around cultivating more satisfying relationships, just as anxieties about financial resources stimulate saving and earning solutions. Within our various anxieties are always the seeds of their solution. We often know intuitively what we need to do.

As you look back over your anxiety and reflect on the conflicts you have uncovered, notice the solutions that emerge, and write them down. Perhaps you know you need to speak up more in your relationships, change your lifestyle, or make a bold career move. Often, big solutions come to mind quickly, but they immediately get shrouded in layers of complications, fears, and other reasons why you can't. Remember, actions that provoke anxiety are often the very ones we need to consider carefully; they are often signaling something important that we care about.

Think of this like the ultimate brainstorming exercise. Keep going until you run out of ideas. And when it feels like you have run out of ideas, try again a bit more. The idea is to source your anxiety as close as possible for as many solutions as you can generate and keep a list. Don't worry about organizing them now, just get them down. Make sure that your solutions are *within your control*.

Key questions to ask in identifying solutions:

- What solutions would diminish my anxiety?
- What can I do to alter or prevent the things that I am afraid of?
- What can I control? What can't I control?

- What solution would help me feel more comfortable with my situation?
- How do I want to feel? What actions are in my control that would help ensure this?
- What do I need to do but am afraid of doing?
- What do I wish I were able to do?
- What do I wish I had already done?
- What action comes to mind that I immediately dread?
- What would I do if I weren't afraid?

## Building Block 3: Prioritize solutions

Now that you have potential solutions in front of you, it is time to figure out what solutions make the most sense and which are less feasible. While it is not critical to rank your anxieties and action steps, doing so can engage your executive thinking, which delivers a greater sense of control. It also breaks your actions down into manageable steps rather than overwhelming you.

Are there some solutions that would solve more than one of your anxieties? These solutions are the most valuable and should be ranked higher. Perhaps you worry that your health is suffering from your poor lifestyle choices, which also negatively impacts your work performance and relationships. When you have your list, ask yourself which solutions appear the most important? Which ones seem the easiest to manage? Look for the action items that rise to the top of the pile, in spite of how frightening they might feel.

Key questions to help prioritize solutions:

- Which solutions solve the most important conflicts?
- Which solutions do I feel comfortable implementing?
- Which solutions feel too scary to implement?
- What would it take to implement a scary solution?

# Pillar Five: Taking Action

Anxiety offers the energy you need to forge solutions, and it stubbornly won't give up until you engage it. Now that you have identified anxiety's message and identified action steps, you are moving into action. Don't be surprised if you start to notice a resurgence of avoidance, confusion, or resistance. It's the moment of truth, and the physical sensations of anxiety are your body readying itself for action, not telling you to stop.

## Building Block 1: Dismantle resistance

Even if you are sold on the benefits of action, you still might not know where to start, how to start, or even be willing to take that leap. Your mind might be cluttered with all the compelling reasons why not to act. This is anxiety doing its job: fueling conflict, discomfort, and also the energy and discomfort to solve it. Resistance is your body's way to protect itself from pain and discomfort. Maybe the steps you've delineated are too big, or maybe the goal is too lofty and threatening. Aim to make steps so small that resistance is kept in check.

The best action plans involve small steps—no less than five parts. If you are struggling to change your eating habits, break the beginning into small parts. Start by planning out a menu and then a shopping list. After this step, then figure out how to get home in time to cook and create strategies to avoid ordering takeout or attacking the whole refrigerator. Or a new exercise routine can begin with you determining what you need and like to do. Then procure the necessary equipment or clothing. After this, create a schedule and come up with strategies to keep that schedule. These are all action steps that are each small enough to bypass resistance. They also help build *momentum*. Picture yourself doing these smaller tasks. Notice how manageable they are. Know that you are prepared.

Key questions to break solutions into manageable parts:

- How can solutions be broken into small pieces?
- If any of the pieces still feel scary, in what way can I break them down further?
- What is a step small enough that I can do it without resistance?

## Building Block 2: Take the leap

You have your steps delineated, you know when and how you will execute them, and you are now ready to act. Be aware of your old tricks that help you avoid your discomfort. Maximize calming techniques if anxiety spikes, breathing deeply and evenly, minimizing distractions, and telling yourself *I can do this*.

This is the time for courage—the belief in something greater than your fear. You have done the work of understanding and prioritizing how to use your anxiety, you have planned how you will act, and you have assessed your resistance for any final clues that are worth heading. You have ruled out any good reason to abstain from action, and now is the time to engage anxiety's energy. It is time to act.

Key questions to review for courage:

- What purpose do I care more about than my anxiety?
- Can I reframe my anxiety as excitement for this opportunity to take control and solve this problem?
- Can I remind myself it's okay to be anxious, that this is courage, and I am stretching myself?
- How can I be gentle with my anxiety, and my effort, while not allowing myself to avoid?
- If not now, when? And how?

## Building Block 3: Build momentum

Once you face your fears and take smart action, you will feel your anxiety diminish. This can happen immediately upon taking that first step or be more gradual. As first steps evolve into next steps, momentum takes hold and the effort needed diminishes. It's like any new habit—speaking in public, exercising more, or getting to bed earlier—the more you do it, the easier it gets. The original anxiety is no longer needed to spur action, so it diminishes. Momentum is the great blessing of behavioral change. If solutions are well considered and sustainable, they quickly become self-reinforcing.

## Building Block 4: Resolve anxiety

The last, and perhaps most important, thing to notice in this process is the resolution of your initial anxiety. Breathe, take it in, and notice the positive change. Taking action drives down your anxiety; once its aim is achieved, its purpose is fulfilled. Anxiety for this conflict is no longer needed once action is underway, momentum is engaged, and space is created for focus to other priorities. To the degree that anxiety feels confining, draining, and distressing, its relief brings space, energy, and joy.

**Your Anxiety Tool Kit**

Making Your Anxiety Work for You!

## 1
### RECOGNIZING ANXIETY

Reframe Your Thinking

Notice How Anxiety Speaks to You

Contextualize Your Anxiety

## 2
### IDENTIFYING ANXIETY

Hear Anxiety's Message

Name Your Anxiety

Decode Anxiety's Message

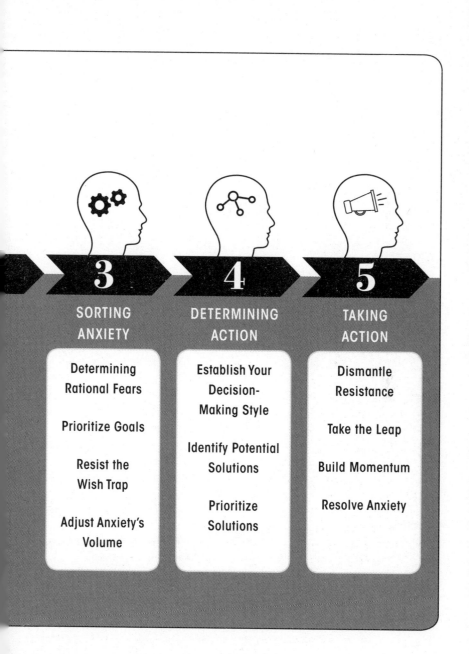

**3**

SORTING
ANXIETY

Determining
Rational Fears

Prioritize Goals

Resist the
Wish Trap

Adjust Anxiety's
Volume

**4**

DETERMINING
ACTION

Establish Your
Decision-
Making Style

Identify Potential
Solutions

Prioritize
Solutions

**5**

TAKING
ACTION

Dismantle
Resistance

Take the Leap

Build Momentum

Resolve Anxiety

# Notes

## Introduction

1    Viktor Frankl, *Man's Search for Meaning* (Boston: Beacon Press, 2006).

2    Ellen Hendriksen, "Anxiety, Depression, or Both?" Scientific American, May 19, 2016, https://www.scientificamerican.com/article/anxiety-depression-or-both/.

## Chapter One

1    Jane Wagner, *The Search for Signs of Intelligent Life in the Universe* (New York: Harper Collins, 1986), 18.

2    T. M. Luhrmann, "The Anxious Americans," *New York Times*, July 18, 2015, https://mobile.nytimes.com/2015/07/19/opinion/sunday/the-anxious-americans.html.

3    Ruth Whippman, "America the Anxious," *New York Times*, September 22, 2012, https://opinionator.blogs.nytimes.com/2012/09/22/america-the-anxious/?_r=0.

4    "Facts & Statistics," Anxiety and Depression Association of America, last modified August 2017, https://www.adaa.org/about-adaa/press-room/facts-statistics.

5    "Highlights: Workplace Stress & Anxiety Survey," Anxiety and Depression Association of America, accessed July 1, 2017, https://www.adaa.org/workplace-stress-anxiety-disorders-survey.

6    "Who's stressed in the U.S.? Adult Stress Levels from 1983–2009 Described," Science Daily, June 11, 2012, www.sciencedaily.com/releases/2012/06/120611153228.htm.

7    Seth Stephens-Davidowitz, "Fifty States of Anxiety," *New York Times*, August 6, 2016, http://www.nytimes.com/2016/08/07/opinion/sunday/fifty-states-of-anxiety.html.

8    Mihaly Csikszentmihalyi, *Flow: The Psychology of Optimal Experience* (New York: HarperCollins, 2008), 33.

9    Matthew B. Crawford, *The World Beyond Your Head: On Becoming an Individual in the Age of Distraction*, (New York: Macmillan, 2015), 16.

10    Susan Weinschenk, "Why We're All Addicted to Texts, Twitter and Google," *Psychology Today*, September 11, 2012, https://www.psychologytoday.com/blog/brain-wise/201209/why-were-all-addicted-texts-twitter-and-google.

11    "What Is the Tiny Life Movement?" The Tiny Life, accessed June 24, 2017, http://thetinylife.com/what-is-the-tiny-house-movement/.

12    Kathleen D. Vohs, et al., "Making Choices Impairs Subsequent Self-Control: A Limited-Resource Account of Decision Making, Self-Regulation, and Active Initiative," *Journal of Personality and Social Psychology* 94, no. 5 (2008): 883–898.

13    Barry Schwartz, "More Isn't Always Better," *Harvard Business Review*, June 2006, https://hbr.org/2006/06/more-isnt-always-better.

14    Louis Menard, "The Prisoner of Stress," *The New Yorker*, January 27, 2014, https://www.newyorker.com/magazine/2014/01/27/the-prisoner-of-stress.

15    Maria Konnikova, "When It's Bad to Have Good Choices," *The New Yorker*, August 1, 2014, http://www.newyorker.com/science/maria-konnikova/bad-good-choices.

16    Eric Barker, "This Is the Best Way to Overcome Fear of Missing Out," *Time*, June 7, 2016, http://time.com/4358140/overcome-fomo/.

17    Amit Chowdhry, "Research Links Heavy Facebook and Social Media Usage to Depression," *Forbes*, April 30, 2016, https://www.forbes.com/sites/amitchowdhry/2016/04/30/study-links-heavy-facebook-and-social-media-usage-to-depression/#126cdee64b53.

18    Liu yi Lin, et al., "Association Between Social Media Use and Depression Among U.S. Young Adults," *Depression and Anxiety* 33 (January 2016): 323–331, http://onlinelibrary.wiley.com/doi/10.1002/da.22466/abstract.

19    Elle Hunt, "What Are 'Read Receipts' and How Can I Stop Them Destroying My Life?" The Guardian, March 17, 2017, https://www.theguardian.com/culture/2017/mar/17/i-know-theyve-seen-my-message-so-why-havent-they-replied.

20    Alan Watts, *The Wisdom of Insecurity: A Message for an Age of Anxiety* (New York: Random House, 2011), 52.

21    Kristine Phillips, "Ruth Bader Ginsburg on Trump's presidency: 'We Are Not Experiencing the Best of Times,'" *Washington Post*, February 24, 2017, https://www.washingtonpost.com/news/the-fix/wp/2017/02/24/ruth-bader-ginsburg-on-trumps-presidency-we-are-not-experiencing-the-best-of-times/?utm_term=.84cfd06523f3.

22    Edie Weiner and Arnold Brown, *FutureThink: How to Think Clearly in a Time of Change* (Upper Saddle River, NJ: Prentice Hall, 2006), 24.

23    Charles Hugh Smith, "Social Change Will Upend the Status Quo," *Washington's Blog*, January 10, 2018, http://www.washingtonsblog.com/2018/01/social-change-will-upend-status-quo.html.

24    Robert L. Leahy, "How to Think about Terrorism," *Psychology Today*, January 10, 2015, https://www.psychologytoday.com/blog/anxiety-files/201501/how-think-about-terrorism.

25    Ginia Bellafante, "Yes, the World Is Going Berserk, but Inner Peace Is Still Possible," *New York Times*, July 20, 2016, http://nyti.ms/2ahCdKo.

26    "Xanax: The Dangerous Benzodiazepine," Novus Detox, accessed April 5, 2017, https://novusdetox.com/xanax-the-dangerous-benzodiazepine.

27    Stephens Davidowitz, "Fifty States of Anxiety."

28    Steven M. Platek, Julian Paul Keenan, and Todd K. Shackelford, eds., *Evolutionary Cognitive Neuroscience* (Cambridge, MA: MIT Press, 2006).

29    "Binge Drinking," Centers for Disease Control and Prevention, accessed July 10, 2014, last modified October 11, 2013, http://www.cdc.gov/vitalsigns/BingeDrinkingfemale/.

30    Tanya Mohn, "Arrests of Women for Drunken Driving Are on the Rise," *New York Times*, September 4, 2009, http://wheels.blogs.nytimes.com/2009/09/04/arrests-of-women-for-drunken-driving-are-on-the-rise/?_php=true&_type=blogs&_php=true&_type=blogs&_r=1.

31    Andrew Solomon, *The Noonday Demon: An Atlas of Depression* (New York: Simon & Schuster, 2011), 226.

32    Cynthia L. Ogden, et al., "Prevalence of Obesity Among Adults and Youth: United States, 2011–2014," Centers for Disease Control and Prevention, November 2015, https://www.cdc.gov/nchs/data/databriefs/db219.pdf.

33    "Overweight and Obesity Statistics," National Institute of Diabetes and Digestive Kidney Diseases, August 2017, https://www.niddk.nih.gov/health-information/health-statistics/overweight-obesity.

34    "Statistics about Diabetes," American Diabetes Association, last updated July 19, 2017, http://www.diabetes.org/diabetes-basics/statistics/.

35    James A. Levine, "What Are the Risks of Sitting Too Much?" Mayo Clinic, September 4, 2015, http://www.mayoclinic.org/healthy-lifestyle/adult-health/expert-answers/sitting/faq-20058005.

36    David Hinkley, "Average American Watches 5 Hours of TV Per Day, Report Shows," *NY Daily News*, March 5, 2014, http://www.nydailynews.com/life-style/average-american-watches-5-hours-tv-day-article-1.1711954.

37    "Digital Set to Surpass TV in Time Spent with US Media," eMarketer, August 1, 2013, http://www.emarketer.com/Article/Digital-Set-Surpass-TV-Time-Spent-with-US-Media/1010096.

38    Jacqueline Howard, "Americans Devote More Than 10 Hours a Day to Screen Time, and Growing," CNN, July 29, 2016, http://www.cnn.com/2016/06/30/health/americans-screen-time-nielsen/.

39    Robert M. Sapolsky, *Why Zebras Don't Get Ulcers* (New York: Holt Paperbacks, 2004), 334.

40    "Relaxation Drinks the Next Billion Dollar Industry," Bloomberg TV, accessed July 1, 2017, http://www.bloomberg.com/video/relaxation-drinks-next-billion-dollar-industry-rWwSLjvBTwS_dGV6eiZfBA.html.

41    "Higher Anxiety Linked to What You're Probably Doing Right Now," PsyBlog, accessed July 10, 2017, http://www.spring.org.uk/2015/06/increased-anxiety-linked-to-simple-behaviour-youre-probably-doing-right-now.php.

42    Megan Teychenne et al., "The Association between Sedentary Behaviour and Risk of Anxiety: A Systematic Review," BMC Public Health, June 19, 2015, http://bmcpublichealth.biomedcentral.com/articles/10.1186/s12889-015-1843-x.

## Chapter Two

1    Benedict de Spinoza, *On the Improvement of the Understanding/The Ethics/Correspondence* (Dover Publications, 1955), 101.

2  Michael A. Tompkins, *Anxiety and Avoidance: A Universal Treatment for Anxiety, Panic, and Fear* (Oakland, CA: New Harbinger Publications, 2013), 23.

3  Sue Shellenbarger, "Rethink Your After-Work Routine to Make the Transition Home a Happy One," *Wall Street Journal*, February 10, 2015, https://www.wsj.com/articles/rethink-your-after-work-routine-to-make-the-transition-home-a-happy-one-1423611601.

4  Jon Kabat-Zinn, *Full Catastrophe Living*, 2nd ed.,(New York: Random House, 2013), xxvii.

5  Thea Singer, *Stress Less: The New Science That Shows Women How to Rejuvenate the Body and the Mind* (London: Penguin, 2010), xvi.

6  Jean M. Twenge, Liqing Zhang, Charles Im, "It's Beyond My Control: A Cross-Temporal Meta-Analysis of Increasing Externality in Locus of Control, 1960–2002," *Personality and Social Psychology Review* 8, no. 3 (2004): 308–319.

7  David Eagleman, *Incognito: The Secret Lives of the Brain* (New York; Random House, 2011), 26.

8  Christopher Chabris and Daniel Simons, "Gorilla Experiment," The Invisible Gorilla, accessed September 14, 2017, http://www.theinvisiblegorilla.com/gorilla_experiment.html.

9  Eagleman, *Incognito*, 28.

10  Malcolm Gladwell, *Outliers: The Story of Success* (New York, Hachette, 2008).

11  "Learn Why We Must Keep Our Minds on Driving and Off Our Cell Phones," National Safety Council, accessed June 23, 2017, http://www.nsc.org/learn/NSC-Initiatives/Pages/Understanding-the-Distracted-Brain.aspx.

12  Daniel Goleman, *Focus: The Hidden Driver of Excellence* (New York: Harper Collins: 2014), 20.

13  "Learn Why We Must Keep Our Minds on Driving," National Safety Council; Marcel Adam Just, Timothy A. Keller, and Jacquelyn Cynkar, "A Decrease in Brain Activation Associated with Driving When Listening to Someone Speak," *Brain Research* 1205 (April 18, 2008): 70–80, doi:10.1016/j.brainres.2007.12.075.

14  Maria Popova, "The Difficult Art of Self-Compassion," Brain Pickings, accessed April 23, 2017, https://www.brainpickings.org/2016/09/05/school-of-life-self-compassion/.

15  Tompkins, *Anxiety and Avoidance*, 43.

16  Heidi Grant Halvorson, *Succeed: How We Can Reach Our Goals* (New York: Penguin, 2011), 11.

17  Anne Lamott, *Bird by Bird: Some Instructions on Writing and Life* (New York: Anchor, 1995), 31.

## Chapter Three

1  *Sherlock*, episode 10, "The Abominable Bride," directed by Douglas Mackinnon, written by Mark Gatiss and Steven Moffat, aired January 1, 2016, on BBC One.

2  Salam Ranabir and L. Reetu, "Stress and Hormones," *Indian Journal of Endocrinology and Medicine* 15, no.1 (2011): 18–22, http://www.ncbi.nlm.nih.gov/pmc/articles/PMC3079864/.

3  Casey Schwartz, "A Neuroscientist Argues That Everybody Is Misunderstanding Fear and Anxiety," The Cut, July 23, 2015, https://www.thecut.com/2015/07/everybody-misunderstanding-fear-and-anxiety.html?mid=facebook_scienceofus.

4  Schwartz, "A Neuroscientist Argues That Everybody Is Misunderstanding Fear and Anxiety."

5  "Understanding the Stress Response," Harvard Health Publishing, last modified March 18, 2016, http://www.health.harvard.edu/staying-healthy/understanding-the-stress-response.

6  Joseph LeDoux, "Coming to Terms with Fear," *Proceedings of the National Academy of Sciences*

*of the United States of America*, January 9, 2014, http://www.cns.nyu.edu/ledoux/pdf/PNAS
-2014-LeDoux-1400335111.pdf.

7 Eagleman, *Incognito*, 68.

8 Joseph LeDoux, *Anxious: Using the Brain to Understand and Treat Fear and Anxiety* (New York:
Penguin, 2015), 134.

9 Cornelia Herbert et al., "Emotional Self-Reference: Brain Structures Involved in the Processing of
Words Describing One's Own Emotions," *Neuropsychologia* 49, no. 10 (August 2011): 294–2956.

10 "Anxiety," American Psychological Association, accessed August 14, 2017, http://www.apa.org
/topics/anxiety/.

11 Patricia Pearson, *A Brief History of Anxiety...Yours and Mine* (New York: Bloomsbury, 2009),
9–10.

12 American Psychiatric Association, *Diagnostic and Statistical Manual of Mental Disorders (DSM-
5)*, 5th ed., (Washington, DC: APA Publishing, 2013), 189.

13 American Psychiatric Association, *DSM-5*.

14 Thierry Steimer, "The Biology of Fear- and Anxiety-Related Behaviors," *Dialogues in Clinical
Neuroscience* 4, no. 3 (September 2002): 231–249.

15 "What Is Stress?" The American Institute of Stress, accessed September 4, 2017, http://www
.stress.org/what-is-stress/.

16 "What Is Stress?"

17 Bruce McEwen, *The End of Stress as We Know It* (New York: Dana Press, 2002), 2–3.

18 Norman Doidge, *The Brain That Changes Itself: Stories of Personal Triumph from the Frontiers of
Brain Science* (New York, Penguin, 2007), 164.

## Chapter Four

1 Carl Rogers, *On Becoming a Person: A Therapist's View of Psychotherapy* (Boston: Houghton
Mifflin Harcourt, 1961), 17.

2 Allan V. Horowitz, *Anxiety: A Short History* (Baltimore: The Johns Hopkins University Press,
2013), xiii.

3 Horowitz, *Anxiety: A Short History*, 6.

4 Robert Eno, *The Analects of Confucius*, University of Indiana, 2015, http://www.indiana
.edu/~p374/Analects_of_Confucius_(Eno-2015).pdf.

5 Rodney Taylor, "Confucius and the Age of Anxiety," Huffington Post, June 18, 2014, http://
www.huffingtonpost.com/rodney-l-taylor-phd/confucius-and-the-age-of-_b_5508311.html.

6 Derek Lin, trans. *Tao Te Ching: Annotated and Explained* (Woodstock, VT: SkyLight
Illuminations, 2006).

7 "Stoicism," *Stanford Encyclopedia of Philosophy*, April 15, 1996, https://plato.stanford.edu
/entries/stoicism/.

8 Soren Kierkegaard, trans. Alastair Hannay, *The Concept of Anxiety: A Simple Psychologically
Oriented Deliberation in View of the Dogmatic Problem of Hereditary Sin* (New York: Liveright,
2015), 187.

9 George Miller Beard, *American Nervousness: Its Causes and Consequences, a Supplement to Nervous
Exhaustion* (New York: Putnam, 1881).

10   "Neurasthenia and the Culture of Nervous Exhaustion: Introduction," University of Virginia, accessed August 17, 2017, http://exhibits.hsl.virginia.edu/nerves/.

11   "Neurasthenia," University of Virginia.

12   Beard, *American Nervousness*, vi.

13   "Neurasthenia," University of Virginia.

14   William James, *The Gospel of Relaxation* (New York, Henry Holt & Company, 1889), 45.

15   James, *The Gospel of Relaxation*, 48.

16   James, *The Gospel of Relaxation*, 70.

17   William James, *Psychology: A Briefer Course* (Cambridge: Harvard University Press, 1984), 133.

18   Charles Darwin, *On the Origin of the Species* (London: John Murray, 1859), 208.

19   Darwin, *On the Origin of the Species*.

20   McEwen, *The End of Stress as We Know It*, vii.

21   Sigmund Freud, *Introductory Lectures on Psychoanalysis* (New York: W. W. Norton & Company, 1933), 488.

22   LeDoux, *Anxious: Using the Brain to Understand and Treat Fear and Anxiety*, 4.

23   Stephen P. Thornton, "Sigmund Freud (1856–1939)," *Internet Encyclopedia of Philosophy*, accessed July 21, 2017, http://www.iep.utm.edu/freud/.

24   Sigmund Freud, "Inhibitions, Symptoms and Anxiety, the Institute of Psychoanalysis," *Sigmund Freud Selected Writings* (New York: W. W. Norton & Company, 1997), 371.

25   Albert Ellis, *Reason and Emotion in Psychotherapy: Comprehensive Method of Treating Human Disturbances* (New York: Citadel Press, 1996).

26   Rachel Rosner, "Aaron T. Beck's Drawings and the Psychoanalytic Origin Story of Cognitive Therapy," *History of Psychology* 15, no. 1, (2013): 1–18.

27   C. R. Rogers, *On Becoming a Person: A Therapists View of Psychotherapy* (New York: Houghton Mifflin, 1961), 174.

28   Abraham Maslow, *The Farther Reaches of Human Nature* (New York: Penguin, 1971), 24.

29   Maslow, *The Farther Reaches of Human Nature*, 33.

30   J. J. Froh, "The History of Positive Psychology: Truth Be Told," *NYS Psychologist* 16, no. 3 (2004): 18–20.

31   Martin Seligman, *Authentic Happiness: Using the New Positive Psychology to Realize Your Potential for Lasting Fulfillment* (New York: Simon & Schuster, 2002), 28.

32   Martin Seligman and Mihaly Csikszentmihalyi, "Positive Psychology: An Introduction," *American Psychologist* 55, no. 1, (January 2000): 5–14.

## Chapter Five

1   Kay Redfield Jamison, *An Unquiet Mind: A Memoir of Moods and Madness* (New York: Random House, 1996), 5.

2   Jan Hoffman, "Good News about Worrying," *New York Times*, November 2, 2015, https://well.blogs.nytimes.com/2015/11/02/while-waiting-for-test-results-worrying-may-help-in-the-long-run/.

3   Diane Musho Hamilton, "Calming Your Brain during Conflict," *Harvard Business Review*, December 22, 2015, https://hbr.org/2015/12/calming-your-brain-during-conflict.

4      Steven Pinker, *How the Mind Works* (New York: W. W. Norton & Company, 1999), 371.

5      Rick Hanson, *Hardwiring Happiness: The New Brain Science of Contentment, Calm and Confidence* (New York: Random House, 2013), 4.

6      Sarah Banks et al., "Amygdala—Frontal Connectivity during Emotion Regulation," *Social Cognitive and Affective Neuroscience* 2, no. 4, (December 2007): 303–312.

7      Sapolsky, *Why Zebras Don't Get Ulcers*, 210.

8      Sapolsky, *Why Zebras Don't Get Ulcers*, 212.

9      Jeffrey Schwartz and Sharon Begley, *The Mind and the Brain: Neuroplasticity and the Power of Mental Force* (New York: HarperCollins, 2002), 371.

10     S. Löwel and W. Singer, "Selection of Intrinsic Horizontal Connections in the Visual Cortex by Correlated Neuronal Activity." *Science* 255, no. 5041 (January 1992): 209–212. The phrase itself was first coined by Siegrid Löwel.

11     Hanson, *Hardwiring Happiness*, 10.

12     Erin O'Donnell, "A Better Path to High Performance," *Harvard Magazine*, May–June 2014, http://harvardmagazine.com/2014/05/a-better-path-to-high-performance.

13     Bruce Goldman, "Study Explains How Stress Can Boost Immune System," Stanford Medicine, June 21, 2012, https://med.stanford.edu/news/all-news/2012/06/study-explains-how-stress-can-boost-immune-system.html.

14     McEwen, *The End of Stress as We Know It*, 149.

15     McEwen, *The End of Stress as We Know It*, 149.

16     Schwartz and Begley, *The Mind and the Brain*, 368.

17     Doidge, *The Brain that Changes Itself: Stories of Personal Triumph from the Frontiers of Brain Science*, xix-xx.

18     Schwartz and Begley, *The Mind and the Brain*, 101.

19     Sapolsky, *Why Zebras Don't Get Ulcers*, 154.

20     Alina Tugend, "The Contrarians on Stress: It Can Be Good for You," *New York Times*, October 3, 2014, https://www.nytimes.com/2014/10/04/your-money/the-contrarians-on-stress-it-can-be-good-for-you-.html?_r=0.%20).

21     Hermann Nabi et al., "Increased Risk of Coronary Heart Disease among Individuals Reporting Adverse Impact of Stress on Their Health: The Whitehall II Prospective Cohort Study," *European Heart Journal* 34, no. 34 (September 2013): 2697–2705.

22     Bret McKay and Kate McKay, "Managing Stress Arousal for Optimal Performance: A Guide to the Warrior Color Code," The Art of Manliness, August 15, 2013, http://www.artofmanliness.com/2013/08/15/managing-stress-arousal-for-optimal-performance-a-guide-to-the-warrior-color-code/.

23     Csikszentmihalyi, *Flow: The Psychology of Optimal Experience*, 68.

24     Colleen Merrifield and James Danckert, "Characterizing the Psychophysiological Signature of Boredom," *Experimental Brain Research* 232, no. 2 (February 2014): 481–491.

25     Tugend, "The Contrarians on Stress."

26     Jeongok Logan et al., "Allostasis and Allostatic Load: Expanding the Discourse on Stress and Cardiovascular Disease," *Journal of Clinical Nursing* 17 (April 2008): 201–208.

27     Luhrmann, "The Anxious Americans."

28    Shawn Achor, *The Happiness Advantage: The Seven Principles of Positive Psychology That Fuel Success and Performance at Work* (New York: Random House, 2010), 26.

29    Philip Perry, "The Bad News: Trauma Can Be Inherited. The Good News—So Can Resilience," Big Think, accessed October 21, 2017, http://bigthink.com/philip-perry/the-bad-news-trauma-can-be-inherited-the-good-news-so-can-resilience.

30    John Bowlby, "The Nature of a Child's Tie to Its Mother," *International Journal of Psycho-Analysis* 39, no. 5 (September–October 1958): 350–373.

31    Shelley Taylor et al., "Biobehavioral Responses to Stress in Females: Tend-and-Befriend, Not Fight-or-Flight," *Psychological Review* 107, no. 3 (July 2000): 411–429.

32    Taylor et al., "Biobehavioral Responses to Stress in Females."

33    Bernadette von Dawans et al., "The Social Dimension of Stress Reactivity," *Psychological Science* 23, no. 7 (July 2012): 829.

34    Elaine N. Aron, *The Highly Sensitive Person: How to Thrive When the World Overwhelms You* (New York: Random House, 1997).

## Chapter Six

1    Ashton Applewhite, Tripp Evans, Andrew Frothingham, *And I Quote: The Definitive Collection of Quotes, Sayings, and Jokes for the Contemporary Speechmaker*, rev. ed. (New York: Thomas Dunne Books, 2003).

2    Daniel Wenger, "Ironic Processes of Mental Control," *Psychological Review* 101, no. 1 (1994): 34–52. Wegner's model of ironic process in mental control that is a primary source on thought suppression actually has the opposite effect.

3    Evan Forman et al., "A Comparison of Acceptance- and Control-Based Strategies for Coping with Food Cravings: An Analog Study," *Behavior Research and Therapy* 45, no. 10 (November 2017): 2372–2386.

4    Ernst Koster, "The Paradoxical Effects of Suppressing Anxious Thoughts during Immanent Threat," *Behavior and Research Therapy* 41, no. 9 (September 2003): 1113–1120.

5    C. S. Carver et al., "Assessing Coping Strategies: A Theoretically Based Approach," *Journal of Personality and Social Psychology* 56 (1989): 267–283.

6    Elisha Goldstein, "Finding Your True Refuge: An Interview with Tara Brach," Psych Central, accessed November 3, 2017, http://blogs.psychcentral.com/mindfulness/2013/02/finding-your-true-refuge-an-interview-with-tara-brach-phd/.

7    Tompkins, *Anxiety and Avoidance*, 3.

8    Martin Seif, "How Can I Overcome My Fear of Flying?" Anxiety and Depression Association of America, accessed August 22, 2017, https://www.adaa.org/living-with-anxiety/ask-and-learn/ask-expert/how-can-i-overcome-my-fear-of-flying.

9    Kabat-Zinn, *Full Catastrophe Living*, i.

10    Brené Brown, *Rising Strong: The Reckoning. The Rumble. The Revolution.* (New York: Penguin Random House, 2015), 50.

11    Alexandra Dingemans et al., "The Effect of Suppressing Negative Emotions on Eating Behavior in Binge Eating Disorder," *Appetite* 52 (2009): 51–57.

12      Dingemans et al., "The Effect of Suppressing Negative Emotions on Eating Behavior in Binge Eating Disorder."

13      "Anxiety Disorders," American Psychiatric Association, accessed March 21, 2017, http://dsm .psychiatryonline.org/doi/abs/10.1176/appi.books.9780890425596.dsm05.

14      David Biello, "Inside the Debate about Power Posing: A Q&A with Amy Cuddy," TED, February 22, 2017, http://ideas.ted.com/inside-the-debate-about-power-posing-a-q-a-with-amy-cuddy/.

15      Goldstein, "Finding Your True Refuge: An Interview with Tara Brach."

16      Edward Selby, "Avoidance of Anxiety as Self-Sabotage: How Running Away Can Bite You in the Behind," *Psychology Today*, May 4, 2010, https://www.psychologytoday.com/blog/overcoming -self-sabotage/201005/avoidance-anxiety-self-sabotage-how-running-away-can-bite-you.

17      LeDoux, *Anxious: Using the Brain to Understand and Treat Fear and Anxiety*.

18      LeDoux, *Anxious: Using the Brain to Understand and Treat Fear and Anxiety*, 103.

19      LeDoux, *Anxious: Using the Brain to Understand and Treat Fear and Anxiety*, 142.

20      Sapolsky, *Why Zebras Don't Get Ulcers*.

21      Hanson, *Hardwiring Happiness*, 23.

22      *Stress—Portrait of a Killer*, National Geographic, DVD, 20th Century Fox, November 18, 2008.

23      William Stixrud, *Self-Propelled: Helping Kids Develop Internal Motivation*, 2011, audio, https:// www.learningandthebrain.com/store/product/908/35_548/self-propelled-helping-kids-with -executive-dysfunction-find-internal-motivation.

## Chapter Seven

1       Brown, *Rising Strong*, 4.

2       Carol S. Dweck, *Mindset: The New Psychology of Success* (New York: Random House, 2006).

3       Clifton Parker, "Stanford Research: The Meaningful Life Is a Road Worth Traveling," *Stanford Report*, January 1, 2014, http://news.stanford.edu/news/2014/january/meaningful-happy -life-010114.html.

4       Mark Twain, *Pudd'nhead Wilson* (Dover Thrift Edition, 1999), 60.

5       Peter J. Norton and Brandon J. Weiss, "The Role of Courage on Behavioral Approach in a Fear-Eliciting Situation," *Journal of Anxiety Disorders* 23, no. 2 (March 2009): 212–217.

6       Daniela Schiller, "Snakes in the MRI Machine: A Study of Courage," Scientific American, July 20, 2010, https://www.scientificamerican.com/article/snakes-in-the-mri-machine/.

7       Patricia L. Lockwood et al., "Neurocomputational Mechanisms of Prosocial Learning and Links to Empathy," *Proceedings of the National Academy of Sciences of the United States of America 113*, no. 35 (June 2016): 9763–9768.

8       Tim Newman, "Brain's Empathy Center Identified," *Medical News Today*, August 16, 2016, https://www.medicalnewstoday.com/articles/312349.php.

9       Lucius Annaeus Seneca, *Moral Letters to Lucilius*, Letter 13.

10      Parker, "Stanford Research: The Meaningful Life Is a Road Worth Traveling."

11      Sapolsky, *Why Zebras Don't Get Ulcers*, 4–5.

12      Robert M. Sapolsky, "How to Relieve Stress," *Greater Good Magazine*, March 22, 2012, https:// greatergood.berkeley.edu/article/item/how_to_relieve_stress.

13      Brown, *Rising Strong*, xviii.

14 Lisa Feldman Barrett, *How Emotions are Made: The Secret Life of the Brain* (New York: Houghton Mifflin Harcourt, 2017), xii–xiii.

15 Barrett, *How Emotions are Made*, 203.

16 Daniel Pink, *Drive: The Surprising Truth about What Motivates Us* (New York: Penguin Random House, 2009), 145.

17 Pink, *Drive*, 7.

18 Pink, *Drive*, 145.

19 Richard M. Ryan and Edward L. Deci, "Self-Determination Theory and the Facilitation of Intrinsic Motivation, Social Development, and Well-Being," *American Psychologist* 55, no. 1 (January 2000): 68–78, https://selfdeterminationtheory.org/SDT/documents/2000_RyanDeci_SDT.pdf.

20 Ryan and Deci, "Self-Determination Theory and the Facilitation of Intrinsic Motivation."

21 Edward L. Deci et al., "A Meta-Analytic Review of Experiments Examining the Effects of Extrinsic Rewards on Intrinsic Motivation," *Psychological Bulletin* 125, no. 6 (1999): 627–668.

22 Jeremy Jamieson et al., "Mind Over Matter: Reappraising Arousal Improves Cardiovascular and Cognitive Responses to Stress," *Journal of Experimental Psychology* 141, no. 3 (2012): 417–422.

23 Adam Galinsky and Maurice Schweitzer, *Friend and Foe: When to Cooperate, When to Compete, and How to Succeed at Both* (New York: Penguin Random House, 2015), 47.

24 "Commuters 'Suffer Extreme Stress,'" *BBC News*, last modified November 30, 2004, http://news.bbc.co.uk/2/hi/uk_news/4052861.stm.

25 Paul Willner, "The Chronic Mild Stress (CMS) Model of Depression: History, Evaluation, and Usage," *Neurobiology of Stress* 6 (February 2017): 78–93.

26 Sapolsky, *Why Zebras Don't Get Ulcers*, 392.

27 William C. Sanderson, Ronald M. Rapee, David H. Barlow, "The Influence of an Illusion of Control on Panic Attacks Induced via Inhalation of 5.5% Carbon Dioxide-Enriched Air," *Archives of General Psychiatry* 46, no. 2 (1989): 157–162, doi:10.1001/archpsyc.1989.01810020059010.

28 Courtney Pierce Keeton, Maureen Perry-Jenkins, and Aline G. Sayer, "Sense of Control Predicts Depressive and Anxious Symptoms Across the Transition to Parenthood," *Journal of Family Psychology* 22, no. 2 (April 2008): 212–221, https://www.ncbi.nlm.nih.gov/pmc/articles/PMC2834184/.

29 Neal Krause and Sheldon Stryker, "Stress and Well-Being: The Buffering Role of Locus of Control Beliefs," *Social Science & Medicine* 18, no. 9 (1984): 783–790, http://www.sciencedirect.com/science/article/pii/0277953684901059.

30 V. Molinari and P. Khanna, "Locus of Control and Its Relationship to Anxiety and Depression," *Journal of Personality Assessment* 45, no. 3 (June 1981): 314–319, http://www.ncbi.nlm.nih.gov/pubmed/7252756.

31 Irwin N. Sandler and Brian Lakey, "Locus of Control as a Stress Moderator: The Role of Control Perceptions and Social Support," *American Journal of Community Psychology* 10, no. 1 (1982): http://onlinelibrary.wiley.com/doi/10.1007/BF00903305/full.

32 R. Hoehn-Saric and D. R. McLeod, "Locus of Control in Chronic Anxiety Disorders," *Acta Psychiatrica Scandinavica* 72, no. 6 (December 1985): 529–535, http://www.ncbi.nlm.nih.gov/pubmed/4083058.

33      Bruce S. McEwen, "Central Effects of Stress Hormones in Health and Disease: Understanding the Protective and Damaging Effects of Stress and Stress Mediators," *European Journal of Pharmacology* 583, no. 2–3 (April 7, 2008): 174–185.

34      Ceylan Isgor et al., "Delayed Effects of Chronic Variable Stress During Peripubertal-Juvenile Period on Hippocampal Morphology and on Cognitive and Stress Axis Functions in Rats," *Hippocampus* 14, no. 5 (2004): 636–648, http://onlinelibrary.wiley.com/doi/10.1002/hipo.10207/full.

35      Chris Hadfield, "What I Learned from Going Blind in Space," TED talk, March 2014, https://www.ted.com/talks/chris_hadfield_what_i_learned_from_going_blind_in_space.

36      K. Sweeny et al., "Two Definitions of Waiting Well," *Emotion* 16, no. 1 (February 2016): 129–143, https://www.ncbi.nlm.nih.gov/pubmed/26461244.

37      Holger Ursin, Eivind Baade, and Seymour Levine, eds. *Psychobiology of Stress: A Study of Coping Men* (New York: Academic Press Inc., 1978).

38      Sapolsky, *Why Zebras Don't Get Ulcers*, 258.

39      Barrett, *How Emotions Are Made*, 152.

## Chapter Eight

1       Alia J. Crum, Peter Salovey, and Shawn Achor, "Rethinking Stress: The Role of Mindsets in Determining the Stress Response," *Journal of Personality and Social Psychology* 104, no. 4 (2013): 716–733, doi: 10.1037/a0031201.

2       Kelly McGonigal, *The Upside of Stress: Why Stress Is Good for You, and How to Get Good at It* (New York: Penguin Random House, 2016), 11.

3       Honor Whiteman, "Unhappiness, Stress 'Does Not Cause Ill Health, Mortality,'" Medical News Today, December 10, 2015, http://www.medicalnewstoday.com/articles/303766.php.

4       Abiola Keller et al., "Does the Perception that Stress Affects Health Matter? The Association with Health and Mortality," *Journal of Health Psychology* 31, no. 5 (September 2012): 677–684.

5       Keller, "Does the Perception that Stress Affects Health Matter?"

6       "Fellow's Research on Stress Featured in TED Talk," Harvard Medical School, accessed April 30, 2018, https://www.populationmedicine.org/node/462.

7       Kelly McGonigal, "How to Make Stress Your Friend," TED talk, June 2013, https://www.ted.com/talks/kelly_mcgonigal_how_to_make_stress_your_friend/transcript?language=en.

8       Lise T. Gustad et al., "Symptoms of Anxiety and Depression and Risk of Acute Myocardial Infarction: The HUNT 2 Study," *European Heart Journal* 35, no. 21 (June 2014): 1394–1403, https://academic.oup.com/eurheartj/article/35/21/1394/582852.

9       Achor, *The Happiness Advantage*, 69.

10      Sandra Blakeslee, "Placebos Prove So Powerful Even Experts Are Surprised: New Studies Explore the Brain's Triumph Over Reality," *New York Times*, October 13, 1998, http://www.nytimes.com/1998/10/13/science/placebos-prove-so-powerful-even-experts-are-surprised-new-studies-explore-brain.html.

11      Blakeslee, "Placebos Prove So Powerful Even Experts Are Surprised."

12      Fabrizio Benedetti, Elisa Carlino, and Antonella Pollo, "How Placebos Change the Patient's Brain," *Neuropsychopharmacology* 36, no. 1 (January 2011): 339–354, https://www.ncbi.nlm.nih.gov/pmc/articles/PMC3055515/.

13      Jo Marchant, *Cure: A Journey into the Science of Mind Over Body* (New York: Crown, 2016), 35.

14      Daniel Siegel, *Mindsight: The New Science of Personal Transformation* (New York: Random House, 2010), xi.

15      Nicole Llewellyn et al., "Reappraisal and Suppression Mediate the Contribution of Regulatory Focus to Anxiety in Healthy Adults," *Emotion* 13, no. 4 (2013): 610–615, http://psycnet.apa .org/psycinfo/2013-16564-001/.

16      Ellen O'Donnell, "Fredrickson Describes Nourishing Power of Small, Positive Movements," NIH Record, accessed January 30, 2018, https://nihrecord.nih.gov/newsletters/2013/05_10_2013 /story3.htm.

17      Amrisha Vaish, Tobias Grossmann, and Amanda Woodward, "Not All Emotions Are Created Equal: The Negativity Bias in Social-Emotional Development," *Psychological Bulletin* 134, no. 3 (May 2008): 383–403, https://www.ncbi.nlm.nih.gov/pmc/articles/PMC3652533/.

18      Kyle Benson, "The Magic Relationship Ratio, According to Science," The Gottman Institute, October 4, 2017, https://www.gottman.com/blog/the-positive-perspective-dr-gottmans -magic-ratio/.

19      Tony Schwartz, "Overcoming Your Negativity Bias," *New York Times*, June 14, 2013, https:// dealbook.nytimes.com/2013/06/14/overcoming-your-negativity-bias/?_r=1.

20      Hanson, *Hardwiring Happiness*, 7.

21      Elif Batuman, "How to Be a Stoic," *The New Yorker*, December 19 & 26, 2016, http://www .newyorker.com/magazine/2016/12/19/how-to-be-a-stoic.

22      Eagleman, *Incognito*, 64.

23      A. W. Brooks, "Get Excited: Reappraising Pre-Performance Anxiety as Excitement," *Journal of Experimental Psychology: General* 1443, no. 3 (June 2014): 1144–1158, http://www.hbs.edu /faculty/Pages/item.aspx?num=45869; Olga Khazan, "Can Three Words Turn Anxiety into Success?" *The Atlantic*, March 32, 2016, http://www.theatlantic.com/health/archive/2016/03 /can-three-words-turn-anxiety-into-success/474909/.

24      Jeremy P. Jamieson et al., "Turning the Knots in Your Stomach into Bows: Reappraising Arousal Improves Performance on the GRE," *Journal of Experimental Social Psychology* 46, no. 1 (January 1, 2010): 208–212, https://www.ncbi.nlm.nih.gov/pubmed/20161454.

25      Jamieson et al., "Turning the Knots in Your Stomach into Bows."

26      Llewellyn et al., "Reappraisal and Suppression Mediate the Contribution of Regulatory Focus to Anxiety in Healthy Adults."

27      Jeremy P. Jamieson, Matthew K. Nock, and Wendy Berry Mendes, "Mind over Matter: Reappraising Arousal Improves Cardiovascular and Cognitive Responses to Stress," *Journal of Experimental Psychology: General* 141, no. 3 (August 2012): 417–422.

28      Diana Yates, "To Suppress or to Explore? Emotional Strategy May Influence Anxiety," Illinois News Bureau, May 13, 2013, https://news.illinois.edu/blog/view/6367/204813.

29      Llewellyn et al., "Reappraisal and Suppression Mediate the Contribution of Regulatory Focus to Anxiety in Healthy Adults."

30      Sally A. Moore, Lori A. Zoellner, and Niklas Mollenholt, "Are Expressive Suppression and Cognitive Reappraisal Associated with Stress-Related Symptoms?" *Behaviour Research and Therapy* 46, no. 9 (September 2008): 993–1000; Benjamin P. Chapman et al., "Emotion

Suppression and Mortality Risk Over a 12-Year Follow-Up," *Journal of Psychosomatic Research* 75, no. 4 (October 2013): 381–385.

31    Solomon, *The Noonday Demon: An Atlas of Depression*, 65.

32    Ed Yong, "Self-Control Is Just Empathy you're your Future Self," December 6, 2016, *The Atlantic*, https://www.theatlantic.com/science/archive/2016/12/self-control-is-just-empathy-with-a-future-you/509726/.

33    Martin Seligman and John Tierney, "We Aren't Built to Live in the Moment," *New York Times, May 19, 2017*, https://www.nytimes.com/2017/05/19/opinion/sunday/why-the-future-is-always-on-your-mind.html.

34    Frankl, *Man's Search for Meaning*, 66.

## Chapter Nine

1     C. G. Jung, *The Collected Works of C.G. Jung: Civilization in Transition*, 2nd ed., vol. 10, trans. Gerhard Adler and R. F. C. Hull (Princeton University Press, 1970).

2     Drake Baer, "Why Psychologists Say Anxiety Is the 'Shadow' of Intelligence," The Cut, September 15, 2016, https://www.thecut.com/2016/09/psychologists-say-anxiety-is-the-shadow-of-intelligence.html.

3     Ronald Najman, "Excessive Worrying May Have Co-Evolved with Intelligence," SUNY Downstate Medical Center Newsroom, April 13, 2012, http://www.downstate.edu/news_releases/2012/news_release_full11.html.

4     Barrett, *How Emotions are Made*, 222.

5     Barrett, *How Emotions are Made*, 225.

6     Sara Gilgore, "Local Nonprofit Scores Big on 'Ellen,'" *Washington Business Journal*, June 19, 2017, http://www.bizjournals.com/washington/news/2017/06/19/this-local-exec-went-from-foster-care-to-the-u-s.html.

7     Lisa J. Burklund et al., "The Common and Distinct Neural Bases of Affect Labeling and Reappraisal in Healthy Adults," *Frontiers in Psychology*, no. 5(2014): 221, https://www.ncbi.nlm.nih.gov/pmc/articles/PMC3970015/; Katharina Kircanskit, Matthew D. Lieberman, and Michelle G. Craske, "Feelings into Words: Contributions of Language to Exposure Therapy," *Psychological Science* 23, no. 10 (2010): 1086–1091, http://www.scn.ucla.edu/pdf/Kircanski(2012)PsychSci.pdf; M. D. Lieberman et al., "Subjective Responses to Emotional Stimuli during Labeling, Reappraisal, and Distraction," *Emotion* 11, no. 3 (June 2011): 468–480, https://www.ncbi.nlm.nih.gov/m/pubmed/21534661/, C. Herbert, B. M. Herbert, and P. Pauli, "Emotional Self-Reference: Brain Structures Involved in the Processing of Words Describing One's Own Emotions," *Neuropsychologia* 49, no. 10 (August 2011): 2947–2956, https://www.ncbi.nlm.nih.gov/pubmed/21756925.

8     Bruce McEwen, "Physiology and Neurobiology of Stress and Adaptation: Central Role of the Brain," *Physiological Reviews* 87, no. 3 (July 2007): 873–904, http://physrev.physiology.org/content/87/3/873.

9     Pinker, *How the Mind Works*, 372.

10    Amy F. T. Arnsten, "Stress Impairs Prefrontal Cortical Function in Rats and Monkeys: Role of

Dopamine D1 and Norepinephrine α-1 Receptor Mechanisms," *Progress in Brain Research* 126 (2000): 183–192, https://www.ncbi.nlm.nih.gov/pubmed/11105647.

11 John Hughlings Jackson, "The Evolution and Dissolution of the Nervous System," lecture, 1884, http://www2.psykl.med.tum.de/klassiker/hughlings_jackson_croonian_2.html.

12 Sarah J. Banks et al., "Amygdala-Frontal Connectivity During Emotion Regulation," *Social Cognitive and Affective Neuroscience* 2, no. 4 (December 2007): 303–312, https://www.ncbi.nlm.nih.gov/pmc/articles/PMC2566753/.

13 Ann Gill Taylor, "Top-Down and Bottom-Up Mechanisms in Mind-Body Medicine: Development of an Integrative Framework for Psychophysiological Research," *Explore (NY)* 6, no. 1 (January 2010): 29, https://www.ncbi.nlm.nih.gov/pmc/articles/PMC2818254/.

14 McEwen, "Physiology and Neurobiology of Stress and Adaptation."

15 Rajita Sinha et al., "Dynamic Neural Activity during Stress Signals Resilient Coping," *Proceedings of the National Academy of the Sciences* 113, no. 31 (August 2, 2016): 8837–8842, http://www.pnas.org/content/113/31/8837.full.pdf.

16 Elizabeth D. Kirby et al., "Acute Stress Enhances Adult Rat Hippocampal Neurogenesis and Activation of Newborn Neurons via Secreted Astrocytic FGF2," eLife, April 16, 2013, https://elifesciences.org/articles/00362.

17 C. Cosi et al., "Repeated Restraint Stress Increases BDNF Plasma Levels in Rat: Effects of Milnacipran, Preqabalin, and Duloxetine," *Neuroscience Meeting Planner*, no. 457.20 (2009), http://www.neuroact.com/publications/analgesia-snri/161-repeated-restraint-stress-increases-bdnf-plasma-levels-in-rat-effects-of-milnacipran-pregabalin-and-duloxetine-poster.html.

18 Kara E. Hannibal and Mark D. Bishop, "Chronic Stress, Cortisol Dysfunction, and Pain: A Psychoneuroendocrine Rationale for Stress Management in Pain Rehabilitation," *Physical Therapy* 94, no. 12 (December 2014): 1816–1825, https://www.ncbi.nlm.nih.gov/pmc/articles/PMC4263906/; McEwen, "Physiology and Neurobiology of Stress and Adaptation."

19 Shelley E. Taylor, "Tend and Befriend: Biobehavioral Bases of Affiliation Under Stress," *Current Directions in Psychological Science* 15, no. 6 (December 2006): 273–277, https://wesfiles.wesleyan.edu/courses/PSYC-317-jwellman/Week%207%20-%20Oxytocin/Taylor%202006.pdf.

20 Hal Arkowitz, "Is Depression Just Bad Chemistry?" Scientific American, March 1, 2014, https://www.scientificamerican.com/article/is-depression-just-bad-chemistry/.

21 A. Ohman, A. Flykt, and F. Esteves, "Emotion Drives Attention: Detecting the Snake in the Grass," *Journal of Experimental Psychology: General* 130, no. 3 (September 2001): 466–478, https://www.ncbi.nlm.nih.gov/pubmed/11561921.

22 "Talking to Yourself in the Third Person Can Help You Control Stressful Emotions," MSU Today, July 26, 2017, http://msutoday.msu.edu/news/2017/talking-to-yourself-in-the-third-person-can-help-you-control-stressful-emotions/.

23 LeDoux, "Coming to Terms with Fear."

24 LeDoux, *Anxious: Using the Brain to Understand and Treat Fear and Anxiety*, 35.

25 Taylor, "Tend and Befriend."

26 Taylor, "Tend and Befriend."

27 "Fred Rogers: Look for the Helpers," YouTube, uploaded April 15, 2013, https://www.youtube.com/watch?v=-LGHtc_D328.

28      C. Cosi et al., "Repeated Restraint Stress Increases BDNF Plasma Levels in Rat."

29      F. S. Dhabhar et al., "Stress-induced Redistribution of Immune Cells—from Barracks to Boulevards to Battlefields: A Tale of Three Hormones—Curt Richter Award Winner," *Psychoneuroendocrinology* 37, no. 9 (September 2012): 1345–1368, doi: 10.1016 /j.psyneuen.2012.05.008.

30      A. Harvey et al., "Threat and Challenge: Cognitive Appraisal and Stress Responses in Simulated Trauma Resuscitations," *Medical Education* 44, no. 6 (June 2010): 587–594, https://www.ncbi .nlm.nih.gov/pubmed/20604855.

31      M. D. Seery, "Challenge or Threat? Cardiovascular Indexes of Reilience and Vulnerability to Potential Stress in Humans," *Neuroscience and Biobehavioral Reviews* 35, no. 7 (June 2011): 1603–1610, https://www.ncbi.nlm.nih.gov/pubmed/21396399.

32      Mark P. Mattson, "Hormesis Defined," *Ageing Research Reviews* 7, no. 1 (January 2008): 1–7, https://www.ncbi.nlm.nih.gov/pmc/articles/PMC2248601/.

33      Sonja Lyubomirsky, *The How of Happiness: A New Approach to Getting the Life You Want* (New York: Penguin, 2008), 20.

34      Lyubomirsky, *The How of Happiness*, 39.

35      Löwel and Singer, "Selection of Intrinsic Horizontal Connections in the Visual Cortex by Correlated Neuronal Activity."

36      John Sweller, "Cognitive Load Theory, Learning Difficulty, and Instructional Design," *Learning and Instruction* 4 (1994): 295–312, doi: 10.1016/0959-4752(94)90003-5.

37      Richard M. Shiffrin and Walter Schneider, "Controlled and Automatic Human Information Processing: II. Perceptual Learning, Automatic Attending, and a General Theory," *Psychological Review* 84, no. 2 (March 1977): 127–190, http://psych.indiana.edu/tradition/Shiffrin_and _Schneider_1977.pdf.

38      Prinz and Wehrenberg, *The Anxious Brain*, 9.

39      Joshua Green, *Moral Tribes: Emotion, Reason, and the Gap Between Us and Them* (New York: Penguin Press, 2013), 15, 133–134.

40      Charles Duhigg, *The Power of Habit: Why We Do What We Do in Life and Business* (New York: Random House, 2012), 20.

41      Feldman Barrett, *How Emotions are Made*, 26.

## Chapter Ten

1       Lydia Belanger, "25 Inspirational Quotes from Bill Clinton on His 70th Birthday," *Entrepreneur*, August 19, 2016, https://www.entrepreneur.com/article/281175.

2       Yasmin Anwar, "How the GGSC Helped Turn Pixar 'Inside Out,'" *Greater Good Magazine*, June 19, 2015, https://greatergood.berkeley.edu/article/item/how_ggsc_turned_pixar_inside_out.

3       Kira M. Newman, "Do Mixed Emotions Make Life More Meaningful?" *Greater Good Magazine*, April 25, 2017, https://greatergood.berkeley.edu/article/item/do_mixed_emotions_make _life_more_meaningful.

4       Gregg Henriques, "A Periodic Table of Behavior for Psychology," *Psychology Today*, June 2, 2017, https://www.psychologytoday.com/blog/theory-knowledge/201706/periodic-table -behavior-psychology.

5       Gregg Henriques, "Clarifying the Nature of Anxiety and Depression," *Psychology Today*, March 28, 2016, https://www.psychologytoday.com/blog/theory-knowledge/201603/clarifying-the -nature-anxiety-and-depression.

6       Galinsky and Schweitzer, *Friend and Foe*, 134.

7       Watts, *The Wisdom of Insecurity*, 75.

8       Julian F. Thayer et al., "A Meta-Analysis of Heart Rate Variability and Neuroimaging Studies: Implications for Heart Rate Variability as a Marker of Stress and Health," *Neuroscience and Biobehavioral Reviews* 36 (2012): 747–756, http://kinova.nu/index_htm_files/implications -for-heart-rate-variability-as-a-mark.pdf.

9       Sean A. Guillory and Krzysztof A. Bujarski, "Exploring Emotions Using Invasive Methods: Review of 60 Years of Human Intracranial Electrophysiology," *Social Cognitive and Affective Neuroscience* 9, no. 12 (December 1, 2014): 1880–1889, fig. 3, https://www.ncbi.nlm.nih.gov /pmc/articles/PMC4249472/figure/nsu002-F3/.

10      J. D. Gabrieli, R. A. Poldrack, and J. E. Desmond, "The Role of Left Prefrontal Cortex in Language and Memory," *Proceedings of the National Academy of Sciences* 95, no. 3 (February 1998): 906–913, https://www.ncbi.nlm.nih.gov/pubmed/9448258; http://www.loc.gov/loc /brain/emotion/Davidson.html.

11      Dale Archer, *Better than Normal: What Makes You Different Can Make You Exceptional* (New York: Random House, 2012), 92.

12      Schwartz and Begley, *The Mind and the Brain*, 66.

13      Malcolm Gladwell, *Blink: The Power of Thinking without Thinking* (New York: Back Bay Books, 2005).

14      Daniel Kahneman, *Thinking Fast and Slow* (New York: Farrar, Straus and Giroux, 2011).

15      John Medina, *Brain Rules: 12 Principles for Surviving and Thriving at Work, Home, and School* (Seattle, WA: Pear Press, 2008), 174.

16      Paul J. Zak, "How Stories Change the Brain," *Greater Good Magazine*, December 17, 2013, https://greatergood.berkeley.edu/article/item/how_stories_change_brain.

17      Simone Ravicz, "The Secret Upside to Stress," Happify Daily, accessed January 30, 2018, http:// my.happify.com/hd/secret-upside-to-stress/.

18      H. Selye, "Stress and Distress," *Comprehensive Therapy* 1, no. 8 (December 1975): 9–13, https:// www.ncbi.nlm.nih.gov/pubmed/1222562.

19      Derek Thompson, *Hit Makers: The Science of Popularity in an Age of Distraction* (New York: Penguin Press, 2017), 132.

20      Jonathan Gottschall, *The Storytelling Animal: How Stories Make Us Human* (New York: Houghton Mifflin Harcourt, 2012), 83.

21      Gottschall, *The Storytelling Animal*, 83.

## Chapter Eleven

1       Rainer Maria Rilke, *Letters to a Young Poet* (New York: W. W. Norton & Company, 1934), 21.

2       Baer, "Why Psychologists Say Anxiety Is the 'Shadow' of Intelligence."

3       Kevin Rathunde, "Toward a Psychology of Optimal Human Functioning: What Positive Psychology Can Learn from the 'Experiential Turns' of James, Dewey, and Maslow,"

*Journal of Humanistic Psychology* 41, no. 1 (2001): 136,http://journals.sagepub.com/doi/pdf/10.1177/0022167801411008.

4     Richard P. Bagozzi, Utpal M. Dholakia, and Suman Basuroy, "How Effortful Decisions Get Enacted: The Motivating Role of Decision Processes, Desires, and Anticipated Emotions," *Journal of Behavioral Decision Making* 16, no. 4 (October 2003): 273–295, http://onlinelibrary.wiley.com/doi/10.1002/bdm.446/abstract.

5     Amanda Phingbodhipakkiya, "Why Having a Plan B Can Sometimes Backfire," TED, June 22, 2017, http://ideas.ted.com/why-having-a-plan-b-can-sometimes-backfire/.

6     Charles Duhigg, *Smarter Faster Better: The Transformative Power of Real Productivity* (New York: Random House, 2017), 236.

7     John D. Salamone and Mercè Correa, "The Mysterious Motivational Functions of Mesolimbic Dopamine," *Neuron* 76, no. 3 (November 8, 2012): 470–485, https://www.ncbi.nlm.nih.gov/pmc/articles/PMC4450094/.

8     Asociación RUVID, "Dopamine Regulates the Motivation to Act, Study Shows," ScienceDaily, January 10, 2013, https://www.sciencedaily.com/releases/2013/01/130110094415.htm.

9     J. D. Salamone et al., "Effort-Related Functions of Nucleus Accumbens Dopamine and Associated Forebrain Circuits," *Psychopharmacology* 191, no. 3 (April 2007): 461–482, https://www.ncbi.nlm.nih.gov/pubmed/17225164/.

10    S. Cabib and S. Puglisi-Allegra, "The Mesoaccumbens Dopamine in Coping with Stress," *Neuroscience and Biobehavioral Review* 36, no. 1 (January 2012): 79–89, https://www.ncbi.nlm.nih.gov/pubmed/21565217/.

11    Siri Leknes and Irene Tracey, "A Common Neurobiology for Pain and Pleasure," *Nature Reviews Neuroscience* 9 (April 2008): 314–320; D. D. Price, "Sensory-Affective Relationships among Different Types of Clinical and Experimental Pain," *Pain* 28, no. 3 (March 1987): 297–307, https://www.ncbi.nlm.nih.gov/pubmed/2952934.

12    Medina, *Brain Rules*, 173.

13    Christine Carter, "Grit Needs Passion, Not Fear," *Greater Good Magazine*, August 30, 2016, https://greatergood.berkeley.edu/article/item/grit_needs_passion_not_fear.

14    McEwen, "Physiology and Neurobiology of Stress and Adaptation"; Elizabeth D. Kirby et al., "Acute Stress Enhances Adult Rat Hippocampal Neurogenesis and Activation of Newborn Neurons via Secreted Astrocytic FGF2," eLife, April 16, 2013: https://elifesciences.org/articles/00362.

15    Farzin Shamloo and Sébastien Hélie, "Changes in Default Mode Network as Automaticity Develops in a Categorization Task," *Behavioural Brain Research* 313 (October 15, 2016): 324–333, doi: 10.1016/j.bbr.2016.07.029.

16    R. L. Buckner, J. R. Andrews-Hanna, and D. L. Schacter, "The Brain's Default Network: Anatomy, Function, and Relevance to Disease," *Annals of the New York Academy of Sciences* 1124 (March 2008): 1–38, https://www.ncbi.nlm.nih.gov/pubmed/18400922.

17    Robert P. Spunt, Meghan L. Meyer, and Matthew D. Lieberman, "The Default Mode of Human Brain Function Primes the Intentional Stance," *Journal of Cognitive Neuroscience* 27, no. 6 (2015): 1116–1124, http://www.mitpressjournals.org/doi/pdf/10.1162/jocn_a_00785.

18    Roy F. Baumeister and Kathleen D. Vohs, "Self-Regulation, Ego Depletion, and Motivation,"

*Social and Personality Psychology Compass* 1, no. 1 (November 2007): 115–128, doi: 10.1111 /j.1751–9004.2007.00001.

19    Sweller, "Cognitive Load Theory, Learning Difficulty, and Instructional Design."

20    Tara Bennett Goleman, *Emotional Alchemy: How the Mind Can Heal the Heart* (New York: Three Rivers Press, 2001).

21    Bradley Elliot, "What Causes a 'Butterflies in the Stomach' Sensation?" *Discover*, February 21, 2017, http://blogs.discovermagazine.com/crux/2017/02/21/butterflies-in-the-stomach -science/#.WWzKD9MrJE4.

22    Stacy Lu, "How Chronic Stress is Harming Our DNA," *American Psychological Association* 45, no. 9 (October 2014): 28, http://www.apa.org/monitor/2014/10/chronic-stress.aspx.

23    McEwen, "Physiology and Neurobiology of Stress and Adaptation."

24    N. D. Volkow et al., "Dopamine in Drug Abuse and Addiction: Results from Imaging Studies and Treatment Implications," *Molecular Psychiatry* 9, no. 6 (June 2004): 557–569, doi: 10.1038 /sj.mp.4001507.

## Chapter Twelve

1    Benjamin Disraeli, *Lothair* (University of California Libraries, 1870).

2    Mihaly Csikszentmihalyi, *Flow: The Psychology of Optimal Experience* (New York: Harper Perennial Modern Classics, 2008).

3    T. Gilovich et al., "The Experience of Regret: What, When, and Why," *Psychological Review* 102, no. 2 (April 1995): 379–95, https://www.ncbi.nlm.nih.gov/m/pubmed/7740094/.

4    Randall Neely, "Strangers Write Their Biggest Regret on Public Board. All Use the Same 3-Letter Word," Inspire More, July 2, 2016, http://www.inspiremore.com/biggest-regret/.

5    Jeffrey Kahn, *Angst: Origins of Anxiety and Depression* (New York: Oxford University Press, 2013), 182.

6    Marwa El Zein, Valentin Wyart, and Julie Grèzes, "Anxiety Dissociates the Adaptive Functions of Sensory and Motor Response Enhancements to Social Threats," eLife, December 29, 2015, https://elifesciences.org/articles/10274.

7    Thayer et al., "A Meta-Analysis of Heart Rate Variability and Neuroimaging Studies."

8    Joseph LeDoux, "For the Anxious, Avoidance Can Have an Upside," Opinionator, April 7, 2013, https://opinionator.blogs.nytimes.com/2013/04/07/for-the-anxious-avoidance-can-have-an -upside/?_r=1.

9    Edie Weiner, "Adaptability: The Skill that Will Never Be Digitized or Outsourced," Big Think, accessed January 30, 2018, http://bigthink.com/in-their-own-words/adaptability-the-skill -that-will-never-be-digitized-or-outsourced.

10    Alexander M. Penney, Victoria C. Miedema, Dwight Mazmanian, "Intelligence and Emotional Disorders: Is the Worrying and Ruminating Mind a More Intelligent Mind?" *Personality and Individual Differences* 74 (2015): 90–93, doi: 10.1016/j.paid.2014.10.005.

11    Sweeny et al., "Two Definitions of Waiting Well."

12    Tsachi Ein-Dor and Orgad Tal, "Scared Saviors: Evidence that People High in Attachment Anxiety Are More Effective in Alerting Others to Threat," *European Journal of Social Psychology* 42, no. 6 (2012): 667–671, doi: 10.1002/ejsp.1895.

13     Philippe Goldin et al., "Randomized Controlled Trial of Mindfulness-Based Stress Reduction Versus Aerobic Exercise: Effects on the Self-Referential Brain Network in Social Anxiety Disorder," *Frontiers in Human Neuroscience* 6 (2012): 295, doi: 10.3389/fnhum.2012.00295.

14     Christine Carter, *The Sweet Spot: How to Accomplish More By Doing Less* (New York: Ballantine, 2015), 95.

15     Marina Watson Peláez, "Plan Your Way to Less Stress, More Happiness," *Time*, May 31, 2011, http://healthland.time.com/2011/05/31/study-25-of-happiness-depends-on-stress-management/.

16     C. Grillon et al., "Mental Fatigue Impairs Emotion Regulation," *Emotion* 15, no. 3 (June 2015): 383–389, doi: 10.1037/emo0000058.

17     M. L. Phillips et al., "Neurobiology of Emotion Perception II: Implications for Major Psychiatric Disorders," *Biological Psychiatry* 54, no. 5 (2003): 515–528.

18     James D. Murphy, *Flawless Execution: Use the Techniques and Systems of America's Fighter Pilots to Perform at Your Peak and Win the Battles of the Business World* (New York: Harper Business, 2005), 124.

19     Peter M. Gollwitzer, "Implementation Intentions: Strong Effects of Simple Plans," *American Psychologist* 54, no. 7 (July 1999): 493–503, http://www.psych.nyu.edu/gollwitzer/99Goll _ImpInt.pdf.

20     Andrew Taggart, "On the Ulysses Effect: Insight, Foresight, and Ingenuity," September 14, 2011, https://andrewjtaggart.com/2011/09/14/on-the-ulysses-effect-insight-foresight-and-ingenuity/.

21     Nathanael J. Fast et al., "Illusory Control: A Generative Force Behind Power's Far-Reaching Effects," Stanford Graduate School of Business Research Paper Series (December 2008): https://www0.gsb.columbia.edu/mygsb/faculty/research/pubfiles/11639/illusory_control.pdf.

22     Albert Bandura, "Self-Efficacy Conception of Anxiety," *Anxiety, Stress, and Coping* 1, no. 2 (1988).

23     American Friends of Tel Aviv University, "Finding Relief in Ritual: A Healthy Dose of Repetitive Behavior Reduces Anxiety, Says Researcher," ScienceDaily, November 2, 2011, https://www .sciencedaily.com/releases/2011/09/110922093324.htm.

24     A. Bandura, "Self-Efficacy Mechanism in Human Agency," *American Psychologist* 37, no. 2 (1982): 122–147.

25     Susan Nolen-Hoeksema, Blair E. Wisco, and Sonja Lyubomirsky, "Rethinking Rumination," *Perspectives on Psychological Science* 3, no. 5 (2008): 400–424, http://sonjalyubomirsky.com /wp-content/themes/sonjalyubomirsky/papers/NWL2008.pdf.

26     Goleman, *Focus*, 14.

27     Sweeny et al., "Two Definitions of Waiting Well."

28     Sweeny et al., "Two Definitions of Waiting Well."

29     Galinsky and Schweitzer, *Friend and Foe*, 43.

30     David A. Havas et al., "Cosmetic Use of Botulinum Toxin-A Affects Processing of Emotional Language," *Psychological Science* 21, no. 7 (July 2010): 895–900, https://www.ncbi.nlm.nih .gov/pmc/articles/PMC3070188/.

31     Eric Jaffe, "The Psychology Study of Smiling," *Observer*, December 2010, https://www .psychologicalscience.org/observer/the-psychological-study-of-smiling.

32     T. L. Kraft and S. D. Pressman, "Grin and Bear It: The Influence of Manipulated Facial

Expression on the Stress Response," *Psychological Science* 23, no. 11 (2012): 1372–1378, doi: 10.1177/0956797612445312.

33    Amy Cuddy, Caroline Ashley Wilmuth, and Dana R. Carney, "The Benefit of Power Posing Before a High-Stakes Social Evaluation," Harvard Business School working paper, no. 13–027 (September 2012), http://dash.harvard.edu/handle/1/9547823.

34    Stephen J. Dubner, "How to Get More Grit in Your Life," prod. Christopher Werth, *Freakonomics Radio*, May 4, 2016, http://freakonomics.com/podcast/grit/.

35    Carter, *The Sweet Spot*, 197.

## Chapter Thirteen

1    Matthew D. Lieberman, *Social: Why Our Brains Are Wired to Connect* (New York: Crown Publishers, 2013), 9.

2    Matthew D. Lieberman and Naomi I. Eisenberger, "Pains and Pleasures of Social Life," *Science* 323 (February 13, 2009): 890–891.

3    Lieberman, *Social*, 19.

4    Lieberman, *Social*, 220.

5    Harari, *Sapiens: A Brief History of Humankind*, 10.

6    Kahn, *Angst*, 219.

7    Sheldon Cohen and Thomas A. Willis, "Stress, Social Support, and the Buffering Hypothesis," *Psychological Bulletin* 98, no. 2 (September 1985): 310–357.

8    Lu, "How Chronic Stress Is Harming Our DNA," 28.

9    Tara Brach, "Attend and Befriend—Healing the Fear Body," lecture, accessed January 31, 2018, https://www.tarabrach.com/attend-and-befriend-healing-the-fear-body-audio/.

10    F. Ozbay et al., "Social Support and Resilience to Stress: From Neurobiology to Clinical Practice," *Psychiatry* 4, no. 5 (2007): 35–40, http://psycnet.apa.org/record/2007-07464-009.

11    Nicholas Christenfeld et al., "Social Support Effects on Cardiovascular Reactivity: Is a Stranger as Effective as a Friend?" *Psychosomatic Medicine* 59 (1997): 388–398.

12    J. Holt-Lunstad, T. B. Smith, and J. B. Layton, "Social Relationships and Mortality Risk: A Meta-Analytic Review," *PLOS Medicine* 7, no. 7 (2010).

13    Krzysztof Kaniasty, "Social Support and Traumatic Stress," *PTSD Research Quarterly* 16, no. 2 (Spring 2005): 1–8, https://www.ptsd.va.gov/professional/newsletters/research-quarterly/v16n2.pdf; E. J. Ozer et al., "Predictors of Posttraumatic Stress Disorder and Symptoms in Adults: A Meta-Analysis," *Psychological Bulletin* 129, no. 1 (January 2003): 52–73, https://www.ncbi.nlm.nih.gov/pubmed/12555794; R. E. Dinenberg et al., "Social Support May Protect Against Development of Posttraumatic Stress Disorder: Findings from the Heart and Soul Study," *American Journal of Health Promotion* 28, no. 5 (2014): 294–297, https://www.ncbi.nlm.nih.gov/pubmed/23941102; A. L. Coker et al., "Social Support Protects against the Negative Effects of Partner Violence on Mental Health," Journal of Women's Health and Gender-Based Medicine 11, no. 5 (June 2002): 465–476, https://www.ncbi.nlm.nih.gov/pubmed/12165164.

14    S. Dixit, V. Chauhan, and S. Azad, "Social Support and Treatment Outcome in Alcohol Dependence Syndrome in Armed Forces," *Journal of Clinical and Diagnostic Research* 9, no. 11 (November 2015), https://www.ncbi.nlm.nih.gov/pmc/articles/PMC4668508/; Rebecca K.

Sripada et al., "Social Support and Mental Health Service Use among Individuals with PTSD in a Nationally-Representative Study," *Psychiatric Services* 66, no. 1 (January 2015): 65–71, https://www.ncbi.nlm.nih.gov/pmc/articles/PMC4283571/; Ralf Schwarzer and Anja Leppin, "Social Support and Health: A Meta-Analysis," *Psychology & Health* 3, no. 1 (1989): 1–15, http://www.tandfonline.com/doi/abs/10.1080/08870448908400361.

15      Shawn Achor, "Positive Intelligence," *Harvard Business Review*, January–February 2012, https://hbr.org/2012/01/positive-intelligence.

16      Maija Reblin and Bert N. Uchino, "Social and Emotional Support and Its Implication for Health," *Current Opinions in Psychiatry* 21, no. 2 (March 2008): 201–205.

17      Sourya Acharya and Samarth Shukla, "Mirror Neurons: Enigma of the Metaphysical Modular Brain," *Journal of Natural Science, Biology, and Medicine* 3, no. 2 (2012): 118–124.

18      Lea Winerman, "The Mind's Mirror," *Monitor on Psychology* 36, no. 9 (October 2005): 48.

19      Winerman, "The Mind's Mirror."

20      Christine Comaford, "Angry Customers? Don't Flip—Do This," Forbes, June 11, 2016, https://www.forbes.com/sites/christinecomaford/2016/06/11/stop-ignoring-the-massive-roi-potential-of-angry-customers/#1a166e2d4de1.

21      Emma Bryce, "How Emotions Are 'Made': Why Your Definition of Sadness Is Unlike Anyone Else's," *Wired*, March 23, 2017, http://www.wired.co.uk/article/lisa-feldman-barrett-emotions.

22      H. Haker et al., "Mirror Neuron Activity during Contagious Yawning—an fMRI Study," Brain Imaging Behavior 7, no. 1 (March 2013): 28–34, https://www.ncbi.nlm.nih.gov/pubmed/22772979.

23      Rose McDermott, James H. Fowler, and Nicholas A. Christakis, "Breaking Up is Hard to Do, Unless Everyone Else is Doing it Too: Social Network Effects on Divorce in a Longitudinal Sample," *Social Forces* 92, no. 2 (October 18, 2009): 491–519.

24      Cindy Kuzma, "Are You Suffering from Secondhand Stress?" *Shape*, accessed January 31, 2018, http://www.shape.com/lifestyle/mind-and-body/are-you-suffering-secondhand-stress.

25      Daniel Yudkin, "The Isolating Effects of Anxiety," *Scientific American*, June 16, 2015, https://www.scientificamerican.com/article/the-isolating-effects-of-anxiety/.

26      "New Friendship Study Has Great Message for Social Anxiety Sufferers," PsyBlog, accessed January 31, 2018, http://www.spring.org.uk/2014/11/new-friendship-study-has-great-message-for-social-anxiety-sufferers.php.

27      James W. Pennebaker, "Expressing Feelings," in *Opening Up: The Healing Power of Expressing Emotion* (The Guilford Press, 1997), http://www.byui.edu/counseling-center/self-help/stress-management/feelings.

28      Lieberman, *Social*, 220.

29      Zak, "How Stories Change the Brain."

30      Kelly McGonigal "How to Make Stress Your Friend."

31      Jill Suttie and Jason Marsh, "5 Ways Giving Is Good for You," *Greater Good Magazine*, December 13, 2010, http://greatergood.berkeley.edu/article/item/5_ways_giving_is_good_for_you.

32      Kelly McGonigal, "How to Overcome Stress by Seeing Other People's Joy," *Greater Good Magazine*, July 5, 2017, https://greatergood.berkeley.edu/article/item/how_to_overcome_stress_by_seeing_other_peoples_joy.

33    Lian T. Rameson, Sylvia A. Morelli, and Matthew D. Lieberman, "The Neural Correlates of Empathy: Experience, Automaticity, and Prosocial Behavior," *Journal of Cognitive Neuroscience* 24, no. 1 (2011): 235–245, http://www.scn.ucla.edu/pdf/Rameson(2012) JOCN.pdf.

34    Tristen K. Inagaki and Naomi I. Eisenberger, "Neural Correlates of Giving Support to a Loved One," *Psychosomatic Medicine* 74 (2012): 3–7.

35    Sapolsky, *Why Zebras Don't Get Ulcers*, 407.

36    Paul J. Zak, "Why Inspiring Stories Make Us React: The Neuroscience of Narrative," *Cerebrum: the Dana Forum on Brain Science* (2015): 2.

37    Jennifer L. Goetz, Dacher Keltner, and Emiliana Simon-Thomas, "Compassion: An Evolutionary Analysis and Empirical Review," *Psychological Bulletin* 136, no. 3 (May 2010): 351–374.

38    Travis Bradberry, "How Complaining Rewires Your Brain for Negativity," *Entrepreneur*, September 9, 2016, https://www.entrepreneur.com/article/281734.

39    Carolien Martijn et al., "Getting a Grip on Ourselves: Challenging Expectancies about Loss of Energy after Self-Control," *Social Cognition* 20, no. 6 (2002): 441–460; D. M. Wegner et al., "Paradoxical Effects of Thought Suppression," *Journal of Personality and Social Psychology* 53, no. 1 (July 1987): 5–13.

40    Ryan J. Giuliano and Nicole Y. Y. Wicha, "Why the White Bear Is Still There: Electrophysiological Evidence for Ironic Semantic Activation during Thought Suppression," *Brain Research* (February 2010): 62, doi: 10.1016/j.brainres.2009.12.041.

41    Dacher Keltner, *Born to Be Good: The Science of a Meaningful Life* (New York: W. W. Norton, 2009), quoted in Susan Cain, *Quiet: The Power of Introverts in a World That Can't Stop Talking* (New York: Broadway Paperbacks, 2013), 144.

42    Yasmin Anwar, "Easily Embarrassed? Study Finds People Will Trust You More," Berkeley News, September 28, 2011, http://news.berkeley.edu/2011/09/28/easily-embarrassed/.

43    Brené Brown, *Daring Greatly: How the Courage to Be Vulnerable Transforms the Way We Live, Love, Parent, and Lead* (New York: Avery, 2012), 68–70.

44    Keith Hampton et al., "The Cost of Caring," Pew Research Center, January 15, 2015, http:// www.pewinternet.org/2015/01/15/the-cost-of-caring/.

## Chapter Fourteen

1    Helen Fisher, Arthur Brown, and Lucy L. Brown, "Romantic Love: An fMRI Study of a Neural Mechanism for Mate Choice," *The Journal of Comparative Neurology* 493 (2005): 58–62; Helen Fisher, "The Tyranny of Love: Love Addiction—An Anthropologist's View," in *Behavioral Addictions: Criteria, Evidence, and Treatment*, eds. Laura Curtiss Feder and Ken Rosenberg (London: Academic Press, 2014).

2    Brené Brown, "Listening to Shame," TED Talk, March 2012, https://www.ted.com/talks /brene_brown_listening_to_shame/transcript.

3    Lisa S. Matthews, K. A. S. Wickrama, and Rand D. Conger, "Predicting Marital Instability from Spouse and Observer Reports of Marital Interaction," *Journal of Marriage and Family* 58, no. 3 (August 1996): 641–655.

4    J. K. Kiecolt-Glaser et al., "Love, Marriage, and Divorce: Newlyweds' Stress Hormones

Foreshadow Relationship Changes," *Journal of Consulting and Clinical Psychology* 71, no. 1 (February 2003): 176–88.

5   "Bride's 'Cold Feet' May Predict Divorce," LiveScience, September 16, 2012, https://www .livescience.com/23196-woman-s-doubts-before-wedding-may-predict-divorce.html.

6   Joanne Davila and Thomas N. Bradbury, "Attachment Insecurity and the Distinction between Unhappy Spouses Who Do and Do Not Divorce," *Journal of Family Psychology* 15, no. 3 (2001): 371–393.

7   V. Michelle Russell, Levi R. Baker, and James K. McNulty, "Attachment Insecurity and Infidelity in Marriage: Do Studies of Dating Relationships Really Inform Us about Marriage?" *Journal of Family Psychology* 27, no. 2 (April 2013): 242–251.

8   Tiffany Dufu, *Drop the Ball: Achieving More by Doing Less* (New York: Flatiron, 2017), 15.

9   Alois Stutzer and Bruno S. Frey, "Does Marriage Make People Happy, or Do Happy People Get Married?" *Journal of Socio-Economics* 35, no. 2 (2006): 326–347.

10   Abigail Geiger, "Sharing Chores a Key to Good Marriage, Say Majority of Married Adults," Pew Research Center, November 30, 2016, http://www.pewresearch.org/fact-tank/2016/11/30 /sharing-chores-a-key-to-good-marriage-say-majority-of-married-adults/.

11   Jon Kabat-Zinn, *Wherever You Go, There You Are: Mindfulness Meditation in Everyday Life* (New York: Hyperion, 1994), 108.

12   Gary Chapman, *The 5 Love Languages: The Secret to Love That Lasts* (Chicago: Northfield Publishing, 2015), 15.

13   Carolyn Hax, "If You Want Family Time, You'll Have to Make Accomodations," *The Washington Post*, June 1, 2017, https://www.washingtonpost.com/lifestyle/style/carolyn-hax-if-you-want -family-time-youll-have-to-make-accommodations/2017/05/31/c924b618-457e-11e7-98cd -af64b4fe2dfc_story.html.

14   L. S. Newman, K. J. Duff, and R. F. Baumeister, "A New Look at Defensive Projection: Thought Suppression, Accessibility, and Biased Person Perception," *Journal of Personality and Social Psychology* 72, no. 5 (May 1997): 980–1001.

15   John Gottman and Nan Silver, *The Seven Principles of Making a Marriage Work: A Practical Guide from the Country's Foremost Relationship Expert* (New York: Harmony Books, 2015), 19–24.

16   Melissa S. Hawkins, Sybil Carrère, and John Gottman, "Marital Sentiment Override: Does It Influence Couples' Perceptions?" *Journal of Marriage and Family* 64 (February 2002): 193–201.

17   Gottman and Silver, *The Seven Principles of Making a Marriage Work*, 71.

18   P. J. Miller, S. Niehuis, and T. L. Huston, "Positive Illusions in Marital Relationships: A 13-Year Longitudinal Study," *Personality and Social Psychology Bulletin* 32, no. 12 (December 2006): 1579–1594.

19   David Levine, "Anthropologist and Love Expert Helen Fisher on the Mysteries of Love," Elsevier, July 29, 2014, https://www.elsevier.com/connect/anthropologist-and-love-expert -helen-fisher-on-the-mysteries-of-love.

20   T. N. Bradbury and F. D. Fincham, "Attributions in Marriage: Review and Critique," *Psychological Bulletin* 107, no. 1 (January 1990): 3–33.

21   Sandra L. Murray and John G. Holmes, "A Leap of Faith? Positive Illusions in Romantic Relationships," *Personality and Social Psychology Bulletin* 23, no. 6 (June 1997): 586–604.

22 Justin A. Lavner, Benjamin R. Karney, and Thomas N. Bradbury, "Newlyweds' Optimistic Forecasts of Their Marriage: For Better or For Worse?" *Journal of Family Psychology* 27, no. 4 (2013): 531–540.

23 T. L. Huston et al., "The Connubial Crucible: Newlywed Years As Predictors of Marital Delight, Distress, and Divorce," *Journal of Personality and Social Psychology* 80, no. 2 (February 2001): 237–252.

24 Helen Fisher, quoted in Tara Parker-Pope, *For Better: How the Surprising Science of Happy Couples Can Help Your Marriage Succeed* (New York: Dutton, 2010), 173.

25 Gottman and Silver, *The Seven Principles of Making a Marriage Work*, 183.

26 "Takotsubo Cardiomyopathy (Broken-Heart Syndrome)," Harvard Women's Health Watch, last modified April 9, 2016, https://www.health.harvard.edu/heart-health/takotsubo -cardiomyopathy-broken-heart-syndrome.

27 "Is Broken Heart Syndrome Real?" American Heart Association, last modified December 12, 2017, http://www.heart.org/HEARTORG/Conditions/More/Cardiomyopathy/Is-Broken -Heart-Syndrome-Real_UCM_448547_Article.jsp#.WaCTq8bMxN0.

28 Scott Edwards, "Love and the Brain," *On the Brain*, accessed January 31, 2018, http://neuro .hms.harvard.edu/harvard-mahoney-neuroscience-institute/brain-newsletter/and-brain -series/love-and-brain.

29 "The Rejected Brain," The Anatomy of Love, accessed January 31, 2018, https:// theanatomyoflove.com/the-results/the-rejected-brain/.

30 Sheryl Sandberg and Adam Grant, *Option B: Facing Adversity, Building Resilience, and Finding Joy* (New York: Knopf, 2017), 24–25.

31 Amy Krouse Rosenthal, "You May Want to Marry My Husband," *New York Times*, March 3, 2017, https://www.nytimes.com/2017/03/03/style/modern-love-you-may-want-to-marry -my-husband.html.

32 Sam Roberts, "Amy Krouse Rosenthal, Children's Author and Filmmaker, Dies at 51," *New York Times*, March 13, 2017, https://www.nytimes.com/2017/03/13/style/amy-krouse-rosenthal -dies-modern-love.html.

## Chapter Fifteen

1 David Eagleman, *The Brain: The Story of You* (New York: Pantheon Books, 2015).

2 Christine Carter, "How Not to Have a Breakdown," *Greater Good Magazine*, January 9, 2012, http://greatergood.berkeley.edu/raising_happiness/post/How_Not_Breakdown.

3 D. W. Winnicott, "The Theory of the Parent-Infant Relationship," *The International Journal of Psychoanalysis* 41 (1960): 585–595.

4 Meghan Crosby Budinger, Tess K. Drazdowski, and Golda S. Ginsburg, "Anxiety-Promoting Parenting Behaviors: A Comparison of Anxious Parents with and without Social Anxiety," *Child Psychiatry and Human Development* 44, no. 3 (June 2013): 412–418, quoted in "8 Fascinating Facts about Anxiety Worth Knowing," PsyBlog, accessed January 31, 2018, http://www.spring .org.uk/2013/10/8-fascinating-facts-about-anxiety.php.

5 J. P. Lougheed, P. Koval, and T. Hollenstein, "Sharing the Burden: The Interpersonal Regulation of Emotional Arousal in Mother–Daughter Dyads," *Emotion* 16, no. 1 (2016): 83–93.

6       Allan N. Schore, "Effects of a Secure Attachment Relationship on Right Brain Development, Affect Regulation, and Infant Mental Health," *Infant Mental Health Journal* 22, no. 1–2 (2001): 7–66.

7       Beatrice Beebe, "My Journey in Infant Research and Psychoanalysis: Microanalysis, a Social Microscope," *Psychoanalytic Psychology* 31, no. 1 (2014): 4–25.

8       Korin Miller, "Postpartum Anxiety May Be More Common Than Postpartum Depression—What You Need to Know," Self, April 12, 2017, http://www.self.com/story/postpartum-anxiety.

9       Daniel J. Siegel, *Brainstorm: The Power and Purpose of the Teenage Brain* (New York: TarcherPerigee, 2014), 22.

10      Carl Jung, *The Theory of Psychoanalysis* (1913).

11      Pearson, *A Brief History of Anxiety…Yours and Mine,* 16–17.

12      C. Izard et al., "Emotion Knowledge as a Predictor of Social Behavior and Academic Competence in Children at Risk," *Psychological Science* 12, no. 4 (July 2001): 352; Susanne A. Denham, "Social Cognition, Prosocial Behavior, and Emotion in Preschoolers: Contextual Validation," *Child Development* 57 (1986): 194–201.

13      Pearson, *A Brief History of Anxiety…Yours and Mine,* 27.

14      S. O. Walker et al., "Nature, Nurture, and Academic Achievement: A Twin Study of Teacher Assessments of 7-Year-Olds," *British Journal of Educational Psychology* 74, no. 3 (September 2004): 323–342.

15      W. Thomas Boyce and Bruce J. Ellis, "Biological Sensitivity to Context: I. An Evolutionary–Developmental Theory of the Origins and Functions of Stress Reactivity," *Development and Psychopathology* 17 (2005): 271–301.

16      Cain, *Quiet,* 111–112.

17      Dawn Huebner, "Rethinking Anxiety: Learning to Face Fear," Tedx Talk, June 22, 2015, https://www.youtube.com/watch?v=jryCoo0BrRk.

18      McEwen, "Physiology and Neurobiology of Stress and Adaptation."

19      Matthew D. Lieberman, "Education and the Social Brain," *Trends in Neuroscience and Education* 1 (2012): 3–9.

20      Katty Kay and Claire Shipman, *The Confidence Code: The Science and Art of Self-Assurance—What Women Should Know* (New York: Harper Business, 2014), 91.

21      Judy Schoenberg, Kimberlee Salmond, and Paula Fleshman, *Change It Ip!: What Girls Say about Redefining Leadership* (Girl Scout Research Institute, 2008), 19.

22      Robert Preidt, "Pre-Test Jitters Might Boost Scores: Study," HealthDay News, October 12, 2012, https://www.hometownpharmacywi.com/patient-resources/article_modal/669575/pre-test-jitters-might-boost-scores-study.

23      Gerardo Ramirez and Sian L. Beilock, "Writing about Testing Worries Boosts Exam Performance in the Classroom," *Science* 331, no. 6014 (January 14, 2011): 211–213.

24      Lisa Heffernan, "What I've Learned: When Teens Lie," *The Washington Post,* February 24, 2015 https://www.washingtonpost.com/news/parenting/wp/2015/02/24/what-ive-learned-when-teens-lie/.

25      Po Bronson and Ashley Merriman, *Nurture Shock: New Thinking About Children* (New York: Twelve, 2009), 139.

26     Eagleman, *The Brain*, 16.

27     Amanda E. Guyer et al., "Neural Circuitry Underlying Affective Response to Peer Feedback in Adolescence," *Social Cognitive and Affective Neuroscience* 7, no. 1 (January 2012): 81–92.

28     "Women and People Under the Age of 35 at Greatest Risk of Anxiety," University of Cambridge, June 6, 2016, http://www.cam.ac.uk/research/news/women-and-people-under-the-age-of-35 -at-greatest-risk-of-anxiety.

29     Jan Hoffman, "Anxious Students Strain College Mental Health Centers," *New York Times*, May 27, 2015, https://well.blogs.nytimes.com/2015/05/27/anxious-students-strain-college -mental-health-centers/.

30     PennState Center for Collegiate Mental Health, Annual Report 2016, https://sites.psu.edu /ccmh/files/2017/01/2016-Annual-Report-FINAL_2016_01_09-1gc2hj6.pdf.

31     "Stress in America: Missing the Health Care Connection," American Psychological Association report, February 7, 2013, https://www.apa.org/news/press/releases/stress/2012/full-report.pdf.

## Chapter Sixteen

1     Alain De Botton, *Status Anxiety* (New York: Vintage, 2005), 6.

2     Robert Sanders, "Researchers Find Out Why Some Stress Is Good for You," Berkeley News, April 16, 2013, http://news.berkeley.edu/2013/04/16/researchers-find-out-why-some-stress -is-good-for-you/; Roman Duncko et al., "Acute Exposure to Stress Improved Performance in Trace Eyeblink Conditioning and Spatial Learning Tasks in Healthy Men," *Learning Memory* 14, no. 5 (May 2007): 329–335.

3     Claudia Batten, interview with the author, July 2014.

4     Csikszentmihalyi, *Flow*, 3.

5     Irene Levine, "Mind Matters: Anxiety in the Workplace," *Science*, September 10, 2010, http:// www.sciencemag.org/careers/2010/09/mind-matters-anxiety-workplace.

6     Arthur C. Brooks, "A Formula for Happiness," *New York Times*, December 14, 2013, http:// www.nytimes.com/2013/12/15/opinion/sunday/a-formula-for-happiness.html?src=me&ref =general&_r=1.

7     Julia Keller, "The Mysterious Ambrose Redmoon's Healing Words," *Chicago Tribune*, March 29, 2002, http://articles.chicagotribune.com/2002-03-29/features/0203290018_1_chicago -police-officer-terry-hillard-courage.

8     National Safety Council, *Understanding the Distracted Brain: Why Driving While Using Hands-Free Cell Phones Is Risky Behavior*, April 2012, http://www.nsc.org/learn/NSC-Initiatives /Pages/Understanding-the-Distracted-Brain.aspx.

9     Christopher Ingraham, "America's Top Fears: Public Speaking, Heights, and Bugs," *The Washington Post*, October 30, 2014, https://www.washingtonpost.com/news/wonk /wp/2014/10/30/clowns-are-twice-as-scary-to-democrats-as-they-are-to-republicans/?utm _term=.180887486eef.

10    Emma Fierberg and Alana Kakoyiannis, "Learning to Celebrate Failure at a Young Age Led to This Billionaire's Success," *Business Insider*, May 31, 2017, http://www.businessinsider.com /sara-blakely-spanx-ceo-offers-advice-redefine-failure-retail-2017-5.

11    J. K. Rowling, "The Fringe Benefits of Failure, and the Importance of Imagination," Harvard

commencement speech, June 5, 2008, https://news.harvard.edu/gazette/story/2008/06/text
-of-j-k-rowling-speech/.

12    Achor, *The Happiness Advantage*, 178.

13    Design Thinking Bootcamp, Stanford Graduate School of Business, https://www.gsb.stanford
.edu/exec-ed/programs/design-thinking-bootcamp/.

14    Sapolsky, "How to Relieve Stress."

15    Achor, *The Happiness Advantage*, 74.

16    Carl R. Anderson, "Locus of Control, Coping Behaviors, and Performance in a Stress Setting: A
Longitudinal Study," *Journal of Applied Psychology* 62, no. 4 (1977): 446–451.

17    T. A. Judge, "Relationship of Core Self-Evaluations Traits—Self-Esteem, Generalized Self-
Efficacy, Locus of Control, and Emotional Stability—with Job Satisfaction and Job Performance:
A Meta-Analysis," *Journal of Applied Psychology* 86, no. 1 (February 2001): 80–92.

18    Sapolsky, *Why Zebras Don't Get Ulcers*, 262.

19    Tugend, "The Contrarians on Stress: It Can Be Good for You."

20    Goleman, *Focus*, 23.

21    Mihaly Csikszentmihalyi, *Beyond Boredom and Anxiety: Experiencing Flow in Work and Play* (San
Francisco: Jossey-Bass, Inc., 1975).

22    Brian Sutton-Smith, "The Opposite of Play Is Not Work—It's Depression," Stanford University
Neurosciences Institute, May 29, 2015, https://neuroscience.stanford.edu/news/opposite
-play-not-work-it-depression.

23    Breena Kerr, "Depression Among Entrepreneurs Is an Epidemic Nobody Is Talking About,"
The Hustle, October 26, 2015, https://thehustle.co/depression-among-entrepreneurs-is-an
-epidemic-nobody-is-talking-about.

24    Planning & Progress Study 2017, Northwestern Mutual Newsroom, https://www
.northwesternmutual.com/about-us/studies/planning-and-progress-study-2017.

25    Northwestern Mutual, "Millennials: Conflict between Instinct to Save and Urge to Spend
Is Elevating Anxiety," Cision, August 10, 2017, https://www.prnewswire.com/news
-releases/millennials-conflict-between-instinct-to-save-and-urge-to-spend-is-elevating-anxiety
-300502217.html.

26    Marcel Schwantes, "The Work-Life Balance Rituals That Help Richard Branson, Warren Buffett,
and Oprah Winfrey Stay Successful," Inc. Southeast Asia, August 4, 2017, http://inc-asean.com
/the-inc-life/work-life-balance-rituals-help-richard-branson-warren-buffett-oprah-winfrey-stay
-successful/.

27    Conor Friedersdorf, "Why PepsiCo CEO Indra K. Nooyi Can't Have It All," *The Atlantic*, July
1, 2014, http://m.theatlantic.com/business/archive/2014/07/why-pepsico-ceo-indra-k-nooyi
-cant-have-it-all/373750/.

28    Sheryl Sandberg, *Lean In: Women, Work, and the Will to Lead* (New York: Knopf, 2013).

29    Gloria Steinem, in "Introduction," Tiffany Dufu, *Drop the Ball*.

30    Christopher Peterson, *A Primer in Positive Psychology* (New York: Oxford University Press,
2006), 127.

31    Paul Assaiante and James Zug, *Run to the Roar: Coaching to Overcome Fear* (New York: Portfolio,
2010), 1–5.

32     Phil Jackson and Hugh Delehanty, *Eleven Rings: The Soul of Success* (New York: Penguin, 2014), 269.

## Chapter Seventeen

1      William James, letter to his wife, Alice Gibbons James, *Letters to William James from Various Correspondents and Photograph Album, 1865–1929* (Cambridge, MA: Harvard University, 1865–1929).

2      Lenore E. A. Walker, *The Battered Woman Syndrome*, 4th ed. (New Yorker: Springer, 2016).

3      Louis Cozolino, *The Neuroscience of Psychotherapy: Healing the Social Brain*, 3rd ed. (New York: W. W. Norton, 2002), 262.

4      B. L. Thompson and J. Waltz, "Self-Compassion and PTSD Symptom Severity," *Journal of Traumatic Stress* 21 (2008): 556–558, doi:10.1002/jts.20374.

5      Post Traumatic Stress Disorder Fact Sheet, Sidran Institute, accessed January 31, 2018, https://www.sidran.org/resources/for-survivors-and-loved-ones/post-traumatic-stress-disorder-fact-sheet/.

6      Megan C. Kearns et al., "Early Interventions for PTSD: A Review," *Depression and Anxiety* 29, no. 10 (October 2012): 833–842.

7      Thayer et al., "A Meta-Analysis of Heart Rate Variability and Neuroimaging Studies."

8      McEwen, *The End of Stress as We Know It*, 124.

9      J. T. Mitchell, "When Disaster Strikes…The Critical Incident Stress Debriefing Process," *Journal of Emergency Medical Services* 8, no. 1 (January 1983): 36–39.

10     Kearns et al., "Early Interventions for PTSD."

11     William Frey, *Crying: The Mystery of Tears* (1985).

12     Paul J. Zak, *The Moral Molecule: The Source of Love and Prosperity* (New York: Dutton, 2012); Judith Orloff, "The Health Benefits of Tears," *Psychology Today*, July 27, 2010, https://www.psychologytoday.com/blog/emotional-freedom/201007/the-health-benefits-tears.

13     Victor Hugo, *Les Miserables*, trans. Charles E. Wilbour (New York: Modern Library, 1992), 1,056.

14     Brené Brown, *The Gifts of Imperfection: Let Go of Who You Think You're Supposed to Be and Embrace Who You Are* (Center City, MN: Hazelden, 2010), xiv.

15     J. W. Pennebaker and S. K. Beall, "Confronting a Traumatic Event: Toward an Understanding of Inhibition and Disease," *Journal of Abnormal Psychology* 95, no. 3 (1986): 274–281.

16     Jeff Jaeger et al., "Trauma Narratives: It's What You Say, Not How You Say It," *Psychological Trauma* 6, no. 5 (2014): 473–481.

17     Louis Cozolino, *The Healthy Aging Brain: Sustaining Attachment, Attaining Wisdom* (New York: W. W. Norton, 2008), 151.

18     "Psychology of Flight Anxiety," SOAR: Conquer Fear of Flying, accessed February 7, 2018, http://www.fearofflying.com/store/psychology-of-flight-anxiety.shtml.

19     Achor, *The Happiness Advantage*, 17.

20     R. G. Tedeschi and L. G. Calhoun, "Posttraumatic Growth: Conceptual Foundations and Empirical Evidence," *Psychological Inquiry* 15 (2004): 1–18.

21     C. vanOyen Witvliet, T. E. Ludwig, and K. L. Vander Laan, "Granting Forgiveness or Harboring Grudges: Implications for Emotion, Physiology, and Health," *Psychological Science* 12, no. 2 (March 2001): 117–123.

# Chapter Eighteen

1 Marianne Williamson, *A Return to Love: Reflections on the Principles of "A Course in Miracles"* (New York: Harper Collins, 1992).

2 Claire Adams and Mark R. Leary, "Promoting Self-Compassionate Attitudes Toward Eating Among Restrictive and Guilty Eaters," *Journal of Social and Clinical Psychology* 26, no. 10 (2007): 1120–1144.

3 Kristen D. Neff, "The Science of Self-Compassion," in *Wisdom and Compassion in Psychotherapy: Deepening Mindfulness in Clinical Practice*, eds. C. Germer and R. Siegel (New York: Guilford Press, 2012), 79–92.

4 Ashley Batts Allen and Mark R. Leary, "Self-Compassion, Stress, and Coping," *Social and Personal Psychology Compass* 4, no. 2 (February 1, 2010): 107–118.

5 Hanson, *Hardwiring Happiness.*

6 Robert Emmons, "Why Gratitude Is Good," *Greater Good Magazine*, November 15, 2010, https://greatergood.berkeley.edu/article/item/why_gratitude_is_good.

7 Robert Emmons, "Pay It Forward," *Greater Good Magazine*, June 1, 2007, https://greatergood.berkeley.edu/article/item/pay_it_forward.

8 Sharon Begley, "Rewiring Your Emotions," *Mindful*, July 27, 2013, https://www.mindful.org/rewiring-your-emotions/.

9 Barbara L. Fredrickson, "The Undoing Effect of Positive Emotions," *Motivation and Emotion* 24, no. 4 (December 2000): 237–258.

10 Achor, *The Happiness Advantage*, 49.

11 Yi-Yuan Tang, Britta K. Hölzel, and Michael I. Posner, "The Neuroscience of Mindfulness Meditation," *Nature Reviews Neuroscience* 16 (2015): 213–225.

12 J. I. Cea Ugarte, A. Gonzalez-Pinto Arrillaga, and O. M. Cabo Gonzalez, "[Efficacy of the Controlled Breathing Therapy on Stress: Biological Correlates]," *Revista de Enfermeria* 33, no. 5 (May 2010): 48–54.

13 H. S. Song et al., "The Effects of Specific Respiratory Rates on Heart Rate and Heart Rate Variability," *Applied Psychophysiology and Biofeedback* 28, no. 1 (March 2003): 13–23.

14 David Frausto Peña et al., "Vagus Nerve Stimulation Enchances Extinction of Conditioned Fear and Modulates Plasticity in the Pathway from the Ventromedial Prefrontal Corext to the Amygdala," *Frontiers in Behavioral Neuroscience* 8 (2014): 327.

15 "What Happens in Vagus," Cleveland Clinic Wellness, accessed February 1, 2018, http://www.clevelandclinicwellness.com/programs/NewSFN/pages/default.aspx?Lesson=1&Topic=5&UserId=00000000-0000-0000-0000-000000000705.

16 Gian Mauro Manzoni et al., "Relaxation Training for Anxiety: A Ten-Years Systematic Review with Meta-Analysis," *BMC Psychiatry* 8 (2008): 41.

17 Herbert Benson, *The Relaxation Response* (New York: HarperTorch, 2000).

18 K. Kukkonen-Harjula et al., "Haemodynamic and Hormonal Responses to Heat Exposure in a Finnish Sauna Bath," *European Journal of Applied Physiology and Occupational Physiology* 58, no. 5 (1989): 543–550.

19 L. Lindgren et al., "Physiological Responses to Touch Massage in Healthy Volunteers," *Autonomic Neuroscience: Basic and Clinical* 158, no. 1–2 (December 2010): 105–110.

20    T. M. Mäkinen et al., "Autonomic Nervous Function during Whole-Body Cold Exposure Before and After Cold Acclimation," *Aviation, Space, and Environmental Medicine* 79, no. 9 (September 2008): 875–882.

21    Mladen Golubic, "Practices to Tame the Flame," Center for Lifestyle Medicine Wellness Institute, Cleveland Clinic, presentation October 27, 2014.

22    Sue McGreevey, "Mindfulness Meditation Training Changes Brain Structure in 8 Weeks," Massachusetts General Hospital news release, January 21, 2011, http://www.massgeneral.org /News/pressrelease.aspx?id=1329.

23    Alyson Ross and Sue Thomas, "The Health Benefits of Yoga and Exercise: A Review of Comparison Studies," *The Journal of Alternative and Complementary Medicine* 16, no.1 (2010): 3–12.

24    Elsevier, "New Non-Invasive Form of Vagus Nerve Stimulation Works to Treat Depression," ScienceDaily, February 4, 2016, https://www.sciencedaily.com/releases/ 2016/02/160204111728.htm.

25    "Alpha Brain Waves—Everything You Need to Know," Binaural Beats Freak, accessed February 7, 2018, https://www.binauralbeatsfreak.com/brainwave-entrainment/alpha-brain-waves -everything-you-need-to-know.

26    "What's the Evidence?" Transcendental Medicine, accessed February 1, 2018, http://www .tm.org/research-on-meditation.

27    Transcendental Meditation, "Transcendental Meditation Technique: A Complete Introduction," YouTube, January 29, 2014, https://www.youtube.com/watch?v=fO3AnD2QbIg.

28    Ruth Buczynski, "Tara Brach Shares One Way to Find True Refuge," National Institute for the Clinical Application of Behavioral Medicine, accessed February 1, 2018, http://www.nicabm .com/finding-true-refuge-with-tara-brach/.

29    Google, "Mindfulness with Jon Kabat-Zinn," YouTube, November 12, 2007, https://www .youtube.com/watch?v=3nwwKbM_vJc.

30    Philippe R. Goldin and James J. Gross, "Effects of Mindfulness-Based Stress Reduction (MBSR) on Emotion Regulation in Social Anxiety Disorder," *Emotion* 10, no. 1 (February 2010): 83–91.

31    Philippe Goldin, Wiveka Ramel, and James Gross, "Mindfulness Meditation Training and Self-Referential Processing in Social Anxiety Disorder: Behavioral and Neural Effects" *Journal of Cognitive Psychotherapy* 23, no. 3 (August 2009): 242–257.

32    "Acceptance and Commitment Therapy," GoodTherapy.org, last modified October 25, 2017, http://www.goodtherapy.org/learn-about-therapy/types/acceptance-commitment-therapy.

33    Kristin Wong, "The Benefits of Talking to Yourself," *New York Times*, June 8, 2017, https:// mobile.nytimes.com/2017/06/08/smarter-living/benefits-of-talking-to-yourself-self-talk.html.

34    E. Kross et al., "Self-Talk as a Regulatory Mechanism: How You Do It Matters," *Journal of Personality and Social Psychology* 106, no. 2 (2014): 304–324.

35    Alyson Shontell, "A 69-Year-Old Monk Who Scientists Call the 'World's Happiest Man' Says the Secret to Being Happy Takes Just 15 Minutes a Day," *Business Insider*, January 27, 2016, http://www. businessinsider.com/how-to-be-happier-according-to-matthieu-ricard-the-worlds-happiest -man-2016-1.

36 Richard J. Davidson, *The Emotional Life of Your Brain: How Its Unique Patterns Affect the Way You Think, Feel, and Live—and How You Can Change Them* (New York: Plume, 2013), 214.

37 Davidson, *The Emotional Life of Your Brain,* 214.

38 Richard J. Davidson and Antoine Lutz, "Buddha's Brain: Neuroplasticity and Meditation," *IEEE Signal Processing Magazine* 25, no. 1 (January 2008): 174–176.

39 Paul J. Zak, "Why Inspiring Stories Make Us Reach: The Neuroscience of Narrative," *Cerebrum* (2015): 2.

40 M. Oaten et al., "Longitudinal Gains in Self-Regulation from Regular Physical Exercise," *British Journal of Health Psychology* 11, no. 4 (November 2006): 717–733.

41 Seung-Schick Yoo et al., "The Human Emotional Brain without Sleep—a Prefrontal Amygdala Disconnect," *Current Biology* 17, no. 20.

42 Alice G. Walton, "The Fascinating Connections between Gut Bacteria, Weight and Mood," *Forbes,* July 6, 2017, https://www.forbes.com/sites/alicegwalton/2017/07/06/the-fascinating-connections-between-gut-bacteria-weight-and-mood/#2aa9a780f97f.

43 P. Salmon, "Effects of Physical Exercise on Anxiety, Depression and Sensitivity to Stress—A Unifying Theory," *Clinical Psychology Review* 21, no. 1 (2001): 33–61.

44 Sapolsky, *Why Zebras Don't Get Ulcers,* 401.

45 Larissa Ledochowski et al., "Acute Effects of Brisk Walking on Sugary Snack Cravings in Overweight People, Affect and Responses to a Manipulated Stress Situation and to a Sugary Snack Cue: A Crossover Study," *PLOS ONE* 10, no. 3 (March 11, 2015).

46 Oaten et al., "Longitudinal Gains in Self-Regulation from Regular Physical Exercise."

47 Brad Stulberg, "How Exercise Shapes You, Far Beyond the Gym," The Cut, June 29, 2016, https://www.thecut.com/2016/06/how-exercise-shapes-you-far-beyond-the-gym.html.

48 John M. Grohol, "Need to Form a New Habit? 66 Days," Psych Central, last modified October 7, 2009, https://psychcentral.com/blog/archives/2009/10/07/need-to-form-a-new-habit-66-days/.

49 Jeffrey M. Jones, "In U.S., 40% Get Less than Recommended Amount of Sleep," Gallup News, December 19, 2013, http://www.gallup.com/poll/166553/less-recommended-amount-sleep.aspx.

50 L. Xie et al., "Sleep Drives Metabolite Clearance from the Adult Brain," *Science* 342, no. 6156 (October 18, 2013): 373–377.

51 Emily Underwood, "Sleep: The Brain's Housekeeper," *Science* 342, no. 6156 (October 18, 2013): 301.

52 Kimberly Babson and Matthew Feldner, eds., *Sleep and Affect: Assessment, Theory, and Clinical Implications* (London: Academic Press, 2015).

53 Yasmin Anwar, "Tired and Edgy? Sleep Deprivation Boosts Anticipatory Anxiety," Berkeley News, June 25, 2013, http://news.berkeley.edu/2013/06/25/anticipate-the-worst/.

54 Yoo et al., "The Human Emotional Brain without Sleep."

55 American Academy of Sleep Medicine, "Extra Sleep Improves Athletic Performance," ScienceDaily, June 10, 2008, https://www.sciencedaily.com/releases/2008/06/080609071106.htm.

56 Christine Carter, "The Quiet Secret to Success," *Greater Good Magazine,* September 2, 2013, https://greatergood.berkeley.edu/article/item/the_quiet_secret_to_success.

57 Alan E. Hoban et al., "Microbial Regulation of MicroRNA Expression in the Amygdala

and Prefrontal Cortex," *Microbiome* 5 (2017): 102, quoted in Kimberly Truong, "Could Gut Health Affect Anxiety?" Refinery29, September 5, 2017, http://www.refinery29.com/2017/09/170947/gut-health-anxiety-mental-health.

58    B. Wansink, "The Office Candy Dish: Proximity's Influence on Estimated and Actual Consumption," *International Journal of Obesity* 30 (2006): 871–875.

59    "A Slim by Design Home," Slim by Design, accessed February 7, 2018, http://www.slimbydesign.com/free-resources/home.

60    Tamara Bucher et al., "Nudging Consumers Towards Healthier Choices: A Systematic Review of Positional Influences on Food Choice," *British Journal of Nutrition* 115, no. 12 (June 28, 2016): 2252–2263.

61    Achor, *The Happiness Advantage*.

62    Samual M. McClure et al., "Time Discounting for Primary Rewards," *Journal of Neuroscience* 27, no. 21 (May 23, 2007): 5796–5804.

63    Yong, "Self-Control is Just Empathy with Your Future Self."

64    Yong, "Self-Control is Just Empathy with Your Future Self."

## Conclusion

1    Carlos Castaneda, *Journey to Ixtlan: The Lessons of Don Juan* (New York: Washington Square Press, 1991), 184.

2    Winifred Gallagher, *Rapt: Attention and the Focused Life* (New York: Penguin, 2009), 1.

3    Anne Lamott, *Bird by Bird: Some Instructions on Writing and Life* (New York: Anchor, 1995), 28.

# Other Places to Access Help

**Crisis Call Center/National Suicide Prevention Lifeline:** This 24/7/365 crisis line provides safe, nonjudgmental, professional support for individuals in any type of emotional crisis. Support resources are also available for help in supporting a loved one, as well as best practices for professionals. For phone support in the United States, including special support for veterans, call 1-800-273-8255. Text support can be accessed by texting ANSWER to 839863. Online options for chatting in English, Spanish, and for Deaf and Hard of Hearing at suicidepreventionlifeline.org/.

**Anxiety and Depression Association of America (ADAA):** Whether you are looking for online information or the help of a trained professional in your area, this international nonprofit is a leader in education, training, and research for anxiety, depression, and related disorders. Find out more at adaa.org/finding-help.

**American Psychological Association (APA):** APA is the leading scientific and professional organization representing psychology in the United States, with 115,700+ researchers, educators, clinicians, consultants, and students as its members. It established and governs professional standards of conduct and offers online public information about anxiety and mental health, as well as a directory of psychologists searchable by location. Learn more at apa.org/helpcenter/anxiety.aspx.

**National Alliance of Mental Illness (NAMI):** The largest American grassroots mental health organization, NAMI provides information, educational programs, and advocacy dedicated to building better lives for those affected by mental illness. Online support in accessing help can be found at nami.org/find-support or by calling the NAMI help line at 1-800-950-NAMI (1-800-950-6264). For email support, contact info@nami.org or text NAMI to 741741.

**PsychCentral:** The internet's largest and oldest independent mental health online resource run by mental health professionals provides trusted information and more than 250 support groups to consumers. Visit psychcentral.com/ for more information.

**Psychology Today:** This popular psychology media outlet offers a large, searchable network of therapists in the United States, Canada, and the United Kingdom that can be filtered by location, expertise, insurance, types of therapy, age groups, and more. Find out more at psychologytoday.com/us/therapists.

• •

For further information, help, and inspiration, check out my
website at AliciaClarkPsyd.com or connect with me on Twitter
and Facebook @DrAliciaClark.

# Index

**A**

Abusive relationships, 247, 319–321

Acceptance, 100, 332–333

Acceptance commitment therapy (ACT), 341

Action, 103, 208–228

    *See also* Momentum

    Anxiety Tool Kit strategies for, 374–381

    client stories, 208–210, 211–212, 216–218

    cultivating curiosity and interest, 227–228

    "faking it till you make it," 29, 225–227

    identifying action steps, 215–216

    insight plus energy equation, 210–211

    leaning into discomfort, 213–215

    low-hanging fruit strategy, 226

    making a plan, 218–220

    managing vs. actively coping, 215

    as reward, 212–213

    strategies for staying on track, 220–222

    taking control and, 103, 124, 223–224

    thinking vs. ruminating, 224–225

Active coping, 215, 323

Addiction

    dopamine and, 194, 203–205

    love as, 251, 269

Adolescence, 8, 282–284, 288–292

Adrenaline, 31, 202–203, 220

Advice giving, 265

"Affect labeling," 237

Alarm clock metaphor, 159, 176

Alcohol abuse, 14

Alcoholics Anonymous, 47, 112, 144

Alone, fear of being, 205–206, 230

Altruism, 161

Ambivalence, 170–171, 261, 365

Amygdala, 34

activation of threat system by, 32, 154–155

as attentional prioritizing system, 70, 159

"bottom up" vs. "top down" theory, 155–156

damaged/missing, 178

moderating response of, 173–174, 215, 336–337, 338

myth of "primitive brain" and, 65–67

triggering of, by memory of past trauma, 325–326

"Amygdala hijack" theory, 65–66

Ancient wisdom, 46–47, 62

Anger, 40, 88, 179–182, 256, 268, 315, 329, 363–364

Angst, 36

Antianxiety medications, 3, 12–14, 41, 108, 110, 136, 157–158

Anxiety

as cognitive construct, 34, 152–154, 160

definition of, 35

forms of, 354–356

lack of, 177, 178

purpose of, 19–21, 93–94

terminology for, 2, 34–38

United States, statistics on, 2–3

Anxiety, fear of. *See* Secondary anxiety

Anxiety disorders, 2–3, 23, 35, 125

Anxiety reappraisal, 72–73, 139–141

Anxiety Tool Kit, 352–381

Anxiety vs. fear, 35–36

Art forgeries, 178–179

Astronauts, 127–128

Athletes, 25, 73, 297–298, 315

Attend-and-befriend response, 85–86, 161, 232

Attention, 4, 24–26, 198–200, 302

Attentional prioritizing system, 159

*Authentic Happiness* (Seligman), 60

Automaticity, 165–169, 171–172, 198–200, 222

Autonomic anxiety response, acute, 33, 40–41, 80–81

Autonomic nervous system, 31, 154–155

Autonomy, 120–122

Availability heuristic, 11

Avoidance behavior, 23

See also Avoidance myth; Numbing behavior

abusive relationships and, 319–320

Anxiety Tool Kit strategies for, 365–367

children and, 287–288, 289

client stories, 42–43, 89–91, 103–105, 113–114, 208–210, 270

financial anxiety and, 311

love and relationships and, 252, 257, 263–264

phobias and, 93, 326–327

social support and, 235–237, 245–247, 270–271

vs. taking action, 103

whisper anxiety and, 42–44, 208–210, 356

in workplace, 113–114, 208–210, 301

Avoidance myth, 89–105

See also Secondary anxiety

fallacy of, 91–93

"letting it go," concept of, 94–95

natural function, repression of, 93–94

negative effects of, 96–102

redirection and, 95–96

Awareness, 137–139, 298

**B**

Baby's cry metaphor, 184–185, 207

Back-to-nature movement, 6, 49

Backup plans, 192–193

Balancing work and home-life, 313–314, 327–328

Basketball/gorilla experiment, 25

Beard, George, 48–49

Behaviorism, 55–56, 62

Belly breathing, 336, 337

Benefits of anxiety, xix–xx, 76–77, 183

See also Motivation; Performance, boost for

challenge response, 162, 202–203

memory formation and, 70–71

as needed jolt out of automaticity, 166–167, 176–177, 196, 198–200

nuanced awareness and perception, 177

protective effects, 73, 77, 156–157, 162

reframing your thinking about, 19–23, 73, 171–173

"Big girl pants" strategy, 113–114

Binaural beats, 339

Biofeedback, 338–339

Blind patients, studies on, 74

Boredom, 80, 179–181, 216–218, 257, 307–308

Botox, study on, 226

"Bottom up" vs. "top down" theory, 155–156

Brain, 322

    *See also* Amygdala; Prefrontal cortex; Threat response

    autonomic nervous system, 31, 154

    "bottom up" vs. "top down" theory, 155–156

    chemistry of, 156–158, 202–203

    construction of emotions/anxiety by, 34, 120, 152–154, 160

    default mode network, 198, 231

    emotions and thoughts, interconnectedness of, 334

    empathy and, 114–115, 233–235

    fully engaging, for controlling response to anxiety, 162–164

    healthy attachment in children and, 280

    layers of, 150–151

    locus of control and self-esteem, 125–126

    myth of permanence and immutability, 71–76

    plasticity and automaticity, 164–169, 171–172, 196, 198–200

    play, role of, 308

    positive psychology and, 60–61

    "primitive brain" theory, 65–68, 150–152

    right vs. left hemisphere, 174

    sleep and, 344–345

    social connections and, 230–232

"Brain changers," 286

"Brake pedal" for threat response, 31, 158–159

Bravery. *See* Courage

Breathing techniques, 335–337, 338

Broken heart syndrome, 269

Bullying, 288

Burnout, 197

Bus metaphor, 201–202

"Butterflies" in stomach, 31, 35, 202–203

"Button" pushing, 254, 268, 325–326, 364–365


C

Calming strategies, 40, 335–343, 373

Card player study, 177–178

Career. *See* Work and career

Caring, 87–88, 184–185

Car metaphor, 31, 158–159

Catharsis, 53, 241, 323, 324

Challenge response, 162, 203

Change blindness, 24–25

Character, imagining anxiety as, 29

Chatter anxiety, 41–42, 183, 189–191, 355

Checklists, 221–222

Chemistry, 156–158, 202–203

Childhood, love languages of, 262–263

Childhood, traumatic experiences in, 325–326

Children, anxiety in, 284–294

    *See also* Adolescence; Parenting

    being different, 287–288

    developmental stages and, 280, 282–283, 288–293

    healthy attachment and, 280

    millennials, 290–292, 293

    school performance, 290

    sensitive children, 286–287

Chinese philosophy, 46–47

Choice, anxiety of, 5–7

Choice architecture, 347–348

Choice vs. wishes, 264, 304, 320–321, 372–373

City life, 11–12

Classical conditioning, 55–56

Cognitive behavioral therapy (CBT), 74, 370

Cognitive theory, 56–57, 62, 124, 199

Cold water exposure, 337–338

Collaboration, in workplace, 306

College students, studies of, 24, 92, 125, 219, 293

Communication, 268, 275

    *See also* Complaining; Social media

    constructive criticism, 244

    expressing feelings, 237–239, 251, 260, 359–361

    pitfalls of, 238–239, 245–249

    storytelling as tool of, 241–243

"talking it out," as calming technique, 343

    test taking and, 290

    trauma, coping with, 322–325

Commuters, study of, 122–123

Compassion, 249

    anxiety as, 184–185

    constructive criticism and, 244

    expressing emotions and, 237, 238–239, 260

    helping others, 161, 240

    in romantic relationships, 271–272

    for self, 27–29, 321, 331–333

    storytelling and, 242–243, 246–247

    stress response and, 161

Compassion meditation, 342

Complaining, 117, 129, 243–245, 265

Completion, fear of, 301

Compliments, 253

Compulsive behaviors, 204–205, 223, 312

Confidence, 99–102, 226, 227, 289, 299–301

Conflict, in the workplace, 303–304

Conflict avoidance. *See* Avoidance behavior

Confucius, 46

Confusing behavior, 365–366

Constructive criticism, 244

Contextualizing anxiety, 356–357

Control, xvii, 10–11, 106–130, 179
  See also Naming emotions/anxiety
  autonomy and, 120–122
  client stories, 106–109, 117–119,
    129–130
  coping with trauma and, 329
  courage and, 112–115
  facing challenges to, 125–129
  feeling of helplessness/being stuck,
    23, 24, 71–72, 109–110
  happiness and, 121–122
  vs. inaction/indecision, 115–117
  leaning into discomfort, 119–120
  managing vs. active coping, 215
  mind-set, 110–112
  perception of, 23–24, 71–73,
    122–125
  taking action and, 103, 124,
    223–224
  of threat response, 158–159,
    162–164
  in workplace, 117, 121, 129–130,
    307, 310
Coping, active, 215, 323
Coping and soothing strategies,
  330–348
Cortisol, 32, 157, 202–203, 323
Courage, 112–115, 301, 320,
  321, 380
Creativity, 306, 308
Crisis situations, 317–329
Criticism, constructive, 244
Criticism, of partner, 265–266

Crying, 182–183, 323–324
"Cuddle hormone." See Oxytocin
Curiosity, 227–228

**D**

Danger vs. fear, 127–128, 287
Darwin, Charles, 51–53, 62
Dating, 109, 252–255
Decision-making, 154, 170–171,
  195, 216, 260–261
  See also Action; Control
Decision-making style, 374–375
Default mode network, 198, 231
"Defense mechanisms," 53, 54
Dendrites, 164–165
Depression, 209, 268, 293, 308
  anxiety, linked to, xviii
  control and, 24, 125
  social media and, 8
  substance abuse and, 14
  vagus nerve stimulation and, 339
  work and, 299, 309
Design thinking, 306
Diabetes, 15
Diagnostic and Statistical Manual
  of Mental Disorders (DSM-V),
  xviii, 36, 45, 98
Dieting, 96
Digestion, 203
Digital communication styles,
  8–9
Digital usage, 15

Disappointing others, fear of, 291, 305

Discomfort, leaning into, 119–120, 183–184, 213–215, 344

Disfluency, 183

Distraction, myth of anxiety as, 68–71

Distractions as cause of anxiety, 26, 302

Divorce, 256, 267

Domestic violence, 319–321

Dopamine
    antianxiety medications and, 13, 14, 157–158
    anxiety, connection to, 194–196, 220
    avoidance behavior and, 100–101
    misdirected choices and, 203–205, 347–348, 366–367
    social media and, 4–5

Dreams, 185–188, 257–258, 327–328, 368–369

Drivers in traffic, study of, 122–123

Drug use. *See* Substance abuse

Duchenne smile, 226

**E**

Ellis, Albert, 57, 370

Embarrassment, 245

*Emotional Intelligence* (Goleman), 60–61

Emotions and feelings, 13, 28, 306
    *See also* "Button" pushing; Complaining; Naming emotions/anxiety; *Specific emotion*
    affecting, through thoughts, 334
    anxiety as escalator of, 180–181, 363–364
    anxiety hidden in, 179–184
    as cognitive constructions, 120, 152–154, 160
    as contagious, 232–235
    crying, 182–183, 323–324
    expressing, 237–239, 251, 260, 359–361
    "faking it till you make it," 29, 225–227
    families and, 234, 275
    healthy attachment in children and, 280
    leaning into discomfort, 119–120
    loss and grief, 268–272
    purpose of, 172–173
    sixth sense, 177–179, 253
    "talking it out," as calming technique, 343
    trauma, coping with, 322–325
    "undoing effect" and, 334–335
    writing down, 324–325

Empaths, 87

Empathy, 182, 306
    brain and, 114–115, 233–235

constructive criticism and, 244

courage, linked to, 114–115

developing habit of, 240

expressing emotions and, 237,
238–239, 260

helping others, 240, 303

parenting and, 278–281, 291

in romantic relationships, 266–267,
271–272

self-control and, 147, 348

social anxiety and, 235, 236–237

storytelling and, 241–243

Energy plus insight equation,
210–211

Energy source, anxiety as, 134,
192, 194, 214, 220–221

Entrepreneurs, 309–310

Envy. *See* Jealousy

Epigenetics, 83, 84

Eustress, 183, 298

Evolutionary tools of survival,
101–102, 149–150, 198,
230–232

Evolution theory, 51–53, 66

Exam anxiety, 185, 290

Excitement, 72–73, 139–141

Exercise, 344

Existentialists, 47–48, 62

Expectations, letting go of, 95,
264, 275–277, 350–351

Extroverts, 374–375

**F**

Facial expressions, 226

Failure, fear of, 192–193,
217–218, 225, 301

Failure, growing through, 305

"Fake it till you make it," 29,
225–227

"Falling up," 329

Family. *See* Children; Parenting

Family genetics, 82–84

Family members, sharing of
emotions between, 234

Fantasies. *See* Wishful thinking

Fatigue, 220–222, 344–345,
347–348, 366

Fault finding, in partner,
265–266

Fear, definition of, 35–36

Fear circuit, 32

Fear of missing out (FOMO), 8

Feelings. *See* Emotions and
feelings

Fight-or-flight response. *See*
Threat response

Financial anxiety, 310–312

Fire-alarm fallacy, 69–70

Fire trauma as metaphor, 17–18

Fixed vs. growth mind-set,
109–110

Flow, 80, 298, 302

Flying, fear of, 71, 75–76, 93,
326–327

Food. *See* Nutrition; Overeating

Forcing solutions, 27–28

Forgiveness, 329

Freud, Sigmund, 53–55, 62

Friendships, 235–237, 248–249, 266

    *See also* Social support

Frowning, 226

Frustration, 179–181, 216–218

Fuel, anxiety as, 189–207

    *See also* Motivation

Future, anxiety about, 144–148, 293–294, 311–312

## G

Galvanic skin response (GSR), 292

"Gas pedal" for threat response, 31, 154–155

Gateway behaviors, 209–210

"Generation Squeeze," 274

Generosity, 114–115, 239, 244

Genetics, 67, 82–84

Gentle behaviors. *See* Calming strategies; Self-care; Self-compassion

Glucocorticoids, 323

Goals, 193, 212–213

    *See also* Action; Future, anxiety about; Motivation

    dopamine and, 196

    online programs for achieving, 222

    prioritizing, 371–372

Golden Rule, inverting, 29

Goleman, Daniel, 60–61

"Good enough" parenting, 275–277

Google news alerts, 214–215

Gorilla/basketball experiment, 25

Gratitude, 333–334

Greece, ancient, 47

Grief, 268–272

Grit, 227

Groove, 227

Grounding, 335

Growth vs. fixed mind-set, 109–110

Guilt, 39, 47, 257–258, 327–328

"Gut" reactions, 152

## H

Habits, 25–26, 193–194

    Darwin's views on, 52

    empathy as, 240

    riverbed metaphor, 167–169

    shifting from automaticity to plasticity, 164–169, 171–172, 196, 198–200

    strategies for building/changing, 220–222, 347–348

    threat response as, 33

    time needed to form, 344

Handling anxiety/emotions, ability to, 97–98, 132–133, 180–182, 358, 363–364

Happiness, 227–228, 308
  control and, 121–122
  flow state and, 80, 298
  intentional activity, influence of,
    163
  vs. meaningfulness, 111–112
  meditation and, 342
  myths about, 298–299
  positive psychology and, 60
Health anxiety, 117–119, 129,
  201–202, 317–319
Health effects of stress/anxiety,
  73, 77–78, 134–135, 307, 334
Healthy habits, 344–348
Heart rate, 32, 268, 338–339
Help, asking for, 43, 258–259
Helping others, 85–86, 161, 240,
  303, 323, 342
Helplessness, xviii, 23, 24,
  109–110, 124
Help-seeking behavior, 85, 157,
  161, 232
"Highlighter pens," tears as,
  182–183, 323
"High reactive" children, 286–287
Hindbrain. See Reptilian brain
Hippocampus, 67, 125–126
Historical perspectives, 45–62
Honking horn metaphor, 64–65
Hormesis, 162
Hormones, 32–33, 156–158
Hot-button issues, 367–368
  See also "Button" pushing

Housework, shared, 258–259
HPA (hypothalamic–pituitary–
  adrenal) axis, 32–33, 154
Humanism, 58–59, 62
Hunter-gatherer ancestors,
  83–84, 115–116
Hypothalamic–pituitary–adrenal
  (HPA) axis, 32–33, 154


I

Identifying anxiety, 30–31
  See also Dreams; Naming
    emotions/anxiety; Pushed
    "buttons"; Recognizing anxiety
  Anxiety Tool Kit strategies for,
    357–369
  baby's cry metaphor for, 184–185, 207
  client stories, 170–171, 174–176,
    186–188
  compassion and, 184–185
  detangling from other emotions,
    179–184
  as escalator of emotions, 180–181,
    363–364
  hearing the message, 19–23, 171–
    172, 176–177, 357–358
  investigating ourselves, 173–174
  sixth sense, 177–179, 253
Ignoring anxiety. See Avoidance
  behavior
Imaginary fixations, 264,
  281–282

Imbalance, myth of, 64–65,
    157–158
Immune system, activation of,
    73, 77, 157, 162
Impulsive behaviors, 43, 311
Inaction/indecision, 115–117,
    213
"Inattentional blindness," 24–25
Inconsistent behavior, 365–366
Industrial Revolution, 48–49, 62
Infidelity, 256, 257–258
Information seeking, 10–11
Innovation, 298, 306, 308
Insecurity, 256–257
Inside Out (movie), 172
Insight, concept of, 137
Insight plus energy equation,
    210–211
Intelligence, 149–150, 216
Interpersonal conflict, in the
    workplace, 303–304
Intimacy. See Sex
Introverts, 374–375
Intuition, 177–179, 253
Irrational catastrophic thinking,
    370
Irrational vs. rational fears,
    44, 57, 182, 284, 297, 327,
    370–371
Irritability, 181–182, 216–218
Israel study on anxiety coping,
    223
Israel study on courage, 114–115

**J**
James, William, 49–51, 62
Jealousy, 174–176, 218
Job. See Work and career
Judgment, fear of, 174–176, 236,
    246, 290–292

**K**
Kierkegaard, Soren, 47–48

**L**
Language, 30, 34, 343
        See also Naming emotions/anxiety
        dreams and, 186
        identifying anxiety, 367–368
        love, childhood influences on,
            262–263
        trauma, healing from, 324–325
Lao Tzu, 46–47
Leadership, and girls, 289
Learned helplessness, xviii, 24,
    124
Learning, process of, 55–56, 72,
    101–102, 164–166
Left brain vs. right brain, 174
"Letting it go," concept of, 94–95
Limbic brain, 151
Lion roaring metaphor, 315
Load sharing, 279–280
London taxi drivers, 67, 126
Loneliness, 108–109, 180,

205–206, 229–230, 235–237,
    270–271
"Lone wolves," 258–259, 296
Loss, 268–272
Love and relationships, 250–273
    anxiety as propeller in, 251, 267
    childhood influences on, 262–263
    client stories, 86–87, 254–255,
        257–258, 259–261, 270–272
    dating, 109, 252–255
    domestic violence, 319–321
    focusing on faults, 265–266
    fueling connection, 266–268
    loss and grief in, 268–272
    previous relationships, influence of,
        261–264
    ratio of positive vs. negative inter-
        actions, 138
    sharing feelings, 238–239, 251, 260
    stressors/conflict in, 86–87, 256–
        257, 268
    trusting/sharing responsibilities,
        258–259
    wishful thinking and, 264, 267, 321
Loving yourself, 321
Low-hanging fruit strategy, 226
Low self-esteem, 100, 125–126,
    299–301
Lying by teenagers, study on, 291


**M**

Magic of momentum, 210

Manageable steps, breaking
    actions into, 144–145, 209,
    378–379
Marriage. *See* Love and
    relationships
Maslow, Abraham, 58–59
Matthieu, Ricard, 342
Meaningfulness, 111–112, 121
Medial prefrontal cortex, 34, 195,
    240, 345
Medications, antianxiety, 3,
    12–14, 41, 108, 110, 136,
    157–158
Meditation, 338, 339–342
Memory formation, 70–71,
    325–326
Mesoaccumbens circuit, 195
Message. *See* Identifying anxiety;
    Signal
Metacognition, 97
Millennials, 5, 290–292, 293,
    310–311
Mindful action, 210
Mindfulness, 100, 137, 339–342
Mind-set, 77–78, 110–112,
    133–137
Mirror neurons, 233–235
Misdirection, 203–206
Momentum, 193–194, 209–210,
    226, 379, 380–381
Money, anxiety about, 310–312
Monkey and green banana
    metaphor, 27

Motivation, 28, 271

  *See also* Energy source, anxiety as; Momentum

  anxiety, related to, 191–193, 214

  client stories, 189–191, 196–198, 201–202, 205–206

  dopamine, role of, 194–196, 220

  misdirected choices and behaviors, 203–206

  physical readiness for action, 202–203

  romantic relationships and, 251, 262

  shifting from automaticity to plasticity, 198–200

  strategies for staying on track, 220–222, 347–348

  taking control and, 121–122

  test taking and, 290

Multitasking, 26, 302

Myers-Briggs Type Indicator, 374–375

Myths, 63–88

  *See also* Avoidance myth

## N

Naming emotions/anxiety, 219

  accessing social support and, 237, 343

  Anxiety Tool Kit strategies for, 358–361

  children and, 285–286, 290

  lowering threat response by, 34, 173–174

  as process of cognitive construction, 153–154, 160, 343

Navy SEAL training, 76–77, 126

Negative reinforcement, 100

Negativity bias, 101–102, 138

Neocortex, 151

Neural Darwinism, 72

Neural pathways, 72, 164–169

Neurasthenia, 48–49

Neurosis, 59

Neuroticism, 83

Neurotransmitters, 157–158, 194–196

Newlyweds, 267

News, 11, 214–215

Nocebo, 136

Norepinephrine, 33

Numbing behavior, 14–15, 43, 143, 204–205, 366–367

Nutrition, 345–347

## O

Obesity, 14–15, 204–205

Obsessing vs. thinking, 224–225

Office politics, 307

"One day at a time" strategy, 144–145

Online programs for achieving goals, 222

"Option stress," 5–7

Overeating, 14–15, 96, 143,
    204–205, 331–332
Oxytocin, 33
    expressing emotions and, 182–183,
        239
    social engagement, promotion of,
        85, 157, 161
    storytelling and, 242–243
    stress response and, 85, 157

**P**

Panic disorder study, 124
Panic/panic attacks, 81, 96–99,
    106–109, 117–119, 281–282,
    326, 335
Parachute trainees study,
    128–129
Parasympathetic nervous system,
    31, 158–159, 335–337
Parenting, 84–85, 231, 273–294
    *See also* Adolescence
    anxiety in children and, 284–294
    client stories, 281–282, 284, 293–294
    communication and connection,
        275
    empathy and attachment, 278–281,
        291
    facing down childhood fears,
        287–288
    "good enough," power of, 275–277
    love "languages" of childhood and,
        262–263

    millennials and, 290–292, 293
    school performance and, 290
    sensitive children and, 286–287
    stages of child development and,
        280, 282–283, 288–293
    teaching and modeling behavior,
        274–275, 277
    uptick of stress in, 273–274
    wishes vs. reality, 274
Pavlov, Ivan, 55
Perception, 131–148
    awareness and, 137–139
    client stories, 131–133, 142–143,
        146–147
    of control, 23–24, 71–73, 122–125
    mind-set and, 77–78, 110–112,
        133–137
    reappraising technique, 72–73,
        139–141
    time horizon and, 144–147
Perfectionism, 227, 277, 350–351
Performance, boost for, 297–298,
    315–316
    challenge response and, 162, 203
    fear of failure and, 192–193, 305
    perception and, 131–133, 142
    "sweet spot" of, 79–80, 132, 162
    test taking and, 290
Performance anxiety, 302–303
Performance limitation, myth of,
    78–81
Persistence, 227
Personal care. *See* Self-care

Personifying your anxiety, 29

Phobias, 93, 326–327

Physical behavior, using to influence feelings, 225–227

Physiological response, 31–33, 35, 156–160, 202–203

Pilots vs. commuters, stress response of, 122–123

Planning, contingency, 128, 192–193, 225

Planning action, 218–220

Plasticity, 60, 66, 164–169, 171–172, 196, 200, 336

Play, role of, 308

Poison ivy study, 136

Politics, 9–11, 367–368

Positive, focusing on, 137–139

Positive illusions, 266–267

Positive psychology, 60–61, 62

Post partum anxiety (PPA), 281–282

Posttraumatic growth, 329

Post-traumatic stress disorder (PTSD), 320, 321–322

Power, sense of, 99–100, 122

Power imbalance, 260–261

Powerlessness, 24, 99–100, 372–373

Power posing, 227

Practice, optimal, 25

Prefrontal cortex, 52, 345

    "bottom up" vs. "top down" processing, 155–156

    dopamine and, 195

    mediation of anxiety by, 34, 215, 240

    right brain vs. left brain, 174

    threat response, trumped by, 70, 155

    vagus nerve stimulation and, 336–337

Pregnancy, 281–282

Presidential election of 2016, 10

"Primitive brain," 65–68, 150–152

    *See also* Amygdala

Proactive coping, 215, 323

"Processing anxiety," 55

Processing emotions. *See* Naming emotions/anxiety

Procrastination, 43, 44, 208–210, 301

Projection, 265–266

Prostress, 183

Psychodynamics, 54–55

Public speaking, 40, 51, 232–233, 279–280, 302–303, 341–342

Purpose, sense of, 121, 307–308

Pushed "buttons," 254, 268, 325–326, 364–365


**R**

RAIN acronym, 340

Rational emotive behavior therapy, 57

Rational vs. irrational fears, 44, 57, 182, 284, 297, 327, 370–371

Read receipts, 8–9

Reappraising technique, 72–73, 139–141

Recency bias, 11

Recognizing anxiety, 30–31

    *See also* Identifying anxiety

    Anxiety Tool Kit strategies for, 353–357

    fire alarm metaphor, 69–70

    manifestations of, 38–44

    paying attention, 24–26

    physical experience of, 31–33, 35, 202–203

    terminology and, 2, 34–38

Redirection, 95–96

Reframing your thinking about anxiety, 19–23, 73, 171–173, 353–354

Rejection, fear of, 8–9, 230, 232–233, 235–237, 246, 252–253, 291, 303

Relationships. *See* Love and relationships; Social support

Relaxation industry, 15–16

Relaxation strategies. *See* Calming strategies

Religion, 47–48

Repetition, 126–127

Reptilian brain, 65–68, 150–152

Resilience, 126–127, 227, 329

Retirement, 106–109, 299, 311–312

Reverse placebo, 136

Right brain vs. left brain, 174

Risk taking, 298

Ritualistic behaviors, 223

Riverbed metaphor, 167–169

Rogers, Carl, 58

Rogers, Fred, 161

Romantic relationships. *See* Love and relationships

Routines, 221–222, 227

Ruminating vs. thinking, 224–225, 324

## S

Sadness, 172, 181

Safety behaviors, 312

Schemas, 57

Scientific progress, 53

Screen time, 15

SEAL training, 76–77, 126

Secondary anxiety, 92, 96–99, 131–133, 135, 180, 326

Second person, referring to yourself in, 236, 341–342

Secrets, 324–325

Sedentary lifestyle, 15, 16

Self-acceptance, 58

Self-actualization, 59

Self-care, 197, 201–202, 284, 328

    checklists, 221–222

healthy habits, 344–348

pushing yourself too far at work, 309–310

Self-compassion, 27–29, 321, 331–333

Self-control, 96, 147, 348

Self-destructive behavior, 365–366

Self-determination theory, 121

Self-esteem, 100, 125–126, 299–301, 351

Selfishness, 86–88, 327–328

"Self-sabotage," 100

Self-talk, 113–114, 341–342, 367–368

Seligman, Martin, 60

Selye, Hans, 36–37

Sensitivity, 87, 286–287

Serenity prayer, 111, 112, 223, 264

Serotonin, 14, 157–158

Sex, 14, 195, 258, 267–268

Shame, 245–247, 249, 277, 319–320

    See also Stigma of anxiety

Shop window study, 292

Signal, 19–21, 170–188

    See also Identifying anxiety

"Signal anxiety," 54

Sixth sense, 177–179, 253

Skinner, B.F., 56

Sleep, 344–345

Smartphones, 8–9, 15

    See also Social media

Smiling, 226

Snakes in MRI, study of, 114–115

Social anxiety

    in children and youth, 278, 289, 291, 292, 294

    client stories, 229–230, 235–237

    overview, 235

    power poses and, 227

Social connections, and adolescence, 288, 289, 290–292

Social learning theory, 223

Social media, 4–5, 8–9, 249, 252, 290–292

Social support, 229–249

    See also Compassion; Complaining; Empathy

    accessing, by expressing feelings, 237–239

    avoidance of, 235–237, 245–247, 270

    client stories, 229–230, 235–237

    in crisis situations, 322–324

    as evolutionary tool of survival, 230–232

    helping others, 85–86, 161, 240, 303, 323, 342

    myth of withdrawal and isolation, 84–86

    oxytocin and, 85, 157, 161

    physical and mental health benefits of, 232–235

    pitfalls of securing, 238–239, 245–249

seeking the right people for, 247–249

storytelling and, 241–243

tend-and-befriend response, 85–86, 161, 232

in workplace, 247, 306–307

Soothing and coping strategies, 330–348

Soothing behaviors. *See* Addiction; Numbing behavior

Sorting step, in Anxiety Tool Kit, 369–374

Sports, 25, 73, 315

Statistics on anxiety, 2–3

Stigma of anxiety, xix, 21–22, 214, 285

Storytelling, 241–243

Strength building, 162

Stress, definition of, 36–37

"Stressed out," 21–22

Stress hormone. *See* Cortisol

Stress-induced cardiomyopathy, 269

Stress response, 156–157, 161, 183, 288, 292, 323, 338

    *See also* Threat response

Subgenual anterior cingulate cortex (sgACC), 114–115

Substance abuse, 14, 209, 233, 366

Success, in workplace, 305, 309

Sugar, 14–15, 204

Survival tools. *See* Evolutionary tools of survival

"Sweet spot," 79–80, 132, 162

Sympathetic nervous system, 31–33, 154–155

Synapses, 164


**T**

Talking it out, 343

Taxi drivers, 67, 126

Tears, 182–183, 323–324

Teenagers, 8, 282–284, 288–292

Television viewing, 15

Tend-and-befriend response, 85–86, 161, 232

Terminology, 2, 34–38

Test taking, 185, 290

Texting, 8–9

Thinking vs. ruminating, 224–225, 324

Third person, 160, 341–342

Thought systems, competing, 179

Threat response (fight-or-flight response)

    *See also* Amygdala; "Button" pushing; Yelling anxiety

    anxiety, differentiated from, 32, 159–160

    avoidance behavior and, 91

    "bottom up" vs. "top down" theory, 155–156

    "brake pedal," parasympathetic nervous system as, 31, 158–159 calming strategies, 40, 335–343, 373

vs. challenge response, 162, 203

chemistry of, 156–158, 202–203

dopamine, role of, 194–196

engaging whole brain and, 162–164

fear and, 35–36

"gas pedal," sympathetic nervous system as, 31, 154–155

memory formation and, 70–71, 325–326

misdirected choices and, 203–206

physical experience of, 31–33, 35, 202–203

"primitive brain" framework for, 65–68, 150–152

right brain vs. left brain, 174

as survival tool, 149–150

vs. tend-and-befriend response, 85–86, 161, 232

triggering of, by memory of past trauma, 33, 325–326

Tibetan monks, 342

Tiger metaphor, 115–117

Time horizon, 144–148, 293–294, 311–312

Tiny house movement, 6

Tiredness. See Fatigue

"Top down" vs. "bottom up" theory, 155–156

Transcendental meditation (TM), 339

Trauma, 17–18, 80–81, 319–326

Triune brain theory, 150–152

Trust, 239, 242–243, 258–259

Tuning out, 198

"Twenty-second rule," 347

U

Ulysses Effect, 222

Uncertainty. See Discomfort, leaning into

Unconscious, 54–55

Underload, 307–308

"Undoing effect," 334–335

United States, anxiety in, 2–3

Urbanization, 48–49

Urban life, 11–12

V

Vagus nerve, 336–337, 339

Valium, 136

Vasopressin, 32–33

"Volume control," 180

Vulnerability, 236, 238, 243, 246–247, 251

W

Waiting, anxiety of, 128, 224–225

"Waiting" dreams, 186–188

Warm water exposure, 337

Weight loss, 96, 143

Whispering anxiety, 168, 219–220

    client stories, 42–43, 208–210, 284, 299–301

    disfluency and, 183–184

    health concerns and, 319

    identifying, 43–44, 356

    relationships and, 256–257

Wishful thinking, 314

    abusive relationships and, 320–321

    Anxiety Tool Kit strategies for, 372–373

    parenting and, 274

    in romantic relationships, 264, 267, 321

    in workplace, 304

Withdrawal. *See* Avoidance behavior

Women, balancing work and home-life, 313–314

"Woody Allen gene," 83

Work and career, 22, 186, 214, 295–316

    *See also* Performance, boost for; Retirement

    avoidance behavior and, 113–114, 208–210, 301

    balancing home-life and, 313–314, 327–328

    boredom in, 216–218, 307–308

    client stories, 38–39, 41–43, 117, 129–133, 142, 170–171, 189–191, 196–198, 208–210, 216–218, 295–296, 299–301, 311–312

    common anxieties in, 301–303

    complaining at, 117, 129, 243–245

    dealing with difficult people, 303–304

    financial anxiety and, 310–312

    growing through failure, 305

    happiness and personal well-being, 298–299

    irrational vs. rational fears, 297

    play, role of, 308

    risks of pushing too far, 309–310

    social interactions and, 247, 306–307

    taking control and, 117, 121, 129–130, 307, 310

Worry, definition of, 37–38

Writing down feelings, 324–325, 359–361


**Y**

Yelling anxiety, 38–41, 170–171, 284, 325–326, 330–331, 355

Yerkses Dodson Curve, 79–81, 162

Yoga, 332, 338

Young adults, 292–294

Youth. *See* Children

# Acknowledgments

Writing a book can be a surprisingly vulnerable process that can spark anxiety in even the most confident person. There have been many anxious moments of this project, and translating them into solutions has required consistent practice of the principles outlined in this book, including reliance on the people around me.

Sitting down to catalog the people who have helped bring this book to life is a powerful exercise in gratitude quite unlike any other. There have been so many people over the years who have supported and shaped the ideas of these pages it is impossible to list them all. It is with deep appreciation that I wish to thank the many clients, professionals, and loved ones who have shared their insights and experiences that have helped form the concepts described here. I am so grateful for your ongoing inspiration.

I want to thank my wonderful agent, Rachel Ekstrom Courage, who was among the earliest believers in this project and has patiently shepherded it—and me—through its many iterations in becoming the book it is today.

To my enormously talented writing partner, Jon Sternfeld, your organizational vision and gifted writing has transformed these ideas and experiences into something immeasurably better. Your resourcefulness, patience, and partnership not only made this project possible, but fun.

To my brilliant editor, Shana Drehs, who has guided this project with a steadfast vision and an even hand that has made this book a more accessible version of itself at every turn. Thank you for believing in the project and bringing your editing genius to the project. To the larger publishing team at Sourcebooks who have visually translated my ideas and partnered with me to help get the word out, I am deeply appreciative.

To Melanie Gorman, marketing and branding expert, together with her Tango team, who has long been a source of encouragement, thank you. Your ongoing support and can-do attitude motivates me to do my part in making the world a better place.

To my colleagues, thought leaders, and scientists who tirelessly aim to help people achieve better health and happier lives, your work invigorates me. A huge thank-you to neuroscientists Yaisa Andrews-Zwilling, PhD, and Daniel Zwilling, PhD, for their review of the manuscript.

And to numerous other authors and literary professionals who have generously shared precious time and sage advice, thank you. I will continue to pay it forward.

This book is also a direct result of a very special group of women who have embraced, energized, and challenged me to think bigger and stretch farther than I thought was possible. The power of another's belief in you cannot be overstated, especially in the face of anxiety. My tribe is deep and broad, and I am profoundly grateful for its strength, vitality, and love.

My family, along with dear friends, remains an ongoing source of strength and support, for which I am so grateful. Thank you for continuing to show up and share in life's twists and turns and do so with grace and humor. It is hard to express my appreciation for the love and support I continuously feel.

To my children, who have tolerated more distraction than was probably fair, shared in every disappointment and success along the way, and indulged discussions of feelings since you could actually talk, thank you Your fresh perspective, brave hearts, and love nourish me at every turn. I am so proud to be your mom.

To my dear husband, Michael, who has supported this project in confidence and doubt, who partnered in facing its many demands, and who demonstrates every day how powerfully love can arouse courage, thank you from the bottom of my heart. Building and sharing a life with you has been my greatest accomplishment and my deepest blessing.

Finally, to my community of clients, friends, and virtual acquaintances who face and use anxiety every day to improve your lives, thank you for sharing your stories and trusting me in your growth. You have inspired these pages, and they are dedicated to you.

# About the Authors

**Alicia H. Clark** is a licensed psychologist specializing in anxiety and relationships. Clark has served as adjunct clinical faculty at the Chicago School of Professional Psychology, and her work has been featured in hundreds of online, print, and video publications worldwide. She lives in Washington, DC, with her husband and two children. For more information, visit AliciaClarkPsyD.com.

**Jon Sternfeld** is a writer whose books include *Crisis Point: Why We Must—and How We Can—Overcome Our Broken Politics in Washington and Across America*, with Senators Tom Daschle and Trent Lott, and *A Stone of Hope: A Memoir* with Jim St. Germain. Sternfeld lives in New York.